Walter MacLeod

A List of persons concerned in the Rebellion transmitted to the Commissioners of Excise

By the several supervisors in Scotland

Walter MacLeod

A List of persons concerned in the Rebellion transmitted to the Commissioners of Excise
By the several supervisors in Scotland

ISBN/EAN: 9783337216689

Printed in Europe, USA, Canada, Australia, Japan

Cover: Foto ©ninafisch / pixelio.de

More available books at **www.hansebooks.com**

A LIST OF PERSONS
CONCERNED IN
THE REBELLION

TRANSMITTED TO THE COMMISSIONERS OF EXCISE
BY THE SEVERAL SUPERVISORS IN SCOTLAND
IN OBEDIENCE TO A GENERAL LETTER OF
THE 7TH MAY 1746
AND A SUPPLEMENTARY LIST WITH
EVIDENCES TO PROVE THE SAME

With a Preface by
THE EARL OF ROSEBERY

and Annotations by the
REV. WALTER MACLEOD

EDINBURGH
Printed at the University Press by T. and A. Constable
for the President of the Scottish History Society
1890

CONTENTS

	PAGE
PREFACE by the Earl of Rosebery,	vii
LIST OF REBELS,	1
SUPPLEMENTARY LIST, with Evidences,	297
APPENDIX by the Rev. Walter Macleod—	
I. Analysis of the List,	357
II. Biographical Notes,	363
Notes on Supplementary List, .	386
III. Illustrative Documents, .	390

PREFACE

The list here printed is the bare official record of our last historical romance. There were afterwards in Great Britain Gordon Riots, and Bristol Riots, and Peterloo itself—these, though tragic, were ephemeral: but the march of the Highlanders on London in 1745 was a civil war, perhaps the most picturesque and the most difficult to realise of all such conflicts. For the tale in brief is this:—

A hundred and forty-five years ago a French-born prince of British origin leaves Belleisle and lands in the Western Highlands. He is alone with seven followers, and a handful of louis d'ors, but his name with its traditions, and his own gallant bearing, rally round him a few chiefs and their followers. He presses forward, followed by a ragged but terrible tail, disperses in five minutes regular troops, to whom his army are as Mohawks, and seizes Edinburgh. There he holds Court in low-lying Holyrood, commanded by the Castle, which is garrisoned by his foes, and defeats in another burst another regular army. Thence, little stronger, he dashes into England as far as Derby. He spreads consternation throughout the kingdom, and strikes the very heart of the Empire. In London there is Black Friday, the realm seems at the mercy of a raid, and it seems the toss of a die whether England shall be Guelph or Stuart. Then the wild foe is mysteriously paralysed. The confused advance is followed by a precipitate retreat. The Highlanders hurry back with a dismal haste, downcast and draggled: further and further, past Glasgow, past Falkirk, till they are lost in the mists of the North whence at last there comes news that they have been crushed, and harried, and slaughtered, and that their leader has disappeared.

Then ensues that famous flight of the romantic youth through the vague unknown country, pressed and pursued, in caves, in huts, in women's clothing; passing through penniless Highlanders with a reward on his head that meant wealth for a clan: but, faithfully served, escaping back to the Continent and to a long ignominy. He disappears for a decade and emerges a changed man: bloated, drunken, half-imbecile, half-brute, and so he ends his life. Then again, by a magic unconscious touch of History, he is transmuted for ever into a paladin, with a tradition and a worship which have always hallowed his smallest relics as of a hero or a saint. The secret of the fascination is not impenetrable. Recklessness, which is one of the most engaging qualities of private life, loses no part of its grace on a larger stage. Charles came alone, relying on his ancestral rights and his charm of manner. The throne he claimed for his father was occupied by an elderly German, for whom no one felt enthusiasm, or even liking or respect. A Popish prince was of course a danger, and few except wild Celts, obedient to their chiefs, would risk life for such a cause. But there was at least equal indifference for the reigning family, and doubtless many who held aloof would not have grieved in their hearts had the spirited adventurer been successful. Charles Edward has the immortal advantage of passing into history side by side with George the Second. Nor does that exhaust his good fortune. He was opposed and defeated by a prince of his own age, his superior doubtless in point of ability, but as infinitely his inferior in all that graces mankind; nay, unhappily distinguished from ordinary humanity by so rare a lust of slaughter, and so bloodthirsty a brutality, that the victor of Culloden is much less to be envied than the vanquished.

In view, then, of the weakness and unpopularity of the reigning family, and of his gallant bearing and hereditary rights, the wonder is not that Charles should have collected so many adherents as that they should have been so few. He secured, indeed, south of the Forth no support worth speaking of. But as a Pretender in Scotland he had one fatal defect. His faith and his training were those of a Papist. His grand-uncle, under similar circumstances, had signed the Covenant. Such a proceeding would indeed have been excessive in 1745. Subscription to the Covenant was out of date. But had Charles been able to renounce Roman Catholicism as he afterwards did, and anticipated by five years the abjuration of 1750, he might have swept Scotland. For his grandfather, as Duke of York, was the last sovereign the Scots had seen; and though his residence had been nothing less than genial and gracious, the Hanoverian kings had no more contemplated holding a Court at Holyrood than the Emperor Nicholas at Warsaw. The Union was still unpopular. The country was still poor. A name like that of Stewart, borne by a Protestant prince of engaging presence, would have raised the nation in its cause. But religion outweighed all else. Sixty years had not elapsed since Claverhouse had harried the servants of God : it was not seventy since the young Chevalier's grandfather had sat and gloated over the sufferings of the saints in the Council Chamber at Holyrood. The very assurances of toleration and goodwill that the Regent brought from his father were dated from Rome. He himself could not be brought to attend the service of the Kirk. It was well at his entry to receive him with waving hats and huzzas, well to gaze at his shadow of pageantry, well to watch his daily reviews. There was a pleasing excitement in the street whose one end faced the frowning Castle, with its Hanoverian garrison, while the other touched the Palace, where the Pretender held his Court. There could not but be curiosity to see the handsome features of the grandson of James the Second, and the great-grandson of Charles the First—the representative of such gallant hopes and such solemn memories. But for all that, the population, capable of such sudden frenzy as that which hanged Porteous eight years before, remained cold and apathetic. The all-powerful clergy deserted their pulpits and the city at his approach. Nothing could be more significant or more sinister. There were few recruits. The gracious face of the young Prince remained melancholy and overcast. Fate had already written failure upon it.

While in Edinburgh there was apathy, in the Covenanting West there was open hostility. Glasgow raised a regiment against him. Another county once more vindicated its claim to a supremacy of whiggery, for whereas Ayr alone of Scottish burghs petitioned in favour of the Union, Ayrshire is said to have been the only Scottish county that sent not a man to join the Pretender. Throughout the Lowlands, indeed, there was no encouraging sign. And when Charles marched into England, not to bring but to find encouragement, he found none except at Manchester, so soon to be known by so different a political doctrine.

Whence then came his followers? It was essentially an army of clans. There were, no doubt, some few non-juring Episcopalians, men, like Balmerino, who believed in divine right; men in the mood for adventure, living in poverty at home, whose condition might possibly be made better, but could hardly in any event be made worse; men, like Elcho, who knew not why they joined, men of impulse, dare-devils, malcontents: such as are found in every hazardous enterprise. There were noble souls, like Perth and Tullibardine and Pitsligo, who could understand no other cause, to whom it was a religion and a martyrdom. But these were exceptions. The army that invaded England was practically a gathering of clans: so much so that, had young Lochiel taken his brother's advice, and avoided meeting the Prince, there would in all probability have been no rising at all. Some chiefs agreed to join, and that fact meant so many thousand men—in many cases reluctant, it is said, to leave their homes, and in most cases eager to return to them after a victory, but still the loyal servants of the head of their sept.

PREFACE.

Why the chiefs rose is less difficult to understand. They had not been spoiled by the sovereigns who succeeded James II. There had been the massacre of Glencoe. There had been the Union, profoundly distasteful to men half-proud, half-barbarous, but supremely independent. There had been the rising of 1715. There had been the Disarming Acts of 1716 and 1725. There had been the Malt Tax. They had no money, no industry: they were at the head of a great number of half-starved, warlike dependents. There was no prospect except in action. Repose meant inanition. Movement might be fatal, but it might not; and at any rate it would be exciting. Add to these lower motives the natural sympathy with a lonely gallant young prince claiming his birthright, with an appeal to their chivalry, and we can hardly feel surprised at their decision.

But why, we ask ourselves, should this movement have alarmed the powerful Government of London? That it did so is abundantly clear. Putting Black Friday on one side, we know that the battle of Falkirk, fought when the Highlanders were in full and hurried retreat, appalled the Court. The only smiling faces were those of the dauntless old King and the malicious but comforted Cope. The best excuse for the cruelty of the repression is the reaction after extreme terror that was then felt. The fact is that no one knew how the dynasty stood. It might be rooted in the hearts of the people or it might not. There was nothing to endear it except Protestantism, nothing personal or traditional. It might be that the quiescence of the nation meant a dull devotion to the existing state of things. But it might also be a perilous indifference; it might even be that the whole nation might rise in a moment, that Charles might cause a ferment as great as the Excise Bill. At any rate, it was certain that on one side there was enthusiasm; on the other, at most, staid conviction. A struggle between these two forces does not always end as it ought. We do not need to believe that Newcastle shut himself up to consider which was likely to be the winning side.

He, though Secretary of State, had no real means of knowing what the mind of the people might be. We do not even know now. We think that there was general apathy: that the failure of the rebellion of 1715 had cowed the Jacobites and kept them from coming openly forward: but we are told that the Welsh were moving to join the Pretender at Derby, and we have strong reason to believe that princes like Beaufort were affected to the cause, which was besides so powerful as to guide the whole policy of Sir R. Walpole to its repression. A majority of the nation was not necessary for success; a bold minority would secure foreign intervention. In all probability, had Charles not retreated from Derby, ten thousand Frenchmen would have attempted a descent on southern England and changed the face of our history. Moreover, a Jacobite army at the gates of London might have roused all those forces of disorder which afterwards showed themselves so potent. If Lord George Gordon could make the metropolis tremble, the roughs that he afterwards utilised might have made Charles Edward a Regent or a King.

But these were not the sole causes of panic. The troops of Cope and Hawley were not dispersed in a moment by such enemies as they had been accustomed to meet. The Highlanders who, uttering an inhuman shout, and clothed in an unknown garb, dashed on with their broadswords, inspired the same horror as the North American Indians that cut Braddock to pieces, or the Huns that followed Attila.

They could not be considered fellow-citizens and subjects. They ate oatmeal mixed with the blood of their kine; their ploughs were attached to the tails of their oxen; their diseases, engendered by a wretched way of life, spread even more panic in England than their arms. Their language was as unintelligible as an African dialect. They were, to the English, barbarians who represented the unknown which is terrible. Taking all, then, into consideration, we may come to the conclusion that the instinct of Charles was right to press onward from Derby, and that the rebellion represented a much more serious danger than we, sitting in our nineteenth-century arm-chairs and counting noses, are apt to reckon.

But on him and his there was a curse that blighted all. At Derby and at Falkirk he was compelled to retreat when he had the fairest chances of success. When a declaration of Protestantism might have served his cause he withheld it: when it was a matter of indifference to everybody he made it. The confidence which he denied to the only general he lavished on the only traitor in his army. When it was represented to him that his mistress was not merely a scandal, but a spy, he risked his adherents, and lost his cause by retaining her, not because he liked her, but because he did not choose to follow advice. When his appearance was of importance, he retired into impenetrable seclusion; when it was repellent, he showed himself nightly in public. There is nothing more to be said. The spell that hung over the froward fanaticism of James ruined the bright promise of his grandson. The despairing exclamation with which the last emissary sent by the Jacobites to Charles Edward closed the account between Great Britain and the exiled family expresses the general verdict of mankind, 'What has your family done, sir, thus to draw down the vengeance of Heaven on every branch of it through so many ages?' It is this dark shadow of destiny, this long historical tragedy, which have given a fascination to the Stuart story. It is the cause for which many thousands of brave men willingly faced exile and ruin and death, for which they were attainted and hanged and massacred; round which the sweetest poetry of Scotland has wound itself, and which the legends of the people embalm. It is not then out of place to print this list of the martyrs of that hapless, hopeless faith.

And now, as to the lists themselves. They are of course imperfect. Clanranald's men of Moidart are, for instance, not included. A very curious list of these, with their respective weapons, is preserved in Father Macdonald's *Moidart; or*

Among the Clanranalds, pp. 171-4. But some of the clans supposed to be detailed are very sparingly given. There are, for instance, only 21 Frasers detailed, with their chief, Lord Lovat, and 24 from the Elgin district, which is an obviously inadequate return. It is probable that some lists are still missing. There is an official printed list 'of noblemen, gentlemen, and others, who have been attainted, and adjudged to be guilty of high treason, for levying war against His Majesty within this realm, since the 24th day of June 1745.' It is drawn up or certified by Mr. D. Moncrieffe, Deputy Queen's Remembrancer, and bears the date of September 24, 1747, when it was published. It begins by reciting those attainted by the 19th of George II., of whom there are 42. It proceeds to give the list in four certificates, two of them under the hand of Henry Masterman, Esq., Clerk of the Crown. The first of these, dated July 24, 1747, contains 51 names, those found guilty of high treason by virtue of His Majesty's special commission of Oyer and Terminer and Gaol Delivery in and for the county of Surrey. The second, dated July 25, 1747, contains 78 names, those found guilty by the same special commission for the county of Cumberland. The third, of the same date, gives those found guilty at York, 70 in all. The fourth is under the hand of Ashley Cowper, Esq., Clerk of Parliament, and sets forth that the Earls of Kilmarnock and Cromartie, Lords Lovat and Balmerino, had been found guilty of high treason, 203 in all. There are scarcely any English names, except that of the hapless Townley, forsaken in the shambles of Carlisle. Some of the Surrey descriptions have a quaint ring: 'Thomas Chadwick, otherwise Chaddock, gentleman, otherwise tallow-chandler; Thomas Furnival, gentleman, otherwise chapman; James Gadd, otherwise Gad, gentleman, otherwise printer, otherwise typefounder; Thomas Siddall, gentleman, otherwise peruke-maker: Alexander M'Growther, the elder, otherwise called Robinson, otherwise Robison, otherwise Robertson, gentleman, otherwise farmer, otherwise yeoman' (the law seems determined to get hold of the hunted M'Growther somehow); 'George Ramsay, gentleman, otherwise labourer,' and so forth.

As to the present list, the Rev. Walter Macleod, to whose interesting Appendix we are so much indebted, tabulates the names, and finds them insufficiently Celtic: hinting indeed that the Highland host is something of a phantom. But to that it must be replied that the list is obviously deficient: that the districts named are not in the main purely Highland districts; that, however, Scotsmen north of the Forth would in 1745 be essentially Highlanders, and that as a matter of fact the eye-witnesses of the Pretender's army speak of Highlanders, and nothing else—that is, men who in garb and appearance and language, and indeed for all practical purposes, were Highlanders: indeed in Home's *History of the Rebellion*, p. 104, an eyewitness goes out of the way to say that all the Pretender's followers at the battle of Prestonpans were distinctively Highlanders. 'The volunteer answered that most of them seemed to be strong, active, and handy men; that many of them were of a very ordinary size, and, if clothed like low country men, would (in his opinion) appear inferior to the king's troops; but the Highland garb favoured them much, etc., etc.' Again, p. 137, 'When the rebels began their march to the southward they were not 6000 men complete: they exceeded 5500, of whom 400 or 500 were cavalry; and of the whole number not quite 4000 were real Highlanders, who formed the clan regiments, and were indeed the strength of the rebel army. All the regiments of foot wore the Highland garb.' Mr. Patullo, the muster-master of the rebel army, on whose statement this sentence is based, does not indeed give any calculation of who were 'real Highlanders'; the inference rather to be drawn from him is that the cavalry were Lowland and the infantry Highland. But in any case, even on Home's showing, it is clear that the great bulk—two-thirds at least—were Highlanders; and though it is probable that some chiefs may have swelled their clan-following by recruiting Lowlanders, and that some of the tenants of Tullibardine and Perth may not have been strictly Highlanders, and although it stands on record that many non-Highland levies joined the rebel standards after the retreat and before Falkirk, it is abundantly clear that the invasion of England was substantially a Celtic raid. Against the general testimony, the fact that the majority of names in these lists are not purely Celtic cannot be allowed to prevail. It would rather seem to prove that clan names were not so strictly adhered to as is generally supposed.

If the lists are deficient it is from no want of care on the part of the Government. Circulars were sent to the parochial clergy (Dunbar's *Social Life in Former Days*, i. 375), desiring them to send in lists of all in their parishes who had *not* been engaged in the late 'wicked and unnatural rebellion.' The deficiency would rather seem to arise from several of the excise districts being omitted. In the Edinburgh Almanack of 1766 there is a 'List of officers in the country collections under the direction of the Commissioners of Excise,' and the districts are given as follows: Aberdeen, Argyle North, Argyle South, Ayr, Caithness, Dumfries, Edinburgh, Fife, Glasgow, Haddington, Inverness, Linlithgow, Perth, Teviotdale. The districts in this book are:—Aberdeen, Argyle North, Ayr, Banff, Caithness, Campbelltown, Dumfries, Dundee, Dunfermline. Duns, Edinburgh, Elgin, Glasgow (2), Haddington, Kelso. Kirkcaldy, Lanark, Linlithgow, Montrose, Old Meldrum, Paisley, Perth, Ross, St. Andrews, Stirling. In the twenty years that elapsed between the two lists it is probable that changes may have been made, but the lists do not apparently cover the same or the whole ground. It does not seem possible, therefore, to carry the matter further than this— that the lists are probably complete in themselves, but that there are not enough of them. There are 2520 names in this list, and few are reckoned as killed. But Charles's army before

PREFACE.

Falkirk was at least 9000, and at Culloden perhaps not less than 8000. In that curious little book, *The Letters of a Volunteer with Cumberland's Army*, the author, on hearsay evidence, estimates the Jacobite loss at Culloden at 2000 killed, besides 222 French and 326 prisoners. Chambers says they lost 1000, one-fifth of their army. President Forbes says they were supposed to have 8000 men at Culloden, 'of whom one-half are probably destroyed or in custody.' The Duke of Argyll, in an article published in 1883, alludes to a manuscript in the British Museum which states that the greatest number of men in arms against the Government did not exceed 11,000. This points to a higher estimate than any that I have seen. But in any case Charles must have had under arms, at one time or another, three, if not four times the number recorded here.

One or two detailed remarks may not be out of place. 'Private man' means 'private soldier.' 'Pedee' (Latin, 'pedisequus') on page 275 is a sort of footboy. Some of the descriptions are curious, and in this respect the Montrose report may be singled out as the most racy and animated. On page 12, the delinquent schoolboy, William Law, will be noticed: on page 18, James Petrie, the 'shirrif deput': on page 23, John Stewart, the 'prompter to rebellion,' and William Troup, the dancing-master: on page 26, James Crichton of Auchengoull, 'created Viscount of Frendraught by the Pretender's son': on page 50, the quaint description of Lord Strathallan: on page 63, the judicious Crawford, portioner of Craill, who secured a knighthood from James and a pension from George: on page 66, the unhallowed duality of Andrew Lothian, who was 'brewer and precentor to the unqualified meetinghouse': on page 68, the disloyal harridan, Mrs. Skeen, and Alexander Stiven, the 'Trone [Tron?] man': on page 92, Sir James Innes the weaver: on page 132, John Berrie, the 'extraordinary salt watchman,' and Bartholomew Bower, the insulting precentor: on page 182, John Mitchell, the ruffian: on page 184, the 'outragious' Rannie:

on page 214, the obscure narrative of Gilbert Gibson: on page 220 and 222, the unlucky substitutes, David Low and George Money: on page 236, Syme, who dwelt by the seaside, but was ' wrong in his judgement,' which on the facts is obvious enough. Throughout it will be found that it was no light matter to wear a white cockade, to drink toasts without reflection, or to speak disrespectfully of King George or the Duke of Cumberland. In the second list, page 297, are some curious details of property, though it will seem hardly possible that Arthur Gordon of Carnoucie (page 308) should really have had an income of £9000 sterling.

Altogether it may be hoped that, for those who take any interest in this last burst of chivalry, these Lists will not have been printed in vain.

LISTS OF REBELLS Transmitted to the Commissioners of Excise by the several Supervisors of Excise in SCOTLAND In obedience to a General Letter of the 7th May 1746

INDEX

Names of districts from which Lists are sent.	Folios[1] of the Book where Lists begin.	No. of Rebels each List contains.
Aberdeen	2	220
Air	292	1
Argyle { north	282	110
south [Campbelltoun]	290	2
Banff	24	200
Caithnes	270	5
Dumfermling	146	19
Dumfries	142	19
Dundee	196	490
Duns	294	4
Edinburgh & Precincts	244	138
Elgine	100	388
Glasgow 1st	272	2
Glasgow 2d	274	17
Haddington	132	59
Kelso	280	5
Kilmarnock		none
Kirkaldy	260	24
Lanerk	84	9
Linlithgow	264	27
Montrose	150	335
Old Meldrum	86	121
Paisley	292	2
Perth	42	115
Ross	72	118
St. Andrews	62	44
Stirling	54	46
		2518
	More	2 come up
		———— from country
		2520

[1] For the folios in the original the pages of this volume are substituted.

A LIST FROM ABERDEEN DISTRICT REBELLION TRANSMITTED TO SUPERVISOR OF

Names.	Designations.	Abode.	Parish.
A.			
James Adamson	Gardner	Drum	Drumoack
John Alexander	Picture Drawer	Aberdeen	Aberdeen
Cosmos Alexander	do.	do.	do.
William Auld	Huxter	do.	do.
James Allan	Town Cadie	do.	do.
James Adam	Gardner	do.	do.
George Alexander	Glover	Spittall	Old Machar
William Aberdeen	Vintiner	Old Aberdeen	do.
James Aberdour	Brazier	do.	do.
Robert Allan	A Servant	do.	do.
James Anderson	Barber	do.	do.
William Adamson	Labourer	Cowlie	Munymusk
B.			
William Burnet	Labourer	Collonach	Strachan

OF PERSONS CONCERN'D IN THE
THE BOARD BY Mr. DAVID STUART,
EXCISE THERE.

County.	Acts of Rebellion and Circumstances.	Where they now are.
Aberdeen	Carried Arms with the Rebells in England and at the Battle of Falkirk, ffrom whence he Carried off a good deal of plunder	Lurking.
do.	Carried Arms with the Rebells in England	Not known.
do.	Carried Arms with the Rebells in England	Not known.
do.	Carried Arms at Inverury and Culloden	Lurking.
do.	Carried Arms at Inverury and Culloden	Prisoner in Aberdeen.
do.	Carried Arms, but deserted and joyned His Royal Highness the Duke at Culloden.	
do.	Acted as an Ensign in the Rebel Army	Lurking.
do.	Acted as a Quarter Master in the Rebel Army	Lurking.
do.	Assisted in uplifting money for the Rebells in Old Aberdeen and was at the Battle of Culloden	Not known.
do.	Carried Arms at the Battle of Culloden	Prisoner in Old Aberdeen.
do.	With the Rebells from the Commencement of the Rebellion	Not known.
do.	Carried Arms at Culloden Battle	Lurking.
Kincardin	Was at Falkirk and Culloden Battles under Arms	Not known.

Names.	Designations.	Abode.	Parish.
Robert Baxter	Labourer	Netherhaugh	Strachan
William Birse	do.	Carlaurg	Birse
Magnus Bridgefoord	do.	Upper Mains of Blairydroyne	Durris
Robert Brand	do.	Banchory	Upper Banchory
John Burnet, Esqr	of Campfield	Campfield	Kincardin
William Baird	Silk dyer	Aberdeen	Aberdeen
Robert Barclay	Merchant	do.	do.
John Bredy	Labourer	Don Bridge	Old Machar
James Bisset	Servant to John Downie	Little Clintarly	Newhills
Peter Byers, Esqr	of Tonley	Tonley	Tonley

C.

John Calder	a young servant	Burnhead	Birss
James Coutts	a poor man	Banchory	Upper Banchory
David Cumming	a Servant	Aberdeen	Aberdeen
John Cristal	Wright	do.	do.
David Coutts, Junr	Wright	do.	do.
David Cristal	do.	Old Aberdeen	Old Machar
George Chalmers	Salmond Fisher	Don bridge	do.
Peter Coutts	Merchant	Aberdeen	Aberdeen

ABERDEEN DISTRICT—*Continued.* 5

County.	Acts of Rebellion and Circumstances.	Where they now are.
incardin	Was at Falkirk Battle, but said to be forced out	Not known.
berdeen	Was at Falkirk Battle, but said to be forced out	
do.	Carried Arms at the Battle of Culloden	
incairden	Carried Arms at the Battle of Culloden	
berdeen	Captain of Artillary in the Rebel Service	Taken prisoner at Carlisle.
do.	Appeared with the first who attempted to proclaim the Pretender, and assisted in unloading the Spanish Ship at Peterhead	Prisoner in Aberdeen.
do.	Lifeguard man to the Young Pretender during the whole Rebellion	Not known.
do.	Carried Arms at the Battle of Culloden	Not known.
do.	Carried Arms at Falkirk and Culloden	Lurking.
do.	A Captain of the Rebells during the whole Rebellion	Lurking.
berdeen	Carried Arms at Culloden, but said to be forced	Not known.
do.	Carried Arms with the Rebells	
do.	Carried Arms at the Battle of Culloden	Killed.
do.	Carried Arms at the Battle of Culloden and was very active in unloading the Spanish Ship at Peterhead & transporting the arms	Lurking.
do.	Carried Arms at Falkirk and Culloden	Not known.
do.	Assisted in unloading the Spanish Ship at Peterhead, was concerned in a Mob in Old Aberdeen, was apprehended and admitted to Bail	Old Aberdeen.
do.	Carried arms at Falkirk and Culloden	Lurking.
do.	Kept guard for the Rebells the night of Inverury Skirmish, and has distinguished himself by talking most disrespectfully of His Majesty	Not known.

LIST OF REBELS FROM

Names.	Designations.	Abode.	Parish.
John Coutts	Baker's Apprentice	Aberdeen	Aberdeen
Robert Calder	Sailor	do.	do.
William Coutts	Boatman	Torry	Nigg
George Craig	Wright	Lonhead	Old Machar
Andrew Clark	Labourer	Wester Co-larly	Echt
D.			
George Durward	Labourer	Band	Birss
Robt. Durward	do.	do.	do.
Thomas Duncan	do.	Tillygarment	do.
Peter Davidson	Servant	Balnacraig	Aboyn
James Dunn	Labourer	Calton of Cockardy	Kinkardin
Alexander Douglas	do.	Coble heugh	Banchory
John Douglas	a Cottar	Glass Well	do.
James Duff	Writer's Apprentice	Hatten	Aughterglass
Alex^r Decorm, Junr	Servant	Aberdeen	Aberdeen
Alex^r Decorm, Senr	Wright	do.	do.
Andrew Deans	Labourer	Hill of Tullicarn	Clunie
John Downie	ffarmer	Little Clintarty	Newhills
Peter Dogood	of Auchenhove	Auchenhove	Lumfannan

ABERDEEN DISTRICT—*Conitnued.*

County.	Acts of Rebellion and Circumstances.	Where they now are.
Aberdeen	Was one of the Mob who broke the Town's Drum when solemnizing the Prince of Wales Birth Day	Not known.
do.	Carried Arms and went North with the Rebells	Not known.
Kincairdin	Assisted in Inlisting men for the Pretender and discharged numbers of People from attending a Fast appointed by Royal Authority	Prisoner in Aberdeen.
Aberdeen	Carried Arms at Culloden	Not known.
do.	Carried Arms at Falkirk and Culloden	Not known.
Aberdeen	Carried Arms at Falkirk but said to be forced	
do.	Carried Arms at Falkirk but said to be forced	
do.	Carried Arms at Falkirk but said to be forced	Not known.
do.	Carried Arms in England & at Falkirk and Culloden	
do.	Carried Arms at Culloden	
Kincardin	Carried Arms at the Battle of Culloden, and there	Kil'd.
do.	Carried Arms at Inverury & Culloden	Not known.
Aberdeen	Carried Arms in the Character of an Officer at Inverury, and was one of those who apprehended Mr. Maitland of Pitrichie	Not known.
do.	Acted as a Lieutenant of the Rebells at the Battle of Culloden & as Collector of the Town Tax of Aberdeen	Lurking.
do.	Acted as a Tidesman for the Rebells in the Port of Aberdeen	Not known.
do.	Carried arms at the Battle of Culloden	Lurking.
do.	Lieutenant in the Rebel Army at the Battle of Culloden	Lurking.
do.	One of the Rebel Officers, was very active in raising large sums of money out of the Parishes of Kincardin, Lumfannan, Touch, Alford, Lochhill, and Midmar	Lurking near his own house.

LIST OF REBELS FROM

Names.	Designations.	Abode.	Parish.
E.			
John Easson	a Cottar	Lorichmore	Strachan
Henry Elphinston, Senr	a discharg'd land waiter	Aberdeen	Aberdeen
Henry Elphinston, Junr	Shipmaster	do.	do.
Michael Edward	Blacksmith	Old Aberdeen	Old Machar
William Edward	Shoemaker	do.	do.
Robert Ewing	Soldier & deserter	Charlestown	Aboyne
Charles Ewing	Labourer	do.	do.
Robert Easson	do.	Formistoun	do.
Peter Ewing	do.	Croft	Glentaner
F.			
Alexander Frazer	Servant	Castle Frazer	Clunie
James Farquharson	of Balmurret	Craigmile	Kincardin
Robert Forbes	Silversmith Apprentice	Aberdeen	Aberdeen
Benjamin Forbes	Merchant	do.	do.
Willm ffindlater	Shoemaker	Spittal	Old Machar
Willm Farquharson	Farmer	Tarland	Tarland
Robert Findlay	Labouring Servant	Balfidie	Birss
Alex^r Tillan	Labourer	Kirktoun	Aboyne
George Forsyth	Servant	Stonywood	Newhills
Francis Farquharson	of Monaltrie	Brachly	Glenmuck
John Farquharson	Farmer	Bogg	Tarland
Henry Farquharson	do.	Whitehouse Miln	Colston
Francis Farquharson	do.	Bogg	Tarland

ABERDEEN DISTRICT—*Continued.*

County.	Acts of Rebellion and Circumstances.	Where they now are.
Kincardin	Carried Arms at the Battle of Culloden.	
Aberdeen	Acted as Tidesurveyor for the Rebels in the Port of Aberdeen	Prisoner at Edinr.
do.	Went to Carlisle with the Rebels, from whence he deserted	Not known.
do.	Carried Arms and went North with the Rebels	Not known.
do.	Assisted in unloading the Spanish Ship at Peterhead and was one of a Mob in Old Aberdeen, was apprehended but	Admitted to Baill.
do.	Carried Arms at Falkirk and Culloden	Kill'd.
do.	Carried Arms at Falkirk and Culloden, and was very active in plundering	Lurking.
do.	Carried Arms at Falkirk & Culloden, and was very active in plundering	Not known.
do.	Carried Arms at Falkirk, but hath not been out since	At home.
Aberdeen	Carried Arms at the Battles of Falkirk & Culloden	Lurking.
do.	Carried Arms in England, a Lieu^t Collonel, and wounded at Falkirk	Lurking.
do.	Carried Arms at Culloden	Lurking.
do.	Carried Arms from the commencement of the Rebellion to the Battle of Culloden	Not known.
do.	Assisted in transport^g the Spanish Arms from Peterhead, surrender'd himself, & now	Admitted to Baill.
do.	Assisted in raising men for the Rebels	Not known.
do.	Carried Arms at Culloden, but said to be forced	Not known.
do.	Carried Arms at the Battle of Culloden	Not known.
do.	Carried Arms at Falkirk and Culloden	Lurking.
do.	A Collonel in the Rebel Army at Falkirk and Culloden, and one of the Chief Raisers of the Men of Aboyne & Cromar	In Inverness Prisoner.
do.	An Ensign at Culloden Battle	Kill'd.
do.	Captain in the Rebel Army at Falkirk & Culloden	Lurking.
do.	Carried arms as an Officer at Culloden	Kill'd.

LIST OF REBELS FROM

Names.	Designations.	Abode.	Parish.
Robert Farquharson	Farmer	Bogg	Tarland
John Frain	do.	Miln of Auchenhove	Lumfanan
Robert Farquharson	Deserter from Lord Loudown's Regim^t	Tullick	Glenmuck
Charles Farquharson	Farmer	Drumnopark	do.
Francis ffarquhar	Servant	Phinzian	Birss
G.			
George Gordon, Esqr	of Halhead	Aberdeen	Aberdeen
Francis Gordon	of Kincardin Miln, Writer	do.	do.
Alex^r Garrioch	Merchant	do.	do.
Francis Gordon	Shoemaker	do.	do.
Willm Gow	Salmond Fisher	Don Bridge	Old Machar
William Garmack	Workman	Lonhead	do.
William Gray	Salmond Fisher	Don Bridge	do.
Lord Lewis Gordon	Lieut^t in the Navy		
Charles Gordon, Esqr	of Blelock	Miln of Gillan	Coull
John Gattahon	Turner	Dyce	Dyce
William Gordon	Farmer	Ferrer	Aboyn
James Glass	a Rebel Officer		Glenmuck
H.			
John Hector	Salmond Fisher	Croves	Old Machar
John Hogg	Extraordinary Tidesman	Aberdeen	Aberdeen
Charles Hacket	Wright Lad	do.	do.
Alexander Hall	Salmond Fisher	Kincoussic	Mary Culter
John Hunter	Labourer	Leyshangie	Kemny

ABERDEEN DISTRICT—*Continued.* 11

County.	Acts of Rebellion and Circumstances.	Where they now are.
Aberdeen	An Ensign at Culloden Battle	Kill'd.
do.	A Serjeant in the Rebel Army	Lurking.
do.	An Ensign in the Rebel Army at the Battle of Culloden	Lurking.
do.	An Ensign in the Rebel Army at Culloden Battle	Lurking.
do.	Carried Arms at Culloden, but said to be forced out.	
Aberdeen	Carried Arms the whole Rebellion, & was Secretary to Lord Pitsligo	Not known.
do.	Acted as General Quarter Master to the Rebels, now in the Highlands	Lurking.
do.	Acted as Ensign during the whole Rebellion	Lurking.
do.	Acted as Ensign during the whole Rebellion	Lurking.
do.	Carried Arms at Culloden	Not known.
do.	Carried Arms at Culloden	Not known.
do.	Carried Arms at Culloden, and was taken prisoner, but	Admitted to Baill.
	Acted as Governour of Aberdeen and Collonel of a Regim^t of the Rebels	Not known.
do.	A Captain and carried Arms at Falkirk, Inverury & Culloden & forced men out of the Earl of Aboyn's Estate	Lurking.
do.	Carried Arms at Cullonden	Lurking.
do.	Carried Arms at Falkirk & Culloden	Lurking.
do.	Was one of those who took the Excise Officers prisoners for to deliver their Books to him	Not known.
Aberdeen	Carried Arms during the whole Rebellion	Prisoner in Old Aberdeen.
do.	Acted as Tidesman for the Rebels in Aberdeen	Not known.
do.	Acted as Collector of the Cess for the Rebells	
do.	Acted as Serjeant to the Rebels	Lurking.
do.	Carried Arms at Culloden	Lurking.

Names.	Designations.	Abode.	Parish.
I.			
James Jaffrey	Joyner	Aberdeen	Aberdeen
Thomas Jaffrey	Under Goaler	do.	do.
John Innes	Wright	do.	do.
John Ingram	Workman	Lonhead	Old Machar
Alex^r Irvine, Esqr	of Drum	Drum	Drumoack
James Innes, Esqr	of Banacraig	Banacraig	Aboyne
Alex^r Imbry		Lochloun	Banchory
K.			
David Keith	Workman	Hardgate	Old Machar
Joseph Kemloe	Blacksmith	do.	do.
William Knows	Salmond Fisher	Nether Banchory	
Robert Knows	do.	Craighead	Nether Banchory
L.			
Joseph Largo	Journyman Sadler	Aberdeen	Aberdeen
Mr. George Law	Nonjurant Minister	do.	do.
Willm Law, his son	A School Boy	do.	do.
Willm Leith	Snuff Grinder	do.	do.
Willm Leith	a Tobacconist	Old Aberdeen	Old Machar
Patrick Logie	Writer	Aberdeen	Aberdeen
George Leith	Salmond Fisher	do.	do.
Charles Longmuir	Labourer	Upper Torie	Nigg
Andrew Lines	do.	Blackhall	Strachan
Willm Ley	Deserter from the Army	Charlestoun	Aboyn
David Lumsden	Farmer	Auchlossan	Lumfanan
John Lumsden	do.	Miln of Cowl	Cowl

ABERDEEN DISTRICT—Continued.

County.	Acts of Rebellion and Circumstances.	Where they now are.
Aberdeen	Carried Arms at the Battles of Falkirk & Culloden	Not known.
do.	Carried Arms at the Battle of Culloden	Lurking.
do.	Acted as Ensign in the Rebel Army during the whole Rebellion	Lurking.
do.	Was at the Battle of Culloden	Not known.
do.	Carried Arms with the Rebels during the whole Rebellion, now in the Highlands	Lurking.
do.	Was in the Rebel Life Guards	Lurking.
do.	Carried Arms at Culloden	Lurking.
Aberdeen	Carried Arms at Culloden	Lurking.
do.	Carried Arms at Culloden	Lurking.
do.	Carried arms during the whole Rebellion	Lurking.
Kincardin	Was Aiding & Assisting to the Rebels in taking Horses	Prisoner in Aberd^n.
Aberdeen	Carried Arms at the Battle of Culloden	Not known.
do.	Carried Arms with the Rebels, was at Stirling Seige & Culloden, now prisoner in	Inverness.
do.	Carried Arms at Culloden	Not known
do.	Carried arms at Falkirk & Culloden, now prisoner in	Aberdeen.
do.	Carried Arms at Culloden, now prisoner in	Elgine.
do.	Acted as Land-Waiter & Officer of Excise in Aberdeen	Lurking.
do.	Acted as Tidesman at Aberdeen	Not known.
Kincardin	Carried Arms at Culloden	Lurking.
do.	Carried Arms as a Serjeant at Inverury & Culloden, now in the Highlands	Lurking.
Aberdeen	Carried Arms as a Serjeant at Inverury & Culloden	Lurking.
do.	Captain of the Rebels	Dead.
do.	Bought & Furnisht Shoes for the Rebels, did not appear in Arms but was very [active] in spiriting up his nighbours to rise in Rebellion	Not known.

LIST OF REBELS FROM

Names.	Designations.	Abode.	Parish.
Thomas Ley	Labourer	Tullick	Glenmuck
John Low	Farmer	Gowry Hall	Aboyn
M.			
Duncan M'Grigor	Farmer	Tarland	Tarland
John M'Lean	Servant to Ja[s] Tower	Ferryhill	Old Machar
Will[m] Moir, Esq[r]	of Loneymay	Nether Miln	Crouden
Robert Mitchell	Barber	Aberdeen	Aberdeen
Robert Muir	Writer	do.	do.
David Marr	Flesher	do.	do.
George Mill	Labourer	Upper Torie	Nigg
James Moir	Shoemaker	Old Aberdeen	Old Machar
Peter Murray	Servant to Wm. Coutts	do.	do.
John Martin	Farmer	Gordon's Mil	do.
Robert Montgomery	A Beggar	Old Aberdeen	do.
Hugh M'Gee	Sailor	Aberdeen	Aberdeen
Alexander Marr	Flesher	do.	do.
Alexander M'Donald	Merchant	do.	do.
Robert Marr	Wright	do.	do.
Thomas Mossman	Writer	do.	do.
Thomas Mercier, Esq[r]	Merchant	do.	do.
James Moir, Esq[r]	of Stonywood	Stonywood	Newhills
Charles Moir	Ship Master	Aberdeen	Aberdeen
Hercules M'Cook.	Shoemaker	Spittal	Old Machar

ABERDEEN DISTRICT—Continued.

County.	Acts of Rebellion and Circumstances.	Where they now are.
Aberdeen	Carried Arms at Inverury & Culloden	Lurking.
do.	Acted as Serjeant to the Rebels at Falkirk, but was not out since	Not known.
Aberdeen	Acted as Ensign, now prisoner at Inverness	Inverness.
do.	Carried Arms at Inverury & Culloden	Not known.
do.	Acted as Deputy Governour of Aberdeen	
do.	A Serjeant & in Arms for the Rebels, was very active in Recruiting & at Culloden Battle	Not known.
do.	One of the Rebel Hussar the whole Rebellion	Not known.
do.	Carried Arms at Inverury & Culloden	Lurking.
Kincardin	Carried Arms at Inverury & Culloden	Lurking.
Aberdeen	Assisted in Unloading a Spanish Ship at Peterhead, was in custody but	Admitted to Baill.
do.	Carried arms during the whole Rebellion, now prisoner in	Old Aberdeen.
do.	Acted as an Ensign at Culloden, now prisoner in	Aberdeen.
do.	Carried Arms at Culloden	Not known.
do.	Carried arms at Culloden	Lurking.
do.	Kept Guard at Aberdeen for the Rebels the night of Inverury Skirmish, now prisoner at	Aberdeen.
do.	Was frequently in Company with the Rebels Governours and assisted in breaking open Letters for which he is now in prison at	Aberdeen.
do.	Acted as Tidesman for the Rebells at Aberdeen	Not known.
do.	Appeared on the Cross at reading the Rebels' Manifesto, wrote the Burgess Tickets to the French Officer, for which absconded, but is now	Admitted to Baill.
do.	Aid du Camp to Lord Pitsligo during the whole Rebellion	Lurking.
do.	A Lieutenent Collonel during the whole Rebellion	Lurking.
do.	Acted as Captain during the Rebellion	Lurking.
do.	Carried Arms at Falkirk & Culloden	Not known.

Names.	Designations.	Abode.	Parish.
Ronald M'Donald.	Servt at Brick Kilns	Old Aberdeen	Old Machar
Alex^r M'Grigor	Workman	Lonhead	do.
James Mitchell	do.	do.	do.
George Mitchell	do.	do.	do.
Gilbert Menzies, Esqr	Son to Mr. Menzies of Pitfodels formerly a French Officer	Pitfodels	Mary Culter
John Menzies David Menzies Willm Menzies James Menzies	Sons of said Mr. Menzies of Pitfodels.	do.	do.
William Mair	Farmer	Blackhall	Strachan
Alexander Million	Shoemaker	Loughtoun	Banchory
Peter Mackie	a Farmer's son	Midbelty	Kincardin
John Moir	Labourer	Auchmore	Midmar
William Middleton	Labourer	Tilabooty	Cowl
Samuel Middleton	Labourer	do.	do.
James Middleton	Labourer	Tilfoody	Aboyn
N.			
James Nivie	Merchant	Aberdeen	Aberdeen
O.			
William Ogg	Labourer	Muryhall	Aboyn
William Ogilvy	Merchant	Aberdeen	Aberdeen
P			
William Philp	Weaver	do.	do.
George Paton	Journyman Shoemaker	do.	do.

ABERDEEN DISTRICT—Continued.   17

County.	Acts of Rebellion and Circumstances.	Where they now are.
Aberdeen	Carried Arms during the Rebellion	Not known.
do.	Carried Arms at Culloden	Not known.
do.	Carried Arms at Culloden, now prisoner in	Aberdeen.
do.	Carried Arms at Culloden, now prisoner in	Aberdeen.
Kincardin	Carried Arms at Culloden Battle	Lurking.
do.	Carried Arms in England & at Culloden	Lurking.
	Carried Arms in England and at Culloden	Lurking.
	Carried Arms during the whole Rebellion	Not known.
	Carried Arms during the whole Rebellion	
do.	Distressed the Country levying money for the Rebels, said to be	Kill'd.
do.	Carried Arms at Culloden	
Aberdeen	Acted as Ensign for the Rebels during the Rebellion	Not known.
do.	Carried Arms at Culloden Battle	Lurking.
do.	Assisted the Rebels in Robing the Country of Arms, but did not go to the Field with them	At Home.
do.	An Active Rebel at all the Engagements & is now lurking	Near Home.
do.	An Active promoter of Rebellion	at home.
Aberdeen	Assisted the Rebels in keeping [guard] during Inverury Skirmish, now prisoner in	Aberdeen.
Aberdeen	Carried Arms with the Rebels	Lurking.
do.	Carried Arms in the Pretender's Life Guards during the whole Rebellion	Lurking.
Aberdeen	Carried arms at the Battle of Culloden	Not known.
do.	Kept guard for the Rebels the night of Inverury Skirmish & was concerned in some Mobs, for which he was apprehended but afterwards	Admitted to Baill.

LIST OF REBELS FROM

Names.	Designations.	Abode.	Parish.
James Petrie	Shirrif Deput	Aberdeen	Aberdeen
Alex^r Paterson	Labourer	Todlochy	Munymusk
R.			
John Robertson	Wright	Aberdeen	Aberdeen
Robert Reid	Merch^t & Son to Sr Alex^r Reid of Barra	Barra	Bourty
James Robb	late Servt to the Shirrif Clerk	Aberdeen	Aberdeen
James Ross	Apprentice	do.	do.
John Ross	Sailor	do.	do.
Hugh Russel	Apprentice	do.	do.
James Ross, Senr	Shirrif Officer	do.	do.
James Ross, Junr, his Son	a Boy	do	do.
Robert Ross	Gardner	do.	do.
Robert Ross	Porter	do.	do.
John Ross	Flesher	do.	do.
John Reid	Stabler	do.	do.
Andrew Richy	Horse Hyrer	Old Aberdeen	Old Macha
Robert Reid	Mason	Aberdeen	Aberdeen
Hugh Ross	Labourer	Wester Clunie	Birss
Alex^r Robertson	do.	Clintary	do.
Alex^r Rieth	Taylor	Gateside	Upper Banchory
James Ramsay	Servant	Boathole	Durris
Robert Reid, Junr	Servant	Charlestoun	Aboyn
Alex^r Ross	Farmer	Tullich	Glenmuck
Donald Reid	Labourer	Inver	Braemarr
S.			
James Stot	Sclater	Aberdeen	Aberdeen

County.	Acts of Rebellion and Circumstances.	Where they now are.
Aberdeen	Aided & assisted the Rebels in all their meetings at Aberdeen; Proclaimed the Pretender and levyed money for the Rebels particularly in the County of Ross	Not known.
do.	Carried Arms at Falkirk and Culloden	Lurking.
Aberdeen.	Carried Arms and was at the Battle of Culloden	
do.	A Rebel officer at Inverury Skirmish & one of those that Apprehended Mr Maitland of Pitrichie	Not known.
do.	Carried Arms the whole Rebellion & was at Culloden Battle	Not known.
do.	Acted as an Ensign in the Rebel Army	Not known.
do.	Acted as an Officer in the Rebel Army	
do.	Carried Arms at the Skirmish of Inverury & was imprisoned, but afterwards	Admitted to Baill.
do.	Carried Arms the whole Rebellion, and is now prisoner at	Inverness.
do.	Acted as a Drummer for the Rebels, now prisoner at	Inverness.
do.	Carried Arms at Culloden	Not known.
do.	Carried Arms at Culloden, now prisoner at	Aberdeen
do.	Carried Arms at Culloden	Lurking.
do.	Carried Arms at Culloden	Not known.
do.	Carried Arms during the Rebellion	Not known.
do.	Was in Arms in a Mob at Aberdeen upon the Prince of Wales' Birth Day	Not known.
do.	Carried Arms at Falkirk & Culloden	
do.	Carried Arms at Falkirk & Culloden	
Kincardin.	Carried Arms at Culloden	Lurking.
do.	Carried Arms at Falkirk	Lurking.
Aberdeen.	Carried Arms at Falkirk & Culloden	Lurking.
do.	Carried Arms at Falkirk and there	Kill'd.
do.	Carried Arms at Falkirk and Culloden	Lurking.
Aberdeen.	Carried Arms the whole time of the Rebellion	Lurking.

Names.	Designations.	Abode.	Parish.
John Shaw	ffidler	Aberdeen	Aberdeen
Willm Steuart	Journyman Baker	do.	do.
John Scott	Sailor	do.	do.
George Steill	Merchant	do.	do.
Daniel Smith	do.	do.	do.
Robert Sandilands	Writer	do.	do.
James Sill	Merchant	do.	do.
Alexander Symers	Gardner	do.	do.
Willm Strachan	Late Clerk to the Comptroller of the Customes	do.	do.
John Sherrif	Barber	do.	do.
James Strachan	Extraordinary Tidesman	do.	do.
James Smith	Workman	Lonhead	Old Machar
Robert Scrogy	Servant Lad	Eshly	Upper Banchory
Robert Smith	do.	Bridge Dy	Strachan
Francis Smith, Senr	do.	Charlestoun	Aboyn
Francis Smith, Junr	do.	do.	do.
James Simpson	do.	do.	do.
Steuart	of Auchoily	Auchoily	Glenmuck
Peter Smith	Labourer	Auchlossan	Lumfanan
Alexander Smith	do.	Dalquhing	Glentaner

ABERDEEN DISTRICT—*Continued.*

County.	Acts of Rebellion and Circumstances.	Where they now are.
Aberdeen	Carried Arms thro' the whole Rebellion and now prisoner in	Aberdeen.
do.	Carried Arms at Culloden	Lurking.
do.	Carried Arms at Falkirk, Inverury, & Culloden; and tho' scarce better than a Boy was very active in distressing the Inhabitants of Aberdeen where he is now in prison	Aberdeen.
do.	Assisted in landing a Spanish Ship at Peterhead, and was Substitute Governour of Aberdeen the time of Inverury Skirmish	Lurking.
do.	Formerly a Sailor in Commodore Anson's Squadron, acted as Lieutenant in the Rebel Service, & was at Inverury & Culloden Battle	Lurking.
do.	Captain in the Rebel Service, was in England, Falkirk, and Culloden, now in the Highlands	Lurking.
do.	A Serjeant in the Rebel Service, & was at the Battle of Culloden	Not known.
do.	Carried Arms at Culloden	Not known.
do.	Acted as Collector of Excise & Customs in Aberdeen for the Rebels, & went north with them	Lurking.
do.	Acted as Tidesman for the Rebels in Aberdeen	Lurking.
do.	Acted as Tidesman for the Rebels in Aberdeen	Lurking.
do.	Carried Arms at Culloden and now prisoner in	Inverness.
Kincardin	Carried Arms at Culloden	
do.	Carried Arms at Culloden	
Aberdeen	Carried Arms at Falkirk & Culloden	Not known.
do.	Carried Arms at Culloden, but said to be forced	
do.	Carried Arms at Culloden, but said to be forced	
do.	Carried Arms the whole Rebellion, Wounded at Culloden & since	Dead.
do.	Carried Arms at Falkirk and Culloden	Lurking.
do.	Carried Arms at Inverury but return'd & laid hold of His Royal Highnesses Proclamation	Not known.

LIST OF REBELS FROM

Names.	Designations.	Abode.	Parish.
John Stewart	Farmer	Borland	Glentaner
Peter Stewart James Stewart Joseph Stewart	} Sons to the above John Stewart	do.	do.
Peter Sanyson	Labourer	Tullich	Glenmuck
T.			
William Troup	Dancing Master	Aberdeen	Aberdeen
Andrew Tilleray	Horse hyrer	Old Aberdeen	Old Machar
John Thomson	Merchant	do.	do.
John Turner	Brick layer	Aberdeen	Aberdeen
Charles Troup	Servant	Pittenkery	Upper Banchory
W.			
Daniel White	Hookmaker	Aberdeen	Aberdeen
Alexander White	do.	do.	do.
Joseph Wilkins	Weaver	Old Aberdeen	Old Machar
George Weir	Workman	Lonhead	do.
William Williamson	Salmond Fisher	Hilhead Blairs	Mary Culter
James Webster	Servant	Balnaboth	Birse
William Walker	Wauker	Waukmill belly	Kincardin

ABERDEEN DISTRICT—*Continued.*

County.	Acts of Rebellion and Circumstances.	Where they now are.
Aberdeen	A prompter to Rebellion who had three sons Engaged therein from one of which he received a Horse taken at Inverness, he also apprehended two of the M'Leods who were making their escape home	Not known.
do.	Enlisted Volunteers with the French and carried Arms at the Battles of Falkirk, Inverury and Culloden, now near their father's house	Lurking.
do.	Was at Falkirk and Culloden	Lurking.
Aberdeen	Acted as Lieutenant at Inverury and Culloden	Lurking.
do.	Carried Arms during the Rebellion	Lurking.
do.	Acted as Ensign at Inverury and Culloden	Lurking.
do.	A Serjeant for the Rebells during the whole Rebellion	Lurking.
Kincardin	Carried Arms at Culloden, but said to be forced out.	
Aberdeen	Carried Arms during the whole Rebellion	Lurking.
do.	Carried Arms the whole of the Rebellion	Lurking.
do.	Carried Arms at Inverury & went north with the Rebels	Not known.
do.	Carried Arms at Culloden	Not known.
Kincardin	Carried Arms at Culloden & prisoner at	Aberdeen.
Aberdeen	Carried Arms at Culloden but said to be forced.	
do.	Carried Arms at Falkirk & Culloden	Not known.

LIST OF PERSONS CONCERNED IN BOARD BY MR. JOHN STUART,

Names.	Designations.	Abode.	County.
A.			
George Abernethie	Merchant & Magistrate	Banff	Banff
Jas. Abercrombie	Farmer	Skeith	Banff
Alex^r Anderson	Laird of Tynot	Tynot	do.
Alex^r Anderson	Servant	Upper Dalachie	do.
James Anderson	Merchant	do.	do.
John Anderson	Gentleman	Craghead	Murray
John Abernethie	Skinner or Taner	Strathbogie	Aberdeen
John Allan	Farmer	Moss side	Banff
Alex^r Anderson	Servant	Knochie Milne	do.
Alex^r Abernethie	Farmer	Tipperty	do.
John Anderson	Younger of Greens	Greens	Aberdeen
B.			
James Bowman	Householder	Portsoy	Banff
James Bowie	Brewer & Maltster	Cullen	Banff
George Bremner	Shoemaker	Fochabers	Murray
John Barclay	do.	do.	do.
Robert Bennet	Merchant	do.	do.
Robert Bremner	Weaver	do.	do.
George Bremner	Shoemaker	Birkinburn	do.
Alex^r Begg	Taner	Akinboe	Aberdeen
Geo^g Bygowan	Servant	Kintore	Aberdeen

THE REBELLION TRANSMITTED TO THE SUPERVISOR OF EXCISE AT BANFF.

Station amongst the Rebels and Acts and Circumstances of Rebellion.	Where they now are.
Captain, assisted in collecting money	Prisoner at Carlisle.
Captain, assisted in collecting the Revenue for the Rebels & gave them Intelligence of Arms	Lurking.
Ensign	Lurking.
A Serjeant and Enlisted men for the Rebels	a Prisoner.
An Ensign & very active in circumveening men into the Rebel service	Not known.
Ensign	Lurking.
Hyred out by the Inhabitants, who were forced so to do by John Gordon of Abochie	Lurking.
Private man & hired out	Not known.
Private man	Lurking.
An Officer & taken at Carlisle	Prisoner.
Volunteer	Not known.
A private man	Not known.
A private man & assisted in plundering the Earl of Findlater's house	Lurking.
A private man	Not known.
A private man	Lurking.
A private man & returned to the Countrey	Lurking.
A private man & returned to the Country	Lurking.
A Volunteer	Lurking.
Private man & hired out	Not known.
Private man & hired out	Not known.

Names.	Designations.	Abode.	County.
George Brember	Wright & a Servant	Carnousie	Aberdeen
James Bicky	Miller's Apprentice	Miln of Turreff	Banff
Willm Brown	Servant	Carnousie Wank Miln	do.
Willm Baird	of Auchmedin	Auchmedin	Aberdeen
C.			
Angus Campbell	Carrier	Banff	Banff
John Chapman	Servant to Sr Wm Gordon of Park	Park	do.
Alexander Clark	Dyster	Fochabers	Murray
Alexander Cowie	Weaver	do.	do.
Thomas Clapperton	do.	do.	do.
Patrick Christy	Farmer	Causartly	Banff
James Crichton	of Auchingoull	Auchingoull	do.
John Cormack	Servant to Darlathis	Darlathis	Aberdeen
D.			
John Duff	Baxter	Banff	Banff
Sir Willm Dunbar	Laird of Durn	Durn	do.
James Donaldson	Servant	Ranass	do
Alex^r Duffus	Messenger	Fochabers	Murray
George Duncan	Servant	do.	do.
James Dawson	Wright	Kinminity	Banff
James Duncan	Servant	Turriff	Aberdeen
Willm Davidson	Taylor	do.	do.
E.			
John Elder	Servant to Sr Wm Gordon of Park	Park	Banff
F.			
Robert Frazer	Carrier & Horse hirer	Banff	Banff
James Farquhar	Farmer	Burnside	do.
Donald Frazer	House holder	Portsoy.	do.
George Forbes	Weaver	Fochabers	Murray
Alex^r ffrazer	Gentleman	Miln of Artlock	Aberdeen

BANFF DISTRICT—Continued.

Station amongst the Rebels and Acts and Circumstances of Rebellion.	Where they now are.
Private man	Lurking.
Private man	Lurking.
Private man	Lurking.
Deputy Lieutenant & Governour of Banff Shire under Lord Lewis Gordon	Not known.
Private man	Not known.
Serving his master who was a Rebel	Not known.
Private man	Prisoner.
Private man was at Culloden Battle and there	Kill'd.
Private man	Prisoner at Carlisle.
Serjeant & was at the Battle of Culloden	Lurking.
A Collonel of the Rebels and created Viscount of Frendraught by the Pretender's Son	Not known.
Recruited men for the Rebels	
Private man	Not known.
Volunteer & would have no Commission	
Assisted the Rebels	Prisoner at Inverness.
A Private man	Lurking.
Private man	Lurking.
Private man & hired out	Lurking.
Private man	Lurking.
Private man, is returned to the Country &	Lurking.
a Servant	Lurking.
a Private man	Not known.
Private man	Lurking.
Private man	
Servant to Lord Drummond	Not known.
Volunteer	

LIST OF REBELS FROM

Names.	Designations.	Abode.	County.
Robert Forbes	Farmer	Corss	Aberdeen
William Fife	do.	Down	Banff
G.			
John Grant	Servt to Sir Wm Gordon	Park	Banff
Sir William Gordon	of Park	Park	do.
Alex^r Gordon	Farmer	Pittenbringan	do.
George Gordon	Blacksmith	Cullen	do.
James Guthry	Servant	Ranass	do.
John Goodbrand	Wright	Cullen	Banff
Humphrey Grant	Weaver	Banff	do.
Alex^r Gordon	Gentleman	Fochabers	Murray
Charles Gordon	Surgeon Apprentice	Aberdeen	Aberdeen
James Gordon	of Clashtirum	Clashtirum	Banff
James Gordon	Gentleman	Birkenbuss	do.
John Gordon	Popish Priest	Press home	do.
William Gray	Salmond Fisher	Fochabers	Murray
James Gordon	Younger of Aberlour	Aberlour	Banff
John Gordon	School Master	Tarrycross	do.
John Gray	Servant	Keith	do.
William Gordon	Farmer	Newmill	do.
Peter Gordon	Inn keeper	Strathbogie	Aberdeen
John Grant	Taylor	do.	do.
Charles Gordon	Gentleman	Beldornie	Banff
Charles Gordon	Younger of Binhall	Binhall	Aberdeen
Charles Gordon	Younger of Terpersie	Terpersie	Banff
George Glashan	Servant	Bagrie Miln	Aberdeen
John Grant	do.	Haddoe	Banff

BANFF DISTRICT—Continued. 29

Station amongst the Rebels and Acts and Circumstances of Rebellion.	Where they now are.
a Lieutenant	made prisoner at Carlisle.
a Volunteer with the Rebels	Not known.
a Servant	Lurking
a Rebel Collonel & very active in distressing the Country by levying money, using very violent measures	Lurking.
A Volunteer in the Pretender's Son's Life Guards	Not known.
Was very active in the Rebel service	a Prisoner.
Assisted the Rebels	Lurking.
a Private man	Lurking.
a Lieutenant in the D. of Perth's Regiment	Not known.
a Captain, assisted in collecting the Revenue for the Rebels and was at the affair of Keith	Not known.
a Captain, assisted in Robing Lord Sinclair near Portsoy, of his Horses &c.	
a Captain & very active in Recruiting men for the Rebels	Lurking.
a Lieutenant & was very active, wounded at Inverury Skirmish	Not known.
Went to Perth with Recruits and afterwards followed the Rebels	
Private man, was at the plundering the Earl of Findlater's house, returned to the Country &	Lurking.
a captain & very active in his station, has been in the Country since Culloden Battle but	Lurking.
Assisted the Rebels, had been a Serjeant in General Cope's Army & deserted	Lurking.
Private man	Prisoner at Carlisle.
a Volunteer	Lurking.
a Volunteer	Lurking.
Hired out by the Inhabitants	Lurking.
a Volunteer	Not known.
Paymaster in Gordon of Glenbucket's Regiment	made Prisoner at Carlisle.
a Volunteer	made Prisoner at Carlisle.
a Private man & hired out	Not known.
a Private man & hired out	

Names.	Designations.	Abode.	County.
James Grant	Fidler	Haddoe	Banff
John Gordon	Farmer	Borter	do.
John Gordon	of Glenbucket	Glenbucket	
James Gordon	of Beldornie	Beldornie	Banff
John Gordon	Farmer	Collonoch	Aberdeen
John Gordon	of Abochie	Abochie	do.
James Gordon	of Conbardie	Conbardie	do.
James Gordon	of Terpersie Senr	Terpersie	Banff
Alex^r Gordon	of Darlathis	Darlathis	Aberdeen
Alex^r Gordon, Junr	of Darlathis	do.	do.
Arthur Gordon	of Carnousie	Carnousie	Banff
George Gill	Shoemaker	Bridgend now at Aberdeen	Aberdeen
John Gillespie	Sclater	Turriff	do.
Alex^r Gill	Servant	Cushny	Banff
John Garvich	do.	Buckholy	Aberdeen
Alex^r Gatt	Servant	Carnusie	Banff
H.			
George Hay	Sailor	Portsoy	Banff
Robert Hendry	Servt to Sir Wm Dunbar	Durn	do.
Andrew Hay	Younger of Raness	Raness	do.
Alexander Hay	Blacksmith	Fochabers	Murray
Alexander Hay	Gentleman	Aswantly	Banff
John Hamilton	do.	Sanston	Aberdeen
Charles Hacket	Farmer	Drachlamiln	do.
Charles Hacket	his Son	do.	do.
George Hay	Younger of Montblery	Montblery	Banff
John Hay	Wright	Dalgaty	Aberdeen
Peter Hepburn	Farmer	Ardin	do.

BANFF DISTRICT—*Continued.* 31

Station amongst the Rebels and Acts and Circumstances of Rebellion.	Where they now are.
Private man	Not known.
Acted as a spy and was taken	Prisoner.
a Lieut. Collonel	
a Volunteer	
a Volunteer	
a Rebel Collonel	Not known.
Acted in the character of an Officer	
a Rebel officer	
a Volunteer	
an Officer in the Rebel Army	
An officer in the Rebel Army	Not known.
Attacked one of the M'Leods on his Escape from the Skirmish of Inverury and attempted to rob him of his Arms till prevented by Mr James Donaldson Merch^t in Turriff & others well affected	Not known.
Acted as a Spy and a Reconitering Officer for the Rebels	Not known.
A Private Man	Lurking.
A Private Man but very oppressive	Not known.
Was aiding & assisting in Robing James Paterson, Carrier in Banff of a Letter from Sir James Grant to the Laird of M'Leod which being carried to Lord Lewis Gordon, occasioned the action of Inverury and the Retreat of the M'Leods	Not known.
a Lieutenant	a Prisoner.
assisted the Rebels	Not known.
Major of Horse to Lord Pitsligo's Regiment	Lurking.
a Private Man	Lurking.
a Volunteer	Not known.
Governour of Carlisle for the Rebels and there made	Prisoner.
a Violent Jacobite & aided & assisted the Rebels	
a Recruiting Officer and Collected the Cess for the Rebels	
a Volunteer	Not known.
a Recruiting Officer, & the principal Person who proclaimed the Pretender at Turriff & drank rebellious healths	
had a Commission from Gordon of Glenbucket to Recruit for the Rebels	

Names.	Designations.	Abode.	County.
Adam Hay	of Asslid	Asslid	Aberdeen
James Hacket	a Farmer's Son	Drachlamiln	do.
I.			
James Joyner	Servant	Towks	Banff
John Innes	Younger of Edingight	Edingight	do.
James Joyner	House holder	Portsoy	do.
Coll. James Innes	Overseer of the highways	Cullen	do.
James Innes	Wig Maker	Fochabers	Murray
William Innes	do.	do.	do.
Patrick Innes	Weaver	Edindiack	Banff
John Ingram	Miller	Perry's Miln	Aberdeen
John Johnston	Servant	Burnend Carnusie	do.
Adam Irvine	late of Bruchly	Down	Banff
K.			
Alexander Kerr	Weaver	Keith	Banff
James King	Servant	Darrow	Aberdeen
L.			
William Laing	Servant	Fochaber	Murray
Alex^r Lesslie	ffarmer	Auchinhanick	Banff
John Lawrance	Mason	Keith	do.
John Leith	Inn Keeper	Strathbogie	Aberdeen
Alex^r Lowper	Mason	do.	do.
Alex^r Leith	Farmer	Collithy	do.
Willm Lorimer	do.	Irnhill	do.
Alexander Leith	Mason	Turriff	do.
Wm Lesslie	a Farmer's Son	Hillhead of Turriff	do.

BANFF DISTRICT—Continued.

Station amongst the Rebels and Acts and Circumstances of Rebellion.	Where they now are.
a Volunteer, was at the Battle of Culloden, & there made	Prisoner.
a private man	Lurking.
Private Man	Lurking.
a Rebel Volunteer, who when he returned home his Father would not harbour	Lurking.
a Private Man	Not known.
Aid du Camp to Ld Ogilvie, threatened the Officer of Excise when doing his duty; he was in the Rebellion Anno 1715	Prisoner at Aberdeen.
a Private Man, but laid down his Arms and now	at Liberty.
a Private Man, was at Culloden Battle and since	a Prisoner.
a Volunteer, & most active in the Rebel service	Lurking.
a Private Man	Not known.
Private Man returned to the Countrey &	Lurking.
Gentleman Volunteer	Lurking.
Private man hired out	Lurking.
Private man	Lurking.
Private Man	Not known.
Ensign	Lurking.
Private man hired out	Lurking.
a Volunteer	Lurking.
Private man hired out	Lurking.
Went into England with the Rebels	Prisoner at Carlisle.
a Private man	Not known.
a private man	Lurking.
a private man and returned to the country but	Lurking.

LIST OF REBELS FROM

Names.	Designations.	Abode.	County.
M.			
Alex^r M'Ra	an Idler	Banff	Banff
Thomas Marr	Mason	do.	do.
W^m M'Donald	Piper	Portsoy	Banff
Alex^r Mackie	Servant	Byers	do.
Donald M'Kay	do.	Fochabers	Murray
John Milne	do.	Boadfoord	Banff
Peter Montgomery	Sadler	Fochaber	Murray
Peter M'Lauchlan	Weaver	do.	do.
Alex^r Mackie	Servant	Keith	Banff
James Mitchell	Weaver	do.	do.
Willm Malcom	do.	do.	do.
James Mair	Servant	Strathbogie	Aberdeen
David Mattheson	Taylor	do.	do.
Donald M'Kenzie	Mason	do.	do.
Willm M'Glashan	Horse hirer	do.	do.
Alexander Man	Servant	Slioch	do.
Alex^r Mitchell	Farmer	Carnwhelp	Banff
Alex^r M'Donald	Servant	do.	do.
Alex^r Morrison	a Farmer's Son	Knockieburn	do.
George Milne, Junr	Son to Geo. Miln, Innkeeper	Turriff	Aberdeen
James Maver	Son to Willm Maver	do.	do.
William Milne	Son to Ja^s Milne, Mason	do.	do.
Willm Morrison	Servant	Darlathis	do.
Alex^r Morrison	Farmer	Muckle Colp	do.
John Morrison	Servant	Aucherless	do.
N.			
William Nicolson	Servant	Strathbogie	Aberdeen

BANFF DISTRICT—Continued. 35

Station amongst the Rebels and Acts and Circumstances of Rebellion.	Where they now are.
a Lieutenant	Not known.
a Private man	Not known.
Piper	
Private Man	Lurking.
Private Man went with the Rebels into England	Kill'd.
Private Man	Lurking.
Private Man	Lurking.
Private Man	Prisoner at Carlisle.
Private Man hired out	Lurking.
a Private Man and hired out	Lurking.
a Private Man and hired out	Lurking.
a Volunteer	Lurking.
Hired out by the Inhabitants and served in the Rebellion	Lurking.
Served in the Rebellion being hired out by the Inhabitants	Lurking.
Carried Arms and was hired out	Lurking.
a Private Man and hired out	Not known.
Private Man	Not known.
a Private Man and was hired	Not known.
a Private Man	Lurking.
Attacked one of the M'Leods & attempted to Rob him of his Arms &ca as mentioned of George Gill	Lurking.
Carried on a Correspondence with the Rebels and Run Express to Lord Lewis Gordon at Aberdeen with Sir James Grant's Letter to the Laird of M'Leod which had been Intercepted by the Rebels	Not known.
a Private Man	Lurking.
a Private Man	Lurking.
a Private Man	Lurking.
a Private Man	Lurking.
A Private man & hyred out	Lurking.

Names.	Designations.	Abode.	County.
P.[1]			
George Paterson	Householder	New Durn	Banff
Hercules Paterson	Surgeon & a discharged Officer of Excise	Keith	do.
Alexr Panton	Innkeeper	Turriff	Aberdeen
O.			
Walter Ogilvy	Writer	Banff	Banff
James Ord	Wig Maker	Cullen	do.
Patrick Ogilvy	Servant	Ardoch	do.
Alexr Ogilvy	Shoemaker	Corridown	do.
R.			
James Robertson	Servant	Wintertoun	Banff
Charles Ross	formerly a Soldier	Fochabers	Murray
Peter Robertson	Piper	do.	do.
John Robison	Innkeeper	Strathbogie	Aberdeen
Thos. Ross	Wright	Miln of Coltithy	do.
John Roy	Servant	Turriff	do.
Alexr Ross	Servant	Down	Banff
Patrick Robertson	do.	Findorn	do.
S.			
James Smith	Writer in Edinb{r}	Newmills of Boyn	Banff
James Stivenson	Servant	Edingight	do.
John Sinclair	Fidler	Newmills of Boyn	do.
Alexr Sutherland	Wright	Fochabers	Murray

[1] O comes after the letter P in the original.

BANFF DISTRICT—Continued. 37

Station amongst the Rebels and Acts and Circumstances of Rebellion.	Where they now are.
a Private Man	Not known.
Acted as an Officer in the Rebel Army, was concerned in Levying Contributions at Keith & gave Orders to the Heretors to pay their Cess	Lurking.
Assisted in robing James Paterson, Carrier in Banff of Sir Ja^s Grant's Letter to the Laird of M'Leod, as mentioned of Alex^r Gatt	Not known.
An Officer in the Rebel Army	Prisoner at Carlisle.
One of the Rebel Hussars	Lurking.
a Private Man & Lurking in the house of Patrick Duff on	Spey side.
a Private Man	Lurking.
a Private Man	Lurking.
a Rebel Serjeant & very active in Recruiting Men	Lurking.
Carried Arms and assisted in Collecting Money for the Rebels	Not known.
Carried Arms, being hyred out by the Inhabitants who were forced thereto by John Gordon of Abochie	Lurking.
Private Man	Not known.
Carried Arms as a private man	Lurking.
Carried Arms as a private man	Lurking.
Carried Arms as a private man	Lurking.
a Volunteer & carried Arms	Lurking.
was active in Robing the Country of Horses, &c.	Not known.
Carried Arms as a private man	Prisoner in Banff.
Carried Arms as a Serjeant	Lurking.

Names.	Designations.	Abode.	County.
George Sutherland	Servant	Fochabers	Murray
Peter Stuart	Gentleman	Oxhill	Banff
Peter Stuart	Gentleman	Tannachie	do.
Adam Simpson	Cottar	Glengerick	do.
Angus Stuart	Farmer	Park begg	do.
John Simpson	do.	Auchinhove	do.
Patrick Stuart	Farmer	Tininder	do.
William Smith	Carrier	Keith	do.
William Shand	a Servant	Causartly	do.
Willm Stodhart	Innkeeper	Keith	do.
James Stewart	Farmer	Strathbogie	Aberdeen
Alex^r Stuart	Horse hyrer	do.	do.
Alex^r Smith	Servant	Drinndolo	do.
George Smith	Farmer	Welcomin	do.
James Steuart	Wigmaker	Turriff	do.
John Skien	Taylor	do.	do.
Wm Scot	Servant	Carnousie	Banff
George Smith	Farmer	Upper Bridge End	Aberdeen
T.			
James Taylor	Shoemaker	Newmills of Boyn	Banff
Willm Taylor	Farmer's Son	Dalochie	do
John Thain	Masson	Strathbogie	Aberdeen
David Tulloch	Farmer	Dunbeenan	do.
W.			
Alex^r Wilson	Servt to Sir Wm Gordon	Park	Banff
David Wilson	Servant to do.	Gardenhead Park	do.
Robt Wilson	Wright	Fochabers	Murray
Alex^r Wright	Subtenant	Glengerick	Banff
James Watson	Merchant	Keith	do.

BANFF DISTRICT—Continued.

Station amongst the Rebels and Acts and Circumstances of Rebellion.	Where they now are.
Carried Arms	Lurking.
Ensign in the Rebel Army & was very active in recruiting men	Lurking.
Ensign in the Rebel Army	Lurking.
Carried Arms but said to be hyred out	Lurking.
Ensign in Roy Stuart's Regiment	Lurking.
Lieutenant, was at the Skirmish at Keith	Lurking.
Carried Arms as a Captain	Lurking.
Carried Arms, was hyred out	Lurking.
Carried Arms, was at Culloden Battle & there taken	Prisoner.
was a Spy on his Royal Highnesses Army & conducted the Rebels to attack the Campbells at Keith	Lurking.
Carried Arms, being hired out	Not known.
Carried Arms, being hired out	Lurking.
Carried Arms, being hired out	Not known.
a Private man & carried Arms	Not known.
Carried Arms	Lurking.
Carried Arms	Lurking.
Carried Arms	Lurking.
Recruited Men for the Rebels & otherwayes assisted them	Not known.
Carried Arms as a private man	Lurking.
an Ensign and very active in the Rebel Service, was also at plundering the Earl of Findlater's house	Not known.
Carried Arms as a private man but said to be hired out by the Inhabitants	Lurking.
Captain, who also collected the Cess and Levyied money for the Rebels	Not known.
Carried Arms as a private man	Not known.
Carried Arms but was forced out by his master	At home.
Carried Arms as a private man & deserted from the Rebels in England	Not known.
Carried Arms as a private man, said to be hired out	Lurking.
Quarter Master in Roy Stuart's Regiment, was at the Battle of Culloden & there	Kill'd.

LIST OF REBELS FROM

Names.	Designations.	Abode.	County.
John Wright	Taylor	Strathbogie	Aberdeen
John Walker	Servant	Drumbulg	do.
Willm Walker	Weaver	Hackhall	do.
John Watt	Servant	Gamry	Banff
Wm Watt	Servant	Auchmedin	Aberdeen
Willm Wilson	Servant to Wm Maver	Turriff	do.

BANFF DISTRICT—*Continued.*

Station amongst the Rebels and Acts and Circumstances of Rebellion.	Where they now are.
Carried Arms, said to be hired by the Inhabitants	Lurking.
A Private Man in the Rebel Service	Not known.
Carried Arms as a private man & was hyred thereto	Not known.
Carried Arms	Lurking.
Carried Arms	Lurking.
Assisted in robing James Paterson, Carrier, of Sir James Grant's Letter as mentioned of Alex^r Gatt	Not known.

A LIST OF PERSONS CONCERNED THE BORD BY MR. LEWIS HAY

Names.	Designations.	Abode.	Parish.
B.			
John Buchanan	Carrier	Auchterarder	Auchterarder
John Balfour	Messenger at Arms	Perth	Perth
James Bayne	Barber	do.	do.
Burt	Shoemaker	do.	do.
Robert Bresdie	Indweller	Muthel	Muthel
John Bowie	Mason	Dunkeld	Dunkeld
John Bannerman	Workman	do.	do.
C.			
David Carmichael	of Balmedie, Coll^r of the Cess	Balmedie	Dron
Lodovick Caw	Surgeon	Creiff	Creiff
Mungo Campbell	late Soldier in Ld John Murray's R^t	do.	do.
Campbell	Son of the Laird of Glenlyon	Glenlyon	Fortingall
John Campbell	of Kinloch	Milton of Strathbran	Little Dunkeld
Duncan Campbell	Brother of the Laird of Dunneves	Dunneves	Fortingall
Matthew Chape	Sadler	Perth	do.
John Carmichael	a Coll^r of the Stent in Perth	Woodend	Kinoull

N THE REBELLION, TRANSMITTED TO SUPERVISOR OF EXCISE AT PERTH.

County.	Acts of Rebellion and Circumstances.	Where they now are.
Perth	Carried Arms as a Volunteer in the Rebel Army	Prisoner at Stirling.
do.	Acted as a Captain in the Rebel Army & was seen in Arms	Lurking.
do.	Acted as a Quarter Master for the Rebels	Lurking.
do.	Seen in Arms with the Rebels	Lurking.
do.	Press'd out by Lord Drummond, but returned &	at Home.
do.	Guarded the Boat of Invar for the Rebels	at home.
do.	Joined & assisted the Rebels	Not known.
Perth	Collected the Land Tax for the Rebels & voluntarly accepted of that office	Lurking.
do.	Acted as Surgeon to Perth's Regim^t & went with the Rebels	Not known.
do.	Acted as Ensign in the Rebel Army	Lurking.
do.	was a Captain in the Rebel Army	Lurking.
do.	Acted as Captain in the Rebel Army	Prisoner at Inverness.
do.	Acted as an Officer in the Rebel Army	Lurking.
do.	Carried Arms with the Rebels	Prisoner in Perth.
do.	Joyned the Rebels and went North with them	Not known.

Names.	Designations.	Abode.	Parish.
Duncan Comrie	Indweller	Woodend of Mevie	Comrie
Alex^r Cuming, Senr	Papist	Miln of Drummond	Muthel
Alex^r Cuming, Junr	do.	do.	do.
John Clark	Mason	Dunkeld	Dunkeld
D.			
Gavin Drummond	Brewer	Auchterairder	Auchterairder
James Drummond	Tenant	Garthlees	
George Drummond	Baxter	Perth	Perth
John Drummond	Messenger at Arms	do.	do.
William Dow		Auchinshelloch	Comrie
John Drummond		Millinow	do.
James Drummond		Comrie	do.
Peter Drummond		Bellnae	do.
Peter Drummond		Millinmow	do.
William Drummond	of Callender	Callender	Monzie
James Drummond	called Duke of Perth	Drummond	Muthel
George Drummond	of Drummawhance	Drummawhance	do.
Ja^s Drysdale		Muthel	do.
John Drummond		Drummond	do.
Ja^s Drummond		Cochquhillie	do.
John Drummond	Valle de Chambre to D. of Perth	Drummond	do.
G.			
Robert Graham	of Garrack	Garrack	Fortavit
Willm Gray	Surgeon Apprentice	Perth	Perth
Peter Graham		Gorthie	Fowls

PERTH DISTRICT—Continued.

County.	Acts of Rebellion and Circumstances.	Where they now are.
Perth	Carried Arms for the Rebels but pressed thereto	Not known.
do.	Went along a Volunteer with the Rebels	Not known.
do.	Went along with the Rebels as a Volunteer	Not known.
do.	took the Excise Officer Prisoner for the Rebels & beat him	surrendered himself.
Perth	was active in forcing people into the Rebellion by the Duke of Perth's order	Not known.
do.	Carried Arms as a Rebel Volunteer	Prisoner in Edin^r.
do.	Carried Arms as a Rebel Volunteer	do.
do.	Acted as Overseer under the French Engineer, said to be pressed	Prisoner in Perth.
do.	Acted as a Lieutenant for the Rebels	Not known.
do.	Carried Arms as a Captain of the Rebells	Lurking.
do.	Carried Arms for the Rebels, said to be pressed	At home.
do.	Volunteer in the Rebel Army	Lurking.
do.	Carried Arms as an Ensign in the Rebel Army	Not known.
Perth	Acted as a Captain for the Rebels	do.
do.	a Rebel General & very active in their service	Not known.
do.	was Prest into the Rebel Service	Not known.
do.	Press'd into the Rebel Service	At home.
do.	a Volunteer in the Rebel Service	At home.
do.	a Volunteer in do. Service	Not known.
do.	a Volunteer in said Service	Not known.
Perth	Levied the Excise at Duns for the Rebels & went along with them	Not known.
do.	Went off with the Rebels as a Volunteer	Prisoner at Edin^r.
do.	Went along with the Rebels as Commissary for their Army	Not known.

LIST OF REBELS FROM

Names.	Designations.	Abode.	Parish.
H.			
Duncan Henderson	Merchant	Perth	Perth
Willm Henderson	Baxter	do.	do.
Willm Harrel		Strothell Miln	Muthel
Thos Hill	Brewer	Dunkeld	Dunkeld
I.			
David Jack	Wright	Dunkeld	Dunkeld
L.			
James Lockhart	Wright	Crieff	Crieff
John Low	Farmer	Ballanloig	Logyrate
James Lindsay	Shoemaker	Perth	Perth
James Lindsay	Shoemaker Apprentice	do.	do.
Martin Lindsay	Writer in Edinburgh	do.	do.
Mr Robert Lyon	Minister	do.	do.
M.			
Willm Murray	Post Master	Crieff	Crieff
Allan M'Donald	Brewer	do.	do.
M'Intyre	Merchant	Burn of Keltney	Fortingall or Dull
Menzies	of Sheen	Sheen	
Alex^r M'Lean	Shoemaker Apprentice	Perth	Perth
John Martin	no Employment	do.	do.
Thos Moncrife	late Excise Officer	do.	do.
Ld George Murray	Brother to Duke of Athole	Tullibardine	Blackfoord

PERTH DISTRICT—*Continued.* 47

County.	Acts of Rebellion and Circumstances.	Where they now are.
Perth	Carried Arms as a Lieutenant of the Rebels	Lurking.
do.	Was a Lieutenant of the Rebels and seen in Arms	Lurking.
do.	Carried Arms as a Volunteer in the Rebel Army	Not known.
do.	Joyned the Rebels	Dead.
Perth	Went along as a Volunteer with the Rebels	Not known.
Perth	A Volunteer with the Rebels in some superior station	Lurking.
do.	Acted in the character of an Officer amongst the Rebels	Lurking.
do.	A Rebel Volunteer & seen in Arms	Prisoner at Inverness.
do.	Seen with the Rebels & in Arms but said to be forced out	Lurking.
do.	Acted as Secretary to Ld Strathallan & Oliphant of Gask	In Edin^r Prisoner.
do.	Went along with the Rebels as Chaplain to their Army	Montrose, Prisoner.
Perth	Carried Arms with the Rebels in some superior station	Not known.
do.	Entered a Volunteer in the Rebel Army	do.
do.	Was in the Rebel Army in the station of an Officer	do.
do.	Acted in the character of an Officer amongst the Rebels	do.
do.	Seen in Arms with the Rebels but said to be press'd	Lurking.
do.	Went off a Volunteer with the Rebells	Lurking.
do.	Acted as Deput Collector of Excise for the Rebels	Lurking.
do.	A Rebel General &c.	Not known.

LIST OF REBELS FROM

Names.	Designations.	Abode.	Parish.
Murray	Younger of Dollaire	Dollaire	Creiff
John M'Leish		Muthel	Muthel
John M'Robie, younger		Drummond	do.
Lewis M'Robie		do.	do.
Donald M'Ewan	Mason	Dunkeld	Dunkeld
John M'Ewan	Residenter in	do.	do.
James Man	Baker	do.	do.
John Man	Shoemaker	do.	do.
John M'farlane	Taylor	do.	do.
N.			
John Napier	Mason	Dunkeld	Dunkeld
Thomas Nicol	Workman	do.	do.
O.			
Laurance Oliphant	of Gask	Gask	Gask
Laurance Oliphant	younger of Gask	do.	do.
P.			
John Powrie	Shoemaker	Perth	Perth
R.			
George Robertson	of Faskily	Faskily	Mullion
Chas. Robertson	Merchant Apprentice	Eastertyre	Little Dunkeld
Ja⁸ Robertson	of Gillichangie	Killichangie	Logyrate
Ja⁸ Robertson, Junʳ	of Killichangie	do.	do.
Robertson	of Blairfetty	Blairfetty	Blair
Donald Robertson	of Woodsheel	Woodsheel	Fortingall
Robertson	Brother to Woodshell	do.	do.
Duncan Robertson	of Drumaheen	Drumaheen	Foss
Robertson	of Strowan	Carie	do.

PERTH DISTRICT—Continued. 49

County.	Acts of Rebellion and Circumstances.	Where they now are.
Perth	went off a Volunteer with the Rebels	Not known.
do.	Carried Arms with the Rebels, press'd out &	returned home.
do.	Went along a Volunteer with the Rebels	Not known.
do.	Went out a Rebel Volunteer	at home.
do.	Carried Arms in the Rebel Army	Lurking.
do.	Carried Arms in Rebel Army	Lurking.
do.	Carried Arms	England, Prisoner.
do.	Carried Arms in Rebel Army but deserted before the Battle of Prestoun	at Home.
do.	Joyned the Rebels on their Retreat Northward	Absconding.
Perth	Employed by the Rebels as a Guard of Invar Boat	At home.
do.	Joyned the Rebels, took the Officer' of Excise Prisoner & beat him	Absconding.
Perth	a Volunteer in the Rebel Army	Not known.
do.	a Volunteer in do.	Not known.
Perth	Went along with the Rebels to England	England, Prisoner.
Perth	Lieut.-Coll. in the Rebel Army, seduced by the Marquis of Tillibardine	Not known.
do.	Acted as an Officer in the Rebel Army	Lurking.
do.	an Officer in said Army but left them before the Battle of Falkirk	at home.
do.	was an Officer amongst the Rebells	Lurking.
do.	was a Rebel Collonel & very active in pressing men into that service	Lurking.
do.	Acted as an Off^r in the Rebel Army	Lurking.
do.	was an officer in said Army	Lurking.
do.	was a Collonel in said Army	Lurking.
do.	was a General in said Army	Lurking.

D

Names.	Designations.	Abode.	Parish.
Thos Robertson	Farmer	Windyedge	Aberdagie
James Rattray	Surgeon Apprentice	Perth	Perth
James Riddoch		Drummond	Muthel
Duncan Roy		do.	do.
Laur Robertson	Mason	Dunkeld	Dunkeld
S.			
Malcon Stuart	Brother of the Laird of Sheerless	Sheerless	Mullion
Chas Stuart, Junr	of Ballachan	Ballachan	Logyrate
Robert Stuart	of Killihassy	Killihassy	Weem
Stuart	of Kennoching	Kennoching	Foss
Stuart	of Bohallie	Bohallie	Weem
Stuart	of Garth	Garth	Dull
Stuart	the Laird of Garth's Brother	do.	do.
Stuart	Weaver	Balmaniel	Logyrate
Stuart, Junr	of Findynet	Findynet	do.
John Stuart	Mercht Apprentice	Perth	Perth
Alexr Stuart	Shirref Officer	do.	do.
Finlay Stuart	do.	do.	do.
John Showster	Indweller	Scoon	Scoon
James Stuart	Living in	Cannband	Comrie
Æneas Sinclair		Comrie	do.
Peter Stalker	Servant to Jon Stalker	Glenlednek	do.
John Stalker		Condie Cleuch	Monzie
The Lord	Strathallan	Machony	Muthel
Willm Smith	Living at	Drummond	do.
William Stuart		Drummond	do.

PERTH DISTRICT—Continued.   51

County.	Acts of Rebellion and Circumstances.	Where they now are.
Perth	was a Captain of the Rebels and seen in Arms	Lurking.
do.	was a Rebel Volunteer	Lurking.
do.	went a Volunteer in the Rebel Army	At home.
do.	went a Volunteer in the Rebel Army	
do.	went in Arms with the Rebels on their Retreat North	Not known.
Perth	Was an Officer in the Rebel Army	Lurking in the Hills.
do.	Acted as Lieut Collonel in the Rebel Army	Lurking in do.
do.	an Officer in said Army & commanded his own Tenents	Lurking in do.
do.	was Major in the Rebel Army & commanded his own Tenents	
do.	Was an Officer in said Army, had the command of his own Tenents	Lurking in the Hills.
do.	Acted as an Officer in said Army commanding his own Tenents	
do.	was an Officer in the Rebel Army	
do.	was also an Officer in the Rebel Army, is sometimes at home but	Lurking.
do.	Acted as an Officer in the Rebel Army	do.
do.	Went off a Volunteer with the Rebels	Lurking.
do.	Employed as Spies & Intelligencers by Lord Strathallan, were active in oppressing the Country & charging the people to pay the Revenue, &c., to the Rebels	at Edinr prisoners.
do.	
do.	was concerned in a Mob & in Arms at Perth on the Annivry of His Majesty Birth Day	Went North wt the Rebels.
do.	Carried Arms with the Rebels but forced out	at home.
do.	Pressed by the Rebels into their service	at home.
do.	Press'd by the Rebels into their service	at home.
do.	Carried Arms as a private man in the Rebel Service but press'd out	at home.
do.		not known.
do.	a Volunteer in the Rebel Service	at home.
do.	Carried Arms in said Service as a Volunteer	Not known.

Names.	Designations.	Abode.	Parish.
James Stuart		Drummond	Muthel
John Scott	Mason	Dunkeld	Dunkeld
James Scott	Workman	do.	do.
James Stuart	Tobacconist	do.	do.
Lau^r Stuart	Cook & Taylor	do.	do.
Robert Stuart	Servant	do.	do.
T.			
James Thomson	Tenant	Potthill	
Robert Thomson	do.	do.	
W.			
David Wilson	Indweller in	Scoon	Scoon
Y.			
James Yuill	Living in	Bridge End	Kinnowl

PERTH DISTRICT—Continued. 53

County.	Acts of Rebellion and Circumstances.	Where they now are.
Perth	Carried Arms as a Volunteer in the Rebel Service	Not known.
do.	Carried Arms in the Rebel Service	surrendered himself.
do.	Carried Arms in do. Service	not known.
do.	Joyned the Rebells & carried Arms	Absconding.
do.	Carried Arms in Service of the Rebels	at Home.
do.	Carried Arms in the Rebels Service	Perth Prison.
Perth	Carried Arms as a Volunteer in the Rebel Service	Prisoners in Stirling.
do.	Carried Arms as a Volunteer in said Service	
Perth	was Armed & in a Mob at Perth on the Anniversary of his Majesty's Birth Day &	went North with the Rebels.
Perth	Appeared in Arms in a Mob at Perth on the Anniversary of His Majesty Birth Day	at home.

A LIST OF PERSONS CONCERNED IN THE
BY MR. THOMAS HOOME, SUPERVISOR

Names.	Designations.	Abode.	Parish.
A.			
Roberte Anderson	Brewer	Carnock	St. Ninians
B.			
Alex^r Buchanan	Son of the Laird of Auchleishie	Auchleishie	Callander
Robt Buchanan	Son of Baillie Buchanan in Boghastle	Boghastle	Callander
Pat^k Buchanan	Brewer	Kilmahog	do.
John Buchanan	do.	do.	do.
Willm Baad	Brewer & Maitster	Letham	Airth
C.			
James Calbreath	Son to Wm Calbreath, Miller	Pows Mill	St. Ninians
D.			
Allan Dow	Labourer	Glenfinglas	Callender
Drummond	Factor to Drummond of Perth		

REBELLION, TRANSMITTED TO THE BOARD OF EXCISE AT STIRLING.

County.	Acts of Rebellion and Circumstances.	Where they now are.
Stirling	Wore a white Cockade & carried Arms in the Service of the Rebells & assisted in robing the Country	at Home.
Perth	Carried Arms as a Captain in the Rebel Service	London, prisoner.
do.	was a Captain in the Rebel Service, at the Battle of Culloden & there	Kill'd.
do.	Joyned the Rebels & went along with them to Crieff	at Home.
do.	Joyned the Rebels & went with them to Crieff	at Home.
Stirling	Assisted the Rebels as a Guide, carried their Arms & secured Boats for them to pass the Forth	at Home.
Stirling	Carried Arms with the Rebels at Falkirk	Lurking.
Perth	Carried Arms with the Rebels, was at the Battle of Culloden & there	Kill'd.
	was very active in seducing Gentlemen from their Duty and Loyalty to his Majesty	at home.

Names.	Designations.	Abode.	Parish.
H.			
John Haddin	of Lendrick	Lendrick	Kilmadock
Alex[r] Haddin	Son of the above John Haddin	do.	do.
John Henderson	Merchant & Brewer	Clackmannan	Clackmannan
David Henderson	Glasier	do.	do.
M[r] Will[m] Harper	Episcopal Minister	Bothkiner	Bothkiner
K.			
James Kincaid	of Degreen	Degreen	Falkirk
L.			
Peter Lockhart	Smith	Bannockburn	St. Ninians
John Lochead	Merchant	Alloa	Alloa
G.[1]			
James Graham	Younger of Airth	Airth	Airth
James Gardner	Servant to said Jas. Graham	do.	do.
M.			
James M'Ewan	Son to John M'Ewen Shoemaker	Stirling	Stirling
John M'farlane	Servant	Glenfinglas	Callander

[1] Alphabetical arrangement as in MS.

STIRLING DISTRICT—*Continued.* 57

County.	Acts of Rebellion and Circumstances.	Where they now are.
Perth	Carried Arms in the Pretender's Son's Life Guards	Not known.
do.	had a Commission in the Rebel Army and went along with them	
Clackmannan	Aided & assisted the Rebels as a Guide & wore a white Cockade	at home.
do.	Drank the Pretender's Son's health as Prince of Wales, & beat the Excise Officer for reproving him	at home.
Stirling	Was very active in aiding & assisting the Rebels & waited of the Pretender's Son at Falkirk	At home.
Stirling	was very active in assisting the Rebels Day & Night, Robed the Country of Horses, drank the Pretender's son as Prince of Wales, wishing Damnation to his Majesty	at home.
Stirling	Drank the same disloyal health, speaking most undecently & maliciously of His Majesty	at home.
Clackmanan	Purchased from the Rebels a very Considerable Quantity of Goods that had been seized for his Majesty's behoof & got them at an under value	at home.
Stirling	Joyned the Rebels when they first pass'd the Forth & carried Arms with them	Lurking.
do.	Killed one of His Majesty's Dragoons at Stirling	Prisoner at Edin^r.
Stirling	Accepted of a Commission in the Rebel Army	Not known.
Perth	Carried Arms with the Rebels in England, and was at Culloden Battle	Lurking.

LIST OF REBELS FROM

Names.	Designations.	Abode.	Parish.
Pat^k M'Grigor	Tradesman	Miltoun	Callander
Alex^r M'Grigor	do.	do.	do.
Dougal M'Grigor	do.	do.	do.
John M'Inhonnel	Brewer	Bridge of Kelty	do.
Willm Murdoch	Wool Merchant	Callander	do.
Donald M'Nab	Farmer	Brae Leing	do.
Alex^r Roy M'Grigor	Labouring Man	Callander	do.
John Roy M'Lauchlan	Brewer	do.	do.
Arch^d M'Laren	Farmer	Curnoch	do.
John M'humish	Pedler	Bridge of Turk	do.
John Murray	Son to Ja^s Murray, Merch^t	Airth	Airth
Alex^r Mill	of Newmilln	Newmill	do.
David Mill	Son to s^d Alex^r Mill	do.	do.
Thomas Mill	do.	do.	do.

O.

P.

Sir Arch^d Primrose	of Dunipace	Dunipace	

R.

John Ritchie	of Sinks	Sinks	St. Ninian's
David Rollo	Son to the Laird of Powis	Powis	do.
James Rollo	do.	do.	do.

STIRLING DISTRICT—*Continued.* 59

County.	Acts of Rebellion and Circumstances.	Where they now are.
Perth	Carried Arms into England with the Rebels, said to be forced	Returned home.
do.	Carried in England with the Rebels, said to be forced	
do.	Carried Arms with the Rebells in England, said to be forced	
do.	Acted as a Serjeant in the Rebel Army	returned home.
do.	Acted as Ensign in the Rebel Army, was thrice forced out & as often deserted	at home.
do.	Carried Arms & first went South & there after North with the Rebels	Not known.
do.	Carried Arms in the Rebel Service & was at Culloden Battle, said to be forc'd	at home.
do.	Went to Edin^r in Rebel Service, took the Benefite of the Indemnity in Novr 1746	at home.
do.	Assisted the Rebels with money being forced thereto or to send a man	at home.
do.	Carried Arms in the Rebel Service & was at Falkirk & Culloden Battles	Lurking.
Stirling	in the Rebel Service from their first crossing the fforth, Lurking in Dollar parish	about Hillfot.
do.	Seized Boats for the Rebels passage. Transported their Arms with horses & abused his Maj^s Soldiers when Prisoners	at home.
do.	Very active in aiding & assisting the Rebells & Transporting their Arms	at home.
do.	was very active in assisting the Rebels, Transporting their Arms	at home.
Stirling	had a Commission amongst the Rebel Hussars.	
Stirling	hath carried Arms in the Rebel Army from Novr 1745 till defeat at Culloden	Not known.
do.	Carried Arms in the Rebel Army till the Defeat of Culloden	Lurking.
do.		

LIST OF REBELS FROM

Names.	Designations.	Abode.	Parish.
James Robertson	Weaver	Bannockburn	St. Ninian's
S.			
John Stuart	of Glat	Glat	Callander
David Stuart	of Ballahallan	Ballachallan	do.
John Stuart	Brewer	Collingtown-gill	do.
John Simpson	Brewer & Malster	Falkirk	Falkirk
Andrew Stiven	Farmer	Ferrytoun	Clackmanan
U.			
James Urquhart	Copper Smith	Stirling	Stirling

STIRLING DISTRICT—*Continued.*

County.	Acts of Rebellion and Circumstances.	Where they now are.
Stirling	did drink the Pretender's Son's health as Prince of Wales, and spoke many things most indecently, scandalously & maliciously of his Prent. Majesty	at home.
Perth	Carried Arms in the Rebel Army	Not known.
do.	had a Commission in the Rebel Army & collected his Majesty's Revenue for them	Lurking.
do.	Went along with the Rebel Army	Not known.
Stirling	very active in procuring Boats for the Rebels to pass to the Forth	at home.
Clackmannan	Carried off two Dragoon Horses from the Battle of Preston	at home.
Stirling	Acted as Commissary for the Rebel Army	Not known.

LIST OF PERSONS CONCERNED IN THE
BY MR. JAMES M'KERRAS SUPERVISOR

Names.	Designations.	Abode.	Parish.
A.			
Andrew Aiton	Indwellar	Craill	Craill
Willm Aiton	do.	do.	do.
Andrew Auchenleck	of Cunnachie	Cunnachie	Monymeal
B.			
John Barnie	Servant to Earl of Kelly	Kelly house	Carnbee
David Brown	Indwellar	St. Andrews	St. Andrews
James Bocik	do.	do.	do.
Alex^r Barclay	Bleacher	Blaeboe	Kimbock
Henry Balfour	Dunboag	Dunboag	Dunboag
C.			
Henry Crawford	Portioner of Craill	Craill	Craill

REBELLION, TRANSMITTED TO THE BOARD OF EXCISE AT ST. ANDREWS.

County.	Acts of Rebellion and Circumstances.	Where they now are.
Fife	Joined the Rebels before Preston Battle & carried Arms, was in the Rebellion 1715	Said to be dead.
do.	Enticed out the above Andrew his Brother, furnished him, E. of Kelly &c. with Arms & spok disrespectfully of His Majesty	at home.
do.	Joined the Rebells & carried Arms from after the Battle of Preston till dispers't, was in Rebell^n 1715	Not known.
do.	Carried Arms with the Rebels as servant to his said Master	Serving Dav^d Aitkin Tenent in Camela & Parish of Carnbee.
do.	Carried Arms in the Rebel service under the Earl of Kelly	Lurking in Fife.
do.	Drank the Pretender's health & influenced John Dewar to engage in Rebellion	at home.
	Carried Arms in the Service of the Rebels & for them Collected the Revenue in Angus	Couper in Fife.
	Furnished one David Weems a Rebel with a Horse	at home.
Fife	Furnish'd the Rebels with money & welcomed them to Town, advised them to secure the Excise Officers & their Books, was in the Rebellion & Knighted by the Pretender 1715 yet has a pension of 55 lib. p. annum from the Trustees for Improvement of Manufactors	at home.

LIST OF REBELS FROM

Names.	Designations.	Abode.	Parish.
Robert Cleland	Merchant	Craill	Craill
George Cleland	Ship Master	Pitenweem	Pittenweem
Eliz^h Crawford or Mrs Rolland	Merchant	Anstruther Wester	Anstruther Wester
Alex^r Chrystie	Servant	South fferry	South fferry
D.			
James Davidson	Servant	Myreside	Faukland
Robert Douglas	Gentleman	Coupar	Coupar
John Deuar	Indweller	St. Andrews	St. Andrews
John Deuar	do.	do.	do.
James Duncan	Inkeeper	Ferry Porton Craigs	Ferry Port-on Craigs
E.			
Erskine	Earl of Kelly	Kelly house	Carnbee
Thomas Erskine	Merchant	Kilrenny	Bouffie
F.			
George Finlay	Heelmaker	Anstruther Easter	Anstruther Easter
H.			
Robert Haxton	Surgeon	St. Andrews	St Andrews
Andrew Hay	do.	Coupar	Coupar
Heleneas Haxton	Gentleman	Rathehills	Kilminny

ST. ANDREWS DISTRICT—*Continued.* 65

County.	Acts of Rebellion and Circumstances.	Where they now are.
Fife do.	These two being Magistrates in their Abodes, diswaded the Traders from allowing Officers of the Revenue to survey or paying them their duties. The latter attended the Rebels collecting & used his authority for them	at home.
do.	Drank the Pretender's Son's health, attended him at Edin^r & sent a Barrel of Gun Ponder to his use	at home.
do.	Carried Arms in the Rebel Service & was active in robing the Country of Arms	not known.
do.	Went Servant to Ld Kilmarnock when he joyn'd the Rebels but bore no Arms	in Faukland, Prisoner.
do.	Collected the Cess for the Rebels, was also in the Rebellion in the year 1715	not known.
do.	Carried Arms in the Rebel Service from Preston Battle under the Earl of Kelly	in Perth, Prissoner.
do.	Carried Arms in the Rebel Service as above	kill'd at Culloden.
	Drank the Pretender's health & success to his arms, was in Rebellion 1715	at home.
do.	Was a Collonel in the Rebel Army from the Commencement of the Rebellion, was at the Battles of Preston, Falkirk, & Culloden & in the End of September headed a Party who collected the Excise in Fife	Lurking in or about his own house.
	has carried Arms in the Pretender's Son's Life Guards from their first raising	not known.
Fife	Refused to drink His Majesty's health, Casting abusive Reflections upon His Sacred Majesty & the Presbyterian Ministers & professing his attachment to the Pretender in the strongest manner	at home.
Fife do. do.	Carried Arms in the Rebel Army during the whole Rebellion	Not known. Lurking in Fife. Lurking in the country.

E

Names.	Designations.	Abode.	Parish.
L.			
Robert Leith	Baillie	Pittenweem	Pittenweem
Andrew Lothian	Brewer & Precentor to the Unqualified Meetinghouse	Cellerdyke	Killrenny
Peter Lindsay	Gentleman	Worminstone	Craill
M.			
Maiden	Surgeon	Craill	Craill
Alexander Middleton	Wright	Leuchars	Leuchars
George M'Gill	Surgeon	Kimbock	Kimbock
O.			
Thomas Oliphant	Wright, late Baillie and present Elder in the Church	Anstruther Wester	Anstruther Wester
Alexander Oram	Vintiner	Coupar	Coupar
P.			
Robert Philp	Shoemaker	Craill	Craill

ST. ANDREWS DISTRICT—*Continued.* 67

County.	Acts of Rebellion and Circumstances.	Where they now are.
Fife	Present Baillie, went in Person to the Brewers & forbid them to pay their Excise to the Officers of the Revenue but to the Rebels, & told them he would protect them for so doeing & he himself attended the Rebells at their Collecting the Revenue 7^{ber} 30, 1745	at home.
do.	pay'd the whole of his own duty & demanded & received the Revenue from others liable therein, which he also pay'd to the Rebels whom he caused use severities on the people, he pray'd for the prosperity of the Rebels & shews himself upon all occasions to be disaffected	at home.
do.	Carried Arms with the Rebels & assisted in levying the Cess & Excise	not known.
do.	Drank the Pretender's health & his Son's & vaunted that he had got 20 libs of their money	at home.
do.	Carried Arms in the Rebel Service from after the Battle of Preston till Culloden	not known.
do.	Assisted in carrying a Barrel of Gun Pouder to the Rebels & drank the Pretender's health	at home.
do.	was very active in Levying the publick money for the Rebels & Compelling people to pay: destribute money to some sick Rebels at Coupar & was alwayes dessaffected	at home.
Fife	Assisted in burning one of his Majesty's Boats, was frequently with the Rebels, drinking the Pretender's health & his sons under Discharges of Fire Arms & is a known enemy to the present Government	at home.

Names.	Designations.	Abode.	Parish.
James Pattie	Servant	Ballcornie	Carnbee
R.			
David Rue	Gentleman	Anstruther	Anstruther
Reid	Spouse to John Skeen	Craill	Craill
S.			
William Sharp	Gentleman	St. Andrews	St. Andrews
Charles Sibbald	do.	do.	do.
Alexr Stiven	Trone man	Leith	South Leith
T.			
William Thomson	Boatman	Pittenweem	Pittenween
W.			
Charles Wightman	Merchant	Anstruther	Anstruther

ST. ANDREWS DISTRICT—*Continued.* 69

Acts of Rebellion and Circumstances.	Where they now are.
went along with the Earl of Kelly at first, & carried Arms till defeat at Culloden	Balcormie, in his Father's, Peter Pattie.
joined the Rebels at the first & carried Arms with them into England	Prisoner at Carlisle.
Gave Fire, Coalls & Tarr to burn one of the King's Boats that was lost in time of the Rebellion, said the two men that Extinguished the flames ought to have had Ropes about their Necks, & is alwayes Exclaiming against the present Goverment	at home.
Carried Arms in the Rebel Service, is but a very young man & Influenced by bad Company	Stirling, prisoner.
Carried Arms in the Rebel Service & was in the Company that proclaim'd the Pretender at Coupar	Lurking in Fife.
Carried a Barrel of Gun pouder to the Pretender's Son & wore a white Cockade	not known.
Twice demanded parties from the Rebels to break the Customhouse & carry off the Goods seized for His Majesty's behoof, but was often refused, this procceded from his affection towards the Smugglers to whom he is servicable both by Sea & Land & is himself remarkably dissaffected to the present Government	at home.
Went with his Wife & waited on the Pretender's son, Entertained the Rebels, had a man in pay in their Service at his own Expense, is said to be factor for the Earl of Kelly, Collected the Excise for him, had the assurance to ask the Excise Officer how he liv'd under his Governm^t & has always been known for a dissaffected person	at home.

Names.	Designations.	Abode.	Parish.
David Weems	Surgeon	Coupar	Coupar
David Weems	Indweller	St. Andrews	St. Andrews
John Wright	Surgeon	Foodie	Darsie

ST. ANDREWS DISTRICT—*Continued.*

County.	Acts of Rebellion and Circumstances.	Where they now are.
Fife	Carried Arms in the Rebel Army, was also in the Rebellion of 1715	Lurking at home.
do.	This the first man who promulgate the Pretender's Manifesto's & had the assurance to go to a minister of the Established Church with	at home.
do.	Joined the Rebel Army after the Battle of Preston & carried Arms with them	not known.

A LIST OF PERSONS CONCERNED IN
BOARD BY MR. LAUR. ANGUS,

Names and Designations.	Abode.	Parish.
A.		
Thos Anderson Ground Officer to Balmaduthy		
B.		
Thos Bruce Servant to the Earl of Cromarty	Newtarbat	Kilmoor
James Bayne Son to Bayne in Knockbelly	Bogg	Urquhart
Simon Brodie lived in Templand		
C.		
Roderick Chisholm 4th son to Chisholm of that Ilk	Erchiles	Kilmorack
John Chisholm Servant to the sd Laird of Chisholm	do.	do.
Alexr Campbell, Tenent & Distiller	Brakahy	do.
Donald Cameron in	Teahrowat	do.
Donald Cameron in	Kilmorack	do.
John Cameron in	do.	do.
John Calder son to Jas Calder Tenent in	Miltoun of Red Castle	Kilernan
E.		
John Erskine, Officer of Excise	Dingwall	Dingwall

THE REBELLION TRANSMITTED TO THE SUPERVISOR OF EXCISE IN ROSS.

County.	Particulars of Facts.
	Forced out several Persons in & about Balmaduthis ground to the Rebel Service.
Cromarty	attended the Earl his Master at Perth and Elsewhere.
Nairn	was in Arms with the Rebels & is now a servant to Donald Rioch in Bogg.
	Carried Arms in the Rebel Service.
Inverness	a Captain in the Rebel Service, headed about Eighty of the Chisholms at the Battle of Culloden, himself and 30 whereof were kill'd upon the Field.
do.	Carried Arms as a Lieutenant in said Company & was wounded at the Battle of Culloden.
do.	was Ensign in said Company & kill'd at the said Battle of Culloden.
do.	Carried Arms at the Battle of Culloden.
do.	Carried Arms at the said Battle of Culloden.
do.	Carried Arms at the Battle of Culloden.
Ross	Carried Arms at the said Battle & has since absconded.
do.	was at Falkirk & Sutherland with the Rebels and threatened to burn some houses in Dingwall in order to force the possessors to go with him to the Rebel Service.

LIST OF REBELS FROM

Names and Designations.	Abode.	Parish.
F.		
Simon Fraser, Lord Lovat	Castle downy	Kiltarlaty
Simon Fraser, Master of Lovat	do.	do.
Fraser younger of Culbocky	Culbocky	do.
William Fraser of Culmiln	Culmiln	do.
Alex' Fraser son to Alex. Fraser of Rilich	Rilich	Kirkhills
Alex' Fraser of Balchreggan	Balchreggan	do.
Simon Fraser of Achnaclouh	Achnaclouh	Kirltarlaty
John Fraser Tenent in Bewly	Bewly	Kilmorack
Simon Fraser Tenent in do.	do.	do.
John Fraser Tenent	Wellhouse	do.
John Fraser Tenent	Tea Wigg	Kilmorack
John Fraser, son to —— Fraser of Moydie	Moydie	do.
Roderick Fraser, Tenent in	Limaire	do.
Alexander Fraser Tenent in	do.	do.
William Fraser Piper to Lord Lovat	Wester Downy	Kiltarlaty
David Fraser Piper to ditto.		
John Fraser Brogmaker	Balnamuick	Urra
Donald Fraser, Son to James Fraser Tenent	Balagalken	Logy & Urquhart
James Fraser Son to do.	do.	do.
John Forbes merchant in Tain	Tain	Tain
Alex' Fraser, Living in Kincardin parish		Kincardin
Hugh Ferguson lately Servant to Ld Nairn		
Hugh Fraser Son to William Fraser, Merchant	Culbocky	Urquhart
G.		
Charles Graham	Tain	Tain
Peter Gow Garder	Bewly	Kilmorack
Alex' Grant Son to Perler Grant	Corromaly	Contine

ROSS DISTRICT—*Continued.*

County.	Particulars of Facts.
Inverness	is supposed to have aided & assisted the Rebels by ordering out his Clan.
do.	was one of the Chief Commanders of the Frasers in the Rebel Service.
do.	was a Captain of the Frasers under Fraser of Inneralachy.
do.	was also a Captain of Do. under Inneralachay & kill'd at Culloden Battle.
do.	was a Captain of the Frasers in the Rebel Service.
do.	was a Captain of Do. in said Service under Inneralachay.
do.	was a Captain of Do. under Do.
do.	a Soldier in the Rebel Service.
do.	a Soldier in said Service & killd at the Battle of Culloden.
do.	a Rebel Serjeant, Living sometimes at home.
do.	was in Arms at the Battle of Culloden, supposed to be kill'd.
do.	in the Rebel Service, supposed to be kill'd at Culloden.
do.	was with the Rebels in Arms.
do.	Carried Arms in the Rebel Service.
do.	Carried Arms in the Rebel Service.
	Carried Arms in said Service.
Ross	Was with the Rebels in Sutherland.
Nairn	Carried Arms in the Rebel Service at the Battle of Falkirk.
do.	Carried Arms in said Service in Sutherland & there kill'd.
Ross	was Storekeeper there to the Rebels.
do.	was a Soldier in Pitcalnie's Rebel Company.
	was with the Rebels, Lurking in the Parish of Callecuden in Cromarty.
Ross	Deserted from the Rebels at Falkirk now in Cullcairn's Company.
Ross	was a Soldier in Cromarty's Regim^t & taken Prisoner in Sutherland.
Inverness	Carried Arms in the Rebel Service being forced out by the Master of Lovat.
Ross	was employed in the Pretender's Service, which Donald Reoch & Kenneth Grant in Contine can witness.

Names and Designations.	Abode.	Parish.
Donald Gollan	Avoch	Avoch
John Glass } Brogmakers in Milton of	Red Castle	Kilernan
Finlay Glass }		
Alex^r Gordon, Lately Merch^t in Cromarty	Cromarty	Cromarty

H.

Andrew Hood } Brothers	Tain	Tain
George Hood }		

M.

Names and Designations.	Abode.	Parish.
Kenneth M'Kenzie, brother of the Laird of Fairburn	Fairburn	Urra
Alexander M'Kenzie of Lentron	Lentorn	Urra
M'Kenzie, Brother to Lentron		
M'Kenzie, Brother to Lentron		
Mr Willm M'Kenzie, brother to the Laird of Kilcoy	Kinnellan	Contine
M'Kenzie, Earl of Cromarty	New Tarbat	Kilmuir
M'Kenzie, Lord M'Leod	do.	do.
Willm M'Kenzie, Brother to Allangrange	Allangrainge	Kilernan
Alex^r M'Kenzie, Tacksman, Killend	Killend	Avoch
Colin M'Kenzie, Late Merch^t in Edinburgh	Brea	Culleculen
Roderick M'Culloch of Glasslich	Glasslich	Fearn
Alex^r M'Kenzie, son to the deceast Lauh^l M'Kenzie Tenent in	Miltown of Ord	Urra
John M'William son to Don^d M'William Tenent	Balavalick	do.
Kenneth Moir, Brogmaker	Miltoun of Ord	do.
John M'Donald	Balnamuik	Loggy
John M'Currathy once Servant to Mr William M'Kenzie		Urra
Alex^r M'Connachy, Son to Alex. M'Connachy in	Balnamuik	do.
Hugh M'Bain, Living in	Bewly	Kilmorack
Farquhar M'Nully, Tenent	Bewly	Kilmorack

ROSS DISTRICT—*Continued.* 77

County.	Particulars of Facts.
Ross	Transported being taken Prisoner.
do.	Carried Arms & both taken Prisoners.
Cromarty	was publicly seen in Arms with the Rebels at Tain.
Ross	{ Both carried Arms as Soldiers in the Earl of Cromarty's Regiment.
Ross	a School Boy, was a Captain in Barrisdale's Rebel Regiment.
do.	was a Major in said Regiment.
Ross	was a Captain of the Mackenzies in the Rebel Service.
Cromarty	was Coll. of a Regim^t in the Rebel Service } both prisoners.
do.	had a Command in the Rebel Army
Ross	was a Captain in Cromarty's said Regiment.
do.	Served as an Officer in the Rebel Army, Witness the Min^r of Cullecuden & Ja^s Grant Officer of Excise.
do.	Served as an Officer in said Army. Witness the above two persons.
do.	Carried Arms & taken prisoner in Sutherland.
do.	was a Lieu^t in Cromarty's Regiment & wounded in Sutherland.
do.	was with the Rebels at Falkirk.
do.	was with the Rebels in Sutherland.
do.	was hired by Alex^r M'Lennan to serve in the Rebel Army for him, he being obliged to find them a man.
do.	Enlisted in his Majesty Service but deserted from Killiwhinning & served the Rebels.
do.	was a private man in Cromarty's Regiment, said to be advanced to a Lieutenant.
Inverness	Said to be forced out into the Rebel Service by the Master of Lovat.
Inverness	Carried Arms in the Rebel Army.

LIST OF REBELS FROM

Names and Designations.	Abode.	Parish.
Alex^r M'Iver, Tenent in Wellhouse near	Bewly	Kilmorack
Roderick M'Lean in	Bridgehouse	do.
John M'William in	Kilmorack	do.
Thomas M'William in	Platchaick	do.
Donald M'Andrew	Fairly	do.
James M'Ildonick	Brackahy	do.
Murdoch M'Kenzie, Son to Colin M'Kenzie late Baillie in	Dingwall	Dingwall
James M'Donald, Tanner in	do.	do.
Murdoch M'Donald, Tenent	do.	do.
Geo^g M'Kenzie Son to John M'Kenzie, Musician	Auchternood	Fettertay
Mr Donald M'Kenzie, Tenent	Inhavanny	do.
Donald M'Intyre in	Milton	Kilmuir
George M'Kenzie } lived at Milton of James M'Clacky } New Tarbat Kenneth M'Lennan }	Kilmuir	do.
Roderick M'Farquhar, Tenent	Spittald of Red Castle	Kileman
John M'ffarquhar his son	do.	do.
Colin M'kenzie, Tenent in Chapleton of Red Castle	Chapletoun	do.
Don^d M'farquhar Son to W^m M'farquhar in West Culmore of	Red Castle	do.
Kenneth M'farquhar, Tenent	Newtoun of Red Castle	do.
Farquhar M'Farquhar, do.	do.	do.
John M'Kenzie son to Thomas M'Kenzie	Barntoun of Red Castle	do.
Donald M'Lennan, Tenent in	Gurgastoun of do.	do.
Murdoch Mitchell, Servant	Balamenoch	Urquhart
Theodore M'kenzie, son to Alex^r M'kenzie, Mason	Easter Culbocky	do.
Alex^r M'kenzie, late Greive to Balmaduthy now at	Coull	Contine
William Man, Servant	Petfoord	Avoch
John Moir	Templand	do.
William Man	do.	do.

ROSS DISTRICT—Continued.

County.	Particulars of Facts.
Inverness	a Serjeant in said Army & was wounded at Culloden Battle.
do.	was with the Rebels.
do.	was with the Rebels & taken Prisoner.
do.	Carried Arms with the Rebels at Culloden.
do.	was with the Rebels in Sutherland.
do.	Carried Arms with the Rebels at Culloden.
Ross	Forced out some of the Inhabitants of Dingwall to go with him to the Rebel Service.
do.	said to be forced into said Service by the said Murdoch M'Kenzie.
do.	said to be forced into said Service by Ditto.
do.	Was in Arms with the Earl of Cromarty in Sutherland.
do.	was a Captain under Cromarty, has absconded since the Battle of Culloden.
Cromarty	a Servant to the Earl of Cromarty in the Rebellion.
do.	Carried Arms in Cromarty's Rebel Regiment.
Ross	was a Captain of the Rebels in Sutherland.
do.	was a Lieutenant of the Rebels in do.
do.	was with the Rebels at the Battle of Culloden.
do.	was with the Rebels in Sutherland.
do.	was with the Rebels & taken Prisoner.
do.	was with the Rebels in Sutherland.
do.	was with the Rebels in do. now Lurking in the Country.
do.	was with the Rebels in Sutherland now Lurking in the Country.
do.	was with the Rebels.
do.	was with the Rebels in Arms.
do.	was Employed in forcing out men into the Rebellion in the Lands late Lord Royston's which he asserts was by his late Master's orders, now Prisoner in Inverness.
do do. do.	} were all in Arms with the Rebels.

Names and Designations.	Abode.	Parish.
N.		
James Niccol	Avoch	Avoch
P.		
Murdoch Paterson, son to John Paterson, Tenent	Lettoch of Redcastle	Kilmuir
Donald Paterson, Senior	East Kessock of do.	do.
Donald Paterson, Junr	Do. of do.	do.
Lauchlane Paterson	Blairdow of do.	Kilernan
Andrew Paterson, son to And^w Paterson, Tenent	Kessock	
R.		
Ronald Ross	Miltown of Ord	Urra
Hugh Ross, Tenent	Balavalich	ffotterty
John Reoch alias Ross, Brother to Don^d Reoch, Tenent	Contine	Contine
John Ross, Mason	Chapletown of Redcastle	Kilernan
James Ross, Tenent	Knockbreak	Kilmuir
George Reid in	Templand	Avoch
Alex^r Reid, Servant	Knockmuir	do.
John Reid Son to John Reid	Petford	do.
Thomas Ross	Tain	Tain
Angus Ross alias M'William	do.	do.
John Robertson	Miltoun of New Tarbat	Kilmuir
William Ross alias Reoch	Tain	Tain
S.		
John Sutherland	Rosskeen	Rosskeen
William Sutherland, Dyster	Barntown	Urra
Callum Stuart, Servant to James Calder	Miltoun of Redcastle	Kilernan

ROSS DISTRICT—*Continued.*

County.	Particulars of Facts.
Ross	was with the Rebels.
Ross, do., do.	were with the Rebels at the Battle of Culloden, Skulking up & down the Country.
do.	was with the Rebels in Sutherland, now Lurking.
	was with the Rebels in Sutherland. Absconding since the Skirmish their.
Ross	was with the Rebels & taken Prisoner in Sutherland.
do.	taken Prisoner at the Battle of Culloden.
do.	was sometime a Sailor with John Reid in Cromarty & to save his Brother's goods, took on him the name of a Rebel Captain under Barrisdale at Tain & Sutherland.
do.	went with the Rebels to Sutherland.
do.	went to Sutherland with the Rebels.
do., do., do.	were with the Rebels.
do., do.	Served in Cromarty's Rebel Regiment, now Enlisted in the Master of Ross his Company.
Cromarty	was a Soldier in Cromarty's said Regiment.
Ross	was a Soldier in Cromarty's said Regiment.
Ross	a Servant to Lord McLeod.
do.	Served in Sutherland under Barrisdale but forced.
do.	went with the Rebels to Sutherland & since absconds.

Names and Designations.	Abode.	Parish.
Kenneth Simpson in	Dunvarny	Urquhart
T.		
Thomas Taylor in	Bridgehouse	Kilmorack
U.		
Kenneth Urquart son to the deceast Thos Urquart	of Cullicuden	Cullicuden
Willm Urquhart late Servt to Willm M'Kenzie	Kennellan	Contine
William Wilson in	New Tarbat	Kilmuir

ROSS DISTRICT—*Continued.*

County.	Particulars of Facts.
Nairn	went about with the Rebels wearing a white Cockade.
Inverness	was at the Battle of Culloden in the Rebel Service.
Cromarty	was with the Rebels & is now lurking about his mother's house in that Parish.
Ross	was with the Rebells at the Battle of Falkirk & in Sutherland.
Cromarty	was a Soldier in the Earl of Cromarty's Regiment.

A LIST OF PERSONS CONCERNED IN THE BY MR. JAMES FERGUSON SUPERVISOR

Names.	Designations.	Abode.	Parish.
B.			
John Bayne	Servant to John Murray of Brughtoun	Brughtoun	Brughtoun
C.			
Andrew Cassie	Late of Kirkhouse	Traquair	Traquair
K.			
James Kerr	Merchant	Peebles	Peebles
M.			
William M'Iver	Factor to the Earl of Traquair	Traquair	Traquair
John Murray	of Brughton	Brughton	Brughton
P.			
John Paton	Servant to Brughtoun	do.	do.
John Piery	Servant to Traquair	Traquair	Traquair
S.			
James Sinclair	Tenent	Stobo	Stobo
W.			
Willm White	Servant to Traquair	Traquair	Traquair

REBELLION, TRANSMITTED TO THE BOARD OF EXCISE AT LANERK.

County.	Acts of Rebellion and Circumstances.	Where they now are.
Tweedale	Joined the Rebels at the very beginning & has been most active in their Service	not known.
do.	Joined the Rebels on their arrival at Edinburgh	Prisoner in the North.
do.	was confined at Edin^r on suspicion of corresponding with the Rebels	out upon Baill.
do.	Suspected of Aiding & assisting the Rebels & therefore	confined at Edin^r.
do.	Joined the Rebels at the very beginning & continued with them during the whole Rebellion, he acted as Secretary to the Pretender's Son	Prisoner at London.
do.	Went out in the Beginning of the Rebellion with his said Master	Not known.
do.	Joined the Rebells when in possession of Edinburgh .	Not known.
do.	About the middle of November 1745 he went after the Rebels to England in quest of some Horses taken from him by them, and as their is no acco^t of him since it is feared he has been oblidged to join them tho' (I'm informed) not his Inclination	Not known.
do.	Joined the Rebels at first on their way from the North	Not known.

A LIST OF PERSONS CONCERNED IN THE
BY MR. JOHN FINLASON, SUPERVISOR
PART OF WHOM ARE RETURNED

Names.	Designations.	Abode.	Parish.
A.			
Thomas Arbuthnot	Mercht & Factor to some Lands here belonging to the Maiden Hospital at Edinr	Peterhead	Peterhead
Thos. Arbuthnot	Sailor	do.	do.
John Abernethie	Overseer of the highwayes	Tyrie	Tyrie
William Angus	Labourer	Old Meldrum	Meldrum
Charles Anderson	Merchant	do.	do.
James Aberdeen	Labourer	Newton	Cruden
B.			
Alexr Bettie	Labourering man	Rothney	Premnay
Robert Bruce	do.	Old Meldrum	Meldrum
Geog Buchan	do.	do.	do.
James Bowman	Farmer	Todelhills	Ellon
James Buchan	Labouringman	Leys	do.
William Bagrie	do.	Gateside	Cruden
John Buchan	do.	Hillhead	do.

REBELLION TRANSMITTED TO THE BOARD OF EXCISE AT OLD MELDRUM. MOST AND LURKING IN THE COUNTRY.

County.	Acts of Rebellion and Circumstances.	Rent of Estate.
Aberdeen	accepted of a Factory from the Rebels upon the Estate which Marischal forfeited in the year 1715. By virtue whereof he called in the Tenents & uplifted some of the Farms for the Rebels and Exerted himself to the utmost of his Power in their Service.	
do.	went out to the Rebellion 1st Octor 1745.	
Aberdeen	Joyned the Rebels at Edinburgh.	
do.	Joined the Rebel Army.	
do.	Assisted in Collecting the Levy money for the Rebels.	
do.	Joined the Rebels after the Battle of Preston.	
do.	Joined the Rebel Army.	
do.	Join'd the Rebel Army.	
do.	Join'd the Rebel Army.	
do.	Joined the Rebels after the Battle of Falkirk.	
do.	Joined the Rebels after the Battle of Falkirk.	
do.	Joined the Rebels after the Battle of Falkirk.	
do.	Joined the Rebel Army after Falkirk Battle.	

Names.	Designations.	Abode.	Parish.
C.			
Charles Cumming	of Kininmount	Kininmount	Longmay
Alex^r Cumming	Farmer his Brother	Crichy	Old Deer
Doctor Cruickshank	Surgeon	Frasersburgh	Frasersburgh
James Cato	house Carpenter	do.	do.
Willm Christy	Ship Master	do.	do.
William Chalmers	Baxter	do.	do.
Geo^g Chein	Sailor	do.	do.
Cumming	of Pitully	Pitully	Pitsligo
Alex^r Craig	Merchant	Roseartie	do.
James Cruickshank	Labouring man	Miln of Bonytown	Rain
John Chives	do.	Rothney	Premnay
Wm Clark	do.	Little Artrachy	Cruden
John Chalmers	Farmer	Methlick	Methlick
D.			
John Dalgearn	Merchant	Auchmungle	New Deer
Peter Duguid	Vintiner	Old Meldrum	Meldrum
John Durward	Sadler	do.	do.
John Douglas	of Fechel	Fechel	Ellon
Alex^r Ditch	Labouring man	Turnilove	Cruden

OLD MELDRUM DISTRICT—*Continued.* 89

County.	Acts of Rebellion and Circumstances.	Rent of Estate.		
		£	sh.	d.
Aberdeen	Joined the Pretender's Son at Edinb^r	150	0	0
do.	Joined the Rebels at Edin^r & was very active in Levying for their Service, Worth of Stock	500	0	0
do.	Joined the Rebel Army at Edinburgh.			
do.	Join'd the Rebel Army.			
do.	⎧ all concerned in apprehending Captain			
do.	⎪ Grant on his way to join Ld Loudoun at			
do.	⎨ Inverness, & carrying him to Achmeden			
	⎪ Lieut. of Banff for the Rebels & all			
	⎩ Joined the Rebels on their way north.			
do.	Joined the Rebels at Edinburgh	300	0	0
do.	Joined the Rebels at Edinburgh, worth money.			
do.	Joined the Rebel Army.			
do.	Joined the Rebel Army.			
do.	Joined the Rebel Army after Preston Battle.			
do.	was at Inverury Skirmish, assisted the Rebels in securing some of the M'Leods taken Prisoners there, went to the Supervisor's Room with three armed men in quest of Books relating to his Majesty's Revenue & was very active in serving the Rebels in every respect.			
Aberdeen	Joined pretty early in the Rebellion & Recruited men for the Rebels.			
do.	was aiding to the Rebels & Enlisted men for their Service.			
do.	went to Aberdeen & brought out the Rebels against the M'Leods at Inverury.			
do.	Joined the Pretender's Standard at Aberdeen & seen at Newburgh with a white Cockade	83	6	8
do.	Joined the Rebel Army after Preston Battle.			

LIST OF REBELS FROM

Names.	Designations.	Abode.	Parish.
F.			
Thomas Forbes	Vintiner	Peterhead	Peterhead
Alexander Forbes	Stabler	do.	do.
Alex^r Falconer	Sailor	Frasersburgh	Frasersburgh
James Ferrier	do.	do.	do.
John Fobes	Lord Pitsligo	Pitsligo	Pitsligo
William Fraser	Brother to Inveralichy	Inveralichy	Longmay
Lewis Farquharson	Labouring man	Foggy Ridge	Rain
John Forbes	do.	Kirk Culsamond	Culsamond
Johnathon Forbes	Farmer	Brux	Kildrumie
George Forrest	Servant to the Countess of Errol	Bowence	Cruden
Willm fforrest	Ground officer to s^d Countess	Gateside	Cruden
John Fullarton	Junr of Dudwick	Bowence	Cruden
David Ferrier	Labouring man	Cotthill	Ellon
James fforbes	do.	Turnerhall	do.
James Forrest	do.	Nethermiln	do.
Willm Forrest	do.	Upper Braehead	Cruden
G.			
Alexander Gill	Shipmaster	Frasersburgh	Fraserburgh
Robert Gordon Junr	of Logie	Logie	Longmay
David Grant		Old Meldrum	Meldrum

OLD MELDRUM DISTRICT—*Continued.* 91

County.	Acts of Rebellion and Circumstances.	Rent of Estate.		
		£	sh.	d.
Aberdeen	Joined the Rebel Army at Edinburgh.			
do.	Went to the Rebellion a Servant to Wm Scott late of Auchtydonald on 1st Octr 1745.			
do.	Joined the Rebel Army.			
do.	Assisted in Apprehending Capt Alex^r Grant going to join Ld Loudoun at Inverness & carrying him to Achmeden Ld Lieu^t of Banff for the Rebels & their Army on their Retreat to the Highlands.			
do.	Joined the Pretender's Son at Edinburgh	400	0	0
do.	Joined the Rebel Army at Edin^r—worth of Stock	1000	0	0
do.	Joined the Rebel Army.			
do.	Joined the Rebel Army.			
do.	Joined the Rebel Army—worth of Stock 22000 Merkes.			
do.	Had a Commiss^n from Moir of Stonywood, Recruited 15 men in s^d Countesses interest for the Rebels. Stayed all that time at her house & joined the Rebel Army before the Skirmish of Inverury.			
do.	Assisted in Recruiting for the Rebel Service.			
do.	Joined the Rebels at Ed^r returned when they left that place, but went out again	166	13	8
do.	Went & joined the Rebels after the Battle of Falkirk.			
do.	Joined the Rebels after the Battle of Falkirk.			
do.	Joined the Rebel Army after the Battle of Preston.			
do.	Joined the Rebel Army after Preston Battle.			
do.	Assisted in apprehending Captain Grant as before mentioned & joined the Rebel Army.			
do.	Join'd the Rebels at Edinburgh	150	0	0
do.	Joined the Rebel Army.			

Names.	Designations.	Abode.	Parish.
H.			
Hay	Countess of Errol	Bowence	Cruden
Adam Hay	of Cairnbanno	Cairnbanno	New Deer
I.			
Sir James Innes	Weaver	Techmurie	Tyrie
K.			
Peter Kilgower	Dyster	Ellon	Ellon
L.			
John Laurence	Merchant	Old Deer	Old Deer
George Legat	Mercht & Taylor	Ellon	Ellon
Laurence Leith	Farmer	New Flinder	Kinethmond
Anthony Leith	do.	Bogs of Leithhall	do.
James Lesslie	Labouring Servant	Old Meldrum	Meldrum
George Lind	do.	do.	do.
George Lind	Smith	do.	do.
John Lesslie		do.	do.
John Laing	Labouring man	Turnerhall	Ellon
M.			
William Moir	Sailor Brother to Invernetty	Peterhead	Peterhead
Robert Middleton	Porter	Frasersburgh	Frasersburgh

OLD MELDRUM DISTRICT—*Continued.* 93

County.	Acts of Rebellion and Circumstances.	Rent of Estate.
		£ sh. d.
Aberdeen	Aided & assisted the Rebels & forced out men into their Service	3000 0 0
do.	Joined the Rebels at Edin^r & Levied several men for their Service on their Retreat North	50 0 0
do.	Joined the Rebels at Edinburgh.	
do.	never fail'd of having a Rejoicing when there was news of the Rebels' Success.	
do.	Proclaimed the Pretender at the Market Cross of Old Deer, Enlisted some men for his Service & joined them himself on their Retreat to the Highlands.	
do.	Alwayes kept a Rejoicing when the Rebels met with Success.	
do.	Joined himself to the Rebel Army.	
do.	Joined himself to said Army	Worth money.
do.	Joined the Rebel Army.	
do.	Joined himself to said Army.	
do.	⎧ Both concerned in going to Aberdeen &	
do.	⎨ bringing out the Rebels against the	
	⎩ Laird of M'Leod and his men at Inverury.	
do.	Joined himself to the Rebel Army after the Battle of Falkirk.	
do.	went out into the Rebellion the 1st Octo^r 1745.	
do.	was often Employed in Carrying Letters to & from the Rebel Army.	

Names.	Designations.	Abode.	Parish.
Alex^r Morrison	Sailor	Frasersburgh	Frasersburgh
James Morrise	Labouring Servant	Ellon	Ellon
Charles Morgan	do.	do.	do.
Alex^r Matheson } David Mattheson }	Labouring men	Old Rain	Rain
Alex^r Merns	do.	Insh	Insh
William Moir	of Longmay Factor to the Countess of Errol	Nethermiln	Cruden
Willm Mitchell	Farmer	Piltachy	Ellon
John Mutch	Labouring man	Elrick	do.
George Mutch	do.	Little Arnage	do.
William Mill	Merchant	Ellon	do.
N.			
Andrew Niddry, Junr	Weaver	Fraserburgh	Fraserburgh
Adam Norald	Labouring Servant	Old Meldrum	Meldrum
Willm Nisbet	Farmer	Waterside	Slains
O.			
Alex^r Ogilvy	of Auchires	Corthie	Rathen

OLD MELDRUM DISTRICT—*Continued.* 95

County.	Acts of Rebellion and Circumstances.	Rent of Estate.
Aberdeen	Concerned in apprehending Captⁿ Alexander Grant going to join Ld Loudoun at Inverness & Carrying him prisoner to the Laird of Achmeden who then acted as Ld Lieutenant of Banff County by Commissⁿ from the Pretender's Son & himself afterwards joined the Rebel Army.	£ sh. d.
do.	⎱ Joined the Rebel Army after the Battle	
do.	⎰ of Preston.	
do.	Joined the Rebel Army.	
do.	Joined the Rebel Army.	
do.	Joined the Pretender's Son at Edin^r was appointed Governour of Aberdeen where he Collected or caused to be Collected the Revenues of Excise & Customs and the Land Tax and did every thing in his Power for the Interest of the Pretender in the most active manner	166 13 8
do.	Joined the Rebel Army after the Battle of Falkirk.	
do.	Joined the Rebel Army after the Battle of Falkirk	
do.	Joined said Army after Falkirk Battle.	
do.	Made great Rejoicings when there was any acco^{ts} of the Rebels' Success.	
Aberdeen	Joined himself to the Rebel Army.	
do.	Joined himself to said Army.	
do.	Joined the Rebel Army at the same time with Longmay, but declared to James Chalmers, Printer in Aberdeen & Geo^g Forbes Merchant there that he was oblidged to take up Arms contrary to his Inclination, having been threatened by the Countess of Errol & Longmay with being turned out of his possession &c. & upon his setting out was furnished by them in a Horse & money to support him.	
Aberdeen	Joined the Pretender's Son at Edinburgh	150 0 0

Names.	Designations.	Abode.	Parish.
Willm Ogilvy	Brother to Auchires	Auchires	Rathen
John Ogilvy	do.	do.	do.
James Oldman	Labouring man	Aldie	Cruden
P.			
Andrew Pirrie	Labouring Man	Ellon	Ellon
Alex^r Peirie	do.	Old Meldrum	Meldrum
Robert Paterson	do.	do.	do.
Charles Peirie	Son to Alex^r Peirie at Miln Auchter	Ellon	Ellon
R.			
Alex^r Ramsay	Merchant	Rosartie	Pitsligo
William Ramsay	Labouring man	Lonhead	Rain
John Robertson	do.	Meiklewartle	do.
Kenneth Ramsay	Labouring Servant	Old Meldrum	Meldrum
John Rannie	do.	do.	do.
Francis Ross, Junr	Surgeon	do.	do.
S.			
John Smith	Labouring Servant	Old Deer	Old Deer
James Smith	do.	do.	do.
John Spens	Labouring man	Miln of Botom	Insh
Alexander Shives	do.	Old Meldrum	Meldrum
James Smith	do.	do.	do.
Alex^r Smith	do.	do.	do.
Thomas Stuart	Gardner to the Countess of Errol	Gateside	Cruden
William Smith	Labouring man	Yondertown	Ellon
Alex^r Scot	do.	Turnilove	Cruden
Wm Sangster	do.	Bullers-buchan	do.
William Scot	Farmer	Blackwater	St. Fergus
John Souter	Labouring man	Ellon	Ellon

OLD MELDRUM DISTRICT—*Continued.* 97

County.	Acts of Rebellion and Circumstances.	Rent of Estate.
Aberdeen do. do.	Joined the Pretender's Son at Edinburgh Joined the Pretender's Son at Edin^r Joined the Rebels after Preston Battle.	have money.
do. do. do. do.	Joined himself to the Rebel Army after the Battle of Preston. Joined the Rebel Army. Joined the Rebel Army. Joined the Rebel Army after the Battle of Preston.	
do. do. do. do. do. do.	All joined themselves to the Rebel Army.	
do. do. do.	Left their Master's Service & Joined the Rebel Army.	
do. do. do.	All carried Arms in the Rebel Service.	
do.	Assisted in Recruiting men for the Rebel Service & threatened to seize the Excise Officer's horse.	
do. do. do. do. do.	All joined & carried Arms in the Rebel Army.	

Names.	Designations.	Abode.	Parish.
T.			
Alex^r Thomson	of Feichfield	Feichfield	Longside
James Thomson	Son to Feichfield	do.	do.
Alex^r Thomson	Sailor	Peterhead	Peterhead
Alex^r Tervas	Merchant	Fraserburgh	Fraserburgh
David Tyrie	Labouring Servant	Ellon	Ellon
David Tyrie, Junr	of Dinnedeer	Dinnedeer	Insh
Robert Taylor	Labouring man	Old Meldrum	Meldrum
John Turras	Smith	do.	do.
James Thain	Servant to John Turras	do.	do.
John Turner, Junr	of Turnerhall	Turnerhall	Ellon
Lady Turnerhall		do.	do.
V, &c.			
James Volume	Surgeon	Peterhead	Peterhead
Thomas Volume	Surgeon to the Countess of Errol	Bowence	Cruden
Alex^r White, Junr	of Ardlahill	Ardlahill	Aberdour
William Wilson	Farmer	Kirkhill	Ellon
Alex^r Wilkin	do.	Kenharichy	do.

OLD MELDRUM DISTRICT—*Continued.* 99

County.	Acts of Rebellion and Circumstances.	Rent of Estate.
		£ sh. d.
Aberdeen	Joined the Pretender's Son at Edin^r & Recruited men for their Service	200 0 0
do.	Joined the Rebel Army with his Father.	
do.	went out in Rebellion the 1st of Octo^r 1745.	
do.	took many Occasions of speaking the strongest Treasonable Language.	
do.	Joined the Rebel Army after the Battle of Preston.	
do.	Joined the Rebel Army	80 0 0
do.	Beat the Drum and Carried French Colours before an Officer who Enlisted men for the Rebel Service.	
do.	Concerned in bringing out the Rebels from Aberdeen against the M'Leods at Inverury.	
do.	was also concerned in bringing out the Rebels against the M'Leods as above.	
do.	Joined the Rebels at Edin^r & Recruited about 20 men for their Service on their Retreat North	300 0 0
do.	was most active in engaging men for her son & sent several after him to the Highlands.	
do.		
do.		
	All joined & Carried Arms in the Rebel Army	30 0 0
do.		
do.		
do.		

A LIST OF PERSONS CONCERNED IN THE
BY MR. JOHN CAMPBELL, SUPERVISOR

Names.	Designations.	Abode.	Cause of Knowledge.
A.			
William Anderson	Wigmaker	Inverness	Information from Arch^d Graham, Gauger
John Allanoch	Merchant	Clashnoer	per Information
B.			
Thomas Bain	Shoemaker	Inverness	Informat^n from said Arch^d Graham
John Bremner	Servant	Jackbarry	Seen by Jno M'Callum Off^r of Excise, Elgine
John Brown		Balindouan	per Information
John Bain, younger		Glenconles	per do.
Arch^d Bain Stuart		Delavoiar	per do.
Angus Brebermackinteer		Achlounie	per do.
John Binnachie	Weaver	Balandie	per do.
James Bowie		Sauie	per do.
C.			
Robert Cuthberth	Shoemaker	Inverness	Inf. from s^d Arch^d Graham
John Clark	Indweller	Ruthven	Seen in Arms by James Brown, Off^r of Excise at Ruthven

REBELLION, TRANSMITTED TO THE BOARD OF EXCISE AT ELGINE.

Acts of Rebellion and Circumstances.	Where at present.
Subordening the Independant Companys to Join the Rebel Army	Inverness.
Carried arms in the Rebel Army as a private man	Clashnaer.
Invigling the Independ^t Companys to join the Rebels	at home.
Carried Arms as a Volunteer in the Rebel Army	not known.
was a private man in Rebel Army, was forced out & deserted	at home.
forced to serve as a private man in said Army & submitted to the King's mercy	at home.
forced out to Serve as a private man in said Army	at home.
served as a private man in said Army & was very active in plundering	at home.
Carried Arms being forced out, has submitted himself	at home.
Deserted from Rebel Army which he had Join'd	at home.
Endeavoured to Trapan the Independent Companys into the Rebellion	at home.
was a Quarter Master in the Rebel Service & very active in his Station	at home.

Names.	Designations.	Abode.	Cause of Knowledge.
John Cumming	Residenter	Inverness	seen by Jn⁰ Grant Ex. officer, Inverness
John Cumming		Tombae	per Information
Lauchlan Cumming		Tomintowll	per do.
Robert Cameron		Keppoch	per do.
John Cruickshank	a Deserter	Dalavoiar	per do.
Robat Cruickshank		do.	per do.
Hector Cruickshank		do.	per do.
Donald Campbell		Foderleter	per do.
John Campbell		do.	per do.
William Coutts		Inverury	per do.
John Cameron		Croftbain	per do.
Evan Cameron	Travelling Taylor		per do.
Alex^r Cameron	Servant to	Balmenoch	per do.
Robert Cruickshank		Badiglashean	per do.
John Cameron	Miller	Ruthven	per do.

D.

Names.	Designations.	Abode.	Cause of Knowledge.
Samuel Douglas	Late Superv^r of Excise	Forress	his Receipts seen
James Dallass	of Cantra	Cantra	Seen in Arms by s^d Arch^d Graham
John Davidson		Inchnakeep	per Information
John Davidson		Achreachan	per do.
John Dow farquharson	Servant in	do.	per do.
Angus Dou Stuart		Achnahayle	per do.
Angus Derg		Tombreck of Foderleter	per do.
James Davidson		Glenconless	per Informa^{tn}
George Davidson		do.	per do.
George Davidson		do.	do.

ELGINE DISTRICT—Continued.

Acts of Rebellion and Circumstances.	Where at present.
Volunterly entered the Rebel Service & got an Officer's Commission	not known.
Was an Officer in the Rebel Army but deserted & has submitted himself	at home.
Carried Arms as a private man	at home.
was a private man in the Rebel Army but forced out, has submitted himself	at home.
Carried Arms as a private man	Dalavoiar.
was forced out in Arms but has submitted himself	at home.
Carried Arms in Rebel Service, being Compell'd	at home.
Carried Arms as a private man, has submitted himself	at home.
Carried Arms as a private man in Rebel Service, has submitted	at home.
Carried Arms as a private man in the Rebel Army	Kill'd.
Carried Arms as a private man or Serjeant in the Rebel Army	at home.
was at the plundering Cullenhouse & carried Arms, working at his Trade	Strathspey.
Carried Arms as a private man	Balmenoch.
was compelled to carry Arms for the Rebels & has submitted himself	at home.
Carried Arms, has submitted to the King's mercy	Ruthven.
Collected the Excise for the Rebels and was very active in his station	Dead.
was Captain in the Rebel Army & Recruited his own Company	Dead.
Compelled to carry Arms in the Rebel Army, has submitted himself	at home.
Carried Arms, has submitted himself.	
Served in the Rebel Army as a private man, has submitted	in the Glens.
Forced into the Rebel Service, has submitted himself	at home.
Served in the Rebel Army & was very active in plundering, has submitted	Tombreck.
Carried Arms in the Pretender's Service	at home.
Carried Arms as a private man	at home.
Carried Arms with the Rebels	at home.

LIST OF REBELS FROM

Names.	Designations.	Abode.	Cause of Knowledge.
F.			
Alex^r Finlay	Weaver	Elgine	Seen by Alex^r Dallas Officer of Ex. Elgine
James Forsyth	Town Officer	Forress	Seen by Arch^d Dunbar, Ex. Officer, Forres
Alex^r Fordyce	Servant	Windyhills	Seen by Wm Porter, Ex. Off^r at Findhorn
Hugh Fraser	Merchant	Inverness	Seen by the above Arch^d Graham
Willm Fraser	of Dalernig	Stratherick	seen per s^d Arch^d Graham
Donald Fraser	Smith	Moy	Seen per do. Graham
Charles Fraser, Junr	of Fairfield	Kinmylies	Seen per do.
Hugh Fraser	Wright	Mirton	Seen per Jno Grant Ex. Officer, Inverness
James Fraser	of Foyers	Stratherrick	Seen per do.
Simon Fraser	Farmer	Dalhaple	Seen per do.
Alex^r ffraser	Culduthel's Brother	Inchnacardoch	Seen per do.
Willm ffraser	Merchant	Fort Augustus	Seen per do.
Hugh Fraser	Farmer	Borlum	Seen per do.
Alex^r Fraser	John Roy's son Tenent	Stratherrick	Seen per do.
John Fraser, Junr	of Bochruben	Castledownie	Seen per do.
Alex^r Fraser	Taxman	Letchune	Seen per do.
Simon Fraser	Vintiner	Stratherrick	Seen per do.
John Fraser	Taxman	do.	Seen per do.
Hugh Fraser	Son to said & Deserter from M'Intoshe's Company	Stratherrick	by Information from do.

ELGINE DISTRICT—*Continued.* 105

Acts of Rebellion and Circumstances.	Where at present.
Carried Arms as a Volunteer in the Rebel Army	not known.
Carried Arms & Recruited men for the Rebels	not known.
Carried Arms as a Volunteer in the Rebel Army	Skulking.
An Adjutant & carried Arms in the said Army	Kill'd.
Carried Arms as an Officer in said Army	not known.
a Captain in the Rebel Army promoted on acco^t of great services	Skulking.
Sold his Lieutenantcy in Cornwallises Reg^t & was Adjutant Genl to the Rebels	not known.
Acted as an Officer in the Rebel Army	not known.
a Captain in said Army & very active in serving that Interest	not known.
a Captain in said Army & very active in his Station	not known.
was a Captain in said Rebel Army, very active in his Station	not known.
Entered the Rebel Service, became a Captain in Enlisting those they hade taken prisoners	not known.
was Captain in said Service & very active in his station	not known.
an Officer in the Rebel Army & very active	Kill'd.
a very active Officer in the Rebel Army, Influenced by Lord Lovat	Lurking.
an Officer in the Rebel Army & violently zealous	not known.
an Officer in said Army & advised Mr Grant to join them also	Kill'd.
an Officer in said Army & active in Enlisting men	not known.
was an Officer in the Rebel Army	Kill'd.

LIST OF REBELS FROM

Names.	Designations.	Abode.	Cause of Knowledge.
Willm Fraser	Farmer	Kirktoun	by Information from Danl M'Laren Ex. Off^r Inverness
John Fraser	Cottar	Englishtoun	by Information from do.
Thomas ffraser	Smith	Englishtown	per Inforⁿ from said Danl M'Laren
John ffraser	Farmer	do.	per Infor. from do.
John Fowler	do.	Kingussie	per do. from Ja^s Browⁿ Ex. Off^r Ruthven
Don^d Farquharson	of Auchrachan	Glenconless	per Information
John Farquharson	of Altery	Eliet	per do.
Robert Farquharson		Mill of Achrachan	per do.
James Fraser		Upper Cults	per do.
Don^d Farquharson	Servant	Glenconless	per do.
Robt Dow Farquharson		Eliet	per do.
Willm Finlay		Cruchly	per do.
James Fleming		do.	per do.
John Fraser		Auchrachan	per do.
John Fleming		Findran	per do.
Patrick Forbes		Balivaler	per do.
John Fleming	Servt to Glenbucket		per do.
And^w Farquharson		Balintom	per do.
John Forbes	Merchant	Candlemore	per do.
Thomas Fraser		Balacharn	per do.
Grigory Farquharson	Tombea	Tombea	Noture in the Country
Cosmus Farquharson	of Tombea, Junr	Tombea	per Information
John Forbes		Wester Achmore	per do.
Forbes		Ballandie	per do.
Robt Fleming		Miln Achdregnie	per do.

ELGINE DISTRICT—*Continued.* 107

Acts of Rebellion and Circumstances.	Where they now are.
Carried Arms & was very active in his Station, but said to be forced out by Ld Lovat	not known.
Carried Arms at Culloden Battle, forced out by Lord Lovat	not known.
Carried Arms at the Battle of Culloden, Compell'd by Lord Lovat	not known.
Carried Arms at said Battle, forced out by Lord Lovat	not known.
Carried Arms, was very active in his Station but forced out by Cluny	at his own house.
a Captain in the Rebel Service & very active in raising men	at home.
Acted as an Officer in the Rebel Army	Prisoner.
An Ensign in the said Army, was at the Spoiling Culloden house	at home.
Carried Arms with the Rebels but has submitted himself	at home.
was Compelled by the Rebels to carry Arms, has submitted	at home.
Carried Arms with the Rebels	not known.
Carried Arms in the Rebel Service	at home.
Carried Arms in said Army, has submitted himself	at home.
forced into the Rebel Service, has submitted	at home.
Carried Arms with the Rebels, deserted them in February 1745	at home.
forced by the Rebels to Carry Arms, has submitted himself	at home.
was very active in raising men for the Rebels, has submitted	w^h Glenbucket.
forced out by the Rebels, has submitted	at home.
Carried Arms with the Rebels, but has submitted himself	at home.
Acted as Serjeant in the Rebel Army	Killed or Prisoner.
Collected the Cess & Excise for the Rebels	Dead.
Carried Arms in the Rebel Army	at home.
Carried Arms in said Army	at home.
Carried Arms in said Army being forced	Killed.
Carried Arms in the Rebel Army	at home.

Names.	Designations.	Abode.	Cause of Knowledge.
Donald Fleming		Miln Achdregnie	per Information; seen in his wounds after Culloden
John Fraser		Balnakeil	per Information
James Ferguson		Tomintoul	per do.
fforbes		Ballandie.	
G.			
John Gordon	of Cordregny	Cordregny	per Information
Patrick Gordon	Son to Ditto	do.	per do.
Lewis Gordon		Milnof Lagan	per do.
Alexr Grant		Nether Clunie	per do.
John Gordon	of Glenbucket	St. Bridget	Noture in the Country
David Gordon	of Kirkhill	Dalavoier	Noture in the Country
John Gordon	Son to Glenbucket	Achreachan	Noture in the Country
Thomas Gordon	of Fodderliter	Fodderliter	per Information
Willm Gordon	Grandson to Glenbucket	Achreachan	per do.
John Grant	of Inverlochy	Inverlochy	per do.
James Gordon		Auchluanie	per do.
John Gordon	of Minmore	Minmore	per do.
Alexr Gordon		Refrish	per do.
Willm Grant	of Blairfinde	Blarfinde	per do.
John Grant	Son to Blarfinde	do.	per do.
Alexr Grant		Logan of Blarfinde	per do.
James Grant		do.	per do.
David Grant	Son to Blarfinde	Blarfinde	per do.
John Grant		Loanbeg	Noture in the Country
John Gordon		Clashmore	per Information
Alexr Grant	Brother to Nevie.		Noture in the Country
John Grant	of Deskie	Deskie	per Information

ELGINE DISTRICT—Continued.

Acts of Rebellion and Circumstances.	Where they now are.
Carried Arms & was at Culloden Battle	at home.
Forced out into Arms by the Rebels	at home.
Carried Arms in the Rebel Army	at home.
Forced by the Rebels to Carry Arms in their Service	at home.
Carried Arms in the Rebel Army, submitted himself	at home.
Carried Arms in do. has submitted himself	at home.
Carried Arms & Collected the Cess for the Rebels	at home.
Carried Arms in the Rebel Army in the Character of an Officer	at home.
Major-General in the Rebel Army & was very active in press^g & Recruiting men	In the hills.
A Lieutenant in the Rebel Army	Dead.
Raised men for the Rebels, took the name of Co^{ll} but was not above a Week with them	at Achreachan.
was a Captain in the Rebel Army under Influence of Glenbucket said to be	in Badenoch.
was a Captain in the Rebel Army	at home.
was Adjutant in said Army	Inverlochy.
ane Officer in said Army	Kill'd.
a Rebel Captain, behaved discreetly & protected the houses of Sr Henry Innes & sev^{ll} Ministers	no Residence.
was Lieutenat in the Rebel Army	at home.
Carried Arms in said Army & has submitted to the King's mercy	at home.
Lieutenant in said Army but deserted	not known.
Lieutenant in said Army	at home.
Ensign in said Rebel Army, submitted himself	at home.
was an Officer of the Rebels	at home.
was Ensign in said Army	Kill'd.
was also Ensign in said Army, has submitted himself	at home.
Ensign in the Rebel Army	Kill'd.
Carried Arms as a private, submitted to the King's mercy	at home.

LIST OF REBELS FROM

Names.	Designations.	Abode.	Cause of Knowledge.
Alex^r Grant	Son to Deskie	Deskie	
John Grant	Son to Ditto	Deskie	
John Gordon	Son to Foderleter	Foderleter	Noture in the Count
George Gordon	Son to Ditto	do.	
Charles Grant	a Deserter	Tomdonach	
William Gordon		Dell	per Information
John Grant	Weaver	Tombreck	per Information
Robt Gauld alias M'Pherson		Ruthven	per do.
Alex^r Gow		do.	per Information
Pat^k Grant		Inshnakap	per do.
John Gordon		Inshnakap	per do.
George Gordon		Newtoun	per do.
John Gordon		Loynavere	per do.
William Grant		Findran	per do.
Mr Wm Grant	a popish Priest	Balivaler	per do.
William Grant		Tomintowle	per do.
George Gordon		do.	per do.
Willm Roy Grant		Balnakeill	per do.
Donald Grant		Easter Galurg	per Information
Don^d Gibenach		Delavoiar	per do.
Peter Grant		do.	per do.
Grigor Grant		do.	per do.
Donald Gordon		do.	per do.
James Grant		Dalnabo	per do.
Thomas Gauld		Auchlounie	per do.
William Grant		Foderleter	per do.
Peter Grant		Do. Wester	per do.

ELGINE DISTRICT—*Continued.* 111

Acts of Rebellion and Circumstances.	Where they now are.
was an Ensign in the Rebel Army	at home.
was a private man in the said Army	at home.
was an Officer in the Rebel Army	Dead.
Carried Arms in the Rebel Army, submitted to the King's mercy	at home.
Lieutenant in the Rebel Army	in the Hills.
a Serjeant in said Army, forced out, & submitted himself	at home.
Carried Arms in said Army but deserted & submitted himself	at home.
private man in said Army, Insulted the country people	at home.
also a private man in said Army & Insulted the country people	at home.
Forced out with the Rebels, has submitted himself	at home.
Carried Arms in the Rebel Army, has submitted	at home.
was a private man in said Army & has submitted himself	not known.
Carried Arms in said Army	Prisoner.
Carried Arms in ditto Army, Submitted	at home.
Directing the Rebels	Balivaler.
a Private man in the Rebel Service, Forced out, has submitted	at home.
a Private man in said Service	Killed.
a private man in the said Service, has submitted to the King's mercy	at home.
Carried Arms, a private man in s^d Rebel Army, forced out, has submitted	at home.
was a private in the Rebel Army, forced out & has submitted himself	at home.
Carried Arms as a private man, being forced out, has submitted	at home.
was a private man in Rebel Army, being forced out, has submitted	at home.
Carried Arms in said Army, has submitted to the King's mercy	Kill'd.
Carried Arms in said Army, has submitted	at home.
Carried Arms in said Army being forced thereto, has submitted	at home.
Carried Arms in said Army, has submitted	at home.
was a Serjeant in said Army & a Recetter of Plunder, has submitted himself	at home.

LIST OF REBELS FROM

Names.	Designations.	Abode.	Cause of Knowledge.
John Grant	Merchant	Tomintoul	per Information
Lewis Grant	Son to Wm Grant	Little Neive	per do.
William Grant	Servant	Clagan	per do.
John Grant		Tamavelan	per do.
John Grant		Upper Drummin	per do.
James Gordon		Croft of Minmore	per do.
William Gordon		Glenrines	per do.
Ja^s Gauldie, Junr		Pitchash	per do.
Alex^r Gordon		Backside of Clashnaver	per do.
Robert Gordon		Nether Clashnaver	per do.
Alex^r Grant		Calier	per do.
Neil Grant		Tomahanan	per do.
Lewis Gaw		Knock of Achnhoil	per do.
Thos Gibenach		Skala	per do.
John Gauld		Achnagara	per do.
Alex^r Gauld		do.	per do.
Peter Grant		Gaulurg	per do.
William Grant	Son to Angus Grant	sometime in Tamvilan	per do.
Willm Grant		Gaulurg	per do.
Ishmael Gordon	Servant		per do.
Lodovick Gordon	Merchant	Elgine	Inf. fm. Rod^k Merchant, Ex. Officer, Elgine
Willm Grant	Wright	Windyhills	from Wm Porter do. at Findhorn
John Gray	Servant	Jromside	from do.
Alex^r Grant	Writer	Inverness	from Arch^d Graham before mentioned
James Gordon	Messenger at Arms	Kingussie Boat	from Ja^s Brown at Ruthven
Alex^r Grant	ffarmer	Croftbain	Information from do.
John Grant	do.	do.	per do. from do.

ELGINE DISTRICT—Continued.

Acts of Rebellion and Circumstances.	Where they now are.
Carried Arms in the Rebel Army, has submitted	at home.
Carried Arms in said Army & was at Spoiling Cullen house, has submitted	not known.
was a private man in said Army	not known.
was also a private man in the Rebel Army	at home.
Carried Arms as a private man or Serjeant in said Army, submitted	at home.
Carried Arms as a private man	at home.
Carried Arms as a private man	at home.
Carried Arms as a private man	at home.
Carried Arms as do. active in Plundering Cullen house, etc. was forced out	at home.
was Serjeant in the Rebel Army	at home.
Carried Arms as a private man in said Army	at home.
Carried Arms as do. in said Army, but forced out	at home.
was a private man in the Rebel Army, was forced	at home.
was a private man in said Army	at home.
was a private man in said Army	at home.
was forced out by the Rebels to carry Arms, has submitted himself	at home.
was forced out into the Rebellion & Twice deserted	at home.
Served as a Soldier in the Rebel Army & was active in plundering the Country	not known.
Carried Arms in the Rebel Army	at home.
Carried Arms in said Army	Lurking.
Carried Arms in the Rebel Horse, was in the Rebellion, 1715	Lurking.
was a Lieutenant in said Army & Enlisted men	Lurking.
Carried Arms in said Army as a Volunteer	Lurking.
was a Captain in said Army	not known.
Prompted out people into the Rebellion & discharged the Min^r for praying for his Majesty	at home.
Carried Arms & was very active, but said to be forced	at home.
Carried Arms & was very active in his Station, but said to be forced out	at home.

LIST OF REBELS FROM

Names.	Designations.	Abode.	Cause of Knowledge.
H.			
Thos Hutcheson	Mercht	Elgine	Inf. from Roderick Merchant
Alexr Hendric	Farmer	Dykeside	from John M'Allum
Thos Houston	do.	Drummyample	from Mr Grant
I.			
Innes	Wright	Coltfield	from Mr Porter at Findhorn
Alexr Innes		Balmdrowan	per Information
John Innes		do.	per do.
Robert Innes		West Foderleter	per do.
K.			
John Kennedy	Servant	Daskie	per Information
Lodovick Kay	Gentleman	Ironside	Inf. from Porter Ex. Officer
L.			
Alexr Leigh	Wigmaker	Elgine	per Inform. from Mr Merchant
Chas. Lesslie	Brother to Findracy	Findracy	per do.
Willm Logie	Porter	Elgine	per do.
Willm Lindsay		Carchley	per Information
Willm Lamb		Achnhoyle	per do.
M.			
John M'Kenzie	Chyrurgeon	Elgin	Inf. from Mr Merchant
Willm M'Kenzie	Residenter	do.	By do.
Peter Matthew	Farmer	Blervie	from Andw Ross Ex. Officer Forress
Alexr Man	Son to Jas Man Farmer	Grange	from do.
John M'Arthur	Brewer	Inverness	from Mr Graham

ELGINE DISTRICT—*Continued.*

Acts of Rebellion and Circumstances.	Where they now are.
Carried Arms as a Volunteer in the Rebel Army	Lurking.
Carried Arms as a Volunteer in said Army	Lurking.
was Adjutant and Paymaster in said Army	not known.
Carried Arms as a Volunteer with the Rebels	Skulking.
Forced out to carry Arms by the Rebels, deserted them in February 1745	at home.
Forced out as above, deserted the 10^h of April 1746	at home.
Forced out by the Rebels to carry Arms, has submitted himself	at home.
Carried Arms as a private man in the Rebel Army	at home.
Acted as an Officer in the Rebel Army	not known.
Active in prompting others to go into the Rebellion	at home.
Recruited for the Rebels & Robed the Country of Arms & was very active at Channery	at Findracy.
was very [active] in giving Intelligence to the Rebels	Lurking.
Carried Arms in the Rebel Army	at home.
Carried Arms in said Army, has submitted himself	at home.
Served as Surgeon in the Rebel Army & was very active	said to be at Edin^r.
Carried Arms in said Army, deluded by David Tulloch	Lurking.
Carried Arms as a Volunteer with the Rebels	not known.
Carried Arms as do. in the said Army	Lurking.
Carried Arms with the Rebels & went with them into England	Prisoner at Carlisle.

LIST OF REBELS FROM

Names.	Designations.	Abode.	Cause of Knowledge.
Don^d M'Donald	Brewer	Inverness	Seen in Arms by Mr Graham
Gillice M'Bain	Brewer	Dalmagarrie	Seen in Arms by do.
Lauchⁿ M'Intosh	Merchant	Inverness	Seen in Arms by Mr Finlay
John M'Lean	Writer	do.	Seen by Mr Grant
Alex^r M'Donald	Residenter	do.	Seen by do.
John M'Javis	of Gartenbeg	Stratherrick	Seen by do.
Alex^r M'Javish	Gartenbeg's Brother	do.	Seen in Arms by do.
Alex^r M'Gillavrae	of Dimmaglass	Dimmaglass	Seen in Arms by do.
Alex^r M'Intosh	Taxman of Elrig	Elrig	Seen in Arms by do.
Alex^r M'Gillawray	Taxman	Petty	Seen in Arms by do.
Robt M'Gillawray	Farmer	do.	Seen in Arms by do.
Arch^d M'Gillawray	Brother to said Robert	do.	Seen in Arms by do.
Angus M'Intosh	of Pharr	Pharr	Seen by do.
Simon M'Intosh	Son to Thos M'Intosh	Daviot	Seen in Arms by do.
Roderick Mitchell	Shoemaker	Fort Augustus	by Information from do.
John M'Laren	Vintiner	do.	by do.
Don^d M'Donald	of Lochgarry	Culachy	seen by do.
Don^d M'Donald	of Scotas	Scotas	By Informa^{tn} from do.
Angus M'Donald	Greenfield	Gariolock	By do.
Ronald M'Donald	Shian	Shian	By do.
John M'Donald	of Arnabee	Arnabee	Seen in Arms by do.
Ronald M'Donald	Brother to Arnabell	do.	By Inform. from do.
Alex^r M'Donald	Octera	Octer	By do.
Allan M'Donald	Son to the Laird of Leek	Leek	Seen in Arms by do.
Alex^r M'Donald	do.	do.	do.

ELGINE DISTRICT—*Continued.* 117

Acts of Rebellion and Circumstances.	Where they now are.
was a pensioner of Chelsea, but carried Arms as Lieu^t in the Rebel Army	not known.
was Major in the Rebel Army & very active in his Station	kill'd.
a Lieu^t Coll. and Enlisted many men	not known.
was an officer in said Army & served voluntarly	Lurking.
Carried Arms as a Volunteer in said Army	not known.
was an officer in the Rebel Army & at the Battle of Falkirk	not known.
was an officer in said Army & active in forcing men into that Service	not known.
was a Collonel in said Army & very active, said to be forced out by Lady M'Intosh	kill'd.
was a Captain in said Army	Lurking.
was Captain in said Army, very active in his Station	killed.
was an Officer in said Army	kill'd.
was an Officer in said Army, Voluntarly engaged	not known.
a Captain in said Army & very active, said to be forced by Lady M'Intosh	kill'd.
Instructed in the Excise, was an officer in the Rebel Army	not known.
Carried Arms, was very active in plundering	not known.
Carried Arms & active in plundering	not known.
was once Lieu^t in Lord Loudon's Regim^t, accepted of a Coll'^{s} Comiss^n from the Rebels	Lurking.
was a Captain in the Rebel Service & Levied the Cess for them	kill'd.
was also a Captain in said Service, assisted in Levying the Cess	not known.
was a Captain in said Army, also assisted in Levying the Cess	not known.
was Captain in said Army & very active in his Station	not known.
was an Officer in the Rebel Army & active in Levying the Cess	not known.
a Captain in said Army & active in Levying do.	not known.
had an Officer's Commission in said Army, was very active	not known.
was a Rebel Officer & very active	not known.

Names.	Designations.	Abode.	Cause of Knowledge.
Donald M'Donald	Lundee	Lundee	Seen in Arms by Mr Grant
Don^d M'Donald	Son to do.	do.	do.
Alex^r M'Donald	Servant	Forth Augustus	do.
Alex^r M'Donald	Vintiner	Laggan	Infor. from do.
Angus M'Bear	Farmer	Faillie	Seen in Arms by Danl M'Laren, Excise Officer at Inverness
Gillies M'Bear	do.	Bananghten	Seen in Arms by do.
Duncan M'Intosh	do.	Drummond	Seen in Arms by do.
Donald M'Bean	do.	Auldaury	By Infor. from do.
Gillies M'Bean	Servant	do.	Seen in Arms by do.
John M'Bean	do.	do.	Seen in Arms by do.
Evan M'Pherson	of Clunie	Clunie	Seen in Arms by Ja^s Brown as men^{td}
M'Pherson, Junr	Farmer	Delwhiny	Seen in Arms by do.
Lewis M'Pherson	do.	Delrady	Seen in Arms by do.
Malcon M'Pherson	Senr of Phoyness	Phoyness	Seen in Arms by do.
John M'Pherson	Elridge	Elridge	Seen in Arms by do.
M'Pherson	of Strathmasy	Strathmassy	Seen in Arms by do.
John M'Pherson	Farmer	Gawamore	Seen in Arms by do.
Donald M'Pherson	do.	Brachachy	Seen in Arms by do.
And^w M'Pherson	Junr of Banachar	Banachar	Seen in Arms by do.
John M'Pherson	Farmer	Pitachuran	Seen in Arms by do.
Hugh M'Pherson	do.	Coraldy	Seen in Arms by do.
Evan M'Pherson	do.	Lagan of Nood	By Information from do.
Lauchlan M'Pherson	Junr of Strathmashie	Strathmashie	Seen in Arms by Ja^s Brown, Ex. Off^r, Ruthven
Kenneth M'Pherson	Merchant	Ruthven	do.
Don^d M'Pherson	do.	do.	do.
Lauch^n M'Pherson	Farmer	Pitmain	do.
Angus M'Pherson	do.	Flichaty	do.
Mal Dow M'Pherson	do.	Ballachroan	do.

ELGINE DISTRICT—Continued.

Acts of Rebellion and Circumstances.	Where they now are.
was a Captain of the Rebels & active in Levying the Cess	not known.
An Officer in the Rebel Army & active in his Station	not known.
Carried Arms as a Volunteer in the Rebel Army	not known.
was an Officer in said Army, Levied the Cess	not known.
an Officer in said Army, was at the Battle of Falkirk	Kill'd.
an Officer in the Rebel Army, forced out by Major M'Bean & was at Falkirk Battle	not known.
an Officer in said Army, was at the Battle of Culloden, forced out by Lady M'Intosh	not known.
was Storekeeper at Aldaury for the Rebels & very active in serving them	not known.
Carried Arms in the Rebel Army, & was very active	not known.
also carried Arms in said Army	not known.
was a Captain in Lord Loudon's Reg^t, became a Coll. in the Rebel Army & forced out others by burning &c.	not known.
was a Lieu^t Collonel of the Rebels & very active	not known.
acted as a Major in the Rebel Army & was active in his Station	not known.
was a Captain in said Army	not known.
was a Lieutenant in said Army	not known.
was a Captain in said Army	not known.
was also a Captain in the Rebel Army	not known.
was Captain in said Army & active in his Station	not known.
Captain in said Army & very active	not known.
was an Officer in said Rebel Army	not known.
was an Officer in said Army	not known.
was an Officer in said Rebel Army	not known.
an Officer in the Rebel Army	not known.
an Officer in said Army, in Edinburgh Castle	Prisoner.
Carried Arms as a Volunteer in the Rebel Army	Lurking.
Carried Arms & was active in his Station	Lurking.
Carried Arms in said Army & very active, said to be	at home.
Carried Arms in said Army & was active	at home.

LIST OF REBELS FROM

Names.	Designations.	Abode.	Cause of Knowledge.
W^m M'Pherson	Farmer	Ringussie	Seen in Arms by Ja^s Brown, Ex. Off^r, Ruthven
Alex^r M'Pherson	do.	do.	do.
Alex^r M'Queen	Smith	Brae Ruthven	do.
Don^d Monro	Farmer	Ruthven	By Information from do.
W^m M'Pherson	Wigmaker	do.	By do.
John M'Pherson	Farmer	Cluny	Seen in Arms by do.
Alex^r M'Pherson	do.	Blarchy beg	do.
W^m M'Pherson	do.	Cato big	By Information from do.
Pat^k M'Alpin		Gaulurg	By Information
Kenneth M'Kenzie	Servant	Dell	per do.
John M'Evan		Balacherach	per do.
George Martin		Tomachlagan	per do.
John M'Kenzie		Ruthven	per do.
Angus M'Donald	Servant	Camdelmore	per do.
Alex^r Martin		do.	per do.
Evan M'Grigor		do.	per do.
Willm Miller		Inshnkep	per do.
James M'Willie	Servant	Cruchley	per do.
David M'Willie		Achrachan	per do.
John M'Person		do.	per do.
W^m M'Grigor		Findran	per do.
Peter M'Donald		Tomintowl	per do.
John M'Allan		do.	per do.
John M'Donald		Redorach	per do.
Grigor M'Grigor		Loipuorn	per do.
Malcom M'Grigor		Auchnahayl	per do.
John M'Grigor		Wester Gaulurg	per do.
John M'Gurman		do.	per do.

ELGINE DISTRICT—Continued. 121

Acts of Rebellion and Circumstances.	Where they now are.
Carried Arms in said Army & was active in his Station	at home.
Carried Arms in said Army & was active	at home.
was a Quarter Master in the Rebel Army	at home.
Carried Arms in the Rebel Service	at home.
was aiding & assisting to the Rebels	at home.
Carried Arms in Rebel Service & was active in his Station	at home.
Carried Arms with the Rebels	at home.
Carried Arms in the Rebel Army	Dead.
was an Ensign in said Army	at home.
Carried Arms in the Rebel Army	at home.
Carried Arms in said Army, was forced out, has submitted to Royal Mercy	at home.
Forced out to carry Arms by the Rebels, has submitted himself	at home.
Carried Arms with the Rebels, has submitted himself	at home.
Carried Arms in Rebel Service	at home.
Carried Arms with the Rebels & is either	Pris^r or Dead.
Carried Arms in the Rebel Army	at home.
Carried Arms in said Army	Braes of Glenlivat.
Deserted from the King's Army & carried Arms with the Rebels	not known.
Carried Arms, was active in plundering the country has submitted	in the Glens.
Carried Arms, was active in plundering, has submitted himself	Milton of Achrachan.
Carried Arms in the Rebel Army	Kill'd.
Forced by the Rebels to carry Arms	at home.
Forced by the Rebels to carry Arms, has submitted himself	at home.
Forced by the Rebels to carry Arms, has submitted himself	Prisoner.
Forced by the Rebels to carry Arms, has also submitted	Loyn Corn.
Forced by the Rebels to carry Arms, has submitted himself	at home.
Forced out by do. to carry Arms, has submitted	at home.
arried Arms in the Rebel Army, has submitted	at home.

LIST OF REBELS FROM

Names.	Designations.	Abode.	Cause of Knowledge.
Malcom M'Grigor		Easter Gaulurg	By Information
Don^d M'Donald		Balintom	per do.
Alex^r M'Donald		Dalnabo	per do.
John M'Pherson		Foderleter	per do.
Alex^r M'Grar		do.	per do.
George Millne		Croft of Inverlochy	per do.
John M'Intosh		East Inveroury	per Information
John M'Donald		Achrachan	per do.
John M'Kenzie	Merchant	Dalmore	per do.
Alex^r M'Lea		Upper Dounan	per do.
John M'Kenzie		Aldinlon	per do.
Willm M'Robie		Morings	per do.
Willm M'Adam	Son to John M'Adam	Shanoal	Noture in the Country
Robt M'Lea	Son to John M'Lea	Coull	per Information
James M'Lea	Servant	Carloch	per do.
Willm M'Robie		Tormachork	per do. Noture in the Country
John M'Lea		Clagan	per Information
Dun M'Willie		East Corrie	per do.
Robt M'Donald	Merch^t	Tarravan	per do.
Willm M'Donald	Taylor	do.	per do.
Alex^r M'Donald	Servant	Minmore	per do.
James Middleton		Ballandie	per do.
Alex^r M'Grigor		Inverachan	per do.
Alex^r Muir		East Pitchash	per do.
James M'Donald		Inveraven	per do.
Peter More		Knockindo	per do.
Angus M'Donald	Servant to	Pitchash	per do.
Alex^r M'Alister		Tamavilan	per do.
Thomas M'Pherson	Servant	Aiknarow	per do.
Robt M'kay		Nether Clashoer	per do.
Alex^r M'Grigor		Balachnockan	per do.

ELGINE DISTRICT—Continued.

Acts of Rebellion and Circumstances.	Where they now are.
Forced out under Arms by the Rebels, has submitted himself	at home.
Forced by the Rebels to carry Arms in their Service	at home.
Carried Arms in the Rebel Service, has submitted	at home.
Carried Arms in said Service but forced, has submitted himself	at home.
Carried Arms in the Rebel Army, but forced, has submitted	at home.
Carried Arms in said Army being compell'd, has submitted himself	at home.
Carried Arms in the Rebel Army	at home.
Carried Arms in said Army, has submitted himself	at home.
Carried Arms in said Army, has submitted himself	at home.
Carried Arms as a Serjeant in the Rebel Army	Middle Dounan.
Carried Arms as a private man in said Army	Kill'd.
Carried Arms in the Rebel Army	Killed.
Forced out by the Rebels to their Service but deserted in Septr 1745	at home.
Carried Arms with the Rebels as a private man	at home.
Carried Arms in the Rebel Army as a private man	Braes of Glenlivat.
Carried Arms in said Army, has submitted himself, keeping Cattle	in the Glens.
Forced out to carry Arms by the Rebels but deserted	at home.
Forced out, has submitted	at home.
Carried Arms with the Rebels, was at the Rifeling Cullen house, submitted	at home.
Carried Arms in the Rebel Army, has submitted himself	skulking.
Carried Arms in said Army	in the Braes.
Carried Arms in said Army	Dead.
Carried Arms & was very active in plundering the country	Left the country.
was Serjean in the Rebel Army	at home.
Carried Arms in said Army	Pitchasch
Carried Arms in said Army	Left the Country.
Carried Arms in said Army	Left the Country.
Forced out into the Rebel Service	at home.
Carried Arms in the Rebel Army	Badenoch.
was Serjeant in said Army & active in Robing the Country	at home.
Carried Arms in said Rebel Army & was active in plundering	at home.

LIST OF REBELS FROM

Names.	Designations.	Abode.	Cause of Knowledge.
Geo. M'Lauchlane		Calur	per Information
John M'kay	Merchant	Balno	per do.
Angus M'Donald	Servant	Tamahanan	per do.
Paul M'Pherson		St. Skola	per do.
John Michie		West Achwauh	per do.
Allan M'Lea		Badiglashean	Noture in the Country
John More		Askimore	per Information
John More, Junr		do.	per do.
John M'Lauchlan		Badivochal	per do.
Coll M'Donald		do.	per do.
James M'Donald		do.	per do.
William M'Lea		Souie	per do.
Geo. M'Donald		Nether Achdregnie	per do.
John Mensat	Weaver	Achdregnie	per do.
James M'donald		Middle Achdregnie	per do.
Wm M'Angus		Letoch	per do.
Allan M'Donald		Dalmloyn	per do.
Alexr M'Pherson		Milton of Achrachan	per do.
Willm M'Hardie		Glen above Achrachan	per do.
N.			
Alex. Nicolson		Inveravon	per Information
P.			
Willm Paton		Tomintowl	per Information
John Perrie		Elgine	Seen in Arms by Alexr Dallas
R.			
Hugh Ross	Turner	Elgine	Seen in Arms by Mr Dallas

ELGINE DISTRICT—Continued.   125

Acts of Rebellion and Circumstances.	Where they now are.
Forced out by the Rebels & carried Arms, has submitted himself	at home.
Carried Arms in the Rebel Army	at home.
Carried Arms in said Army	at home.
Compelled by the Rebels to carry Arms, has submitted	at home.
Carried Arms with the Rebels, has submitted	at home.
a private man in the Rebel Army but deserted & never joined again	at home.
Carried Arms in said Army, has submitted himself	at home.
was in Arms with the Rebels & carried home a great deal of plunder	at home.
Carried Arms in the Rebel Army	Prisoner.
Carried Arms in said Army	Prisoner.
Carried Arms in said Army	at home.
Carried Arms in said Army	at home.
was compelled by the Rebels to carry Arms with them	at home.
Carried Arms in the Rebel Army, was at plundering Cullen house	Nether Achrachan.
Carried Arms in said Army	at home.
Carried Arms in said Army	at home.
Carried Arms in said Army but said to be forced	at home.
Carried Arms in said Army	at home.
Carried Arms in said Army	at home.
Carried Arms in said Rebel Army	Left the Country.
Carried Arms in said Rebel Army, said to be forced	Pris^r or kill'd.
Carried Arms as a volunteer in said Army	Lurking.
Carried Arms as a Volunteer in the Rebel Army	Lurking.

LIST OF REBELS FROM

Names.	Designations.	Abode.	Cause of Knowledge.
Robt Ross	Kirkbeddal	Kirkhill	from M^r M'Callum
Alex^r Reid	Servant	Urquhart	by Infor. from do.
John Ross	Farmer	Forress	Seen officiating by Mr Dunbar
John Rhind	Brewer	Findorn	from Mr Porter
Chas Robertson		Balmlagan	per Information
John Roy Stuart		Tombreck	per do.
Willm Ross		Ruthven	per do.
Donald Reoch, Junr		Culmores	per do.
James Reoch	Servant	Camdelmore	per do.
Donald Reoch		Eliet	per do.
Alex^r Reoch		Galurg	per do.
Grigor Roy M'Grigor		Dalnabo	per do.
John Reoch		West Foderleter	per do.
John Rattray		Balno	per do.
Peter Roy Grant		Badiglashean	per do.
John Roy Grant		Demickmore	per do.
Robt Ross		Tamorlan	per do.
John Ross	Servant	Skalla	per do.
S.			
John Smith	Carter	Elgine	Informⁿ from Mr Dallas
William Stephen	Merchant	do.	Do. from Mr Merchant.
John Smith	do.	do.	per do.
Willm Smith	Farmer	Ortoun	per do. from M^r M'Callum
Willm Smith	Skinner	Forress	per do. from Mr Dunbar
James Syme	Smith	Inverness	per do. from Mr Graham
James Shaw	Servant	Moy	Seen in Arms per do.

ELGINE DISTRICT—Continued.

Acts of Rebellion and Circumstances.	Where they now are.
Volunteer in the Rebel Army, said to be imposed upon when drunk	Lurking.
Carried Arms as a Volunteer in said Army, now in Banffshire	Lurking.
Carried Arms, was keeper of a Magazine for the Rebels & very active	not known.
Informed of proper places & assisted in plundering at Findorn	not known.
Carried Arms in the Rebel Army, submitted himself &	at home.
Forced by the Rebels to carry Arms, has submitted	at home.
fforced by Do. to carry Arms, has submitted	at home.
Carried Arms with the Rebels	at home.
Carried Arm in the Rebel Army	at home.
Carried Arms in said Army being forced	at home.
Carried Arms in the Rebel Army being forced	at home.
A Deserter from the King's Army, was a Serjeant in Rebel Army & a plunderer	at home.
Carried Arms being forced & has submitted	at home.
was Compelled by the Rebels to carry Arms	at home.
Carried Arms in the Rebel Army	at home.
Forced to carry Arms by the Rebels, submitted himself	at home.
Carried Arms in the Rebel Army	at home.
Carried Arms in said Army, has submitted himself	at home.
Carried Arms in the Rebel Army & was very active	at home.
Remarkable for Billating the Rebels on persons well affected to the Governt	at home.
Acted as Store Master for the Rebels	Lurking.
Carried Arms as a Volunteer in the Rebel Army	not known.
Carried Arms as a Volunteer in said Army	not known.
Met the Rebels 2 miles off. Informed of Ld Loudon's Retreat & received a Crown from Lord Kilmarnock for conducting them to Inverness	at home.
Was an Officer in said Rebel Army & at the Battle of Falkirk	not known.

LIST OF REBELS FROM

Names.	Designations.	Abode.	Cause of Knowledge.
John Stuart	Late Baillie	Inverness	Inform^n from Mr Finlay
Hugh Stuart	Gardner	Fort Augustus	per do. from Mr Grant
Alex^r Stuart	Taxman of the Excise	Tamavilan	from the Country
William Stuart		Bregach	per Information
Alex^r Stuart alias Derg		Upper Achlichny	per do.
Don^d Stuart		Ruthven	per do.
John Stuart		Glenconles	per do.
Don^d Stuart		do.	per do.
Pat^k Stuart	Servant	Cruchly	per do.
Allan Stuart		Newtoun	per do.
John Stuart		Findran	per do.
Don^d Stuart		do.	per do.
Don^d Stuart		Auchnahayl	per do.
John Stuart		Terbain	per do.
Robt Smith		Inverary	per do.
John Stuart		East do.	per do.
James Stuart		do.	per do.
Robt Stuart		Dounan	Noture in the Country
John Stuart		Tamavilan	per Information
John Stuart, Junr		Baluhnockan	per do.
Willm Stuart		Clashnaver	per do.
Willm Stuart		West Achivaich	per do.
John Stuart		Achnascra	per do.
And^w Smith		do.	per do.
James Stuart		do.	per do.
Robt Stuart		Badivochal	per do.
Peter Stuart alias Dow		do.	per do.
George Stuart		do.	per do.
Don^d Stuart alias Dow		Glack	per do.
John Stuart alias M'Yoak		Upper Achdregnie	per do.
John Stuart alias Dow		do.	per do.

ELGINE DISTRICT—Continued.

Acts of Rebellion and Circumstances.	Where they now are.
a Volunteer in said Rebel Army & very active, now at Newtoun	Mid Lothian.
Carried Arms, threatened to kill John Grant, Officer of Excise	not known.
was Ensign in the said Rebel Army	no Residence.
was a Captain in said Army & active in raising men	in the Hills.
Carried Arms in the Rebel Army, forced out, has submitted	at home.
Carried Arms & was at the Riffling Cullen house	at home.
Carried Arms being compelled by the Rebels	at home.
was a Rebel Hussar at the Spoiling of Cullen house	at home.
Carried Arms in the Rebel Army	not known.
Carried Arms in said Army	not known.
Carried Arms in said Army	at home.
Carried Arms in said Army	at home.
Carried Arms in the Rebel Army	at home.
Forced to carry Arms in said Army, thrice deserted	at home.
Compelled by the Rebels to carry Arms	at home.
Carried Arms in said Rebel Army	at home.
Forced to carry Arms in said Army	killed.
Carried Arms with the Rebels	at home.
Carried Arms in the Rebel Army	at home.
Carried Arms as a private man in said Army	at home.
Carried Arms in the Rebel Army	Prisoner
Carried Arms in said Army & active in plundering the Country	at home.
Carried Arms, being forced out, has submitted	at home.
Carried Arms, being forced out, has submitted himself	at home.
Carried Arms in the Rebel Army being forced, has submitted	at home.
was Compelled to carry Arms by the Rebels, has submitted	at home.
Carried Arms in the Rebel Army	at home.
Carried Arms in said Army	at home.
Carried Arms in said Army	Dead.
Carried Arms in said Army	at home.
Forced by the Rebels into their Service but deserted	at home.

LIST OF REBELS FROM

Names.	Designations.	Abode.	Cause of Knowledge.
Lewis Stuart	Servant to	Balachnockan	per Information
Robt Stuart		Glenbuckat	per do.
Allan Stuart		Gaulurge	per do.
John Stuart		Delavoiar	per do.
T.			
Mr John Tyrie	a Popish Priest	Clashnaver	Universally known
Duncan Turner		Culmore	per Information
William Turner		Middle Dounan	per do.
Willm Taylor		Crachly	per do.
James Torry	Dyster	Elgine	Infor. from Mr Merchant
Robt Taylor	do.	do.	per do.
Peter Taylor	Farmer	Burnside	Seen p. M^r M'Callum Enlisting men
Robt Tulloch	Bugtoun	Bugtoun	Seen in Arms by Mr Dunbar
James Taylor alias Robertson	ffarmer	Pitmain	Seen in Arms by Mr Brown
W.			
Thos Watson	Servant	Elgine	Seen acting by Mr Dallas
Wm Urquhart	Cooper	Brae Ruthven	Seen in Arms by Mr Brown
Kenneth Urquhart		Upper Cults	per Informat^n
Alex^r Williamson		Croft of Minmore	Noture in the Country

ELGINE DISTRICT—Continued.

Acts of Rebellion and Circumstances.	Where they now are.
Carried Arms as a Serjeant in the Rebel Army	at home.
Carried Arms as a private man	not known.
Carried Arms in the Rebel Army	Kill'd.
Carried Arms in said Army, being forced	at home.
was very active in raising men to go into the Rebellion	at home.
Carried Arms in Rebel Service, has submitted himself	at home.
Carried [Arms] in said Service	at home.
Carried Arms in the Rebel Army, has submitted	at home.
Carried Arms in said Army Voluntarly	Lurking.
Prompting others to go into Rebellion, said to have fled	Banffshire.
a Captain & engaged many men in the Rebel Service	about Banff lurking.
Carried Arms as a Lieut of Hussars	not known.
Carried Arms in the Rebel Army & was very active	at home.
Acted as a Drummer in the Rebel Army voluntarly	Lurking.
Carried Arms in said Army, was very active	at home.
Carried Arms in said Rebel Army	not known.
Carried Arms in said Army, has submitted himself	at home.

A LIST OF PERSONS CONCERNED IN THE
BY MR. GEORGE FAIRHOLM,

Names.	Designations.	Abode.
A.		
Robert Anderson	Younger of Whitburgh	Whitburgh
George Anderson, Junr	Tanner	Haddington
John Anderson	Journyman Sadler	do.
John Anderson	Wright	Seton
Robert Angus	Salt Watchman	West Pans
B.		
John Berrie	Extraordinary Salt Watchman	Prestonpans
Barthol. Bower	Precentor to the Non Jur^t Meeting	Haddington
Alex^r Bouglass	Miln Wright	do.
Thomas Black	Glazier	Mussleburgh
Willm Brown	Salt Officer	Preston pans

REBELLION, TRANSMITTED TO THE BOARD SUPERVISOR AT HADDINGTON.

Acts of Rebellion and Circumstances.	Where they now are.
was one of the Rebel Gen¹ Quarter masters, joined them before Preston Battle & conducted them to attack the King's Army there the night before the Battle & continued with them all along till dispers'd	Lurking in the Country.
Joined the Rebels when they went for England, got a Captain's Commissⁿ & was with them till the end	Kill'd or Lurking.
Voluntarly joined the Rebels when they went to England	not known.
Joined the Rebel Army after Preston & continued with them till after Culloden Battle	fled this country.
Acted as Salt Officer & uplifted the Salt Duty for Behoof of the Rebels	Continues a Watchman.
Acted as Salt Watchman for the Rebels while in this Country	at home.
Carried Messages & Commissions for the Rebels & publickly Insulted the well affected to the Government	at home.
was with the Rebels the most part of the Time they were in this Country but deserted them when they went to England	at home.
was Serjeant in the Rebel Artillary & with them during the whole Rebellion	Killed or absconding.
Acted first as Officer & then as Collector of the Salt Duty under the Rebels but absconded on their going for England	Prisoner.

LIST OF REBELS FROM

Names.	Designations.	Abode.
Walter Brodie	Shoemaker	Blance
David Brodie	Chaplain to Lady Blantyre	Leadington
Andrew Brown	Baillie of the Regality	Dalkeith
C.		
Arch^d Corser	Weaver	Fisheraw
Patrick Crombie	Workman	Haddington
Chas Crookshanks	Extr. Salt Watchman	Cockenzie
Robert Crighton	Salt Watchman	do.
James Cairns	Extrord^y Salt Watchman	Prestonpans
D.		
Charles Duncan	Servt to Dutchess of Gordon	Prestonhall
John Dick	Flesher	Prestonpans
Hendry Davidson	Mason	Tranent
James Dodds	Tenent	Setonhill
Thomas Donaldson	Schoolmaster	Haddington
John Denhame	Gardner	do.
E.		
Arthur Elphingston	Lord Balmerino	Mountainhall
James Elphingston	Regality Baillie	Dalkeith

HADDINGTON DISTRICT—*Continued*.

Acts of Rebellion and Circumstances.	Where they now are.
Joined the Rebel Army & gave Information upon the Neighbourhood of Conceal'd Arms	not known.
Said to have carried Arms in the Rebel Service at the Battle of Preston	Supposed at home.
Did conjunctly w^t Ja^s Elphinston levie upwards of 50£ of Excise which was paid to the Rebels except a small Ballance which remains in the Clerks hands, but was Compelled under pain of Military Execution	Dead.
Joined the Rebels, went with them to England & deserted them on their Retreat from thence	Lurking.
Joined the Rebels soon after Preston Battle & gave Information of Persons well affected to the Government	not known.
Acted as Salt Watchman under the Rebels during their Abode in this country	at home.
Acted as Salt Officer & Collector for the Rebels during their stay in this Country	Prestonpans.
Did the same as Robert Crighton	at home.
Went North before the Battle of Falkirk & Joined Lord Lewis Gordon's Core	none known.
Joined the Rebels on their march for England	Prisoner at Edin^r.
was with the Rebels at Preston Battle in Elcho's Regiment, went with them to England & there deserted	the Neighbourhood.
Joined the Rebels in the Pretender's Son's Life Guards	said to be Prisoner.
Acted as Salt Officer and uplifted the Duty for the Rebels	Prisoner.
Carried Arms at Preston Battle, left the Rebels when they went to England	at home.
Joined the Rebels & was with them during the whole Rebellion, was also in the Rebellion 1715 & pardoned	Prisoner at London.
In Company with And^w Brown Collected 50£ of Excise for the Rebels, being Compelled, Witnes John Murray's Letter	at home.

LIST OF REBELS FROM

Names.	Designations.	Abode.
F.		
Joseph Forbes	Journyman Wright	Haddington
John Finlayson	Salt Watchman	West pans
H.		
Alex^r Henderson	portioner of Tranent	Tranent
James Hay	Residenter in	Haddington
I.		
Charles Irvine	Residenter in	Prestonpans
K.		
Lauchlane King	Salt Watchman	Edmonstoun pans
L.		
James Lesslie	Gentleman to the Dutchess of Gordon	Prestonhall
Alex^r Lilly	Journyman Wright	Haddington
Robert Lindsay	Weaver	do.
Charles Lauder	Procurator	do.
John Lawrie	Salt Watchman	Prestonpans

HADDINGTON DISTRICT—*Continued.* 137

Acts of Rebellion and Circumstances.	Where at present.
Joined the Rebels about the Time of Preston Battle and continued with them till dispers'd, said to be Influenced by Joseph Robertson non jurant Minister at Haddington, his uncle	not known.
Acted as Salt Watchman for the Rebels during their stay in the Lothians	at home.
Joined the Rebels, conducted them the most advantageous way through Tranent the night be[fore] Preston Battle, for which he received a Guinea from Sullivan a Chief Commander; he publickly Insulted the well affected in Tranent, vaunted of his being a Serjeant of the Rebel Artillary, and continued with them till dispers'd	Lurking & said to be got into England.
Joined the Rebel Army at Edinb^r & Continued with them till after the Battle of Falkirk	not known.
Acted as Salt Officer and uplifted Dutie for the Rebels during their stay at Edinburgh	at home.
Acted as Watchman under the Rebels during their stay in that part of the Countrey	at home.
Went North before the Battle of Falkirk & Join'd the Rebels under Lord Lewis Gordon	Lurking in Edin^r.
Carried Arms with the Rebels & came to Haddington well mounted, supposed to be a Spye	in Prison.
was a Volunteer with the Rebels at Preston Battle, deserted when they went to England	at home.
Acted as Salt Officer & Coll^r for the Rebels, said to have been with them at Perth before they came to Edin^r	at home.
Continued in the exercise of his Office under the Rebels	at home.

Names.	Designations.	Abode.
M.		
Rod[k] M'kenzie	Timber Merchant	Fisheraw
William M'kenzie	Saltman	Cockenzie
Will[m] Mitchell	do.	do.
P.		
Andrew Porteus	of Burnfoot	Burnfoot
Samuel Porteus	Salt Watchman	Prestonpans
Janet Primrose	Spouse to John Primrose Late Officer of Excise	Dalkeith
Rob[t] Penston	Gardner	Tranent
R.		
Joseph Robertson	Non Jurant Minister	Haddington
Rob[t] Robertson	Brewer	Ormiston
Christ[r] Ramsay	Labourer	Seton
John Riddell	of Grange in Fife	Inverask
Thomas Redpath	Salt Officer	Prestonpans

HADDINGTON DISTRICT—Continued.

Acts of Rebellion and Circumstances.	Where they now are.
Joined the Rebel Army at Edinburgh, supposed to have continued with them till dispers'd	not known.
Continued in the Exercise of his Office for the Rebels	at home.
do.	at home.
Joined the Rebels in the Pretender's Son's Life Guards at Edinr & continued with them till the end	Prisoner.
Continued in Exercise of his Office & uplifted the Dutie for the Rebels	at home.
Closs attended her Husband & the Rebels & uplifted £1. 6. 5. of Excise from two Compounders in this District	at Dalkeith.
Assisted in Conducting the Rebels through Tranent the night before Preston Battle & gave them intelligence	at home.
Aided & assisted the Rebels & influenced people to join them, particularly George Anderson and Joseph Forbes his own nephew before mentioned. He also sollicited the Pretender's Son the Monday after Preston Battle for an Order to preach in Haddington kirk, who replied 'that was going on too fast.'	
The Day of Preston Battle Drank the Pretender's & his Son's healths by the names of King James & Prince of Wales, & Success to their Arms, Expressing his attachment to their Interest in the strongest manner & went several Times out with the Rebels and assisted in Robing the Country of Horses	Prisoner.
Went with the Rebels to England & continued with them till dispers'd	fled the Country.
Joined in the Pretender's son's Life Guards before Preston Battle & continued in the Service to the end	not known.
Continued in the Exercise of his Office & uplifted the Duty for the Rebels, now employ'd as formerly &	at home.

Names.	Designations.	Abode.
James Reid	Salt Watchman	Cockenzie
William Rannie	do.	Prestonpans
S.		
Andrew Sherriff	Brewer & Maltster	Prestonpans
Wm Sinclair	Salt Watchman	do.
T.		
Hector Thomson	Salt Watchman	Edmonston pan
James Thomson	Brewer & Maltster	Dalkeith
Arch^d Todd	Weaver	Mussleburgh
Thomas Todd	Town Clerk	do.
V.		
Patrick Veitch	Carter	Elphingtoun
John Waddell	Ship Master	Preston Pans

HADDINGTON DISTRICT—Continued.

Acts of Rebellion and Circumstances.	Where at
Continued in the exercise of his office for the Rebels	at home.
do.	at home.
Acted as Salt Officer and uplifted the Duty for the Rebels during their stay at Edin^r	Leith.
Continued in the Exercise of his Office for the Rebels	at home.
Did Salt Officer's Duty & uplifted the money for the Rebels while they Continued there	at home.
Went from Dalkeith with the Rebels in their way to England with a white Cockade & Tartan plaid, pretends he went in quest of a cart & horses which went off with the Rebel Baggage two Days before, but notwithstanding he assum'd the authority of one of their Officers & with a party extorted Victualls for himself & Horses without payment, particularly at the Laird of Kirkeant's and other places in Gallow water, where & at Ginglekirk he assisted the Rebels in taking Horses, but deserted before they entered England	at home since.
Joined the Pretender's Son's Life Guards before they went for England & continued with them till dispers'd	Prisoner.
Collected the Excise in Mussleburgh and Fisheraw to the Extent of £66, 16$sh.$ 11$d.$, & applied it in part paym^t of 250£ imposed by the Rebels on these places as a Contribution all at his own hand with[out] any authority	at home.
Voluntarly engaged with the Rebels to drive their Carriages when they went to England and continued with them till their defeat at Culloden	Lurking.
Acted as Salt Officer & uplifted the Duty for the Rebels during their stay at Prestonpans	at home.

LIST OF PERSONS CONCERNED IN THE BOARD BY MR. JAMES

Names.	Designations.	Abode.	County.
B.			
Gavin Brown	of Bishoptoun	Millhead	Nithsdale
C.			
Willm Carruthers	Servt to Kirkconnal	Kirkconnal	Kirkubright Stewartry
D.			
Erskine Douglas	Surgeon	Hillhead	Annandale
Francis Douglas	Sailor		Stewartry
H.			
John Henderson	of Castlemains	Castlemains	do.
I.			
Ja^s Lesslie Johnston	of Knockhill	Knockhill	do.
Andrew Johnston	his eldest son		
James Irvine, Junr	of Gribton	Gribton	Nithsdale
Edwd Irvine	of Wysbie	Wysbie	Stewartry of Annandale

THE REBELLION, TRANSMITTED TO ROSS, SUPERVISOR AT DUMFRIES.

Acts of Rebellion and Circumstances.	Where they now are.
Attended the Pretender's Son at Dumfries with a white Cockade & gave him what assistance he could.	
Attended his Master in the Rebellion but left them in England	Kirkconnal.
Brothers to Sir John Douglas of Hillhead, Carried Arms with the Rebels from the time that they left Edin^r to their repassing the Forth	Lurking.
Was committed at Carlisle for drinking Treasonable healths; set at Liberty & made Jail Keeper by the Rebels on their getting possession of that place; made his escape when his Royal Highness the Duke retook that City, & now since the Battle of Culloden has been apprehended & is	Prisoner in Carlisle.
Carried Arms with the Rebels from the Time they left Edin^r till dispers'd	Lurking.
Carried Arms in the Rebel Service	not known.
Guided the Rebels & their Baggage from Ecclefechan to Graitney on their way to Carlisle	at home.

Names.	Designations.	Abode.	County.
John Irvine	of Whitehill	Whitehill	Stewartry of Annandale
Willm Johnston	of Lockarby	Whitewinehaws	do.
William Irvine	of Gribton	Gribton	Kirkcudbright Stewartry
M.			
James Maxwell	of Kirkconnal	Kirkconnal	do.
Willm Maxwell	of Carruchan	Carruchan	do.
Willm Maxwell	son to James Maxwell of Barncleugh	Dumfries	Nithsdale
Willm Maxwell, Esq.	Called Earl of Nithsdale	Terragles	do.
Lady Katharine Maxwell	Spouse to the above Willm Maxwell	do.	do.
Sir Willm Maxwell	of Sprinkell	Sprinkell	Annandale Stewartry
Willm M'Ghie	Glazier	Dumfries	Nithsdale

DUMFRIES DISTRICT—*Continued.* 145

Acts of Rebellion and Circumstances.	Where they now are.
was active in pressing horses for the service of the Rebels on their march from Moffat to Carlisle, & threatened the Constables that would not give their assistance	at home.
was very assisting to the Rebels in their march through Annandale to England & when some of their Baggage they left at Blackfoord was carried off by the country people, caused intimation to be made at several Church Doors that if they did not return it they should suffer military execution	at home.
Refused in a publick Company to drink his Majesty's health; went a considerable way to wait on the Pretender's Son but miss'd him and it's the general opinion of the country that he forc'd out his son into the Rebellion	at home.
Served in the Pretender's Son's Life Guards till the Defeat at Culloden	not known.
Accepted of a Captain's Commission from the Pretender's Son & acted as Chief Engineer at Carlisle when the same was beseig'd by His Royal Highness	not known.
Carried Arms with the Rebels	Prisoner.
Went to Edin^r & waited some time upon the Pretender's son	at home.
Attended the Young Pretender most of the time he was at Edin^r and Dumfries, was most active in promoting his Interest and had the principal hand in engaging Wm Maxwell of Carruchan to join the Rebels. She likewise made a present of a horse & chaise to the Person commonly called Duke of Perth	at home.
Entertained one called Major Brown & Willm Maxwell of Carruchan, two Rebels, after they had made their escape over the Walls of Carlisle, & provided them in Horses to carry them to the Rebel Army at Glasgow	at home.
was employed by the young Pretender to go from Dumfries to Carlisle to Reconnitre the King's Army & bring forward Rebel Stragglers, which he did	Prisoner.

K

A LIST OF PERSONS CONCERNED IN THE BOARD BY MR. ROBT. OGILVY,

Persons' Names.	Designations.	Abode.	Parish.
A.			
John Allan	Wright & Glasier	Alloa	Alloa
B.			
Charles Blaw	Son to Castlehill	Castlehill	Culross
Mr Henry Bruce	of Clackmanan	Clackmanan	Clackmanan
Mr James Bruce	Gentleman	do.	do.
C.			
James Callander	Late Deacon of the Baxters	Innerkeithing	Innerkeithing
Daniel Cameron	Coachman to Countess of Kincardin		Dumfermling
Willm Comry	Stewart to Earl of Murray	Duniebrisle	Duniebrisle
Francis Craich	Brewer & Merchant	Clackmanan	Clackmanan

THE REBELLION TRANSMITTED TO SUPERVISOR AT DUMFERMLING.

Acts of Rebellion and Circumstances.	Where they now are.
Joined the Rebels about the Time of Preston Battle, was made Serjeant of Artillary & continued with them till dispers'd	not known.
Came over with Lord John Drummond & joined the Rebels now at Stirling	Prisoner.
Joined the Rebels at Edin^r & was made an Officer in their Army	not known.
Joined Do. at Edin^r in the Pretender's Son's Life Guards	not known.
Joined the Rebels at Edin^r but Sickened & left them before the Battle of Falkirk	Left the Country.
Carried Arms at Preston Battle in the Rebel Army, after that returned to his service, but was very active in carrying messages for the Rebels	not known.
Joined the Rebels when first at Perth & continued with them till dispers'd	not known.
Combin'd with the Rebels at Edin^r & Clackmanan, gave them Information of Arms conceal'd & of Horses which they took, aided in oppressing the country by causing them provide Victualls &c. and assisted in collecting the Excise upon a Sabbath Day. Caused the Excise Officer be apprehended & Imprison'd for three days, publickly Insulted the well-affected & aided & assisted the Rebels several other way too tedious here to relate	at home.

LIST OF REBELS FROM

Persons' Names.	Designations.	Abode.	Parish.
H.			
John Henderson	Brewer & Merchant	Clackmanan	Clackmanan
David Henderson	Brewer & Glazier	do.	do.
M & V.			
James Main	Brewer	Alloa	Alloa
Francis Masterton	of Parkhill		do.
Robert Mercer of Aldie	Brother to Lord Nairn		
John Marshall	Labouring man	Alloa	Alloa
John Marshall	Writer	Kinross	Kinross
Alexr Monteith	Sorter of Yearn	do.	do.
Anthony Murray	of Grange		Culross
John Murray	Late Clark to Collector of the Customs	Alloa	Alloa
William Verly	Carpenter	do.	do.
	No. 19.		

DUMFERMLING DISTRICT—*Continued.* 149

Acts of Rebellion and Circumstances.	Where they now are.
Combined with the Rebels, got from them out of the Warehouse at Leith, Goods which had been Seized by the king's officers, shewed himself very Zealous for the Pretender's Interest, had a hand in Imprisoning the Excise Officer as above mentioned & often beat, oppressed, & insulted the well affected	at home.
Served the Rebels as a Spy & message Bearer. Furnished their Army with necessaries & spoke very treasonable Language, he received from them as a reward, Brandy etc. out of the Custom house of Alloa & had a hand in Imprisoning the Excise Officer in manner above mentioned	at home.
Joined the Rebels before Preston Battle & went with them to England	London, Prisoner.
Joined do. on their coming to Edin^r & got a Commission in their Army	not known.
Joined early in the Rebellion, was active in forcing out others & was made a Collonel	do.
Joined the Rebels after Preston Battle & continued with them	do.
Gave the Rebells Intelligence of Arms hid in the country &c.	at home.
Joined the Rebels & continued with them	not known.
Joined the Rebel Army after Preston Battle & continued with them	do.
Joined do. at the Beginning. Assisted in Collecting the Excise at Clackmanan & continued with them	do.
Was of great use to the Rebels in passing the Forth at Alloa, was overseer to the workmen who built them a Boat & assisted in providing victualls &c. for them	absconded.

A LIST OF PERSONS ENGAGED IN THE
BY MR. ARCHD. STUART, EXAMINER,

Names.	Designations.	Abode.	Parish.
A. More	of this Letter in folio	74th ommitted here.	
William Archer	Taylor	Arbroath	Arbroath
James Abbot	Dyster	do.	do.
James Anderson	Fisher	Ferryden	Craig.
John Anderson	Servant	Bonneton	do.
William Anderson		Johnshaven	Benholm
Alexr Anderson		do.	do.
James Andrew	son to Davd Andrew	Drumellie	Fordon
James Aiton	Mason	Nether Tenements of Caldhame	Brechin
John Adam, Junr	Shoemaker	Brechin	do.
John Aiton		at Kincraig	do.
John Aikenhead	merchant	Brechin	do.

REBELLION, TRANSMITTED TO THE BOARD OFFICIATING AT MONTROSE.

County.	Acts of Rebellion and Circumstances.	Where at present.
Forfar	Kept Guard for the Rebels has submitted to His Majesty's mercy	at home.
do.	Carried Arms for do. was hired by a Tenent	not known.
do.	Carried Arms as a Volunteer in the Rebel Army	Lurking.
do.	Carried Arms in said Army, was at Falkirk Battle & Inverury Skirmish, now in his mother's	wounded.
Mearns	Carried Arms in do. & was at the Engagements of Inverury & Culloden	not known.
do.	This man was forced out, returned before the Battle of ―― & presented himself to the Min^r	at home.
	Carried Arms with the Rebells, but deserted & has submitted himself	at home.
	Was Serjeant in Ld Ogilvie's Regim^t. Assisted in Guarding the Hazard sloop Prisoners. Levied men & accompanied the Rebels to Stirling. Left them about the Time of His Royal Highnesses Proclama^n dated at Montrose & delivered up his Arms to Mr Scot of Rossie	at home.
	Was Serj^t in Ogilvie's Regim^t & at the Battles of Inverury, Falkirk & Culloden	Lurking.
	Was also Serj^t in said Regim^t & att said three Battles	do.
	Was Lieu^t or Ensign in said Regim^t. Levied men & money & collected the Cess of Brechin for the Rebels, was also at the Battles of Inverury, Falkirk & Culloden	Lurking.

LIST OF REBELS FROM

Names.	Designations.	Abode.	Parish.
Charles Anderson	Shoemaker	Brechin	Brechin
David Anderson	Workman	do.	do.
Robert Allan	Son to Thos Allan	Keithock	do.
John Adamson	Shoemaker	Brechin	do.
James Allardice	Tenent	Drums	do.
David Arsil		at Kincraig	do.
B.			
George Bruce	Butcher	Brechin	Brechin
James Bruce	Son to the sd George	do.	do.
James Bowman	Residenter	do.	do.
David Bruce	Butcher	do.	do.
John Bruce	do.	do.	do.
George Brechin	Son to Jas Brechin, Taylor	Muir of Achenblae	Fordon
Alexr Brechin	Son to Alexr Brechin in	do.	do.
James Brechin	do.	do.	do.
Robert Betty	Son to John Bettie in	Drumellie	do.
William Brand	Merchant	Auchenblae	do.

MONTROSE DISTRICT—Continued.   153

County.	Acts of Rebellion and Circumstances.	Where they now are.
	Carried Arms & delivered them up about the Time of his R.H.'s proclama^{tn} at Montrose	at home.
	Do. & delivered them up as above	at home.
	Do. & delivered them up as above	at home.
	Carried Arms in Rebels Service	Prisoner.
	Made Prisoner on Information & sent North	Prisoners.
	Do.	
	Acted as Serj^t Major in Ld Ogilvie's Regim^t Assisted in taking Horses, Arms &c. & the Hazard Sloop. Levied men & money, helped to land & Escorte the French ammunition & Arms, was Deputy Governor of the Town of Brechin when the Rebels lay at Stirling, went North some way with them, then returned to Brechin & laid down his Arms, has given seal^d Informations & on that acco^t only is permitted to stay	at his own house.
	Carried Arms in the Rebellion has not delivered them up	not known.
	Do. but delivered them up on his Royal Highness Proclamation at Montrose	at home.
	Made prisoners on Information & sent North	Prisoners.
	Carried Arms in the Rebel Army	not known.
	Do. but has presented himself to the Min^r of the Parish & submitted at mercy	at home.
	Carried Arms in said Army but deserted	not known.
	Do. & submitted to His Majesty's mercy	at home.
	Contributed all in his power to the Ringing the Kirkbell & publishing the Pretender's Manifesto at Fordon Cross. Offer^d money to any body that would read it & when one was found was a formal witness thereto himself.	at home.

LIST OF REBELS FROM

Names.	Designations.	Abode.	Parish.
Francis Bell	at Denmiln of	Fordon	Fordon
David Bumoss		Johnshaven	Benholm
Peter Barclay	of Johnstone	Johnstone	Laurence Kirk
Robert Barclay	Gentleman	Balmyheuen	Mary Kirk
David Buchan	Servant	Milton of Glenask	Lochlee
David Bennet	do.	Hatton Miln	Kinnel
John Brown	Farmer	Boysham	do.
Sir Alex^r Bannerman	of Elsick	Elsick	Feteresso
James Barclay	a Farmer's Son	Finlastown	do.
David Barclay	Brewer	Arbroath	Arbroath
John Brown	Tenent	Bolsham	Kinnell

MONTROSE DISTRICT—*Continued.* 155

County.	Acts of Rebellion and Circumstances.	Where at present.
	Went to Drumlithie & in the night time forced one Jame Edie out of his house & compell'd him to drink the Pretender's Son's health as Prince of Wales	at home.
Mearns	Served a Volunteer in the Rebel Army	not known.
Kincardin	Went to Edin^r to wait on the Young Pretender, & on his return assumed the character of one of his Justices of the Peace, used violent means to enlist men & oblidged the Brewers in Laurance Kirk to pay him their Excise, which he carried to Stonehive to the Rebels Collector. Lifted arms himself & assisted in Guarding the Arms & Ammunition of the Rebels	at home.
do.	Carried Arms at the Battle of Culloden & said to be	kill'd.
do.	Was at the taking of the Hazard Sloop & came in Arms & made prisoners of severall affected Persons about Fettercairn for not paying Levy money to the Rebels	at home.
Forfar	Carried Arms at Inverury & Falkirk & went to the north with the Rebels	not known.
do.	Carried Arms as Lieu^t was active in decoying others into the Rebellion, compelling some & oppressing others that would not join them, was at Culloden Battle & there said to be	kill'd.
Mearns	Acted as Lord Lieu^t of the County of Merns under the Rebels, was active in serving their Interest & yet moderate to the Country	Lurking.
do.	Carried Arms as a volunteer in the Pretender's Son's Life Guards, was moderate	Lurking.
Forfar	Hoised a white fflag on the Shore at Arbroath & apprehended one of the Hazard Sloop's crew making his escape & causd him be severely whiped	Stirling, Prisoner.
do.	Carried Arms as a Lieu^t in Provost Patrick Wallace's Company & Levied money for the Rebels	not known.

Names.	Designations.	Abode.	Parish.
William Baird	Gardner	Montrose	Montrose
Andrew Beattie	Rope Maker	do.	do.
Peter Beattie	Ship Master	do.	do.
John Bryan	Residenter	do.	do.
George Bisset	Mariner	Stonhaven	Dunnoter or Fetresso
John Buchan	do.	do.	do.
Andrew Bremner	Cowper	do.	do.
Robert Bremner	Mariner	do.	do.
William Bremner	Square Wright	do.	do.
William Buock	Servant	Lawriston	Mariton
C.			
George Carnegy	Merchant Apprentice	Montrose	Montrose
Charles Carnegy	Sailor	do.	do.
David Campbell		in Mains of Glenfarquhar	Forden Div[n]
Thomas Clark	Servant	Morphie	Logie
David Crole	Weaver	Bonykettle	Fettercairn
Alex[r] Catenoch	Servant	Landends	do.

MONTROSE DISTRICT—Continued. 157

County.	Acts of Rebellion and Circumstances.	Where at present.
Forfar	At Montrose beheaved most Insolently gave abusive & threatening Language to the late Magistrates & the Excise Off[rs]. Carried Arms in England, at Falkirk & went North with the Rebels	Lurking.
do.	Carried Arms at Inverury & Falkirk & went North with the Rebels	Lurk[g].
do.	Assisted as Pilot in bringing into Montrose the French Ship on of Oct[r] 1745 and attended the Rebels at the Cross of Montrose on the Young Pretender's Birth Day	Lurking.
do.	Went North Servant to John Scott Governour of Montrose for the Rebels	do.
Kincardin	Was singularly active in piloting in the French Ship to Stonhaven and was Gunner at Deforcing His Majesty's Ships	Prisoner.
do.	Stood with a match & called to one of His Majesty's Ships in Stonhaven Bay that if she came near he would give her a warm Reception	at home.
do.	Was on Guard at Stonhaven for the Rebels & forced Arms from the Country People which he carried to them	at home.
do.	Carried Arms & went North with the Rebels	Lurking.
do.	Carried Arms & forced horses &c. from the Country to carry arms to the Rebels	at home.
Forfar	was hired by his Master & carried Arms at Inverury & Falkirk & went North	Lurking.
Forfar do.	Carried Arms in the Pretender's Son's Life Guards were in Eng[d] & at ffalkirk & went North	Lurking.
	Compelled one Ja[s] Eddie to drink the Pretender son as P[r] of Wales holding a drawn Cutlace over his head	at home.
Kincardin	Carried Arms at Culloden Battle, returned to	his Fay[rs] house.
do.	Do. during the whole Rebellion	at home.
do.	Carried Arms during the whole Rebellion	do.

LIST OF REBELS FROM

Names.	Designations.	Abode.	Parish.
Robt Crookshanks		Johnshaven	Benholm
James Carnegy	of Findaury	Findaury	Brechin
James Carnegy	Surgeon	Brechin	Brechin
James Carnegy	Mason	do.	do.
Robert Carnegy	Weaver	Tenements of Caldhame	do.
John Chalmers	Servant	Kinnels Miln	Kinnel
David Cowie	do.	Rossie	Craig
John Cosky	young man	Binaves	Kinnel
Thomas Crighton	Mason	Arbroath	Arbroath
Alexr Crighton, Senr	Shoemaker	do.	do.
James Crighton		do.	do.
James Coupar		do.	do.
John Chalmers		Drunkendiel	St. Vigeans
James Caird	Servant to Geo. Miln	Balcathie	Arbirlot
Willm Chalmers	Subtenent's son	Mains of Uris	Dunnotter
Willm Cruickshank	Sub Tenent	Nether Crigie	do.

MONTROSE DISTRICT—Continued.

County.	Acts of Rebellion and Circumstances.	Where at present.
Mearns	Do. as a volunteer in the s^d Rebell Army	not known.
	Acted as Ld Lieutenant Deput of the County of Angus, appointed Governours of Towns & Factors on the forfieted Estates of South Esque & Panmuir. Raised himself men & money out of those Estates as well as the rest of the Country by all the methodes of violence & oppression: assisted in guarding the Hazard Sloop; forced people to take Arms & guard the Prisoners of the said Sloop. Joined the Rebels at Stirling & went with them to Inverness	Lurking.
	Acted as Surgeon to Ld Ogilvie's Regim^t bore Arms assisted in guarding the Hazard Sloop prisoners in Brechin & was with the Rebels at Stirling & Inverness	not known.
	Carried Arms in the Rebellion, has not as yet delivered them up	Lurking.
	Do. do.	do.
Forfar	Carried Arms with the Rebels & was with them in the North, now serving the	Laird of Brunton
do.	Listed with the Rebels but deserted & never was in any Battle	not known.
do.	was hired out & carried Arms at Inverury & Falkirk and went north with the Rebels	Lurking.
do.	Joined the Rebels, went with them to England & was very active in raising men	Lurking.
do.	Kept Guard in Arbroath for the Rebels	
do.	Carried Arms with the Rebels into England	
do.	Kept Guard for the Rebels & collected the Cess by their order	
do.	Carried Arms into England with the Rebels	Lurking.
do.	Went to Dundee in arms with his master	Balcathie, Lurking.
Merns	Voluntary, carried Arms with the Rebels but was moderate	Lurking.
do.	Do. & was most outrageous	

LIST OF REBELS FROM

Names.	Designations.	Abode.	Parish.
John Cargil	Tobacconist	Stonhaven	Dunotter or Fetteresso
James Collison	Bellman	do.	do.
Alex^r Cashie	Merchant	do.	do.
Peter Cashnie	do.	do.	do.
Robt Cooper, Senr	Shirrif Officer	do.	do.
Robt Cooper, Junr	Sailor	do.	do.
Willm Collie	Carrier	do.	do.
D.			
John Durie	Merchant	Stonehaven	
Alex^r Duncan	do.	do.	
James Duncan	Shoemaker	do.	
John Duncan	do.	do.	
David Dury	Fewer	do.	
Andrew Deary	Subtenent	Glesla	Dunotter
James Deary	Servant	Dunnottre	do.
James Duncan	Subtenent	Henwells	Fetteresso
James Duncan	do.	Shetrawhead	do.
James Deans	a Smith's son	Cowie	do.
David Dennies	Young man	Binaves	Kinnel
John Duncan	Brewer	Arbroath	Arbroath
Alex^r Duncan	Taxman of the Customs	do.	do.
John Dorwood	Weaver	do.	do.
David Dorwood	Land labourer	do.	do.
George Deakers	Residenter	Montrose	Montrose

MONTROSE DISTRICT—Continued.

County.	Acts of Rebellion and Circumstances.	Where at present.
Kincardin	Carried Arms, Mounted Guard & pressed horses to carry arms to the Rebel Army	at home.
do.	Carried Arms & mounted Guard for the Rebels	do.
do. do.	Carried Arms in the Rebel Service & was active in pressing horses to carry arms to them	do.
do.	Carried arms and was active in pressing horses for behoof of the Rebels	Prisoner.
do.	Carried Arms & went to the North with the Rebels	at home.
do.	Do. & was active in stoping well affected People & Intercepting Letters, &c.	do.
Kincardin	Carried Arms, bought up Tartans & Shoes & pressed Horses for the Service of the Rebels. Read the Pretender's manifesto publickly upon a Sabbath day, frequently mounted Guard & threatened to force others to follow his example	Lurking.
do. do. do. do.	All carried Arms in the Rebel Army & were active in pressing horses for its Service	at home.
Mearns do. do. do. do.	Were all very oppressive & carried Arms in the Rebel Army, Jas Duncan Henswells said to be forc'd out	Lurking.
Forfar	Was hired to the Rebel Service & Carried Arms at Culloden &c.	Lurking.
do.	Carried Arms for the Rebels & assisted in Collecting the Excise at Dundee	not known.
do.	Spoke Treasonably, calling his Majesty an Usurper	in Prison.
do.	Carried Arms with the Rebels	at home.
do.	Assisted the Rebels in keeping the King Tender from unrigging some Ships	not known.
do.	Was Drumer at Inverury Skirmish & Falkirk Battle & went North with the Rebels	Lurking.

L

LIST OF REBELS FROM

Names.	Designations.	Abode.	Parish.
William Douglas	Piper	Drumlithie	Fordon Division
Alex^r Duthie	Smith	Brechin	Brechin
Willm Dear	Meal Monger	do.	do.
John Davidson	Servant	do.	do.
John Duncan	Merch^t & Stamp master	do.	do.
James Dease	Merchant	do.	do.
Willm Duncan	Farmer	Bent of Balbegnie	Fettercairn
Robt Duncan	Servant	Bonykettle	do.
Robt Duncan	Farmer	Milton of Glenask	Lochlee
E.			
James Edward	Residenter	Ferryden	Craig
James Essie, Senr	Weaver	Arbroath	Arbroath
John Edgar, you^r	of Keithlock	Keithlock	Brechin
John Erskine	Merch^t Apprentice	Montrose	Montrose
F.			
John Fettes	Maltman	Montrose	Montrose

MONTROSE DISTRICT—Continued. 163

County.	Acts of Rebellion and Circumstances.	Where at present.
Kincardin do. do.	Went to Stonehaven to assist a French against a British Warrship that had chas'd her in there	at home.
	Assisted the Rebels in taking the Hazard Sloop but left them immediately thereafter	at home.
	Was engaged in the Rebellion & has not delivered up his arms	Lurking.
	Was with the Rebels, but delivered up his Arms on his R^l H's proclam^n at Montrose	at home.
	Apprehended upon Information & sent North with a Guard	Prisoners.
	Carried Arms for the Rebels during the Rebellion	at home.
	Assisted in taking the Hazard Sloop & came in Arms & made prisoners of several well affected persons about Fettercairn for not paying their assessments to the Rebels	at home.
Forfar	Listed voluntarly with the Rebels & carried Arms at the Battle of Culloden	Lurking.
do.	Carried Arms at Falkirk, has submitted himself at mercy	at home.
	Entered into the Pretender's Son's Life Guards at Edin^r & contin^d with them till dispers'd	Lurking.
Forfar	Commanded a Company in the Rebel Army. Received & conveyed the French Arms to the Rebel Army, for which purpose harrassed the Country for Horses & Carts, he was at the Skirmish of Inverury & affair of Falkirk & went North with the Rebels	Lurking.
Forfar	Was at Inverury & Falkirk & went North with the Rebels, while at Montrose he behaved most rudely harassing on all occasions such as he look't on to be friends to the Government	Lurking.

LIST OF REBELS FROM

Names.	Designations.	Abode.	Parish.
John Framan		Miltown	St. Cyrus
John Forbes		Bervie	Bervie
James Forret	Smith	Stonehaven	
James Fordue	Wright	Arbroath	Arbroath
Willm Ferguson	disch^d Excise Officer	do.	do.
Robert Ferrier	ffarmer	do.	do.
John Ferrier	Cottar	Cotton of Little Curcary	Farnel
David Fethes	Servant	West Fithie	do.
John Fraser	do.	Rossie	Craig
John Fraser	a Stranger, lodged w^t	Wm Crighton Paddocks Mire	Kinnel
James Finlay	Son to Dav^d ffinlay, Workman	Cairntoun	Fordon Divⁿ
David Fraser	Son to Alex. Fraser, Tenent	West Cowlie	do.
Alex^r Falconer	Farmer	Birnie	Forden
David fferrier	Merchant	Brechin	Brechin

MONTROSE DISTRICT—*Continued.* 165

County.	Acts of Rebellion and Circumstances.	Where at present.
Kincardin do.	Carried Arms in the Rebel Army as Volunteers, returned &	Lurking.
	Carried Arms mounted Guard and pressed Horses for the Rebel Service	at home.
Forfar	Keeped Guard for the Rebels	} at home.
do.	Acted as Officer of Excise for the Rebels	
do.	Carried Arms as an Ensign of the Rebels & was at the Battle of Falkirk	not known.
do.	being hired carried arms for the Rebels, & was at the Battle of Culloden &c.	Prisoner.
do.	do. do.	Lurking.
do.	Enlisted voluntarly with the Rebels & went with them to the North	do.
do.	Was advised or rather forced by his said Landlord to Enlist with the said Rebels which accordingly he did & went North with them	not known.
Kincardin	Carried Arms in Rebellion but has submitted to his Majesty's mercy	} at home.
do.	do. do.	
do.	Carried arms in Rebellion, was head of a Gang who violently carried off some Leather that had been seized by an Excise Officer & delivered to be Tann'd for his Majesty's use, & since the Battle of Culloden harboured Rebels two of which were found in his houses, for which he was apprehended & carried to Brechin	Prisoner.
	Acted as Deput Governour of the Town of Brechin, practised the highest Tyrrany over the loyal Subjects of the Government in every shape; and particularly extorted men, money, Horses & Arms throughout the whole Country; levyed His Majesty's Excise & gave his own Receipts for the same: was the principal Person who promoted & carried on the affair of taking the Hazard Sloop in which some of the Crew were killed & wounded & the rest made Prisoners and	Supposed to be Lurking amongst the neighbouring Hills.

Names.	Designations.	Abode.	Parish.
James Fotheringham	Fishmonger	Upper Tene-m^{ts} of Caldhame	Brechin
John Firzel	Mason	Nether Tene-m^{ts} of do.	do.
Peter Fairweather	Baker's Servant	Brechin	do.
Hugh Fraser	Smith	Montrose	Montrose
G.			
John Gibson	Chapman in Nether Tenements of	Caldhame	Montrose
David Gouck	Servant	Egypt	Furnel

County.	Acts of Rebellion and Circumstances.	Where at present.
	treated by him in so barbarous a manner as that they must in all probability have perished had it not been for the assistance they received from the Friends of the Government in Montrose, Brechin & elsewhere. He also bore arms in Ld Ogilvie's Regiment, recruited and forced out no less than two Companys of Rebel Militia; was present at the skirmish of Inverury as Captain of one of the said Companys: Burned the Customhouse Boat at Aberdeen: received & conveyed the French Arms and Ammunition to the Rebel Army, for which purpose he harrassed & oppressed the whole country in pressing their Horses & Carts. He joined the main body of the Rebels with his Company at Stirling, accompanyed them to Inverness from whence he returned to Glenesk, raised a great many of the Inhabitants there with a Design to force back Rebel Runnaways & make well affected people prisoners & marched with the said Gleneske to Cortachie in order to force a Garrison of the King's Troops lying there. These facts are well known to every Body in these places of the Country	
-	All Carried Arms in Rebellion, have not delivered them up	Lurking.
Forfar	Carried Arms at Inverury & Falkirk & went North with the Rebels	Prisoner.
	Carried Arms in Rebellion & has not surrendered them	Lurking.
Forfar	Was hired out & Carried Arms at Culloden	Lurking.

LIST OF REBELS FROM

Names.	Designations.	Abode.	Parish.
Alex^r Greig	Merchant	Dysart	Mariton
James Gray	Cottar	Cotton of Gowenhead	Farnel
Willm Gowans	Servant	Kinnels Miln	Kinnel
David Garden, Junr		Lawtoun	Kirkdon
David Gray	Brewer	Arbroath	Arbroath
William Gillespie	Sailor	do.	do.
James Grant	Brewer	do.	do.
James Gray		Temple	Benholm
John Gordon	Surgeon Apprentice	Montrose	Montrose
William Gordon	Writer do.	do.	do.
George Guthrie	Residenter	do.	do.
Willm Gray	Painter	do.	do.
Alex^r Greig	Merch^t Apprentice	do.	do.
Alex^r Garrioch	of Mergie	Mergie	Fetteresso
Willm Gibbon	Merchant	Stonhaven	Stonhaven
Willm Gilmer	Shoemaker	do.	do.
Alex^r Gibbon	Ship Carpenter	do.	do.
Willm Gardner	Servant	Brae of Balfour	Fettercairn

MONTROSE DISTRICT—*Continued.* 169

County.	Acts of Rebellion and Circumstances.	Where at present.
Forfar	Went along as Secretary to Mr Carnegy Junr of Bonny Moon, Dep^t Lieu^t of Angus	not known.
do.	Carried Arms Voluntarly & was at Culloden Battle with the Rebells in the North	Lurking.
do.	Carried Arms being hired & was at Culloden Battle with the Rebels	at home.
do.	Carried Arms as Captain in Ld Ogilvie's Rebel Regiment	not known.
do.	Do. as a private man, kept Guard & assisted in levying money for the Rebels, submitted	at home.
do.	Assisted as Pilot in Sailing a French Ship from Arbroath to Montrose	do.
do.	Carried Arms & was at the Battle of Falkirk	Lurking.
Kincardin	Carried Arms as a Volunteer in the Rebel Army	do.
Forfar } do. }	Carried Arms with the Rebels in England & at Falkirk & went North	do.
do.	Do. being hired & went North	do.
do.	Do. & was at Falkirk Battle	do.
do.	Was Clark to Findaury Dep^t Ld Lieu^t of Forfar County went first to Stirling & then North	do.
Mearns	Practised the highest Tyrrany over the whole Country in General but the Freinds of the Governm^t in particular. Acted as Governour of Stonhaven & press'd out Men & Horses & Extorted money & Arms from the Inhabitants, Collected the Cess, Excise & other Contributions imposed by him upon the Country and at last took up Arms, joined the Rebel Army & went North with them	Lurking.
Kincardin	Assisted in proclaiming the Pretender at Stonhaven, joined the Rebel Army, went to England, was at Falkirk Battle & went North with them	not known.
do.	Carried Arms & went North with the Rebels	kill'd.
do.	Do. & mounted Guards for the Rebels	at home.
do.	Carried Arms in the Rebellion the whole time	at home.

Names.	Designations.	Abode.	Parish.
James Greig	Son to Adam Greig	Bankhead of Ardice	Fordon Division
Robert Gleig	Smith	Drumlithie	Fordon
Adam Gleig	Son to s^d Robert	do.	do.
H.			
James Hood, Junr	Smith	Brechin	Brechin
Adam Hunter	Excise Expectant	do.	do.
James Hunter		Lethan Caltown	St. Vigeans
John Hunter		Newtown of Arbirlot	Arbirlot
Hary Hunter		do.	do.
Robert Henderson	Cottar	Cotton of Ringblythmount	Kinnel
Robert Hodge	Farmer	Fannuksmire	do.

MONTROSE DISTRICT—*Continued.* 171

County.	Acts of Rebellion and Circumstances.	Where at present.
	Carried Arms in Rebellion, returned & submitted	at home.
	Went in Arms to Stonhaven to assist a French Ship laden with arms &c. against one of His Majesty's Ships of War that had chas'd her in there, & read an Intima^{tn} at the Kirk of Glenbervie ordering the people to pay their Excise to the Rebel's Collector	at home.
	Went along with his Father to assist the said French Ship	do.
	Carried Arms in Rebellion	Lurking.
	Survey'd Brechin Division for the Rebels from the End of Septr 1745 to the middle of February 1746, but upon approach of the King's Army left the place, he was taken Prisoner along with Lewis Murray Excise officer in Brechin & confined in the Prison of Montrose, was at last prevailed upon by the strongest threatenings from David Ferrier before mentioned to serve the Rebels in that capacity. He had two motherless Infants & nothing to support himself or them, which probably had push'd him to so desperate & wicked a project	not known.
Forfar	Carried Arms & was at the Battle of Falkirk with the Rebels	
do.	Do. & went north with the Rebels	Lurking.
do.	Do. do.	
Forfar	Carried Arms, was at Culloden Battle, has Carried off his wife & children &	Begging.
do.	Do. & very much distressed the Ministers & other people in the Countrey by taking their Horses, & plundering their Houses, &c. was at Inverury Skirmish & Falkirk Battle & went North with the Rebels	Lurking.

LIST OF REBELS FROM

Names.	Designations.	Abode.	Parish.
George Hay	Residenter	Montrose	Montrose
James Henderson	Ship Master	do.	do.
James Hunter	son to John Hunter	Newbigging	
I.			
Robert Johnston	Sheriff Officer	Stonhaven	Stonhaven
Will[m] Irvine		Fetteresso	Fetteresso
William Jameson	Reedmaker	Montrose	Montrose
Robert Irons	Residenter	do.	do.
Dav[d] Inverarity	Meal Monger	Tenements of Caldhame	Brechin
David Inverarity	Shoemaker	Brechin	do.
K.			
Thomas Keill	Servant to Ja[s] Ferrier	Kintrockat	Brechin
Thomas Kemlar	Miller	Miln of Mundens	Fordon
Alex[r] Kemlar	his Son		Divis[n]
John Key	Taylor	Arbroath	Arbroath
Alex[r] Kerrie	Sailor	Arbroath	do.
John Kerrie	Merchant	do.	do.
Thomas Kinnier	Farmer	Milton Glenesk	Lochlee
James Kemla		Hyndwells	Fetteresso
Gideon Kemlay	Merchant	Stonhaven	

MONTROSE DISTRICT—*Continued.* 173

County.	Acts of Rebellion and Circumstances.	Where at present.
Forfar	Carried Arms, was at Inverury & Falkirk & went North with the Rebels, wounded & in	Montrose Hospital.
do.	Assisted in piloting the French Ship into Montrose & attended the Rebels at the Cross Solemnizing the Young Pretender's Birth day	Lurking.
	Was in Arms with the Rebels, Returned & submitted himself	at home.
	Carried Arms & went North with the Rebels	at home.
Mearns	Do. has submitted & given up his name etc. to the Minister	do.
Forfar	Was Serjeant in the Rebel Army & active in Enlisting men, he Imprisoned several servants who refused to go into his measures, was at Stirling & went North	Lurking.
do.	Carried Arms, was at Falkirk & went North with the Rebels	Montrose Pris^r
	Carried Arms in the Rebellion	Lurking.
	Do. Surrendered his Arms about the time of his R^l H$^{\prime s}$ proclam^n at Montrose	at home.
	Carried Arms, Surrendered on his Royal Highness proclamation at Montrose	at home.
	Went in Arms to Stonhaven to assist the French Ship against the British Man of Warr	do.
Forfar		at home.
do.	All carried Arms in the Rebel Service	not known.
do.		Ed^r Prisoner.
Kincardin	Was at taking the Hazard Sloop, came in Arms & assisted in making Prisoners several well affected persons about Fettercairn for not paying their asscssm^{ts}	at home.
Mearns	Carried Arms as a Volunteer in the Rebel Army	Lurking.
Kincardin	Took up Arms & mounted Guards for the Rebels	at home.

Names.	Designations.	Abode.	Parish.
James Keith	Wright	Stonhaven	
David Keith	Farmer	Invercreunven	
L.			
Willm Leith	Residenter	Brechin	Brechin
David Littlejohn	Servt to Wm Robb	Burkhill	Brechin
William Low	Chapman	Brechin	do.
Alex^r Low	Merch^t	do.	do.
John Leith	Brother to Wm Leith	do.	do.
Thomas Ley		Drumlethie	Fordon Dⁿ
John Louper	Smith	Arbroath	Arbroath
John Laing	Servant	Old Montrose	Mariton
John Lesslie	Merch^t & Farmer	Miln Morphy	St. Cyrus
Willm Lesslie	Mariner	Montrose	Montrose
Dav^d Lyon	Vintiner	do.	do.

MONTROSE DISTRICT—*Continued.* 175

County.	Acts of Rebellion and Circumstances.	Where at present.
Kincardin	Carried Arms, mounted Guards & acted as Ground Off^r on the Estate of Marischal for the Rebels	Lurking.
	Enlisted men for the Rebels	Prisoner.
	Was Lieu^t or Ensign in Ld Ogilvie's 2^d Battalion, assisted in piloting into Montrose one of the French Ships with Arms &c. & in taking the Hazard Sloop, was at Inverury Skirmish & the Battles of Falkirk & Culloden	Lurking.
	Was Engaged in the Rebellion, has not delivered up his Arms	do.
	Surrendered his Arms on His R^l Highnesses Proclamation at Montrose	at home.
	Made prisoner on Information & sent North	Prisoner.
	do.	do.
	Compelled James Eddie to drink treasonable healths & publickly curs'd his Majesty	at home.
Forfar	Kept Guard for the Rebels & carried Arms	not known.
do.	Enlisted with the Rebels & was at Inverury & ffalkirk Battles	Kill'd.
Mearns	Was aiding & assisting in Livering the French Ships at Montrose and Stonhaven, was at Spulzying the Hazard Sloop & carried off some things of value from thence, he broke Mr Freebairn Schoolmaster at St. Cyrus his Doors & assisted the Rebel M'Grigors in plundering his house, he has a house, Horses, Cows & Effects & none of them are yet touched	Lurking.
Forfar	Assisted in piloting into Montrose the French Ships & sailed out Master of the Hazard Sloop after she was taken by the Rebels	Prisoner.
do.	Invited several Gentlemen in Montrose to witness the Rebels solemnizing the Young Pretender's Birth day, gave attendance himself & drank healths along with the Rebels	do.

LIST OF REBELS FROM

Names.	Designations.	Abode.	Parish.
Alex[r] Littlejohn	Physician	Montrose	Montrose
Will[m] Low, Jun[r]	Smith	do.	do.
John Low	Wig Maker	do.	do.
Will[m] Lindsay	Shoemaker	do.	do.
John Lindsay	Surgeon Apprentice	do.	do.
John Lawson, Jun[r]	no designation	Stonhaven	
William Lamb	Stocking Weaver	do.	
James Laurance	Piper	Clochnahill	Dunottre
Thomas Lindsay	Subtenent	Pennywell's	Fetteresso
M.			
Alex[r] Main	Servant	Barn Yards of Dunotter	Dunottre
George Main	do.	Fetteresso	Fetteresso
John Moncur	do.	Feathers	do.
John Mason	Subtenent	Powbare	Fetteresso
John Miln	do.	Skihowhead	do.
Will[m] Mair	Factor to Elsick	Elsick	
John Maul	Writer	Stonehaven	
Peter Maul	Workman	do.	
John Martin	Stocking Weaver	do.	
Bob[t] Mollison	Barber	do.	
James Murray	Cooper	do.	
John Miln	Miln Wright	do.	
Will[m] Morgan	Glover	do.	
John Morgan	Taylor	do.	
Will[m] Middleton	Baxter	do.	
Will[m] Murray	Weaver	do.	

MONTROSE DISTRICT—*Continued.* 177

County.	Acts of Rebellion and Circumstances.	Where at present.
Forfar	Witnessed the above Solemnization & drank healths with the Rebels	Prisoner.
do.	Carried Arms at Falkirk & went North	Lurking.
do.	Was at Stirling & went North as Servant to a French Officer	do.
do.	Carried Arms at Falkirk & went North with the Rebels	do.
do.	Was Lieut in Ld Ogilvie's Regimt, was active in searching for arms, was in England at the Battle of Falkirk & went North with the Rebels	Lurking.
Kincardin do.	Took up Arms & mounted Guards for the Rebels	at home.
do.	Voluntarly served the Rebells with his Musick & went with them	Lurking.
do.	Deserted from the Dutch, carried Arms in the Rebel Army & was very Rigid	do.
Kincardin	Served as a Volunteer in the Rebel Army	Lurking.
do.	Do.	Achortes.
do.	Do. & much oppress'd the Country	Lurking.
do.	Carried Arms as a Volunteer in the Rebel Army & was very Rigid	do.
do.	Do. was tolerably moderate	do.
do.	Was Ensign in the Rebel Army & went to the North with them	Kill'd.
do.	Ensign in Do. Enlisted men, proclaimed the Pretender & went North	Dead.
do.	Carried Arms & went North with the Rebels	Lurking.
do.	Carried Arms, was at Stirling & went North with Do.	Prisoner.
do.	Took up Arms & mounted Guards for the Rebels	at home.
do.	Do. do.	
do. do. do. do.	All took up Arms & Mounted Guards for the Rebels	at home.

M

LIST OF REBELS FROM

Names.	Designations.	Abode.	Parish.
Willm Mackie	Residenter	Montrose	Montrose
Willm Mouat	do.	do.	do.
David Martin	Weaver	Montrose Links	do.
Willm Miln	of Bonnytoun	Montrose	do.
James Mathie	Servant	Old Montrose	Mariton
Alex^r Mill	Shepherd	Bonytoun	do.
John Mill	Vagabound		
Geo: Mill	Tenent	Balcathie	Arbroath
Alex^r Mackie		Arbroath	do.
Duncan Miller	Weaver	Auchmithie	St. Vigeans
James Moodie		do.	do.
James Mason	In	Drumlethie	Fordon Divisⁿ
John Milne	Son to Dav^d Milne	Cotbank	do.
James Mansie	Younger in Ballfield	of Drumlethie	do.
Alex^r Mather	Brewer	Brechin	Brechin

MONTROSE DISTRICT—*Continued.* 179

County.	Acts of Rebellion and Circumstances.	Where they are at present.
Forfar	Carried Arms at Inverury & Falkirk & went North with the Rebels	Lurking.
do.	do. do. do.	Prisoner.
do.	Carried Arms being hired out by a Tenent & went North with the Rebels	do.
do.	Solemnized the young Pretender's Birth day along with the Rebels at the Cross of Montrose	said to be gone to London.
do.	Enlisted voluntarly & carried Arms at Culloden &c. with the Rebels	Lurking.
do.	Carried Arms, was at Culloden &c. said to be hired, now about his own house	Lurking.
	Voluntarly enlisted & went to the Battle of Culloden with the Rebels	Prisoner.
Forfar	Was a Lieut in the Rebel Army & very active in Levying men & money	Lurking.
do.	Carried Arms at Falkirk, has now submitted	at home.
do.	Carried Arms in Rebellion being hired by Tenent to save his Levy money	not known.
do.	Voluntarly Enlisted himself into the Rebel Army, accompanyed them into England, was at Falkirk & went North	Prisoner.
	Was Quarter Master for the Rebels at Drumlethie & bought of His Majesty's Arms from a Deserter. Was concerned in publishing the Pretender's Manifesto at Fordon Cross & in a Mob at Drumlethie where Treasonable Healths were imposed upon the well-affected & enforced by naked Arms & Threatenings	at home.
	Carried Arms in Rebellion, has now submitted himself	at home.
	Went in Arms to Stonhaven to assist the sd ffrench against a British that pursued her	do.
	Carried Arms in Ld Ogilvie's first Battallion, went with it into England, returned to Brechin & Recruited men & violently imprisoned the Excise Officer there: went with the Rebel Army to Inverness where he was advanced to an Ensign	Lurking in the Country.

LIST OF REBELS FROM

Names.	Designations.	Abode.	Parish.
Robert Mackie	Servt to Alex^r Low	Brechin	Brechin
James Mather	Merchant	do.	do.
Mr John Maitland	non Jurant Minister	Carraldston	
David Mathers	Son to Dav^d Mathers	Baker, Brechin	Brechin
George Mathers	do.	do.	do.
David Miller, Junr	Shoemaker	Brechin	Brechin
Robert Mitchell	Brewer & Malster	Johnshaven	Benholme

MONTROSE DISTRICT—*Continued.* 181

County.	Acts of Rebellion and Circumstances.	Where at present.
	was apprehended upon an Information & carried North.	
	Was Ensign in Ld Oglivie's Regim^t, Extorted money, Levyed men and mentained them on his own charges, was at Inverury, Stirling and Inverness, & after the Defeat at Culloden, returned to Brechin & is taken	Prisoner.
	Acted as Factor for the Rebels upon the forfeited Estates of South Esk and Panmuir, squeezed the Tenents in the cruelest manner for money; carried his Insolence and oppression to that hight as to cause put into the Stocks & in Irons several persons well affected to his Majesty upon their refusing to pay him their Rents & afterwards went with the Rebel Army to Stirling. He came originally from the Parish of Fourage in Aberdeenshire.	
	Carried Arms in the Rebellion & have not surrendered them	Lurking.
	do. do.	do.
	Having been forced out deserted from the Rebels without ever acting in the Field and has since been very ready to serve the Government	at home.
Kincardin	Was assisting in livering the French Ships of Arms &c. at Stonhaven & active in serving the French Officers with Express Horses of his own & others, he caused press for that purpose & in searching all passengers for Letters &c., was at Montrose assisting to Spulzie the Hazard Sloop of Warr & carried home some things of Consequence. He was the man who had command of the Party of Rebels that took Mr Thomas Tulloch of Brigton Collector of the Cess in the Mearns & carried him with his Books &c. to the Rebells Ld Lieutenant then Governour of Stonhaven. 'Twas he who forced out and headed a Body of Fishermen with	Prisoner.

Names.	Designations.	Abode.	Parish.
John Mitchell	came from Fetterneer in Aberdeenshire	Johnshaven	Benholme
N.			
James Niccol	Taylor	Arbroath	Arbroath

County.	Acts of Rebellion and Circumstances.	Where they now are.
	whom he apprehended Messrs Gray & Bisset Merchants in Montrose & Perth as they landed from a Warr ship in order to get Intelligence of the Rebells situation in Montrose, & put them into the hands of the Clan M'Grigor which had the Government of that Town. He was principal Director at landing 14 Boats full of Arms & Ammunition at Johnshaven in the night Time & caused a great Fire to be made upon the shore for their direction, he also commanded a party which took two officers of the Excise & delivered them into the hands of the Rebel Hussars: Being asked by some of the Neighbourhood as he went off from Johnshaven in Arms (in which he always was) what his Design was, he answered he was going to shoot the D. of Cumberland with the gun he then had in his hand. Since the 20th of February 1745-6 he has been in Sir Alex^r Bannerman's Company, lay with them some time at Findorn & carried Arms at the Battle of Culloden. The Excise officer with a party took him from behind a Bed and carried him prisoner to Montrose	
Kincardin	This Ruffian is Brother to the above John. Engaged with the first rise of Rebels in this Country & was one of their Lieutenants. He Spulzied the whole country of Arms & took several ministers & country gentlemen's horses which he rode to Death. The most of his Command was forced by himself & he carried Arms at Inverury Skirmish & the Battles of Falkirk and Culloden, is now supposed to be about Fetterneer	Lurking.
Forfar	Carried Arms & mounted Guards for the Rebels	at home.

LIST OF REBELS FROM

Names.	Designations.	Abode.	Parish.
O.			
John Ouchterlony	Writer Apprentice	Montrose	Montrose
John Orkney	Merchant	do.	do.
P.			
Alex. Pyot	Wright	do.	do.
Alex^r Pierson	Ship Master	Arbroath	Arbroath
John Peddie	Merchant	do.	do.
James Peterson	Shirriff Officer	Stonhaven	
R.			
John Ritchie	Pilot	do.	
George Reid	Mason	do.	
Willm Rhind	Workman	do.	
Peter Reid	Brewer	do.	
Alex^r Robertson	Merchant	do.	
Wm Ronald	do.	do.	
John Ronald	Fisher	do.	
Alex^r Robertson	Subtenent	Gallowtoun	Dunottre
Peter Rannie	do.	Mains of Dunottre	do.
James Robertson	Servant	Rossie	Craig
James Retty	do.	Farnel	Farnel
Alex^r Ritchie	Thread maker	Arbroath	Arbroath
Alex^r Robertson	Servant	Letham Cottown	St. Vigeans

MONTROSE DISTRICT—*Continued.* 185

County.	Acts of Rebellion and Circumstances.	Where at present.
Forfar	Carried Arms in the Pretender's Son's Life Guards, was at England & Falkirk	Lurking.
do.	Was active in piloting the French Ships into Montrose & attended the Rebels at Solemnizing the Young Pretender's Birth Day	do.
do.	Carried Arms, was at Falkirk & went North with the Rebels	do.
do.	Assisted in piloting a French ship from Arbroath to Montrose	Prisoner.
do.	Went along with the Rebels to Dundee & assisted in collecting the Excise	at home.
Kincardin	Enlisted & took up Arms with the Rebels, but went not along with them	at home.
do.	Piloted in to Stonhaven a French ship with Arms &c. for the use of the Rebels	do.
do. do. do.	Took up Arms & mounted Guards for the Rebels	at home.
do.	Carried Arms & pressed Horses for the Rebels Service	do.
do.	Do. do.	do.
do.	Carried Arms & went North with the Rebels	Lurking.
Mearns	Carried Arms with the Rebels & very oppressive to the Country	do.
do.	Deserted from the Dutch, was Serjeant in the Rebel Army & very outragious	do.
Forfar	Voluntarly Enlisted, Carried Arms & was at the Battle of Culloden with the Rebels	do.
do.	Carried Arms being hired out & was at Culloden Battle	do.
do.	Carried Arms in the Rebel Army & was at the Battle of Falkirk	
do.	Was hired by a Tenent, Carried Arms & went North with the Rebels	Montrose, Pris^r.

LIST OF REBELS FROM

Names.	Designations.	Abode.	Parish.
Alex^r Reid	Servt to Geo^g Smith	Brechin	Brechin
Geo: Reid	Cottarman	Drums	do.
Peter Richie	Servant	Leuchland	do.
Willm Ritchie	Chapman	Burn of Arrot	do.
Alex^r Ramsay	Shoemaker	Brechin	do.
Robert Reid, Junr	do.	do.	do.
Willm Robertson alias Bickers		Johnshaven	Benholm
Alex^r Robert		Bervie	Bervie

S.

Names.	Designations.	Abode.	Parish.
John Stiven	Wright	Montrose	Montrose
Alex^r Sutherland	Shoemaker	do.	do.
David Smith	Sailor	do.	do.
James Stuart	Merchant	do.	do.
Alex^r Shanks		Chapple Garry	Chapple of Garry
George Smith	Wright	Nether Tenem^{ts} of Caldhame	Brechin
John Sheepherd	Merch^t	Brechin	Brechin

MONTROSE DISTRICT—*Continued.* 187

County.	Acts of Rebellion and Circumstances.	Where at present.
Mearns	Carried Arms in the Rebellion & have not as yet delivered them up	Lurking.
	Do. but surrendered on His Royal Highnesses Proclama^{tn} at Montrose	at home.
	This man engaged with John Mitchell before mentioned, was his Serjeant & became a notorious Robber in the Countries through which he went. He was at Inverury Skirmish & the Battle of Culloden	Lurking.
do.	Carried Arms as a Volunteer in the Rebel Army	kill'd.
Forfar	Was active in Raising men for the Rebels & in oppressing the Countrey for Horses & Carts & Transport the French Arms & Ammunition, also in forcibly carrying off or Stealing Horses from the well affected to the Governm^t	Montrose prison
do.	Carried Arms at Inverury, Falkirk & went North with the Rebels	Lurking.
do.	Do. do. do.	do.
do.	Solemz^d the Pretender's Son's Birth day at Montrose Cross with the Rebels	His mother's house.
Aberdeen	Carried Arms as a Volunteer in the Rebel Army	Lurking.
	Was Lieu^t in Ogilvie's Regim^t and Levied Men for the Rebels. He was at Inverury Skirmish & the Battles of Falkirk & Culloden	not known.
	Bore Arms, was frequently Captain of the Guard over the Hazard Sloop Prisoners. Forced others into that Guard, assisted to Escort the French Arms and Ammunition; was active in making prisoners such as had deserted from the Rebel Army whom he delivered into the hands of the Rebel Officers at Montrose, himself joined Ferrier before men^{td} in Glenesk	Lurking.

LIST OF REBELS FROM

Names.	Designations.	Abode.	Parish.
Andrew Sandyman	Workman	Tenem{ts} of Caldhame	Brechin
George Speed	Servant	Kintrochat	do.
John Smith	Smith	Tenem{ts} of Caldhame	do.
John Scott	Cooper	Brechin	do.
John Strachan	Servant	Bridge End of Brechin	do.
Walter Smart	Workman	Keithock	do.
John Strachan	Butcher	Nether Tenements of Caldhame	do.
John Scott	Merchant	Montrose	Montrose
James Stiven	Apprentice to Wm Smith	Achenblae	Fordon
James Stuart	Brother to Redmyre	Redmyre	do.
David Sheepherd	Servant	Ulysseshaven	Craig
John Sheepherd	do.	Ferryden	do.
Alexr Smith	Farmer	Boysuch Miln	Kinnel
Alexr Smith	Servant	Gitchhorn	Invorkeiler
John Strachan	Cottarman	Cottown of Grange	Kinnel
James Stouter	Brewer	Arbroath	Arbroath
Willm Smith	Threed Maker	do.	do.
Alexr Smith	Barber	do.	do.
David Shanks	Weaver	do.	do.
John Shanks	do.	do.	do.
Dav{d} Scott	Taylor	do.	do.
David Scott	Servant	Balcathie	Arbirlot

MONTROSE DISTRICT—*Continued.* 189

County.	Acts of Rebellion and Circumstances.	Where at present.
	All carried Arms in the Rebellion & have not delivered them up	Lurking.
	Delivered up himself on His Royal Highnesses Prom^n at Montrose	at home.
	Apprehended upon Information and carried North	Prisoner.
Forfar	Acted as Governour of Montrose & Coll^r of the Towns Cess. Sent Letters to severals of the Inhabitants & to some Gentlemen in the Country demanding money by way of Loan for the Pretender's Service & Quartered Rebel Soldiers on such as Refused	Lurking.
do.	Carried Arms in the Rebellion & went with the Rebels	} not known.
do.	Do. do.	
do.	Carried Arms being hired out, was at the Battle of Culloden &c. about his Mother's house	Lurking.
do.	Voluntarly Enlisted & carried Arms at the Battle of Falkirk	Prisoner.
do.	Carried Arms at the Battle of Falkirk, was very active in Raising men & pressing horses for the Pretender's Service & in plundering houses, was a Serjeant	Kill'd.
do.	Was hired & Carried Arms at Falkirk & went North with the Rebels	do.
do.	Carried Arms at Culloden Battle being hired	do.
do.	} All carried Arms in the Rebel Service {	at home.
do.		not known.
do.		do.
do.		do.
do.		Stirling pris^r.
do.		do. do.
do.		Lurking.

LIST OF REBELS FROM

Names.	Designations.	Abode.	Parish.
James Soutor	Servant	Arduthie	Fetteresso
William Smith	Pilot	Stonhaven	Stonhaven
Thomas Stead	Maltster	do.	do.
T.			
Robert Thomson	Factor to Ld Arbuthnot & late Shirriff Deput	Parkside	Arbuthnot
Colin Tindal		Nether Pitforthy	Brechin
David Tindal	Tenent	do.	do.
William Taylor	Brewer	Cottown of Garden	Kirkdon
William Taylor	Mariner	Stonhaven	
W.			
John Welsh	Porter	Clochnahill	Dunottre
Willm Welsh	Servant	Tirntule	Fetteresso
William Walker	Barber	Stonhaven	
Alex^r Wyllie	Dyster	do.	
John Welsh	Mason	do.	

MONTROSE DISTRICT—*Continued*. 191

County.	Acts of Rebellion and Circumstances.	Where they now are.
Mearns	Carried Arms in the Rebel Army, forced out, given up himself to the Minister	at home.
Kincardin	Assisted in piloting the French Ships into the Harbour & carried Arms with the Rebels	at home.
do.	Carried Arms & took Horses for the Rebel Service	do.
do.	This Gentlemen is said to have been very active in Engaging Lord Arbuthnot's Tenents to pay up the Levy money to the Rebels. It's said he was Quarter Master for Lord Pitsligo's men on their march to join the Rebel Army at Edinb^r but upon his waiting upon the Young Pretender & not getting a Station from him suitable to his ambition he returned home & has lived quietly ever since	at home.
	Serjeant in Ld Ogilvie's Regim^t. Carried Arms with the Rebels at Inverury & Falkirk, but left them on their Retreat to the North. Returned & gave up his Arms	at home.
	Made Prisoner on Information & carried to the north	Prisoner.
Forfar	Was with the Rebels in England & till the Defeat at Culloden where he is said to be	Kill'd.
Kincardin	Carried Arms & took Horses for the Rebel Service	at home.
do.	Carried Arms with the Rebels, said to be forced	Lurking.
do.	Carried Arms in Said Army as a Volunteer	do.
do.	Carried Arms & was active in pressing horses for the Rebels	at home.
do.	Carried Arms & acted as Deput Collector for the Rebels in the Mearns	Lurking.
do.	Carried Arms & went North with the Rebels	do.

LIST OF REBELS FROM

Names.	Designations.	Abode.	Parish.
Willm Williamson	Shoemaker	Montrose	Montrose
Robert Wright	do.	do.	do.
Robert Walker	Young man	Boysham	Kinnel
James Watson	Cottar	Highome	Craig
Francis Wyllie	Servant	Pumiln	Farnel
Patrick Wallace	Provost	Arbroath	Arbroath
Thos Watson	Merchant	do.	do.
Thos Wilkie		do.	do.
John Watson	Brewer	do.	do.
David Wilson	do.	do.	do.
Wood	of Allardie	Letham	St. Vigeans
John Webster	Chelsea Pensioner	Arbroath	Arbroath
Andrew Webster	Wright	do.	do.
John Wilson	Son to Thos. Wilson	Farrie	St. Vigeans
Robert Wyllie	Brewer & Merchant	Achenblea	Fordon
Wm Walker	Residenter	do.	do.
William Watson	Son to Wm Watson, late Weaver	Westown of Glenbervie	
William Wisehart	Residing in	Johnshaven	Benholm

MONTROSE DISTRICT—Continued. 193

County.	Acts of Rebellion and Circumstances.	Where they now are.
Forfar	Carried Arms, were at Inverury, Falkirk & went North with the Rebels	Montrose prison.
do.		Lurking.
do.	Behaved discreetly in the Country, was Ensign in Rebel Army, at Falkirk & went North with it	do.
do.	Carried Arms voluntarly & was at Falkirk & Culloden Battles with the Rebels	Arbroath Lurking.
do.	Carried Arms & tho' forced out at first might have escaped, but continued and was at Culloden	Lurking.
do.	had a Commisn as Governour of Arbroath for the Rebels, raised & commanded two Companys of men in their Service & was active in Landing the French soldiers	
do.	Carried Arms in England &c. with the Rebels worth 25 Lib. yearly of Land Rent	Prisoner.
do.	Assisted in piloting a French Ship from Arbroath to Montrose	do.
do.	Carried Arms in the Rebel Army & was in England &c. with them	do.
do.	Carried Arms & kept Guard for the Rebels.	
do.	Was along at Edinr & since in the North with the Rebels, has a 100 Libs of Land Rent.	
do.	Taught the Rebels the Exercise of the Firelock & assisted them in Levying money in the Country	Prisoner.
do.	Carried Arms with the Rebels at Falkirk &c.	
Forfar	Was one of the Rebel Hussars, went with them to England & was taken	Prisoner.
	Proclaimed the Pretender & read his Manifesto at Fordon Cross	at home.
	Concerned in proclaimg Do. publishing his Manifesto at Fordon & Ringing the Bell	do.
	Carried Arms with the Rebels, has submitted to His Majesty's mercy	at home.
Kincardin	Enlisted with Robert Mitchell & assisted in apprehending Messrs Gray & Bisset in manner before mentioned, was in Arms assisting to Liver a French Ship at Stonhaven, went as a Spy to Aberdeen & was taken	Prisoner.

Names.	Designations.	Abode.	Parish.
Alex^r Walker	Residing in	Bervie	Bervie
George Wade	Workman	Brechin	Brechin
James Warden	Drummer	do.	do.
William Webster	Chapman	do.	do.
Charles Willox	Mason in Upper	Tenements of Caldhame	do.
John White	Weaver	Dalladies	Fettercairn
Robert Vallantine	Servant	Johnstone	Laurance Kirk
Y.			
Robert Young	Tenent	Leuchland	Brechin
Walter Young	Sailor	Montrose	Montrose
Alex^r Young	do.	do.	do.
A.			
John Allan	Weaver	Kincardin	Fetteresso
Geo. Abernethie	Servt to Ld Halkerton		Marykirk

MONTROSE DISTRICT—Continued.

County.	Acts of Rebellion and Circumstances.	Where they now are.
Kincardin	Carried Arms for the Rebels as a Volunteer	Lurking.
	Surrendered himself with Arms on his Royal Highnesses proclamⁿ at Montrose	at home.
	was forced to serve the Rebels as Drummer, surrendered on s^d proclamation	do.
	Carried Arms with the Rebels, deserted before the Battle of Culloden & surrended himself to Major Lafusille at Brechin.	
	was apprehended upon Information & carried North	Prisoner.
Kincardin	Carried Arms during the whole Rebellion	at home.
do.	do. for said time	do.
	Acted as Captain in Ld Ogilvie's 2^d Battalion, assisted in taking the Hazard Sloop, Levied men & money for the Rebels, was with them at Inverury Skirmish & the Battles of Falkirk & Culloden	not known.
Forfar	Carried Arms as Serjeant in the Rebel Army & was at Inverury Skirmish & Falkirk Battle & went North	Montrose Pris^r.
do.	Carried Arms & was at Inverury, Falkirk & went North with the Rebels	Lurking.
Kincardin	Carried Arms as Serjeant & was active in taking up horses for the Rebel Service	at home.
do.	Carried Arms with the Rebels during the whole Rebellion	Lurking.

A LIST OF PERSONS ENGAGED IN THE
BY MR. GEO. CRUICKSHANK

Names.	Designations.	Abode.	Parish.
A.			
David Anderson	Servant	Forfar	Forfar
David Aldie	Journeyman Weaver	do.	do.
David Adamson	Chapman	Kirrymuir	Kirrymuir
Thos Alexander	Workman	Bonnygarrow	do.
James Adamson	Farmer	Kingoldram	Kingoldrom
James Anderson	Son to Davd Anderson	Bougiehall	Lintrethan
John Allan	Workman	Pitmody	do.
James Alexander	Servt to Davd Alexander	Garlay	do.
John Anderson	Living at	Navoy	Navoy
John Arrat	Gentleman	Faffirty	Glammis
James Anderson	Single man	Linross	Airly
Thomas Anderson	Servant to Mr. Crighton	Ruthven	Ruthven
David Anderson	Living at	Eassie	Eassie
Laurance Anderson	Servant to Lefenday	Pendreech	Lefenday

REBELLION, TRANSMITTED TO THE BOARD EXAMR. OFFICIATING AT DUNDEE.

County.	Acts of Rebellion and Circumstances.	Where they are for the present.
Forfar	Carried Arms in Ld Ogilvie's Rebel Regiment being hired by the Country	Lurking.
do.	do. in said Regim^t being also hired by do.	do.
Angus	Carried Arms, surrendred them to the Baillie before Falkirk Battle & submitted to mercy	at home.
Angus	do. in Ld Ogilvie's Regim^t being pressed out	do.
do.	Was Serj^t in s^d Regim^t & Extorted money from the Country to Raise men for the Rebels	at home.
do.	Carried Arms in s^d Regim^t—since the Battle of Culloden	come home.
do.	do. as Volunteer in Ogilvie's Regim^t surrendered himself with Arms before Falkirk B.	at home.
do.	do. Deserted the Rebels at Stirling & never joined after	at home.
do.	Carried Arms with the Rebels, hired out by Willm White	not known.
do.	Was Lieut^t in the Rebel Army & burnt the Books & papers in the Custom ho. at Montrose	Fled
do.	Carried Arms in the Rebel Army, hired out by Ja^s Crighton who was Compell'd to do it	not known.
do.	Attended his Master along with the Rebels	Lurking.
do.	Carried Arms, was hired by James Hood	not known.
Perth	Join'd the Rebels as a Volunteer some time before the affair of Falkirk & went North	Lurking.

LIST OF REBELS FROM

Names.	Designations.	Abode.	Parish.
Alex^r Anton	Shoemaker	Meggle	Meggle
John Andrew	Cottar	Cottown of Aflect	Monykie
David Archer	Weaver	Seggiewell	do.
David Auchinleck	Vintiner	Dundee	Dundee
B.			
Thomas Blair	of Glassclone	Dundee	Dundee
James Brown	Taylor	do.	do.
John Blyth	Ship Master	do.	do.
John Brown, Junr	Merchant	do.	do.
Thos. Bire	do.	do.	do.
Allan Bovey	Servant	do.	do.
Patrick Biberny	Mason	do.	do.
Dav^d Butcher	Servant	Pitschellie	Barry
David Baxter	Servt to Jas Kinnie	Onthank	Forgan
James Beg	Cooper	Forgan	
Patrick Buckard	Smith	Benvie	Benvie
Andrew Black	Ground Officer	Alyth	Alyth
David Brown	Merchant	Coupar	Coupar

DUNDEE DISTRICT—*Continued.* 199

County.	Acts of Rebellion and Circumstances.	Where they are for the present.
Perth	Carried Arms, assisted Rattray of Dunoon in oppressing the Country & was at the Battle of Culloden	come home.
Forfar	Carried Arms & was at Falkirk & Stirling with the Rebels, of late surrendred himself	at home.
do.	Deserted from the Royal Army, carried Arms with the Rebels at Falkirk & Stirling	Lurking.
do.	Served in the Rebel Life Guards from after Preston Battle & was at Falkirk &c.	not known.
Forfar	Was Lieu^t Coll., very active in raising men & was at the Battles of Falkirk & Culloden	Prisoner in Bergen in Norway.
do.	Drank the Pretender's health & Confusion to his Majesty King George	Prisoner, Dundee.
do.	Opened the packet & read the Le^{rs} went on the head of a party w^t Carpen^{rs} to Refitt a French ship at Montrose & sent off Lady Strathmore & her Factor Forbes a Rebel to France in his own ship	not known.
do.	Assisted in opening the Packet & Reading the Letters, was Imprisoned at Dundee but	Admitted to Baill.
do.	Was Ensign in the Rebel Army, was at the Battle of Falkirk & went North	not known.
do.	Carried Arms as a Volunteer in do. was at Falkirk Battle & went North	Prisoner.
do.	Do. do.	not known.
do.	Carried Arms with the Rebels, was at Falkirk Battle & Stirling Seige	Prisoner.
Perth	Do. in Ld Ogilvie's Regim^t & was at the Battles of Falkirk and Culloden	at home.
	Carried Arms in said Regim^t & went with them to Perth	do.
Forfar	Do. & was at ffalkirk & Culloden Battles	do.
Angus	Uplifted the Cess for the Rebels & was active in forcing out men to the Rebellion	Lurk^g near home.
Perth	Carried Arms, was at Inverury Skirmish & active in raising men for the Rebels	at home.

Names.	Designations.	Abode.	Parish.
Charles Baillie	Town Baillie	Glamis	Glamis
Andrew Bruce	Ploughman	Braidston	do.
James Brown	do.	Wallflat	do.
David Black	do.	Airly	Airly
William Bell	Ploughman	Kinatie	Airly
William Barnet	do.	Baickie	do.
James Brown	Weaver	Easter Kinordy	Kirrymuir
William Bell	Workman	Clockmill	do.
John Barry	Taylor	do.	do.
Geo^g Barclay	Workman	Kirry Muir	do.
Dav^d Brown	Grandchild to Dav^d Brown	do.	do.
James Barry	Workman		Kingoldram
William Blair	do.	Know	do.
Thomas Brounhills	Labouring Servant	Kinnard	Kinnard
Alex^r Bowar	of Meathie	Meathie	Inverarity
Alex^r Binny	Farmer	Newmill	Tanidys
James Ballingal	Merchant	Forfar	Forfar
Willm Bean	Mason	do.	do.
John Boberno		Mill of Loor	do.
C.			
John Cando	Weaver	Kincairnie	Capoth
Wm Cochran, Junr	Wright	Jackstown	Auchtergaven
Wm Cochran, Senr	Late Factor to Ld Nairn	do.	do.
William Cambell	Sailor, son to ye Shirriff dep^t	Carsgowry	Roswby

DUNDEE DISTRICT—*Continued.* 201

County.	Acts of Rebellion and Circumstances.	What is become of them.
Angus	Accepted of a Captain's Commission from the Rebels but Retracted	at home.
do.	Carried Arms in Rebel Army for Thos Wright being compell'd	not known.
do.	Carried Arms in said Army, said to be forced	do.
do.	Do. do.	Fled.
Angus	Carried Arms in the Rebel Army, said to be forced	fled the country.
do.	Do. do.	do.
do.	Carried Arms in the Rebel Army, surrendered himself & Arms since Culloden Be	at home.
do.	Do. do.	do.
do.	Do. do.	do.
do.	Carried Arms as a Volunteer in Ld Ogilvie's Regim^t	do.
do.	Do. Plundered Gentlemen's & Ministers' houses	do.
do.	Do. in Ld Ogilvie's Regim^t returned since Battle of Falkirk	do.
do.	Do. since Cull^d Battle	at home.
Perth	Bore Arms & went into England with the Rebels & there made	Prisoner.
Forfar	Had a Commiss^n in the Rebel Army & forced out his Tenents into Rebellion	Prisoner.
do.	Was Quarter Master in Ld Ogilvie's Regim^t & very active	Lurking.
do.	Was Ensign in Do. Collected the Excise at Forfar & Granted his Receipts yrfor	do.
do.	Was Soldier in Do. hired by the Country	Prisoner.
do.	Do. do.	Lurking.
Perth	Carried Arms in the Rebel Army	not known.
do.	Was Servant to Lord Nairn, appeared early in Arms in the Rebellion	do.
do.	Was active in perswading the Tenents to raise in Rebellion	at home.
Forfar	Acted as Lieu^t in Ld Ogilvie's Regiment	Bergen, Pris^r.

LIST OF REBELS FROM

Names.	Designations.	Abode.	Parish.
David Cable	Servant	Forfar	Forfar
David Cowtie	Late Baillie in Forfar	do.	do.
Alex^r Chrystie	Servt to s^d Baillie Cowtie	do.	do.
Andrew Cornall	pendickle man	Carsburn	do.
James Crockat	Workman		Kingoldram
Thos. Cairncross	do.		do.
David Clark	do.	Strone	Kirrymuir
Alex^r Clark	do.	Braes Aldallan	Lintrethan
David Cochran	do.	Kirrymuir	Kirrymuir
John Candow	Servt to J^{as} Candow	Longdrum	Lintrethan
James Clark	Servant to Jas. Wright	Berie	do.
David Craik	Son to Dav^d Craik	Nether Seythy	do.
John Craik	Workman	Upper Seithy	do.
James Chaplain	do.	Arronbongue	do.
Thos. Crighton	Brother to Geo: Crighton	Brulzeon	do.
John Calinoch	Servt to Wm Ogilvy	Meikle Kenny	Lintrethan
John Crighton	Servt to Thos. Adam	Cheitlay	do.
David Copens	Workman	Barnton	Kingoldram
Charles Clark	do.	Bank	Kirry Muir
James Crow	Mason	Dundee	Dundee
Alex^r Crichton	Workman	do.	do.
John Cook	do.	do.	do.
James Carnegy	of Balmachy	do.	do.

DUNDEE DISTRICT—*Continued.* 203

County.	Acts of Rebellion and Circumstances.	What is become of them.
Forfar	Carried Arms in said Regiment being hired, has surrendered himself	at home.
do.	Volunteer in Rebel Army, Enticed by Meathie Bowar his Brother in Law	Prisoner.
do.	Carried Arms in Ld Ogilvie's Regim^t hired by the Country	Lurking.
do.	Do. do.	do.
Angus	Carried Arms as a Volunteer in said Regim^t—Since Culloden B.	at home.
do.	Do. do. do.	do.
do.	Press'd to serve in said Regim^t—Since Culloden B.	do.
do.	Carried Arms as a Volunteer in Ld Ogilvie's Regim^t—Since Falkirk B.	do.
do.	Served a Volunteer in said Regiment—Since Culloden Battle	do.
do.	Carried Arms for a Moneth being pressed, but deserted & never join'd again	do.
do.	Delivered up his Arms to the Minister & submitted—Since the Battle of Falkirk	at home.
do.	Do. do.	do.
do.	Deserted the Rebels at Leith but was afterwards forced to assist in raising men	do.
do.	Carried Arms with the Rebels, deserted them at Carlisle & never after join'd	do.
do.	Do. as a Volunteer in Ld Ogilvie's Regiment—Since Culloden B.	do.
Angus	Went along with his Master to the Rebellion but never bore arms: since Culloden	a Prisoner
do.	Press'd out, declar'd to the Minister he had left his Arms & submitted: Since Falkirk	at home.
do.	Carried Arms in Rebellion being press'd, went to England: & at Carlisle	Prisoner.
do.	Carried Arms in Ld Ogilvie's Regim^t being forced: since Culloden	at home.
Forfar	Carried Arms as a Volunteer in Rebel Army, was at Falkirk Battle & went North	Prisoner.
do.	Do. do. do.	do.
do.	Do. do. do.	do.
do.	Was Ensign in the Rebel Army, Carried Arms at Falkirk & went North	not known.

Names.	Designations.	Abode.	Parish.
Alex^r Crichton	Porter	Dundee	Dundee
Thomas Crighton	Surgeon	do.	do.
John Crichton	Sailor	do.	do.
Dr George Colvile	Physician	do.	do.
John Constable	Wright	do.	do.
Willm Crockat	Son to Doctor Crockat	Coupar	Coupar
Alex^r Crook, Senr	Surgeon	do.	do.
Alex^r Crook, Junr	Son to do.	do.	do.
Thomas Chalmers	Son to Willm Chalmers	Whitside	Alyth
James Clark	Sailor	Greenhall	Barry
Thomas Carre	Weaver	Cottown of Afflect	Monykie
Thos Crighton	Gentleman	Ruthven	Ruthven
John Crighton	do.	do.	do.
Thomas Crighton	Ploughman	do.	do.
John Cargill	do.	Bradeston	Airly
And^w Chalmers	do.	Glamiss	Glamiss
Arch^d Cuthbert	do.	Balnamoon	do.
Alex^r Clark	do.	Newtoun of Glamiss	do.
John Clark	do.	Thorntoun	do.
John Catineaugh	do.	Kainie	Gingothrum
John Crighton	do.	Lardean	Airly
Peter Chrystie	do.	Lindertes	do.

DUNDEE DISTRICT—*Continued.* 205

County.	Acts of Rebellion and Circumstances.	What's become of them.
Forfar	Joined the Rebels after Preston & continued with them till disperst, was Imprison'd but	admitted to Baill.
do.	Acted as Surgeon, joined after Preston & carried Arms with the Rebels till after Culloden	near Blair Gowery Lurk^g.
do.	Carried Arms in the Rebel Army	not known.
do.	Physician in the Rebel Army, joined them after Preston & cont^d to the end: in the North	lurking.
do.	Carried Arms & was at Falkirk and Culloden Battles with the Rebels	Lurking.
Perth	Do. & was at Culloden &c. with the Rebels & was active in raising men & money	do.
do.	Surgeon-Major to the Athole Brigade: forc'd out: was in England: has charge of the sick soldiers at Coupar	Keeps his own house at Genl Husk's desire.
do.	his father's servant, was in Arms for the Rebels, he & his Father returned home 5th feb^r 1746	at home.
Perth	Carried Arms in Ld Ogilvie's Regiment; taken at Carlisle	prisoner.
Forfar	Carried Arms in the Rebel Army, was at the Battles of Falkirk & Culloden	Prisoner.
do.	Do. was at Falkirk Battle & Stirling Seige, surrendered himself at Arbroath	at home.
Angus	Son to the Laird of Ruthven, was Lieu^t in the Rebel Army & raised men & money	fled the country.
do.	Son to do. was also Lieu^t & guilty of the same crimes with his Brother	do.
do.	Carried Arms in the Rebel Army, hired by the Country	do.
do.	Do. do.	do.
do.	Do. do.	do.
do.	Do. Hired by a Country man	do.
do.	Do. do.	do.
do.	Do. do.	do.
do.	Enlisted voluntarly & carried Arms with the Rebels	at home.
do.	Carried Arms in Rebellion, hired out by a Country man	not known.
do.	Do. do.	do.

LIST OF REBELS FROM

Names.	Designations.	Abode.	Parish.
Thomas Crighton	Ploughman	Glamiss	Glamiss
Dav^d Cumming		Eassie	Eassie
D.			
John Duncan	Carpenter	Dundee	Dundee
James Dalglish	Labouring man	do.	do.
William Davidson	Journyman Silversmith	do.	do.
Alex^r Duff	Apprentice	do.	do.
Peter Duncan	Workman	do.	do.
Alex^r Douny	Servant	Mire side	Coupar
Gilbert Drummond	Servant to Aldie	Meikleour	Capoth
William Dick	Servt to Kincairnie, Junr	Kincairnie	do.
John Dow	Servt to Ld Nairn	Stanly	Auchtergaven
Andrew Dougal	do.	do.	do.
Drummond	of Logy Almond	Logie Almond	Muneddie
John Doig	Pendickleman	Carseburn	Forfar
John Davie.	Servant to Dodievoe	Dodievoe	Kirrymuir
John Duthie	Weaver	Kirdhill	do.
James Dougal	Surgeon	Kirrymuir	do.
James Duncan	Workman	Balnyboth	do.
James Duncan	do.	Cromuir	do.
Charles Duncan	do.	Haugh	do.
John Duncan	Servt to Thos. Hanton	Easter Coall	Lintreth
John Donald	Do. to Alex^r Farquharson	Ingzeon	do.
David Anderson		Eassie	Eassie
Ebenezer Douny	Ploughman	Blackhill	Glamiss

DUNDEE DISTRICT—Continued. 207

County.	Acts of Rebellion and Circumstances.	What's become of them.
Angus	Carried Arms in Rebellion, hired out by a Country man	fled the Country.
do.	Do. do.	not known.
Forfar	Joined the Rebel Army after Preston Battle & continued with it till the end	not known.
do.	Employed as above	Lurking.
do.	Carried Arms as a Volunteer, was at Falkirk Battle and went North with the Rebels	Dundee, Prisoner.
do.	Carried Arms in the Rebel Army	not known.
do.	Do. do.	do.
Perth.	Do. and was at the Battle of Culloden	at home.
do.	Carried Arms with the Rebels during the whole Rebellion as a Volunteer	Prisoner.
do.	Employed as above	not known.
do.	Employed as above	do.
do.	Employed as above	do.
do.	Suspected of Treason, apprehended & Incarcerate in	Stirling Castle.
Forfar	Served in Ld Ogilvie's Rebel Regim^t hired by the Country	Lurking.
Angus	Carried Arms as a Volunteer in Ld Ogilvie's Regiment	Pris^r at Carlisle.
do.	Employed as above	do.
do.	Acted as Baillie in Kirrymuir under the Pretender's authority	at home.
do.	Carried Arms in Ld Ogilvie's Regim^t, being press'd: since Culloden	do.
do.	Employed as above: do.	do.
do.	Employed as above: do.	do.
do.	Carried Arms as a Volunteer in Ld Ogilvie's Regim^t: do.	do.
do.	Employed as a last above: do.	do.
do.	Carried Arms in the Rebel Army; hired by a Country man in his Room	not known.
do.	Do. do.	do.

LIST OF REBELS FROM

Names.	Designations.	Abode.	Parish.
John Duthie	Ploughman	Newtown of Airly	Airly
Alex^r Dalgairns	do.		
Peter Doctor	do.	Glen Ogilvie	Glamiss
John Deughars	do.	do.	do.
Robert Douglas	do.	Brigton	Kennetles
E.			
John Edward	Workman	Nethertoun	Kirrymuir
Dav^d Edward	do.	Boghead	do.
Alex^r Edward	do.		Kingoldrom
James Edward	do.	Pirsy	do.
Andrew Easson	do.	New Mill	Lintrethan
John Edward	do.	Bottam	do.
Andrew Edward	do.	Newbigging	do.
Alex^r Edward	Labouring man	Hillockhead	do.
John Edward	Tenent	Needs	do.
James Edward	Son to Alex^r Edward	West Revearny	do.
Andrew Edward	Servt to Wm Gruar	Purgave	do.
John Edward	Do. to John Edward Chapman	Greenlamirth	do.
Andrew Edward		Breas	do.

DUNDEE DISTRICT—Continued.

County.	Acts of Rebellion and Circumstances.	What's become of them.
Angus	Carried Arms in the Rebel Army; hired by a Country man in his Room	not known.
do.	Do. do.	do.
do.	Do. do.	do.
do.	Do. do.	do.
do.	Conveening his Tenents to the Rebels & oblidged them to send 9 men into Rebellion	at the Goat Whey.
Angus	Carried Arms in Ld Ogilvie's Regim^t, being forced thereto.—Since Culloden	at home.
do.	Do. do. do.	do.
do.	Carried Arms as a Volunteer in said Regim^t & was at Invernry Skirmish	Killed.
do.	Press'd to serve in said Regim^t, deserted before the Battle of Falkirk	at home.
do.	Press'd to carry Arms w^t the Rebels. Deserted at Carlisle & accepted of Genl Wade's Indemnity	do.
do.	Do. deserted & accepted as above; but was found & press'd again & deserted after Falkirk	do.
do.	Press'd to the Rebel Service; deserted at Dumblain on their Rout west; was press'd again, deserted at Stirling, delivered up his Arms to the Minister. Submitted to his Majesty's mercy & is ever since	at Home.
do.	Compelled to carry Arms w^t the Rebels. Deserted them at Carlisle and never join'd after	at Home.
do.	Press'd to carry Arms in the Rebels, deserted them at Carlisle & would not join again tho' they kindled a fire to burn his house	at home.
do.	Was press'd to the Rebel Service. Deserted & took the benefite of Genl Wade's pro-clam^n	do.
do.	Press'd to serve in Ld Ogilvie's Regim^t. Deserted after Falkirk B.	do.
do.	Employ'd as the last above in every Respect	do.
do.	Was a Volunteer in Ld Ogilvie's Regim^t left them after Falkirk B.	do.

LIST OF REBELS FROM

Names.	Designations.	Abode.	Parish.
John Encie	Labouring Serv[t]	Braidiston	Airly
John Ellis	do.	Cardean	do.
Alex[r] Ellis	do.	Glen Ogilvy	Glamiss
F. David Farquh'ar	Labouring Servant	Lindertes	Airly
Andrew Feithie	do.	do.	do.
Silvester Fenton	do.	Linross	do.
Thomas Filp, Jun[r]	do.	Lindertes	do.
Thomas Filp, Sen[r]	do.	Thorntoun	do.
Joseph Ferguson	do.	Braideston	do.
John Fcithy	Servant to W[m] Smith, Wright	Kirrymuir	Kirrymuir
John Fraser	Maltman	do.	do.
James Findlay	Workman	Mearns	do.
James Findlay	do.	Bruntyleave	do.
David Fenton	Farmer	Little Kenny	Kingoldrum
Will[m] ffroster	Workman	Kincloon	do.
Rob[t] ffletcher	of Balinsho, Jun[r]	Balinsho	Kirrymuir
James Fenton	Workman	Kincloon	Kingoldrum
Alex[r] Furquharson	Farmer	Ingzeon	Lintrethan
John Farquarson	do.	Over Seythy	do.
Alex. ffarquharson	Workman	East Reverny	do.
Silvester Forrester	do.	Ley	do.
Will[m] Farquharson	do.	West Coull	do.
Alex[r] Forbes	Serv[t] to James Craik	Bridge End	do.
James Farquharson	son to Jas. Farquharson	Westertoun	do.
Will[m] ffarquharson	of Broughdurg	Broughdurg	Genacly

DUNDEE DISTRICT—Continued.   211

County.	Acts of Rebellion and Circumstances.	What's become of them.
Angus	Carried Arms voluntarly with the Rebels; was active in forcing out others & oppressing the Country	Bradiston.
do.	Carried Arms in the Rebel Army: being hired by a Country man	not known.
do.	Do. do.	do.
Angus	Carried Arms in the Rebel Army, being hired by a country man	not known.
do.	Employed as the last above in every Respect	do.
do.	Do.	do.
do.	Do.	do.
do.	Do.	do.
do.	Do.	do.
do.	Carried Arms as a Volunteer in Ld Ogilvie's Regim^t.—Since Culloden B.	at Home.
do.	Do. Since do.	do.
do.	Do. do.	do.
do.	Press'd to Bear Arms in said Regim^t do.	do.
do.	Lieu^t in the Rebel Army, extorted money from the Country to raise men with. do.	do.
do.	Carried Arms as Volunteer in Ogilvie's Regim^t do.	do.
do.	Was Major in Ld Ogilvie's Regim^t, neither raised men nor money, made Prisoner	at Bergen.
do.	Voluntarly carried Arms in said Regim^t.—Since Culloden B.	at Home.
do.	Lieu^t in the Rebel Army. Refused to raise men or money tho' ordered do.	do.
do.	Lieu^t in do. Violently press'd men & extorted money for that service. do.	do.
do.	Compell'd to bear Arms in Ld Ogilvie's Regim^t deserted after Falkirk Battle	do.
do.	Employed as the last above in every Respect	do.
do.	Press'd by the Rebels to bear Arms	not known.
do.	Do. said to be drown'd	do.
do.	Press'd to serve in Ld Ogilvie's Regim^t deserted after the Battle of Falkirk	at Home.
do.	was Captain in Do.—Since Culloden Battle	do.

Names.	Designations.	Abode.	Parish.
Robt ffletcher	of Benchy, Junr	Benchy	Forfar
Willm Fodd	Pendickle man	Carsburn	do.
James Fife	Servant	Forfar	Forfar
Thos Fotheringham	of Bandaine	Dundee	Dundee
David ffothering-ham	Merchant	do.	o.
Thomas ffentor	Servt to Willm Marshall	do.	do.
Robt fferguson	Threed maker	do.	do.
Charles ffife	Surgeon	do.	do.
Thos ffotheringham	Merchant	do.	do.
Joseph Ferguson	Weaver	Chapple of Keillor	do.
George Forbes	Factor to Lady Strathmore	Castle Lyon	fforgan
Willm Farquhar	Taylor	Alyth	Alyth
Pat^k ffarquhar	Servant	do.	do.
John Fogo	Farmer	Balmacollie	Auchtergaven
G. James Greig	Tenent	Woodhill	Burray

DUNDEE DISTRICT—*Continued.* 213

County.	Acts of Rebellion and Circumstances.	What's become of them.
Angus	was Major in Ld Ogilvie's Regim^t, made Prisoner at	Bergen.
do.	Carried Arms in do. In the Country	Lurking.
Forfar	Carried Arms in Ld Ogilvie's Regim^t, hired by the Country being forced to send men	Lurking.
do.	Join'd in the Rebel Life Guards after Preston Battle & continued till dispers't, Lurking	about Glenshoe.
do.	Was Governour of Dundee for the Rebels & was very active, managed in a Tyrannical manner	Bergen, Prisoner.
do.	Was a Volunteer at the Battle of Falkirk & went North with the Rebels	not known.
do.	Employed as the last above in all Respects	Dundee, Prisoner.
do.	Acted the Surgeon in the Rebel Army	not known.
do.	Served in the Pretender's Son's Life Guards	do.
do.	Carried Arms with the Rebels, hired by the Country Farmers who were forced thereto	at home.
Perth	Was Master of Horses to the Pretender's Son & at Preston Battle	gone abrode.
do.	Carried Arms in Ld Ogilvie's 2d Battalion	Lurking near home.
do.	Bore Arms for the Rebels at Inverury Skirmish	Lurking.
do.	Was in the Council house of Perth with the Rebels on the annivers^y of his Majesty birth-day but accidentally: He being Ld Nairn's Factor came into Perth that night about some private Business of his Master's, at which instant a Tumult happening 'twixt the Town's People & the Rebels he fled into the Council house fearing violence from the former on his s^d Master's acco^t whom they knew to be in the Rebellion. He never carried Arms nor had any Station in the Rebel Army, this by certain Intelligence	at home.
Forfar	Joined the Rebels at Dundee 13th Jan^ry 1745/6 & carried Arms with them	in Arbroath prison.

LIST OF REBELS FROM

Names.	Designations.	Abode.	Parish.
George Gourlie		Panbridge	Panbridge
James Gourlie		do.	do.
Gilbert Gibson	Weaver	Clayholls	Munykie
John Gibson	do.	Cottown	do.
Andrew Gray	Weaver	Glammis	Glammis
Robert Greenhill	Greive to Brigtoun	Bridgetoun	Kinnettles
James Glenday	do.	Ready	Airly
William Gammack	Clerk	Glammis	Glammis
David Gibson	Porter	Dundee	Dundee
Dav^d Gray	Servant	do.	do.
Dav^d Graham	Merchant	do.	do.
Alex^r Graham	Writer	do.	do.
Robert Guthrie	Merchant	do.	do.
James Gibb	Sailor	do.	do.
George Geigie	Weaver	do.	do.
John Gibson	do.	do.	do.
James Graham	late of Duntroun		
Peter Gleny	Weaver	Pittnepy	Coupar
George Gower	Workman	Alyth	Alyth
Partick Grant	Farmer	Shillhill	Kirrymuir

DUNDEE DISTRICT—*Continued.* 215

County.	Acts of Rebellion and Circumstances.	What's become of them.
Forfar	Carried Arms in the Rebel Army, surrendered them after Culloden B. to the Min^r of the parish	at home.
do.	Did the same as the last above in all respects	do.
do.	Enlisted with the Rebels, never took arms but the Benefite of His Royal Highness's Proclamation & delivered himself up to the Minister	at home.
do.	Carried Arms, was at Falkirk Battle & Stirling Seige, surrendered himself to the Comman^g off^r in Arbroath	at home.
Angus	Carried Arms as a Volunteer in Ld Ogilvie's 2^d Battallion	not known.
do.	Was Serj^t in do. Threatened the Minister on a Sunday for praying for his Majesty	do.
do.	Carried Arms in the Rebel Army for Isobel Cathrae who was forced to hire him	do.
do.	Entertained the Rebels, drunk the Pretender's health &c. Consented to & privitly assisted in Ringing the Bell on the anniversary of the Pret^{rs} son's Birth day	at home.
Forfar	Carried Arms in the Rebel Army at the Battles of Falkirk & Culloden	do. Lurking.
do.	Employed as the last above	Lurking.
do.	Carried Arms in the Rebel Life Guards, was at the Battle of Falkirk &c.	not known.
do.	Employed as the last above	do.
do.	Aided & assisted the Rebels, was active in braking open the post Bagg & Letters &c.	Dundee, prisoner.
do.	Carried Arms in the Rebel Army	not known.
do.	Do.	do.
do.	Do.	do.
do.	Carried Arms in the Pretender's Son's Life Guards	do.
Perth	Carried Arms in the Rebel Army & after his return from Inverury sk^h surren^d them to Mr Alison of Newhall	at home.
do.	Do. in Ld Ogilvie's Regim^t—now Prisoner	at Carlisle.
Angus	Was a Captain in the Rebel Army, forced out Men & extorted money from the country	in the north.

Names.	Designations.	Abode.	Parish.
John Glendy	Weaver	Denhead Logy	Kirrymuir
Donald Gow	Workman	Petewan	Lintrethen
Willm Grower	Servt to Alex^r Farquharson	Cordauch	do.
James Gelletlie	Brewer's Servant	Liff	Liff
John Gray	Weaver	Brankum	Liff
William Gray	of Ballegerno	Balligerno	Inchsture
Willm Greenhill	Gardner	Kirktoun of Lefenday	Lefenday
David Greek	Servt to Stenton	Stenton	Capoth
John Gow	Servant to Aldie	Auchter Gaven	Auchtergaven
Pat^k Grant	Farmer	Sheelhill	Kirrymuir
John Gordon, Junr	Barber and Wigmaker	Forfar	Forfar
H.			
John Hobert	Workman	Nether Shell	Kirrymuir
John Hume	Labouring man	Bandean	Inchture
Andrew How	Weaver	Burnside of Kirkbuddo	Guthrie
David Home	Labouring man	Bandean	Inchture
Charles Horn	Shoemaker	Dundee	Dundee
Francis Henderson	Merchant	do.	do.
Alex^r Henderson	do.	do.	do.
Thomas Haliburton	Wright	do.	do.
John Hutchen	Weaver	Lonend of Loor	Forfar
James Henderson	Servant	Forfar	do.

DUNDEE DISTRICT—Continued. 217

County.	Acts of Rebellion and Circumstances.	What's become of them.
Angus	A volunteer in do. On 1st May surrendered himself & Arms to the Baillie of Kirrymuir	at home.
do.	Being press'd carried Arms with the Rebels, deserted at Carlisle & has submitted to mercy	do.
do.	Carried Arms in Ogilvie's Reg^t being press'd, deserted some time after Falkirk B.	at home.
Forfar	Do. & was at the Battles of Falkirk & Culloden	do.
do.	Employed as the last above. Prisoner	in Perth.
Perth	Was with the Rebels at Stirling, apprehended & now a Prisoner	in Dundee.
do.	Joined the Rebel Army after Preston Battle & continued till their Retreat from Stirling	Lurking.
do.	Employed as the last above	do. near home.
do.	Carried Arms as a Volunteer in the Rebel Army during the whole Rebellion	do. near home.
Forfar	Already entered above.	
do.	Carried Arms as a Volunteer in Ld Ogilvie's Regiment	kill'd.
Angus	Forced to carry Arms in Lord Ogilvie's Regim^t—Since Culloden B.	at home.
Perth	Carried Arms in the Rebel Army—Prisoner	at Carlisle.
Forfar	Carried Arms at the Battle of Falkirk but upon His R.H. proclam^{tn} delivered them up to ye Min^r	at home.
Perth	Do. in the Rebel Army & went to England	Carlisle pris^r
Forfar	Carried Arms as a Serj^t of the Rebels, was at Falkirk Battle & went north with them	not known.
do.	Was aiding & assisting to the Rebels, was Incarcerate but admitted to Baill	at home.
do.	Was aiding &c. Incarcerate & Baill'd & above	do.
do.	Joined the Rebels at Edin^r & carried Arms with them till dispers't	in Glenshoe.
do.	Carried Arms in Ld Ogilvie's Rebel Regiment	Lurking.
do.	Do. in do.	do.

Names.	Designations.	Abode.	Parish.
Patrick Hood	Weaver	Forfar	Forfar
Charles Henderson	Servant	do.	Roscoby
David Hunter	of Burnside	Grang of Monyfieth	Monyfieth
David Haggart	of Cairnmuir	Kirkhill	Capoth
John Hackie	Weaver	Dundee	Dundee
James Henderson	Sclater	do.	do.
William Henderson	do.	do.	do.
Alex^r Henry	Dyster	do.	do.
William Hutcheson	Labouring man	Cossens	Glammis
William Horn	do.	Holmill	do.

J.

George Johnston	Factor to Ld Panmuir	Balfour	
Alex^r Johnstoun	Labouring Servant	Glamis	Glamis
James Johnston	do.	Balgony	do.
William Irvine	do.	Ruthven	Ruthven
Charles Jackson	Brewer	Dundee	Dundee
Alex^r Johnston	Silversmith	do.	do.

K.

John Kinloch	of Kildry, Junr	Kildry	Glenaily
Andrew Kernock	Workman	Craig	Kirrymuir
Sir James Kinloch	of Kinloch	Dundee	Dundee
Robert Kerry	Tenent	Newtoun of Panmuir	Panbridge

DUNDEE DISTRICT—*Continued.* 219

County.	Acts of Rebellion and Circumstances.	What's become of them.
Forfar	Carried Arms in Ld Ogilvie's Rebel Regiment	Lurking.
do.	Do. in do. & was very active —said to be	Kill'd.
Forfar	Carried Arms as a Captain in the Pretender's Son's Life Guards. He was at Preston Battle, went with the Rebels into England & was at the Battle of Culloden	Prisoner at Bergen in Norway.
Perth	In a publick company wish'd confusion to His Maj^y & Army & success to the Rebels	at Home.
Forfar	Carried Arms in the Rebel Army	not known.
do.	Do.	do.
do.	Do.	do.
do.	Do.	do.
Angus	Carried Arms with the Rebels for a Countryman who was oblidged to find them a man	do.
do.	Employed as the last above in every respect	do.
Angus	Was aiding and assisting to the Rebells	Pris^r at Dundee.
do.	Carried Arms in the Rebel Army, hired by another who was oblidged to send a man	not known.
do.	Employed as the last above	do.
do.	Do.	do.
Forfar	Drank the Pretender's health as K. of G. Brettain &c. & His Majesty's confusion &c.	Pris^r in Dundee
do.	Joined the Pretender's Son's Life Guards after Preston, was at Falkirk B. & went North	Pris^r in Bergen.
Angus	Carried Arms as a Capt in Ld Ogilvie's Regim^t	Lurking near home.
do.	Carried Arms in said Regim^t	do.
fforfar	Collonel in do. in 2^d Battallion, joined after Preston Battle, is taken & sent to	Eng^d prisoner.
do.	Enlisted himself and carried Arms in the Rebel Army	In Arbroath pris^r.

LIST OF REBELS FROM

Names.	Designations.	Abode.	Parish.
Alex^r Kinloch	Brother to Sir James above		Meggle
Charles Kinloch	do.		do.
Peter Kinnair	Labouring man	Glenogilvy	Ruthven
L.			
James Lawson	Servt to Sir John Ogilvy	Coldhame	Kirrymuir
John Lundie	Workman	Kirrymuir	do.
James Low	Servt to James Low	Colhaick	do.
Thomas Lawson	Workman	Woodend	do.
Lichton	do.	Buckhood	do.
Alex^r Lacky	do.	Kingoldrum	Kingoldrum
Patrick Lawson	Miller	Bridge End	Lintrethen
James Lawson	Workman	Wester Coull	do.
John Lowthian	do.	Easter Pole	do.
James Lownan	Weaver	Purgavie	do.
David Low	Labouring man	Glamiss	Glamiss
William Livieth	do.	Nayston	do.
John Lawson	do.	Armyfoul	do.
John Livieth	do.	Nayston	do.
John Laird	Workman	Glamiss	Glammis
Patrick Lyon	of Easter Ogle	Easter Ogle	Tanidys
David Lunan	Weaver	Lon End of Loor	Forfar
John Lunan	do.	do.	do.

DUNDEE DISTRICT—*Continued.* 221

County.	Acts of Rebellion and Circumstances.	What's become of them.
Perth	Was Capt in Ld Ogilvie's 2^d Battallion & oppress'd the country by raising men & money.	In Eng^d Prisoner.
do.	was Capt in the Athole Brigade, oppress'd the country as his Brother & suffered the same fate	do.
Angus	Carried Arms with the Rebels for a Farmer who was oblidged to find them a man	not known.
do.	Carried Arms as a Volunteer in Ld Ogilvie's Regiment.—since Culloden B.	come home.
do.	Do. in do. since do.	do.
do.	Do. in do. do.	do.
do.	Press'd to carry Arms in do. do.	do.
do.	Served as a Volunteer in do. Since do.	do.
do.	Served a Volunteer in Ld Ogilvie's Regiment—since Culloden	come home.
do.	Press'd by the Rebels & arms tyed to him, deserted at Carlisle and taken on his way home	at Blackness, Pris^r.
do.	Press'd to serve in Ld Ogilvie's Regim^t	at Carlisle Pris^r.
do.	Being press'd, served in do. surrendered himself & arms to the Min^r after the Battle of Falkirk	at home.
do.	Being press'd served and surrendered as the last above	do.
do.	Carried Arms in the Rebel Army for another who was oblidged either to go himself or find them a man	not known.
do.	Employed as the last above in every respect	not known.
do.	Do.	do.
do.	Do.	do.
do.	Carried Arms as a Volunteer in Lord Ogilvie's 2^d Battallion	do.
Forfar	Had the Station of a Leu^t in Ld Ogilvie's Regim^t	do.
Forfar	Carried Arms in s^d Regim^t being hired by the Country, has surrendered himself to the Min^r of Forfar	at home.
do.	Acted as the last above in all Respects	do.

LIST OF REBELS FROM

Names.	Designations.	Abode.	Parish.
James Lyon	Innkeeper	Dundee	Dundee
Charles Lyon	Son to James Lyon above	do.	do.
Charles Lyon	Silver Smith Apprentice	do.	do.
Andrew Laird	Merchant	do.	do.
Andred Lovall			Panbridge
James Lumgair			do.
William Low	Chapman	Ballbowna	Forgan
Patrick Laird	Vintiner	Meggle	Meggle
Dav^d Lawson	Servant	Alyth	Alyth
Thomas Lawson	Chapman	Alyth	do.
James Laird	Servant to Murrie	Murrie	Errol
M.			
George Money	Ploughman	Armyfoul	Ruthven
Charles Mather	do.	Braideston	Airly
John Miller	do.	Glamis	Glamis
James Mill	do.	do.	do.
James Miles	do.	do.	do.
Thomas Munie	do.	Cossens	do.
John Meal	do.	Newtoun of Glamis	do.
Alex^r Mitchel	do.	Balgony	do.
James Mill	do.	Newtoun of Airly	Airly
Robert Mill	do.	Readie	do.
Thomas Moodie	do.	Bukie	do.
Patrick Moncurr		Navoy	Navoy
Robert Milne	Servant to Wm Smith	Kirrymuir	Kirrymuir
James Milne, Junr	Do. to James Milne	Landends	do.

DUNDEE DISTRICT—*Continued.* 223

County.	Acts of Rebellion and Circumstances.	Where they are at present.
Forfar	Carried Arms in Lord Ogilvie's 2ᵈ Battallion & was active in raising others	about Glenshoe, Lurkᵍ.
do.	Carried Arms in do.	do.
do.	Was a Volunteer with the Rebels, was at the Battle of ffalkirk & went North with them	not known.
do.	Aided & assisted the Rebels, opened the post Bagg Letters &c.	In Dundee Prison.
do.	Carried Arms in the Rebel Army, surrendᵈ to the parish Minʳ on his R.H's proclamⁿ	at home.
do.	Do. surrendered to the Minister of the Parish since the Battle of Culloden	do.
Perth	Carried Arms as Serjeant in Lᵈ Ogilvie's 2ᵈ Battallion	come home.
do.	Lieutenant in sᵈ Battallion. Carried Arms in England & at the Battles of Falkirk & Culloden	about Glenshoe.
do.	Carried Arms in Ogilvie's 1ˢᵗ Battallion & was at the Battle of Falkirk	come home.
do.	Carried Arms in ditto	do.
do.	Carried Arms in the Rebel Army & was at the Battle of Culloden & there taken	Prisoner
Angus	Carried Arms in the Rebel Army, being hired by a Farmer in his Stead	not known.
do.	Do. do.	do.
do.	Do. do.	do.
do.	Do. do.	do.
do.	Do. do.	do.
do.	Do. do.	do.
do.	Do. do.	do.
do.	Do. do.	Returned.
do.	Do. do.	not known.
do.	Do. do.	do.
do.	Do. do.	do.
do.	Do. do.	do.
do.	Carried Arms as a Volunteer in Lᵈ Ogilvie's Regimᵗ till the end	come home.
do.	Employed as the last above	do.

LIST OF REBELS FROM

Names.	Designations.	Abode.	Parish.
Charles Mather	Wright	Kirrymuir	Landends
And^w Moncurr	Weaver	Easter Kinordy	do.
Willm M'Niccol	Workman	Cromby burn	do.
Willm M'Nicoll	do.	Runthyleave	do.
Thomas Milne	do.	Burn of Lidnathy	do.
Willm Malcom	do.		Kingoldrum
Samuel M'Dougal	do.		do.
James Miles	do.		do.
James M'Carro	Servant	Balnakily	Lintrethen
Willm M'Intosh	Servant man	Dundee	Dundee
John Mitchell	Common Workman	do.	do.
Dav^d Morgan	Servant	do.	do.
Willm Moor	Horse hirer	do.	do.
John M'Donald	Servant	do.	do.
James Miller	Horse hirer	do.	do.
Wm Miller	Sailor	do.	do.
Thos. Mitchell	Button maker	do.	do.
John Mitchell	a Boy	do.	do.
Thomas Moodie	Weaver	do.	do.
William Main	Tenent	Newton of Panmuir	Panbridge
Dav^d Mill	Servt to Alex. Medison	Bulzeon	Liff
James Marshall	Officer to the Earl of Airly	Ochterhouse	Ochterhouse
James Miller	Brewer	Coupar	Coupar
Don^d M'Grigor	Town officer	do.	do.
Dav^d Mill	Weaver	Newbigging	Newtyle
James M'Duff	You^r of Forfechy	Farfechy	Tanidys
Pat^k M'Kenzie	Servant	Tarbeig	Forfar

DUNDEE DISTRICT—Continued.

County.	Acts of Rebellion and Circumstances.	Where they are at present.
Angus	Was a Volunteer in s^d Reg^t, deserted & surrendered himself & Arms to the Baillie, 24th April	come home.
do.	A Volunteer in said Regim^t, continued with them till disperst	do.
do.	Press'd to serve in said Regim^t & continued till after Culloden Battle	do.
do.	Do. do.	do.
do.	Do. do.	do.
do.	Carried Arms as a Volunteer in do. & continued till after the Battle of Falkirk	do.
do.	Do. do.	do.
do.	Served in Ogilvie's Regim^t till the end of the Rebellion	do.
do.	Served in do. to the end thereof, being press'd at first	do.
Forfar	Carried Arms in Ld Ogilvie's 2^d Battallion	do.
do.	Drumer in the Rebel Army, was at the Battle of Falkirk & went North	Dundee prison.
do.	Carried Arms as a Volunteer in do., was at Falkirk B. & went North	Do. Prison.
do.	Employed as the last above	not known.
do.	Carried Arms in the Rebel Army	do.
do.	Do.	do.
do.	Do.	do.
do.	Carried Arms as a Serjeant in said Army	Not known.
do.	Acted as a Drummer in do.	do.
do.	Carried Arms as a privat man in do.	do.
do.	Enlisted & carried Arms with the Rebels	Arbroath prison.
do.	Carried Arms in Ld Ogilvie's 2^d Battallion	returned home.
do.	Do. in 1st Battallion	do.
Perth	Joined the Rebels at Dunkeld on their way south & was very oppressive	Glenshoe.
Forfar	Carried Arms in Ld Ogilvie's 2^d Battallion till after Culloden B.	the Highlands.
do.	Do. was at Inverury Skirmish, came home & surrendered his arms to Mr Alison	in Newhall.
do.	Acted as Lieu^t in Ld Ogilvie's Regim^t	Prisoner.
do.	Carried Arms in said Regim^t, being hired by the Country	Lurking.

Names.	Designations.	Abode.	Parish.
Alex^r Man, Junr	Servant	Moss side of Loor	Forfar
John Mitchell	Wright	Forfar	do.
And^w Masterton	Weaver	do.	do.
Robert Mercer	of Aldie	Meikleour	Capoth
Lau^r Mercer	of Lethenday	Pendreich	Lethenday
Mungo Murray	Son to Mr Murray of Kincairnie, was Secretary to the Marq^s of Tullibardine	Kincairnie	Capoth
John M'Ewan	Son to the Laird of Dungarthle	D ngarthle	do.
James Miller	Brewer	5 mile house	Auchtergaven
Alex^r M'Lean	do.	Long Loggie	Meggle
N.			
John Nairn	Lord Nairn	Stanly	Auchtergaven
Thomas Neil	Servt to Stenton, Junr	Stenton	Capoth
John Nash	Servant	Dundee	Dundee
William Nash	do.	do.	do.
David Nevay	do.	Forfar	Forfar
O.			
Thomas Ogilvy	Son to Sir John Ogilvy	Kinordy	Kirrymuir
David Ogilvy	Labourer	Kirrymun	
James Ogilvy	do.	Mearns	c
Thomas Ogilvy	of East Miln	East Miln	Glenaily

DUNDEE DISTRICT—*Continued.* 227

County.	Acts of Rebellion and Circumstances.	Where they now are.
Forfar	Carried Arms & hired as the last above	Lurking.
	Do.	killed.
	Do.	Lurking.
Perth	Acted as a Capt in the Rebel Army during the whole Rebellion	not known.
do.	Carried Arms in do. from a little before Falkirk B. to their dispersing	Dundee prison.
do.	Joined the Rebels a little after their coming to Dunkeld. Gone in women's cloaths to	Edin^r.
do.	Was a Lieut. in the Rebel Army, joined them before Falkirk Battle	not known.
do.	Was in the Mob at Perth on the anniversary of his Majesty's Birth Day, fired on the Town's people & active in Raising Ld Nairn's Tenents into the Rebellion	Perth prison.
do.	Was a Serjeant in the Rebel Army & at the Battles of Falkirk & Culloden	not known.
do.	A General in the Rebel Army in Arms during the whole Rebellion	not known.
do.	a Volunteer in do. In Arms from their coming to Perth to their Retreat from Stirling	do.
Forfar	Carried Arms in the Rebel Army	do.
do.	Do.	do.
do.	Carried Arms in Ld Ogilvie's Regim^t being hired by the Country	Lurking.
Angus	Was Captain in the Rebel Army till disperst, Levyed men & extorted money from the country	come home.
do.	a volunteer in Ld Ogilvie's Regim^t	Carlisle pris^r.
do.	Do. in s^d Regim^t continued with them till the end	Come home.
do.	Captain of the Rebels, was active in raising men & extorting money from the country	come home since Culloden B.

LIST OF REBELS FROM

Names.	Designations.	Abode.	Parish.
Thos. Ogilvy	Farmer	Little Kenny	Kingoldrum
David Ogilvy	of Pool	Pool	Lintrethan
David Ogilvy	Son to Shannaly	Shannaly	do.
Alexr Ogilvy	Son to Alexr Ogilvy	Braes	do.
John Orrok	Land Waiter in the Customs	Dundee	Dundee
Henry Ogilvy	Innkeeper	do.	do.
Peter Ouchterlony	Coffeehouse keeper	do.	do.
John Ouchterlony	Mason	do.	do.
John Ogilvy	of Inshoan	Inshoan	Tanidys
James Ogilvy	Farmer	Mill of do.	do.
John Ogilvy	Farmer	Lochmill	Glamis
John Ogilvy	of Quick	Quick	Cortachy
David Ogilvy	Merchant	Cool	Tannidys
Willm Ogilvy	Servant	Muir of Meathie	Forfar
Willm Ogilvy	Dyster	Forfar	do.
James Ogilvy	Servant	do.	do.
James Ogilvy	Tinker		Barry
Willm Ogilvy	Fewer	Kaince	Kingoldrum
John Ogilvy	of Roughill	Roughill	Glamis
P.			
Alexr Piggot	Servt to Mrs Lyon		Lintrethan
Thomas Prophet	Workman	Balmakity	Kirrymuir

DUNDEE DISTRICT—*Continued.* 229

County.	Acts of Rebellion and Circumstances.	Where they now are.
Angus	Was Lieut in the Rebel Army & guilty of the same crimes with the above	come home since Culloden B.
do.	Served in the Rebel Life Guards & was guilty of the like crimes	Prisr Aberdeen.
do.	Was a Lieut in the Rebel Army, but neither rais'd men nor money—Since Culloden	come home.
do.	Compelled to carry Arms in Ld Ogilvie's Regiment, deserted after Falkirk	at home.
Forfar	Countenanced the Rebels, was Imprisoned at Dundee, but	admitted to Baill & continues in office.
do.	Said to have assisted the Rebels, was Imprisoned at Dundee but admitted to Baill	at home.
do.	Join'd in the Rebel Life Guards after Preston, was at Falkirk B. & went North	not known.
do.	Was a Volunteer with the Rebels at Falkirk Battle & went North with them	do.
do.	Was Captain in Ld Ogilvie's Regiment	Bergen, Prisr
do.	Lieut in do. Enlisted men for the Rebel Service	do.
do.	Acted as Captain in said Regimt	Lurking.
do.	Was Ensign in Do.	Prisoner.
do.	Was a Captain in Ld Ogilvie's Rebel Regiment	Bergen, Prisoner.
do.	Carried Arms in do. forced out by the Laird of Meathie	Lurking.
do.	Do. as a Volunteer in said Regimt	do.
do.	Served & carried Arms in do. being hired by the Country	do.
do.	Carried Arms in the Rebel Army & was at the Battles of Falkirk & Culloden	Prisoner.
Angus	Carried Arms as a Captain in said Army	not known.
do.	Do. as Lieut in Ld Ogilvie's Regt. Oppressed the Country by raising men & money	do.
do.	Was twice press'd to the Rebel Service, his Sister being put in prison before he appeared the last	Came home after Falkirk.
do.	a Volunteer in Ld Ogilvie's Regimt, continued with them till dispers't	come home.

LIST OF REBELS FROM

Names.	Designations.	Abode.	Parish.
Willm Palmer	Son to Palmer	Buckhood Ground	Kirrymuir
Robert Palmer	Workman	Hillside	do.
Robert Palmer	do.	Delairn	do.
John Peddy	do.	Kincloon	Kingoldrum
Alex^r Piggot	do.	Bridge End	do.
Henry Patullo	Merchant	Dundee	Dundee
Andrew Petric	Workman	do.	do.
James Paterson	Common Workman	do.	do.
George Patullo	Merchant	do.	do.
Alex^r Paterson	Officer to the Earl of Airly	Ochterhouse	Ochterhouse
Alex^r Paterson	Servt to Laird of Burnside	Grange of Monyfieth	Monyfieth
John Philp	Carrier	Forfar	Forfar
R.			
John Roy	Servant	Lidnathy	Kirrymuir
Don^d Robertson	Workman	Glenprosin	do.
Charles Rea	do.	Kingoldrum	Kingoldrum
Dav^d Reid	do.	Myrend	do.
Ramsay	do.	Percy	Kirrymuir
John Robertson	of Crandirth	Crandirt	Glenach
Thomas Rough			Eassie
Andrew Renwick	Servant	Kinnettles	Kinettles

County.	Acts of Rebellion and Circumstances.	Where they now are.
Angus	Employed as above	come home.
do.	Employed as above	do.
do.	Press'd into said Regim^t & continued to the end	do.
do.	a Volunteer in Ld Ogilvie's Regim^t where he continued till dispers't	do.
do.	Press'd to carry Arms in Do. & continued to the last,	Inverness, Prisoner.
Forfar	Was Muster Master in the Rebel Army, rose in Arms at the beginning of the Rebellion & was active in disposing of the Goods in the Customhouse for Behoof of the Rebels	Bergen, Pris^r.
do.	Carried Arms as a Volunteer in the Rebel Army & was at the Battles of Falkirk & Culloden	Lurking.
do.	a Volunteer, carried Arms at the Battle of Falkirk & went North with the Rebels	Dundee Prison.
do.	Was Ensign in Sir James Kinloch's Regiment	near Coupar lurking.
Forfar	Carried Arms in the Rebel Army in Ld Ogilvie's 2^d Battalion	Lurking.
do.	Carried Arms in do. went to Eng^d & was at the Battle of Falkirk, after that came home	Dundee Prison.
do.	Carried Arms in Ld Ogilvie's Regiment being hired by the Country	Lurking.
Angus	Press'd to serve in Ld Ogilvie's Regim^t continued till dispers't	come home.
do.	a Volunteer in do. continued to the end	do.
do.	Employed as above	do.
do.	Do.	Pris^r at Carlisle.
do.	Volunteer in the Rebel Army, deserted before the 20th of Octo^r & never join'd after	do.
do.	Captain in Ld Ogilvie's Regim^t & continued to the last	been at home.
do.	Carried Arms in the Rebel Army, being hired by another to serve in his room	not known.
do.	Employed as the last above in every respect	do.

LIST OF REBELS FROM

Names.	Designations.	Abode.	Parish.
James Rea	Servant	Glamis	Glamis
John Roger	do.	Lighton	Airly
Peter Roger	do.	do.	do.
John Robertson	do.	Thornton	Glamis
Alex^r Rough	do.	Glenogilvy	do.
James Robb	do.	Baickie	Airly
Charles Robertson			Novey
Charles Robertson	Farmer	Raimore	Capoth
Alex^r Robertson	of Raimore	Gaey	Douly
John Reoch	Cooper	Stanly	Auchter-gaven
Robert Ramsay	Weaver	Ballmah	Newtyle
Henry Rattray	Servant	Alyth	Alyth
Dav^d Robertson	of Bletton	Bletton	Kirkmichael
James Rattray	of Corb	Corb	do.
John Reoch	Innkeeper	Glen Isla	Glen Isla
James Rattray	Ropemaker	Dundee	Dundee
Alex^r Robertson	Merchant	do.	do.
Charles Rattray	of Dunoon	do.	do.
Charles Rattray	Son to ditto.	do.	do.
David Ramsay	Workman	Fornly	Lintrethan
Willm Roben	Servt to Earl of Airly's 2^d Son	Dundee	Dundee
George Ramsay	Weaver	do.	do.
Willm Reat	Surgeon, son to Dr Reat	do.	do.
Peter Robertson	Apprentice	do.	do.

DUNDEE DISTRICT—*Continued.* 233

County.	Acts of Rebellion and Circumstances.	Where they now are.
Angus	Employed as the last above in every respect	not known.
do.	Do.	do.
do.	Do.	do.
do.	Do.	do.
do.	Do.	do.
do.	Do.	do.
do.	Do.	do.
Perth	Joined the Rebels as a Volunteer before the Battle of Falkirk	Lurking.
do.	Join'd as above & continued to their dispersion	do.
do.	Carried Arms as a Volunteer during the whole Rebellion	do.
Forfar	Carried Arms at Inverury & after that surrendered his Arms to Mr Alison of Newhall	at home.
Perth	Carried Arms in the Rebel Army—& was taken at	Carlisle.
do.	Was a Captain in the Marques of Tullibardine's Regiment	been at home.
do.	Was Major in do. Taken prisoner & carried to	England
Angus	Serjeant in the Rebel Army, left them after their Reatreat from Stirling	Lurk^g near home.
Forfar	Was Clerk to the Deput Governour of Dundee, capable of making discoverys if apprehended	at home.
do.	Assisted in opening the post Bagg & reading the Letters	Confined at home.
do.	Collected the Excise, carried Arms, was at the Battle of Falkirk & went North with the Rebels	not known.
do.	Was Ensign, carried Arms, was at the Battle of & went North with the Rebels	do.
Angus	Press'd into the Rebel Army, deserted before Falkirk B. & surrendered himself	at home.
Forfar	Was a Volunteer in the Rebel Army, at the Battle of Falkirk & went North with the Rebels	not known.
do.	Carried Arms in Rebel Army	do.
do.	Acted as Surgeon in the Pretender's Son's Life Guards	do.
do.	Carried Arms in the Rebel Army	do.

Names.	Designations.	Abode.	Parish.
Duncan Robertson	Merchant	Dundee	Dundee
John Russell	Weaver	Backmuir	Barry
Charles Robertson	Principal Servant to Burnside	Grange of Monyfieth	Monyfieth
William Reid	Groom to Burnside	do.	do.
John Ramsay	Pendicleman	Carseburn	Forfar
James Ramsay	Taylor	Forfar	do.
James Ritchie	Horsehirer	do.	do.
S.			
Duncan Shaw	Factor to Ld Airly	Cortachy	Cortachy
James Stormont	of Pitscanly	Pitscanly	Rosecoby
David Scott	Pendickle man	West Dod	Forfar
Pat^k Simpson	Tenent	Middle do.	do.
Willm Stark	Weaver	Muir of Meathie	do.
Willm Simpson	Workman	Forfar	do.
John Simpson	Servant	do.	do.
Alex^r Stark	do.	do.	do.
Andrew Smith	do.	do.	do.
David Smith	do.	do.	do.
William Seton	Non Jurant Minister	do.	do.
Chas Scott	Ploughman	Glamis	Glamis
John Shunger	do.	Glenogilvy	do.
James Stormond	of Lidnathy	Lidnathy	Kirrymuir

DUNDEE DISTRICT—Continued.

County.	Acts of Rebellion and Circumstances.	Where they now are.
Forfar	Aided & assisted the Rebels, was apprehended & Imprisoned but	admitted to Baill.
do.	Carried Arms, was at the Battles of Falkirk & Culloden & Stirling Seige & wounded	Arbroath prison.
do.	Carried Arms as an Officer in the Rebel Army, was at the Battle of Culloden & there	kill'd.
do.	Attended his Master in England &c. carried [arms] in the Rebellion & was at Culloden Battle	Prisoner.
do.	Being hired by the Country, Carried Arms in Rebellion till the end thereof	come home.
do.	Being armed, went thro' Forfar with Drum & a piper recruiting men for the Rebel Service	Lurking.
do.	Being hired by the Country, carried Arms in Ld Ogilvie's Reg^t till the last	do.
do.	Acted as Deput Lord Lieu^t for the Rebels under his said Master	Lurking in the Country.
do.	Was Ensign in Lord Ogilvie's Regim^t	Prisoner.
do.	Carried Arms in do. being hired by the Country	Lurking.
do.	Do. in said Reg^t said to be forced out by the Laird of Pitcanly his Master	do.
do.	Do. in do. forced by the Laird of Meathie his Master, surrend^d to the Min^r of Forfar	at home.
do.	Carried Arms in Ld Ogilvie's Regim^t being hired by the Country	Lurk^g in the Country.
do.	Employed being hired as the last above	do.
do.	Do.	do.
do.	Do.	do.
do.	Do.	do.
do.	Preached Treasonable Sermons	Prisoner.
Angus	Entertained the Rebels at his house & assisted in Ringing the Bell on the P^{rs} Son's Birth night.	
do.	Carried Arms with the Rebels being hired by another in his room	not known.
do.	Was Ensign in Ld Ogilvie's Regim^t where he continued till diperst	come home.

Names.	Designations.	Abode.	Parish.
John Stiven	Workman	Hirdhill	Kirrymuir
John Stormond	of Kinwhirie	Kinwhirie	do.
James Stormond	Son to Alex^r Stormont	Glenugg	do.
Willm Shaw	of Forter	Forter	Glenaly
Alex^r Schaw	Farmer	Auhavarn	do.
Alex^r Stuart	Gardner	Cookstoun	Kingoldrum
James Stuart	Workman	Kingoldrum	do.
Wm Sampson	do.		Lintrethen
Mr Thos. Syme	Nonjurant Preacher	Ardgath	Errol
Thomas Syme	Workman	Sea Side	do.
Dav^d Stubble	do.	Kettens	Kettens
And^w Seaton	Chapman	Alyth	Alyth
John Smith	of Ballcharry	Ballcharry	do.
Don^d Stuart	Son to Strathgairie, a Schoolboy	Reichep	Capoth
John Stuart	Son to Stenton, Do.	Stenton	do.
Chas. Stuart	of Wester Gowrdie	Wester Gowrdie	do.
John Sangster	Servt to Ld Nairn	Stanly	Auchtergaven
Charles Sheepherd	Shoemaker	Minfield	Forgan
William Sutor	Weaver	Dundee	Dundee
Wm Stiven	Cooper	do.	do.
Dav^d Salter	Victualler	do.	do.
James Schaw	a Servant	do.	do.
And^w Simpson	Sailor	do.	do.
James Stuart	Porter	do.	do.
John Stuart	Son to do.	do.	do.

DUNDEE DISTRICT—*Continued.* 237

County.	Acts of Rebellion and Circumstances.	Where they now are.
Angus	Carried Arms in Ld Ogilvie's Regim^t till dispersed	come home.
do.	Assisted in Escorting Arms to the Rebels	Montrose pris^r.
do.	Carried Arms as a Volunteer in Ld Ogilvie's Regim^t	was at home.
do.	Captain in the Rebel Army, raised men & extorted money from the Country people	come home since Culloden B.
do.	Acted as Captain in Ld Ogilvie's Regim^t	do.
do.	Was Serjeant in do.	do.
do.	Private man in do. Surrendered himself & Arms to the Minister after the Battle of Falkirk	at home.
do.	Serjeant in do. was active in Raising & Imprisoned others to compell them to Enlist	came home since Culloden B.
Perth	Carried Arms & went North with the Rebels	Returned & Lurking.
do.	Do. & was at the Battle of Falkirk with the Rebels, but wrong in his Judgem^t	do.
Forfar	A Volunteer in the Rebel Army & was at the Battle of Falkirk	not known.
Perth	Carried Arms in Ld Ogilvie's 1st Battallion	come home.
do.	Was active in serving the Rebels	Dundee prison.
Perth	Carried Arms from a little before the Battle of Falkirk, seduc'd by Glenbucket	not known.
do.	Employed as the last above. Left them on their return from Falkirk, seduced by do. to leave the School	the Country.
do.	Was a Captain & in Arms during the whole Rebellion with the Rebels	not known.
do.	Was a Volunteer & employed as above	do.
do.	Was a Soldier in Ld Ogilvie's 2^d Battallion	Returned home.
Forfar	Carried Arms in the Rebel Army	not known.
do.	Do.	do.
do.	Aided & assisted the Rebels	Dundee prison.
do.	Carried Arms as a Volunteer with Ld Ogilvie's men	Lurking.
do.	Was Drummer in Lord Ogilvie's 2^d Battallion	Dundee prison.
do.	Carried Arms in ditto Battallion	Lurking about Glenshoe.
do.	Do. in do.	

LIST OF REBELS FROM

Names.	Designations.	Abode.	Parish.
Alex^r Stuart	Merchant	Dundee	Dundee
T.			
John Talbott	Weaver	Dundee	Dundee
Thomas Threepland	Son to Sr Dav^d of Fingask	Fingask	Kinnard
James Thomson	Gardner to Fingask	do.	do.
Willm Taylor	Coachman	Glamis	Glamis
Charles Taylor	Servant	do.	do.
Willm Thomson	Workman	Little Kenny	Kingoldrum
George Thom	do.	Formall	Lintrethen
W.			
John Wagrae	Merch^t Apprentice	Dundee	Dundee
Willm Wood	Journeyman Mason	do.	do.
Alex^r Watson	late of Wallace of Craigie	do.	do.
George Wilkie	Merch^t Apprentice	do.	do.
Dav^d Williamson	Merchant	do.	do.
Sir John Wedderburn	Late of Blackness	Mains of Navey	Newtyle
Wedderburn	Eldest Son to do.	do.	do.
John Wischart	Merchant	Dundee	Dundee
John Williamson	Cooper.	do.	do.

DUNDEE DISTRICT—Continued.

239

County.	Acts of Rebellion and Circumstances.	Where they now are.
Forfar	Assisted in opening the Post Bagg & Reading the Letters, assisted in Fraughting & Supplying with provisions the Ship which carryed off the Rebels to Bergen	at home.
Forfar	Carried Arms in the Rebel Army	not known.
Perth	Was a Captn in the Rebel Army at the Battle of Preston & there	kill'd.
do.	Carried Arms in do. went with them to England & was taken at Carlisle	Carlisle, prisoner.
Angus	Carried Arms in the Rebel Army, Enlisted himself	not known.
do.	Served as a Volunteer in do. & continued to the last	do.
do.	Served a Volunteer in Lord Ogilvie's Regiment	Carlisle, prisoner.
do.	erved as the last above but surrendered himself & Arms to the Minister after Falkirk	at home.
do.	Carried Arms as a Volunteer, was at the Battle of Falkirk & went North	not known.
do.	Employed as the last above in every respect	do.
do.	Was Deputy Gover^{nr} of Dundee, Collected the Cess, Carried Arms, was at Falkirk B. & went North with the Rebels	at Kirkmichael.
do.	Was a Volunteer at the Battle of Falkirk & went North with the Rebels	not known.
do.	Assisted the Rebels, opened the Post Bagg & read the Letters	Dundee prison.
Forfar	Collected the Excise in Perth, Collection for behoof of the Rebels, carried Arms in their Army & was at the Battle of Culloden where he was taken prisoner	England, prisoner.
do.	Carried Arms as Lieu^t in Ld Ogilvie's 1st Battallion	not known.
do.	Carried Arms as do. in do.	Glenshoe, Lurking.
do.	Carried Arms in the Rebel Army	not known.

LIST OF REBELS FROM

Names.	Designations.	Abode.	Parish.
Willm Wintoun	Weaver	Craigtoun	Monykie
Willm Watt	Servant	Greenlawhill	Barry
Dav^d Wilson	Weaver	Cottoun of Loor	Forfar
John Webster	Workman	Forfar	do.
John Webster	Weaver	do.	do.
John Wilkie	Servant	do.	do.
Thomas Watson	Merchant	Kirrymuir	Kirrymuir
George Wilkie	Son to Geo. Wilkie	Auchleishie	do.
John Webster	Mason	Kirrymuir	do.
James White	Workman	West Lidnathy	do.
James Wilson	do.	Inchbraughty	do.
Thos. Wilson	do.	Craigynaig	do.
John Wright	do.	Kingoldrum	Kingoldrum
John White	do.	Kincloon	do.
Chas. Webster	do.		do.
Dav^d Wilkie	do.	Correfie	Lintrethen
John Wilkie	do.	Nether Campsay	do.
John Wright	Servant	Lindertie	Airly
William Watson	do.	Glamis	Glamis
Alex^r White	do.	Cleppithill	do.
Thomas Volumn	Servant	Cossins	do.
James White	Victualler	Meggle	Meggle

DUNDEE DISTRICT— Continued.

County.	Acts of Rebellion and Circumstances.	Where they are.
Forfar	Carried Arms in the Rebel Army, was at Falkirk Battle & Stirling Seige, surrend^d of late to the Commanding officer in Arbroath	at home.
do.	Carried Arms in the Rebel Army, was at the Battle of Falkirk & Stirling Seige	Lurking.
do.	Carried Arms in Ld Ogilvie's Regim^t being hired by the Country	do.
do.	Employed being hired as the last above	taken Prisoner.
do.	Carried Arms as a Volunteer in Ld Ogilvie's Regim^t	Lurking.
do.	Carried Arms in s^d Regim^t being hired by the Country	do.
Angus	Carried Arms as a Volunteer in Ld Ogilvie's Regim^t & continued to their dispersion	come home.
do.	Employed as the last above in every respect	do.
do.	Carried Arms as Serj^t in Ld Ogilvie's Reg^t & continued to the end	do.
do.	Press'd to carry Arms in s^d Regim^t & continued to the End	do.
do.	Carried Arms being press'd as the last above	do.
do.	Do.	do.
do.	Carried Arms as a Volunteer in said Regim^t, continued to the Last	do.
do.	Was three times press'd to carry Arms in s^d Regim^t & as often deserted	do.
do.	Being press'd carried Arms in Ld Ogilvie's Regim^t	Derby, prisoner.
do.	Being press'd carried Arms in do. & was taken prisoner at Carlisle	Carlisle, prisoner.
do.	Served as a private man, surrendered himself to the Min^r after the Battle of Falkirk	at home.
do.	Carried Arms in the Rebel Army being hired by the Country	not known.
do.	Employed and hired as the last above	not known.
do.	Do.	do.
do.	Do.	do.
Perth	Kept a Court as Baron Baillie which he caused fence in the Pretender's name as James the 8th King of Great Brittain &c. & was very active in serving their Interest	at home.

Names.	Designations.	Abode.	Parish.
James Watson	Labouring man	Ketten	Kettens
William Will	Wright	Meggle	Meggle
Y.			
Alex^r Young	Workman	Balintore	Lintrethan
James Young	Servant man	Dundee	Dundee
Robert Young	Residenter	Coupar	Coupar
Dav^d Young	Weaver	Newbiging	Newtyle
Dav^d Yoully	Weaver	do.	do.

County.	Acts of Rebellion and Circumstances.	Where they are.
Forfar	Carried Arms with the Rebels, but deserted going to Falkirk	at home.
Perth	Do. & went to England with the Rebels, was taken in Carlisle	Prisoner.
Angus	Press'd to carry Arms in Ld Ogilvie's Regim^t & deserted after Falkirk Battle	at home.
Forfar	Carried Arms as a Volunteer in s^d Regim^t	not known.
Perth	Carried Arms with the Rebels & was at the Battle of Falkirk & after that	at home.
do.	Do. Being hired by the Country, was at Inverury Skirmish & after that surrend^d himself	do.
do.	Employed as the last above in all respects	do.

A LIST OF PERSONS ENGAGED IN THE
BY MR. EDWARD WYVILL, GENERAL
OF EDINBURGH, PORTSBURGH,

Names.	Designations.	Abode.	Parish.
A.			
James Allan	Merchant	Edinburgh	Edin[r]
Will[m] Aitken	Impost Waiter	do.	do.
John Anandale	Shoemaker	Arbroath	Arbroath
John Aikman	Porter	Leith	Leith
Charles Allen	Cooper's Servant	do.	do.
B.			
Will[m] Brodie	Gunsmith	Canongate	Canongate
John Break	Merchant	Edin[r]	Edin[r]
James Brand	Son to Alex. Brand, Watchmaker	do.	do.
John Bayne	Serv[t] to Murray of Brughton	Brughton	Brughton
John Bowie	Journyman Taylor	Canongate head	Edin[r]
Donald Bain	Labourer	Dunrobin	
William Bain	Inn keeper	Fountainbridge	St. Cuthberts
Pat[k] Buchard	Smith	Benvie	
Tho[s] Boswald	Writer	Edin[r]	Edin[r]

REBELLION, GIVEN IN TO THE BOARD SURVEYOR, AND THE SURVEYORS CANONGATE AND LEITH.

County.	Acts of Rebellion and Circumstances.	Where they now are.
Mid Lothian	Carried Arms in the Pretender's Son's Life Guards	not known.
do.	Accompanyed Ld Elcho as his servant in the Rebellion	do.
Forfar	Carried Arms as a Volunteer in the Rebel Army	do.
Mid Lothian	Assisted in Riffling the Old Stage Coach Lofts of their Horses provisions & carried them to the Rebels whom he likeways assisted in driving their Waggons, &c.	about Leith.
do.	Bore Arms, wore a white Cockade & went into England with the Rebels	not known.
do.	Beat up & Recruited men & Levied money in the Country for the Rebel Service	Lurking in Town.
do.	Carried Arms at the Battle of Preston & wore a white Cockade	at home.
do.	Commanded a party of Rebel Hussars & assisted in levying the Cess at Selkirk &c.	not known.
Tweedale	Had a Command in the Rebel Hussars & was very active in Seizing Horses &c. for their use	Lurk^g about Edin^r.
Mid Lothian	Carried Arms in the Rebel Army	not known.
	Carried Arms in the Rebel Army	not known.
Mid Lothian	Do. & was very active in oppressing the Country by Seizing horses, &c.	do.
	Carried Arms in the Rebel Army	do.
Mid Lothian	Do. in the Pretender's Son's Life Guards	not known.

Names.	Designations.	Abode.	Parish.
Alex^r Banks	Weaver	Bonnington Mills	Leith
Robt Bisset	Brickmaker	Leith	do.
Dav^d Beatt	Merchant	do.	do.
Alex^r Brymer	Baxter	do.	do.
John Brown	Vintiner	do.	do.
Bruce	do.	do.	do.
Robt Brymer	Son to Alex. Brymer Baxter	do.	do.

C.

John Congleton	Surgeon	Edin^r	Edinburgh
John Cairns	Merchant	do.	do.
Mr And^w Craw	Living at	Netherie	
Henry Clark	Gentleman	Canongate	Canongate
Cameron	of Lochiel		
Andrew Cooper	Servt to a Cooper	Leith	Leith
Edwd Callender	Journeyman Goldsmith	Edin^r	Edin^r
Alex^r Coutts	a Goldsmith's Servant	do.	do.
Charles Colquhoune	Wright	Pleasents	St. Cuthberts
And^w Cooper	Son to Dav^d Cooper Gardner	Canongate	Canongate

D.

Robert Drummond	Messenger at Arms	Edinburgh	Edinb^r
Alex^r Davidson	Shoemaker	Cowgate of Edin^r	do.
Walter Drummond	Porter	Leith	Leith

County.	Acts of Rebellion and Circumstances.	Where they now are.
MidLothian	Carried Arms as a Volunteer in the Rebel Army	not known.
do.	Joined the Rebels at Dalkeith & carried Arms	Leith prison.
do.	Carried Arms in the Pretender's Son's Life Guards	not known.
do.	Forced out his son to go into the Rebellion	at home.
do.	With a party of Rebels took a Horse from Thos Mill at Leith	at home.
do.	Went into the Rebellion & carried Arms	not known.
do.	Carried Arms in the Rebellion but forced by his Father	at home.
do.	Carried Arms as a Volunteer in the Rebel Army	not known.
do.	Do.	do.
do.	Carried Arms in the Pretender's Son's Life Guards	do.
do.	Carried Arms in the Rebel Army and Robed Mr Scot's House	Carlisle, Prisoner.
	Was a Coll. in the Rebel Army during the whole Rebellion	not known.
MidLothian	Wore a White Cockade, carried Arms & went to England with the Rebels	do.
do.	Carried Arms as Lieut in the Rebel Army	do.
do.	Carried Arms in the Rebel Army	do.
do.	Do. & was Steward in the Pretender's Son's Cellars & a Commissary for his Army	Lurkg at home.
do.	Carried Arms in the Rebel Army	do.
do.	Carried Arms in the Rebel Army	not known.
do.	Do.	Prisoner.
do.	Carried Arms as a Serjt in Drummond of Perth's Regimt	not known.

Names.	Designations.	Abode.	Parish.
E.			
Alex^r Emly	Shoemaker	Edinburgh	Edinburgh
Erskine	Gentleman	Montrose	Montrose
John Espline	Merchant	Edinb^r	Edinb^r
F.			
John Forbes	Wright	do.	do.
John Falconer	Shoemaker	Pleasents	St. Cuthberths
Gilbert Fife	Taylor	Potterow	Edinburgh
Alex^r Fife	Son to do.	do.	do.
Forbes	Gentleman		
John Ferguson	Taylor & Burges	Edin^r	Edinb^r
John Finlyson	Mathem^k Instrum^t maker	do.	do.
G.			
Richd Giles	Residenter	Canongate	Canongate
Robt Gordon	Alehouse Keeper	Canongate head	Edinb^r
John Goodwillie	Writer	Edinb^r	do.
James Gedd	Printer	do.	do.
James Grant	Do. & News Writer	do.	do.
John Gordon	Weaver	do.	do.
John Graham	Barber	do.	do.
Walter Grant	do.	do.	do.
John Grant	do.	do.	do.
Walter Gordon	Painter	do.	do.
Thomas Gow	Shoemaker	Potteraw	
George Gordon	Inkeeper	West Port Edin^r	St. Cuthberts
Robert Gordon	of Becomie		

EDINBURGH AND PRECINCTS—*Continued.* 249

County.	Acts of Rebellion and Circumstances.	Where at present.
MidLothian	Carried Arms as a Volunteer with the Rebels	Edin^r Lurking.
Forfar	Inlisted Men for the Pretender's Service	not known.
MidLothian	Carried Arms being one of the Rebel Hussars	do.
do.	Carried Arms as a Volunteer in the Rebel Army	not known.
do.	Do. do.	do.
do.	Seen under Arms & in the Livery of the Rebel Life Guards	do.
do.	Employed	do.
	Attended the Pretender's Son under Arms	not known.
do.	Carried Arms in the Rebel Army	do.
do.	was Employed about the Rebel Artillery	do.
do.	Carried Arms in the Rebel Army	not known.
do.	Employed as above	Lurk^g about Ed^r.
do.	Wore Tartans with a White Cockade & assisted in Levying the Revenues &c.	not known.
do.	Acted as printer for the Rebels	Prisoner.
do.	Was Lieu^t in the Rebel Army & printed several Treasonable papers for them	not known.
do.	Carried Arms in the Rebel Army	do.
do.	Carried Arms in do. as a Volunteer	do.
do.	Do. as do.	do.
do.	Do. do.	do.
do.	Carried Arms in the Rebel Life Guards	do.
do.	Carried Arms as a Rebel Hussar	do.
do.	Entered a Volunteer in the Rebel Army	do.
do.	Carried Arms in do.	

LIST OF REBELS IN

Names.	Designations.	Abode.	Parish.
H.			
Thomas Halliburton	Carpenter	Dundee	Dundee
John Henryson	Pupil for the Excise	Edinburgh	Edinburgh
George Hamilton	of Redhouse	Edinb^r	do.
James Hepburn Riccart	of Keith	Canong^t	Canong^t
George Hume	son to Alex^r Hume Writer deceast	Edinburg	Edin^r
Dav^d Hodge	Porter	Leith	Leith
Charles Hacket	Barber	Edin^r	Edin^r
Patrick Hay	Workman	do.	do.
I.			
James Johnston	Late a Cadet in Lee's Regim^t	Edinb^r	do.
Andrew Johnston	Late Servt to the D. of Hamilton	Abbay	Canongate
James Johnston	Son to Jas. Johnston, Merch^t	Edinb^r	Edinb^r
K.			
Arch^d Kennedy	Goldsmith Apprentice	Edinb^r	Edinb^r
Patrick Keir	Wright	Moulhicy hills	St. Cuthberts
Mark Kerr	Pupil for the Excise	Edinburgh	Edinb^r
L.			
Andrew Lumsdaile	Writer	Edinb^r	do.
Simon Lugtoun	Taylor	do.	do.
Alex^r Lindsay	Shoemaker	Canong^t head	do.
James Lauder	Merch^t	Potterow	St. Cuthberts
James Lauder	Merch^t Apprentice	Edin^r	Edinb^r

County.	Acts of Rebellion and Circumstances.	Where they now are.
Forfar.	Carried Arms in the Rebel Army & was active in pressing Horses	not known.
MidLothian	Employ'd as the above—about	Ed^r Lurking.
do.	Was Capt. of Hussars in the Rebel Service	Eng^d prisoner.
do.	Carried Arms in the Rebel Life Guards, said to be Captain	not known.
do.	Carried Arms with the Rebels—said to be in	Eng^d prisoner.
do.	Employed as John Aikman in this List	at home.
do.	Was a Volunteer in the Rebel Army	not known.
do.	Do.	do.
do.	Was a Captain of Volunteers in the Rebel Service	not known.
do.	Carried Arms in the Rebel Army	Carlisle, prisoner.
do.	Was a Captain in the D. of Perth's Regim^t	not known.
do.	Carried Arms in the Rebel Army	not known.
do.	Do.	Lurk^g near home.
do.	Commanded as Lieu^t in the Rebel Army	not known.
do.	Carried Arms in the Rebel Army as a Volunteer	not known.
do.	Employed as the above	Ed^r Prison.
do.	Do.—about	Ed^r Lurking.
do.	Carried Arms in the Rebel Life Guards	not known.
do.	Carried Arms in do.	do.

LIST OF REBELS IN

Names.	Designations.	Abode.	Parish.
M.			
Robert Mitchell	Journeyman Gold-Smith	Edin^r	Edin^r
Anthony Murray	do.	do.	do.
Kenneth M'Kenzie	do.	do.	do.
Marmduke M'Beath	Pouder Flask maker	Canongate	Canongate
Alex^r M'Kenzie	Shoemaker & Shopkeeper	do.	do.
Robert Maxwell	Writer	Edin^r	Edin^r
John Mitchell	Alehouse keeper, Servt to Ld Elcho	Canongate	Canongate
John M'Grigor	Gardner	Back of Canongate	South Leith
Thomas Mitchell	Goldsmith	Potterow	St. Cuthberts
Willm Mushet	Wright	Edinburgh	Edin^r
John M'Naughton	Journeyman Watchmaker	Canongate head	Edinb^r
Mr John Menzies	Gentleman	Edinburgh	do.
Henry Maul	Writer	do.	do.
Pat^k Middleton	Surgeon	do.	do.
James Murray	do.	do.	do.
John Murray	do.	do.	do.
Richd Morrison	Barber	do.	do.
Robert Murray	Writer	Edinb^r	do.
Alex^r Miller	Servt to Ld Geo. Murray	Benvie	
Adolphus Muir	Servt to James Reid	Leith	Leith
Hector M'Lean	do.	do.	do.
Sir David Murray	Knight Baronet	Leith	do.

EDINBURGH AND PRECINCTS—*Continued.*

County.	Acts of Rebellion and Circumstances.	Where they now are.
MidLothian	Carried Arms in the Rebel Army	not known.
do.	Do.	do.
do.	Do.	do.
do.	Was one of the Hussars & very active in Levying money for the Rebels, with them at all the Battles & to the End—about	Ed^r Lurking.
do.	Carried Arms in the Rebel Army	not known.
do.	Do.	at home.
do.	Carried Arms, was at Preston Battle & carried off a Dragoon horse from thence & was in the Rebellion to the end	at home.
do.	Carried Arms & was at the Battle of Preston	not known.
do.	Was in Arms as a Rebel Hussar	do.
do.	Carried Arms in the Pretender's Son's Life Guards	do.
do.	Was at Preston Battle & boasted that he kill'd Co^{ll} Gardner there	Carlisle, prisoner.
do.	Captain of Volunteers in the Rebel Army	not known.
do.	Carried Arms as a Volunteer in the Rebel Army	do.
do.	Carried Arms in the Rebel Life Guards	do.
do.	Carried Arms as a Volunteer in the Rebel Army	do.
do.	Employed as the last above	do.
do.	Served the Pretenders & went along with him as his Barber	Leith prison.
do.	Carried Arms in the Pretender's Son's Life Guards	Carlisle, prisoner.
do.	Served his Master in the Rebellion	not known.
do.	Assisted in pillaging the Old Stage Coach Lofts & carrying off provisions for the Rebel horses	at home.
do.	Was forced out into the Rebellion by his said Master	at home.
do.	Was a Captain of the Rebel Hussars & very active in seizing horses for their use	York, prisoner.

Names.	Designations.	Abode.	Parish.
N.			
David Neavy	Merchant	Edinburgh	Edin^r
James Nicolson	Coffeehouse keeper	Leith	Leith
Robert Nuccol	Mason	Canongate	Canongate
O.			
Walter Orrock	Shoemaker & Council Deacon	Edinb^r	Edinb^r
P.			
John Petrie	Alehouse keeper	Cowgate	do.
Charles Paterson	Carter's Servant	Leith	Leith
John Punton	Porter	do.	do.
James Pith	do.	do.	do.
R.			
James Reid	Innkeeper	Leith	Leith
Adolphus Riddel	Glasier	do.	do.
Robert Rutherfoord	Shoemaker	Potterow	Edinb^r
Alex^r Reid	Journeyman Goldsmith	Edin^r	do.

EDINBURGH AND PRECINCTS—*Continued.* 255

County.	Acts of Rebellion and Circumstances.	Where they now are.
MidLothian	Carried Arms as a Volunteer in the Rebel Army	not known.
do.	had a Commiss^n in the Rebel Army & bore Arms wearing a White Cockade	London, prisoner.
do.	Carried Arms & greatly oppress'd the Country in Seizing horses, Arms &c. for the Rebels' use	about Ed^r lurking.
do.	The Day of Preston Battle came riding furiously up the Canongate with a white Cockade, crying Victory, Victory, the Prince has won the Day, and alighting at the Netherbow Port, shut it against the flying Soldiers, by which means severals of them fell into the hands of the Rebels	at Dubbie side near Leven in Fife.
do.	Carried off several Dragoon horses from Preston Battle, wearing Soldiers accoutraments besmear'd with Blood, & a white Cockade	Carlisle, prisoner.
do.	Assisted in taking & carrying provisions to the Rebel horses & driving their waggons, etc.	about Leith.
do.	Was in the Rebellion & served as Carter to the Rebels	Leith.
do.	Employed as above	do.
do.	Had a Commission from the Rebels as provisor for their Horses, Riffled the Old Stage Coach Lofts of Corn & Hay for their use & managed & directed their Waggons, etc.	at home & appearing publickly.
do.	Employed as Charles Paterson above	at home.
do.	Carried Arms as a Volunteer in the Rebel Army	about Ed^r lurking.
do.	Carried Arms in the Rebel Army	not known.

Names.	Designations.	Abode.	Parish.
James Rutherfoord	Journeyman Goldsmith	Edin^r	Edinb^r
Thomas Robertson	Servt to Peter Spalding, Goldsmith		
S.			
James Smith	Writer	Edin^r	Edinb^r
Andrew Symers	Bookseller	do.	do.
Andrew Swan	Shoemaker	Canongate head	do.
Robert Seton	Son to Wm Seton, Writer to the Signet	Edin^r	do.
James Simpson	Writer	do.	do.
Charles Stuart	Wright	Canongate	Canongate
Archibald Stratton	Watchmaker	Edin^r	Edin^r
Dougald Souter	Messenger at Arms	do.	do.
Alex^r Stivenson	Journeyman Wright	Cowgate of Ed^r	do.
William Spark	Porter	Leith	Leith
George Scott	do.	do.	do.
Alex^r Stiven	do.	do.	do.
Robert Scott	Baxter	do.	do.
T.			
John Tyrie	Carter's Servant	do.	do.
Walter Todd	Tanner	Edinb^r	Edinb^r
Adam Tait	Goldsmith	do.	do.
James Thores	Weaver	do.	do.
W.			
Wilson	Son to Mr Wilson, Ex-Officer	near Dundee	

EDINBURGH AND PRECINCTS—Continued.

County.	Acts of Rebellion and Circumstances.	Where they now are.
MidLothian	Carried Arms in the Rebel Army	at home.
do.	Do.	the City Guard.
do.	Carried Arms in the Pretender's Son's Life Guards	Edin^r, Prisoner.
do.	Carried Arms as a Volunteer in the Rebel Army	not known.
do.	Do.	Ed^r prison.
do.	Carried Arms in the Rebel Life Guards	not known.
do.	Acted as a Clerk to the Rebel Artillary	do.
do.	Was a Lieu^t in the Rebel Army & as such mounted Guard in the Canongate	do.
do.	Seen dismounting Dragoons on their flight from Preston & seizing their Horses &c.	at home.
do.	Carried Arms in the Rebel Army	not known.
do.	Do. & was Wright to the Artillary Carriages	do.
do.	Assisted in taking & carrying Provisions to the Rebels' Horses & driving their carts	at home.
do.	Employed as the last above	do.
do.	Wore a White Cockade publickly (See St. Andrews List)	do.
do.	Carried Arms & prompted the Rebels to pillage the Customhouse of Leith	at home.
do.	Employed as William Spark above	at home.
do.	Carried Arms in the Rebel Army during the whole Rebellion	about Ed^r Lurking.
do.	Carried Arms as a Rebel Hussar	not known.
do.	Was a Volunteer in the Rebel Army	do.
Forfar	Carried Arms and mounted Guard with the Rebels	do.

Names.	Designations.	Abode.	Parish.
Wilson	Innkeeper	Edinburgh	Edinburgh
James Windrum	Son to Windrum of Eyemouth	Abbayhill	South Leith
James Walker	Journyman Candle-maker	Canongate	Canongate
David Wymes	Ld Elcho		
Mr Robt Wright	Gentleman	Edinburgh	Edinburgh
Willm Wilson	Turner	do.	do.
John Wilson	Barber	Canongate	Canongate
William White	Innkeeper	Edin^r	Edin^r

County.	Acts of Rebellion and Circumstances.	Where they now are.
MidLothian	Inlisted Men for the Pretender's Service	not known.
do.	Carried Arms in the Pretender's Son's Life Guards	do.
do.	Carried Arms, was at Preston Battle & wore a White Cockade	at home.
	Was Collonel of the Rebel Life Guards during the whole Rebellion	in France.
do.	a Volunteer in the Rebel Service	not known.
do.	Carried Arms in the Rebel Life Guards	do.
do.	Was a Volunteer in the Rebel Service	do.
do.	Served in the Rebel Train of Artillary	do.

A LIST OF PERSONS CONCERNED IN THE BOARD BY MR. JOHN EXCISE AT

Names.	Designations.	Abode.	County.
A.			
William Aitkin	Servant to Lord Elcho		Fife
B.			
David Boswell	Merchant	Dubbieside	do.
William Balfour	Surgeon	Aberdour	do.
Alexander Balfour	Farmer	Collenburgh	do.
F.			
Duncan Forbes	Indweller	Kirkaldy	do.
G.			
Alexander Gall	Late Salt Officer	Kirkaldy	do.
H.			
Robert Hamilton	Younger of Kilbrachmant	Kilbrachmant	do.
David Houston	Smith	Wester Weems	do.

THE REBELLION, TRANSMITTED TO CAMPBELL, SUPERVISOR OF KIRKALDY.

Acts of Rebellion and Circumstances.	Where they now are.
Accompanied his said Master in the Rebellion	not known.
Joined the Rebels & carried Arms in Ld Pitsligo's Regiment	Lurking.
Joined the Rebels and went into England with them	not known.
Assisted the Rebels & Transported a Cart Load of Arms from Collensburgh to Faukland for their use	at home.
Concealed two Rebells in his house for which was apprehended but liberate	at home.
Joined the Rebels after Preston Battle & with a strong party & great Rigour collected the Excise for them to a considerable extent & granted his Receipts therefor	not known.
Joined the Rebels & was at Preston Battle. Returned home soon after where he has ever since continued. N.B. he is disordered in his Judgment	at home.
Suspected of Treasonable Practices, was apprehended but admitted to Baill	at home.

Names.	Designations.	Abode.	County.
M.			
James Malcolm	Younger of Balbeddie	Balbeddie	Fife
Alexr M'farlane	Scool Doctor	Kinghorn	do.
Robert M'Connie	Brewer	Drumachie	do.
Arch{d} M'Knoby	Servant	Damhead of Aberdour	do.
S.			
Alexr Seton	Merchant	Dubbieside	do.
James Seton	Apprentice to Wm Robertson	Sawmill near Leven	do.
John Stuart	Indweller	Kirkaldy	do.
Christopher Seton	Merchant	Methil	do.
David Seton	Salt Greive to the Laird of Lundin	Drumachie	do.
John Seton	Baxter	Kennoway	do.
T.			
Alexr Tasker	Servant to Mrs Brand	Kinghorn	do.
John Tydieman	Servt to Ld Elcho		do.
W.			
William Wordie	Merchant	Leven	do.
Samuel Wood	Servt to Kilbrachmant Junr	Kilbrachmant	do.
Robert White	Gardner	Linktoun of Arnot	do.
Robert Ushet	Servt to J{no} Stones, Carrier	Aberdour	do.

KIRKCALDY—*Continued.* 263

Acts of Rebellion and Circumstances.	Where they now are.
Joined the Rebels & assisted them in collecting the Excise	not known.
Suspected of assisting in the Escape of the two Rebels found in Duncan Forbes house	Prisoner.
Was engaged in the Rebellion, active in robing the Country of Horses, &c.	hanged by the Rebels.
Joined the Rebels	not known.
Joined the Rebels before Preston Battle, acted as deputy Coll^r of Excise under the Earl of Kelly, & on his Collection was alwayes attended by a strong party of Rebels	Lurking.
Joined in the Earl of Cromarty's Rebel Regim^t & was wounded at the Battle of Culloden	Perth, Prisoner.
Joined the Rebels & continued with them to the End	Escaped to England
Aided & assisted the Rebels & was along with a party searching the Ex: officer's house for himself & Books	at home.
Assisted the Rebels & concealed two of them in his house since their defeat	Lurking.
Joined the Rebels after Preston Battle. Left them in a fourthnight & has since followed his business	at home.
Left his Service & Joined the Rebel Army	not known.
Attended his said Master in the Rebellion	do.
Joined the Rebel Army before Preston in the Pretender's Son's Life Guards	do.
Attended his said Master at Preston Battle	at home.
Engaged himself in the Rebellion	Lurking.
Do.	Prisoner.

A LIST OF PERSONS ENGAGED IN THE BOARD BY MR. CHRISTOPHER EXCISE AT

Names.	Designations.	Abode.	County.
A.			
John Aitkenhead	Younger of Jaw	Slamanan Parish	Stirling
James Ancrum	Salt Greive	Cuffabouts	Linlithgow
B.			
Mr Charles Boyd	Second son to Kilmarnock	Callander house	do.
George Boyd	Servant to do.	do.	do.
Willm Baird	Coalhewer to do.		
D.			
Alexr Dalmahoy	Son to Sir Alexr Dalmahoy	Thirleston	do.
William Donaldson	Gardner	Grange Pans	do.
David Davert	Gardner to Kilmarnock	Callender house	do.
John Denothy	Servt to Mr Charles Boyd, above	do.	do.
G.			
Thomas Glassfoord	Son to Duncan Glasfoord	Ship Mr, Borrowstounness	do.
Walter Graham, son	to the deceased Wal. Graham	Surgeon, Falkirk	

REBELLION TRANSMITTED TO THE SETON, SUPERVISOR OF LINLITHGOW.

Acts of Rebellion and Circumstances.	Where they now are.
Carried Arms in the Rebel Life Guards & was active in Robing the Country of Horses	Lurking.
Assisted in taking & Carrying off two Dragoon horses out of Kinneil parks for the Rebels use	Prisoner.
Acted as a Captain in the Pretender's Son's Life Guards	Lurking.
Carried Arms in the Rebellion	Prisoner.
Do.	Prisoner.
Carried Arms in the Rebel Life Guards, assisted in Carrying off two Dragoon horses from the Parks of Kinneil & in Levying the Excise & Malt Duty for the Rebels	not known.
Servant to the above Alex^r Dalmahoy in the Rebellion	Leith prison.
Carried Arms in the Rebel Service—said to be	kill'd.
Do.	York Goal.
Carried Arms in the Pretender's Son's Life Guards	Lurking.
Acted as Surgeon in the Rebel Army	not known.

LIST OF REBELS FROM

Names.	Designations.	Abode.	County.
H.			
Norwald Home	Brother to Boghall		
James Harvie	Innkeeper	Linlithgow	Linlithgow
K.			
Kilmarnock	Earl William	Callender house	do.
L.			
James Livingston	Late post master	Falkirk	
M.			
John Menzies, son	to Robt Menzies late Innkeeper	St. Ninians	Stirling
Alex^r M'Leod, son	to Mr John M'Leod, Advocate	Muiravenside	
William M'Culloch	Servant to Kilmarnock	Callender house	Linlithgow
Henry Maul	a clark in the Stamp Office	Edinb^r	Mid Lothian
O.			
James Ogston	Weaver	Grange pans	Linlithgow
R.			
James Robertson	Servant to the Laird of Houstoun	Houstoun	
S.			
Charles Shaddon	Coal Grive to Kilmarnock		
James Semple	Weaver	Borrowstouness	Linlithgow

Acts of Rebellion and Circumstances.	Where they now are.
Went to Glasgow & received the money with the Rebels which they Extorted from that City	Lurking.
Carried Arms as Quarter Master in Kilmarnock's Troop	Prisoner.
Was Lieut. Coll. in Pitsligo's Horse & uplifted 12^{sh} & 6^d from a Distiller as his Excise	Beheaded.
Carried Arms in the Rebel Life Guards	Lurking.
Was Paymaster in Menzies of Schian's Regim^t	not known.
Was engaged in the Rebellion	do.
Carried Arms in the Rebellion	Prisoner.
Carried Arms with the Rebels & was most active in Seizing Horses for their use	not known.
Carried Arms in the Rebel Life Guards, assisted in carrying off his Majes. Dragoon Horses from Kinneil parks & in Levying the Excise for the Rebels	not known.
Engaged & went as Groom with Ld George Murray into the Rebellion	do.
Carried Arms in the Rebellion	York Goal.
Do. in Kilmarnock's Troop & was active in seizing horses, &c.	Prisoner.

Names.	Designations.	Abode.	County.
Alex^r Smith	Son to Thomas Smith, Writer	Linlithgow	Linlithgow
Alex^r Smith	Writer	dinburgh	Mid Lothian
W.			
Ninian Wise			
Henry Wardlaw,	son to John Wardlaw, Factor to the Late	Earl of Wigttown,	near Falkirk

LINLITHGOW DISTRICT—*Continued.*

Acts of Rebellion and Circumstances.	Where they now are.
Carried Arms in the Pretender's Son's Life Guards	Lurking.
Carried Arms in the Rebel Life Guards & was active in seizing horses	not known.
Attended his Master in the Rebellion	do.
Served in the Rebel Life Guards & assisted in seizing horses for that Regimt.	do.

A LIST OF PERSONS ENGAGED IN THE BOARD BY MR. WALTER STUART

Names.	Designations.	Abode.
C.		
Hector Campbell	Tenent	Haustrie
M.		
Kenneth M'Keamish	do.	Cathele
S.		
Donald Steuart	do.	Quoycrook
George Sinclair	of Geese	Hoburnhead
Benjamin Sinclair	Tenent	Brackie

REBELLION TRANSMITTED TO THE COLL^R OF EXCISE IN CAITHNESS.

Rebellion and Circumstances.	Where they now are.
Joined the Rebels when in Caithness, but being taken in Sutherland was Shipped for London	Prisoner.
Joined Do. & was in Arms attending Donald Stuart beating up for Volunteers for that Service	not known.
Joined the Rebel Army & beat for men for that Service in the Streets of Thurso attend^d by a party of armed men	do.
Joined the Rebels at Caithness, was taken prisoner in Sutherland & shipped for London	Prisoner.
Joined the Rebels & went to Sutherland with them	not known.

A LIST OF PERSONS ENGAGED IN THE BOARD BY MR. SAMUEL OF GLASGOW

Names.	Designations.	Abode.	Parish.
G. Grigor Grant	Glass grinder	Glasgow	Glasgow
W. Andrew Wood	Shoemaker	do.	do.

REBELLION TRANSMITTED TO THE M'CORMICK, SUPERVISOR 1st DISTRICT.

County.	Acts of Rebellion and Circumstances.	Where they now are.
Lanerk	Joined the Rebels at Glasgow & went off with them	not known.
do.	was a Captain in the Rebel Army, was at the Battle of Culloden & there	taken prisoner.

A LIST OF PERSONS ENGAGED IN THE BOARD BY MR. WILLIAM BLACK, GLASGOW

Names.	Designations.	Abode.	Parish.
B.			
Peter Bell		Glasgow	Glasgow
D.			
Robert Duff	Painter	do.	do.
F.			
Rob[t] Finnie	Serv[t] to Craigbarneth	Burry	Campsie
G.			
John Graham	of Kilmordinny	Clobar, w[t] the Laird of Mains	
John Graham	Painter	Glasgow	Glasgow
Will[m] Gray	Weaver	Gorbals of Glasgow	Meikle Govan

REBELLION, TRANSMITTED TO THE SUPERVISOR OF EXCISE IN 2ND DISTRICT.

County.	Acts of Rebellion and Circumstances.	Where they now are.
Lanerk	Joined in the Rebel Life Guards at Glasgow on their Retreat, Influenced by his mother	Prisoner.
do.	Listed with the Rebels after Preston Battle & continued to the End	do.
	Carried Arms with the Rebels, was at Preston Battle & acted as a Spy in Campsie	fled the country.
Lanerk	Was Aid du Camp to Ld Strathallan & Lieutenant in his Regiment, he was some years ago an Ensign in the Holland Service in a Scots Regim^t	not known.
	Inlisted with the Rebels on their Retreat from Eg^d & left them on their flight to Inverness	at home.
do.	Pedee to one Smith in the Rebel Life Guards who enticed him, he is only 15 years of age & engaged when the main Body lay at Glasgow	not known.

Names.	Designations.	Abode.	Parish.
H.			
Robert Hamilton	Sailor	Woodside near Glasgow	
R.			
Thomas Robertson	Journeyman Barber	Gorbals of Glasgow	Meikle Govan
S. & W.			
James Stirling	of Keir	Calder near Glasgow	Calder
Hugh Stirling	Son to the Laird of Keir	do.	do.
William Stirling	do.	do.	do.
James Stirling	of Craigbarnet	Burry	Campsie

GLASGOW 2ND DISTRICT—*Continued.* 277

County.	Acts of Rebellion and Circumstances.	Where they now are.
Lanerk	Joined in the very beginning of the Rebellion & was in the Life Guards, was in the party that disarmed the well affected in Baldernock, there was a Warrand agt. him prior to the Rebellion for carrying over to the French Service men raised in the Highlands	Fled south.
do.	Inlisted in the Rebel Army & continued to the End	not known.
do.	A zealous ffriend for the Pretender's Interest, was in the Rebellion 1715 & Influenced his two sons after mentioned to join them now by going to Edin^r & presenting them to the Pretender's Son, he was Closs with the Rebels at Glasgow & prompted them to vex & oppress the Inhabitants, on news of the defeat fled his house	Dumbarton Castle pris^r.
do.	Joined the Rebels at or immediately after Battle of Preston, was one of the party which came with Hay to raise the first contribution at Glasgow being 4500 lib. He came South on the defeat at Culloden, was apprehended & Imprisoned in Dumbarton Castle, from thence made his Escape & is now said to be	Isle of Man Prisoner.
do.	Employed by the Rebels as his Brother above & made his Escape from Culloden	not known.
	Carried Arms in the Rebel Life Guards, was wounded at the Battle of Preston & its said he shot a soldier there when the poor man was begging quarter, he committed a great many outrages in the parish of Campsie & Escaped with Hugh Stirling as above, he's possesst of an Estate of 500 mks. yearly	In the Isle of Man prisoner.

Names.	Designations.	Abode.	Parish.
James Stirling	Son to the Laird of Northside	Glasgow	Glasgow
Andrew Sprewl	Writer	Gaudbridge	
Pat^k Stuart	Servt to the Late Coll. Stuart,	Hamilton	Hamilton
Walter Stuart	Servt to Craigbarnet	Burry	Campsie
Robert White	painter	Glasgow	Glasgow

GLASGOW 2ND DISTRICT—*Continued.* 279

County.	Acts of Rebellion and Circumstances.	Where they now are.
Lanerk	Influenced by his Father joined early in the Rebellion, was of the Command that came to Glasgow for money, he was a Volunteer in a Brit^h Reg^t at the Battle of Dettingen	not known.
	Was a Capt in the Rebel ffoot till their dispersion, he used to practise his Business at Ed^r	Prisoner.
Lanerk	Carried Arms in the Rebel Life Guards & was active in seizing horses	not known.
	Carried Arms in the Rebel Army, went to Eng^d with them & returned again	not known.
	Carried Arms amongst the Athole men	Prisoner.

A LIST OF PERSONS ENGAGED IN THE BOARD BY MR. HENRY OF EXCISE

Names.	Designations.	Abode.	Parish.
D.			
Thomas Davidson	Residenter	Kelso	Kelso
K.			
Henry Kerr	of Greden		
M.			
Robert Moir	an Idle young fellow		
S.			
Charles Scot	Brother to Gordonberry		
Francis Scot	Barber	Hawick	Hawick

REBELLION TRANSMITTED TO THE ARMSTRONG, SUPERVISOR AT KELSO.

County.	Acts of Rebellion and Circumstances.	Where they now are.
Teviotdale	Carried Arms with the Rebels but in what Station not known, he is frequently Lunatick & has a wife & several children living upon charity	at home.
do.	Joined the Rebel Army	Prisoner.
	Joined the Rebel Army at Edinburgh	not known.
Tiviotdale	Was sometime Chamberlain to Buccleugh, Joined the Rebel Army	do.
Forrest	Carried Arms with the Rebels & was active in Robing the Country	Lurking.

A LIST OF PERSONS ENGAGED IN THE
BY MR. JAMES M'PHUN, COLLECTOR

Names.	Designations and Abode.
C.	
Alex^r Cameron	of Dungallan
Alex^r Cameron alias	Stronlia, Maryburgh
Angus Cameron	in Maryburgh
Alex^r Cameron	in do.
Alex^r Cameron in	Altavullin in the Braes of Lochaber
Allan Cameron	of Callart
Allan Cameron	of Lundarva
Alex^r Cameron	Drimnasall
Angus Cameron	in Altavullin
Don^d Cameron	of Lochiel
Don^d Carmichael	Excise Compounder at Cuil in Appin
Duncan Cameron	Brewer in Dalmachornra
Duncan More Cameron	Brewer at 9 mile water in Lochaber Braes
Don^d Cameron	Do. in Callart Ferry
Ewen Cameron	Brewer, West Corran, Braes of Lochaber
Ewen Cameron	Do. in Bonarcaig in Lochaber
Ewen Cameron	Do. in Kilmanivaig in do.
Ewen More Cameron	in Maryburgh
Ewen Cameron	Callart's Uncle
Ewen Cameron	Drimnasail's Brother
Ewen Cameron	of Inverlochy
John Cameron	in Corran, Lochaber
John Cameron	Callart's Uncle
John Carmichael	in Achusragan in Appin
John Cameron	Brewer in Corpich
Malcom Carmichael	Change Keeper at Kintalin, Appin
Malcom Cameron	Commonly called Whiskie

REBELLION TRANSMITTED TO THE BOARD OF ARGYLE NORTH COLLECTION.

Acts of Rebellion and Circumstances.	Where they now are.
Was a Standard Bearer in the Rebel Army	not known.
Was a Serjeant in Rebel Army	do.
Soldier in do.	do.
Do.	do.
Do.	do.
Was Captain in the Rebel Army	Prisoner.
Was Officer in do.	kill'd at Preston.
Was at Fort William Seige & there	kill'd.
Was a Soldier in the Rebel Army	not known.
Collonel in do.	do.
Was a Serjeant in do.	kill'd at Culloden.
Carried Arms in do. & is in arrears for his Duties	not known.
An Officer in Rebel Army & in arrears for do.	do.
a soldier in do. & in arrears for do.	do.
Do. & in arrears	do.
Do. do.	do.
Do. do.	do.
Carried Arms in the Rebel Army	do.
Was an Officer in do. at Fort Wm Seige & there made	Prisoner.
A Rebel Officer wounded at Culloden & since	Dead.
a Captain in the Rebel Army	not known.
Carried Arms in the Rebel Army	do.
an Officer in do. was wounded at Culloden & since	Dead.
Carried Arms in the Rebel Army	Not known.
a Serj^t in do. & in arrears for his Duties	do.
Was a Soldier in do. In arrears, said to be	Dead.
Serjeant in the Rebel Army, was at the Battle of Culloden & there	kill'd.

Names.	Designations and Abode.
L.	
Arch^d Leech	near Kirkmichael of Glasrie
M.	
Alex^r M'Lauchlan	in Ladill, Tidewaiter in the Port of Fort W^m
Alex^r M'Lauchlan	Ledsdail, son to the Laird of Corries
Arch^d M'Phun	Taylor in Kirkmichael of Glasrie
Allan M'Lean	Son to Drimnan in Mull
Arch^d M'Coll	from Kintail in do.
Allan M'Lean	Calgarie's Son from Mull
Angus M'Donald	Younger of Glengarry
Alex^r M'Donald	of Glenco
Alex^r M'Donald	of Keppoch
Arch^d M'Inish	in Maryburgh
Arch^d M'Donald	of Clenaig in Lochaber
Arch^d M'Erick	Glenco's piper's nephew
Charles M'Lean	of Drimnan
Donald M'Donald	Brother to Keppoch
Don^d M'Donald	Tirindrish, Brewer in Lochaber
Duncan M'farlan	once in Achtertyre's Company
Dun. Roy M'Lauchlan	in Ballemore in the Island of Kerera
Duncan M'Lauchlan	Donald Og's son
Duncan M'Lauchlan	in Ardachork
Dun. Dow M'Chombich	from Achosrigan, Appin
Dun. M'Herioch	from do.
Donald M'Coll	Smith in Appin
Duncan M'Intyre	Brewer in Lochielhead
Don^d M'Donald	of Sandaig now Lochgarry
Dougald M'Lauchlan	Son to Ewen M'Lauchlan in Inversanda
Don^d M'Donald	Glenco's Brother
Don^d M'Erich	Glenco's Piper
Don^d M'Inish	the Ferryman's Son at Ballechelish
Duncan M'Charmaig	in Achosrigan in Appin
Hugh M'Laren	Brother to Doctor M'Laren in do.
Hugh Roy M'Coll	in Appin
Hugh M'Coll	in Glenstockidal in Appin
Hugh M'Lean	Kilmorie's Son from Mull
Hugh M'Coll	from Aros in Mull
Jas. M'Donald	Glenco's Brother

ARGYLE NORTH COLLECTION—*Continued.*

Acts of Rebellion and Circumstances.	Where they now are.
Carried Arms in the Rebel Army	not known.
Made Major in the Rebel Army, was taken & sent to	London, prisoner.
was Captain in do. & being an Excise Compounder in arrears for his Duties	not known.
Carried Arms in do.	do.
Was an Officer in do.	do.
Carried Arms in do.	do.
was Lieut. in the Rebel Army	do.
was a Collonel in do.	kill'd at Falkirk.
was a Captain in do.	not known.
was Collonel in do.	do.
was a Soldier in do.	do.
was an Officer in do.	do.
Was with the Rebels in Arms	do.
Was an Officer in the Rebel Army	do.
Was a Captain in do.	do.
was a Captain in do. was taken prisoner at Falkirk & sent to	London.
Deserted & Joined the Rebel Army	not known.
Carried Arms in do.	do.
a Soldier in the Rebel Army	do.
Do.	do.
Do.	do.
Do.	do.
Do.	do.
Do. & in Arrears for his Duties	do.
Was Captain in the Rebel Army	do.
Was an Officer in do.	do.
Was an Officer in do.	do.
was with the Rebels	do.
Carried Arms in the Rebel Army	Dead.
Was a Soldier in the Rebel Army	not known.
Do.	do.
Do.	do.
Do.	do.
Was Captain in the Rebel Army	do.
was Soldier in do.	do.
Was an Officer in the Rebel Army	do.

Names.	Designations and Abode.
John M‘Donald	in Inverlochy
John M‘Donald	Brewer in Altavullin
John M‘Kenzie	in Ballachelish
John M‘Coll	Brewer's son at Portnarosh in Appin
John M‘Coll	Sometime in Benderloch
John M‘Kenzie	in Maryburgh
John M‘Lauchlan	Kerera Ferry, Brewer
John M‘Lauchlan	Weaver, in Balimore in Kerrera
John M‘Lean	Brother to Kingerloch
Jas. M‘Lauchlan	in Morvern
Mr Jon M‘Lauchlan	of Kilchoan
Ken. M‘Lauchlan	of Kilinuchanich
Lauchn M‘Lauchlan	of that Ilk
Lauchn M‘Lauchlan	of Inishconel
Lauchn M‘Laren	Doctor in Appin
Lauchn M‘Lean	Natural son to Drimnan
Lauchn M‘Lauchlan	son to the miller of Kilmiln in Appin
M‘Donald	of Kinloch Moidart
Nicol M‘Alman	Brewer in Morvern
Neil M‘Lauchlan	in Balimore in Kerrera
Patk M‘Kaog	in Kerrera
Rond M‘Donald	in Morvern
Rond M‘Donald	Glengarry's Brother in Lochaber
Rond M‘Donald	Clenaig's Brother
Willm M‘Donald	Glengarry's Brother

R.

Duncan Ranken	East Corran near Lochaber

S.

Alexr Stewart	of Invernachyle
Allan Stewart	Brewer in Kilmichael of Glassery
Alexr Stewart	Ardsheil's Cusin German from Morvern
Alexr Stewart	Son to James Stewart, Argour
Allan Stewart	Brother to Invernachyle

ARGYLE NORTH COLLECTION—*Continued.* 287

Acts of Rebellion and Circumstances.	Where they now are.
Soldier in the Rebel Army	not known.
Do.	do.
Carried Arms in the Rebel Army	Prisoner.
Was an Officer in the Rebel Army	not known.
Soldier in Rebel Army, said to be forced out	do.
Soldier in do.	do.
Do.	do.
Do.	do.
Capt in the Rebel Army	kill'd at Culloden.
Old Lieutenant	not known.
Joined the Rebels	do.
Adjutant in the Rebel Army & was very active in raising men	do.
Coll. in do. & Levied the Excise, was at the Battle of Culloden & there	kill'd.
Captain in do. was at Culloden Battle & there	kill'd.
Joined the Rebels	not known.
Was an Officer in the Rebel Army	kill'd at Culloden.
Soldier in do.	not known.
an Officer in do. taken at Lesmahagow on his way to England	Prisoner.
an Officer in do.	kill'd.
a Soldier in do.	not known.
Do.	do.
Do.	do.
Joined the Rebels	do.
was an Officer in the Rebel Army	do.
was a Captain in do.	killed.
Was a Soldier in the Rebel Army	not known.
Was an Officer in the Rebel Army, & active in raising Appin's Tenents	do.
Was a Serj^t in Ld Louden's, taken at Preston by the Rebels & since an Officer in their Army	do.
Was a Captain in the Rebel Army	do.
An officer in do.	do.
a Captain in do.	do.

LIST OF REBELS FROM

Names.	Designations or Abode.
Alex[r] Stewart	Brother to Achnacon
Allan Stewart	Son to Dougald Stewart, Maryburgh
Alex. Stewart	of Ballechalish
Charles Stewart	of Ardsheil
Charles Stewart	Nottary Publick in Maryburgh
Dougald Stewart	in Maryburgh
Don[d] Stewart	Brewer in Tycharnan in Appin
Duncan Stewart	Ardshiel's Uncle from Morvern
Duncan Stewart	Change keeper Inverfolla, Appin
Francis Semple	Late Corporal in Invera's Comp[y]
John Glass Stewart	Brother to Acharn
James Stewart	in Morvern, Ardshiel's Cusin German
James Stewart	in Appin, Ardshiel's Brother
John Stewart	Brewer in Creganich, Lismore Isle
Robert Stewart	Son to Duncan, Appin's Factor
Will[m] Stewart	in Morvern, Ardshiel's Cusin German

ARGYLE NORTH COLLECTION—*Continued.* 289

Acts of Rebellion and Circumstances.	Where they now are.
a Captain in the Rebel Army	not known.
was a Serj^t in the Rebel Army, was wounded at Culloden, was apprehended and sent to	London, prisoner.
was a Captain in do. wounded at Culloden & since	Dead.
was Collonel in do.	not known.
The Pretender's Son's Secretary's Clark	do.
Deserted from Auchtertyre's Company & joined the Rebels	do.
was Serj^t in the Rebel Army	do.
was an Officer in do. at the Battle of Falkirk & there	kill'd.
Joined the Rebels	not known.
Deserted to the Rebels	do.
was a Capt in the Rebel Army, was at the Battle of Culloden & there	kill'd.
was an Officer in do.	not known.
Do.	do.
was Serjeant in the Rebel Army	do.
was a Captain, at Preston Battle & there	killed.
was a Lieut. in the Rebel Army & wounded	not known.

A LIST OF PERSONS ENGAGED IN THE BOARD BY MR. DANIEL OF EXCISE AT

Names.	Designations.	Abode.	Parish.
B. Charles Blackie	Sailor	Campbell-toun	Campbell-toun
C. John Cunison	Officer of Excise	do.	do.

REBELLION, TRANSMITTED TO THE M'DONALD, COLLECTOR CAMPBELLTOUN.

County.	Acts of Rebellion and Circumstances.	Where they now are.
Argyle	Joined the Rebells at Edinburgh, & continued with them till disperst	Pr Dumbarton Castle.
do.	Employed as the above, drunk treasonable Healths & spoke disrespectfully of His Royal Highness the Duke of Cumberland	Prisoner in do.

A LIST OF PERSONS ENGAGED IN THE BOARD BY MR. EDWARD EXCISE AT

Names.	Designations.	Abode.	Parish.
C. William Cochran	of Ferguslie	Paisley	Paisley
W. John Weir	Coal hewer	Cathcart	Cathcart

A LIST OF PERSONS ENGAGED IN THE BOARD BY MR. JOHN HARPER,

Names.	Designations.	Abode.	Parish.
M. John M'Donald	Servant to Captain	Chalmers of	Gadyart

REBELLION, TRANSMITTED TO THE YOUNG, SUPERVISOR OF PAISLEY.

County.	Acts of Rebellion and Circumstances.	Where they now are.
Renfrew	Joined & went along with the Rebels & continued till the Last	Lurking.
Lanerk	Employed as the last above in all respects	Lurking.

REBELLION, TRANSMITTED TO THE SUPERVISOR OF EXCISE AT AIR.

County.	Acts of Rebellion and Circumstances.	Where they now are.
Air	Joined the Rebel Army when first at Perth	not known.

A LIST OF PERSONS ENGAGED IN THE BOARD BY MR. ALEX^R HOME,

Names.	Designations.	Abode.	Parish.
H.			
David Home	Son to the deceast Geo. Home of Whitfield		
Willm Home	Son to Pat^k Home late Maltster	Duns	Duns
L.			
Robt Lauder, Junr	of Bailmouth		
Arch^d Lauder	a Boy, Son to Do.		

REBELLION TRANSMITTED TO THE SUPERVISOR OF EXCISE AT DUNS.

County.	Acts of Rebellion and Circumstances.	Where they now are.
Berwick	Joined the Rebels	Prisoners.
do.	Do.	
East Lothian	Joined the Rebels & went with them to England	not known.
do.	Do.	Prisoner.

LIST OF PERSONS CONCERN'D IN THE REBELLION, WITH EVIDENCES TO PROVE THE SAME, TRANSMITTED TO THE COMMISSIONERS OF EXCISE BY THE SEVERAL SUPERVISORS OF EXCISE IN SCOTLAND

INDEX

Districts.	Folio.[1]
Aberdeen .	298
Argyle, South	326
Banff	308
Caithness	324
Dunse .	326
Dunfermline	348
Dundee	351
Elgin .	334
Edin^r. .	338
Glasgow, 1st & 2^d .	346
Kirkaldy	344
Montrose	320
Old Meldrum	302
Paisley [Newport]	326
Ross	328
Stirling .	316
St. Andrews .	352

N.B.—For Wigton, Air, Kilmarnock, Argyle North, Lanark, Perth, Haddington, Jedburgh, Dumfries, & Lithgow Districts no Lists with Evidences to prove the Facts were sent to the Board. the proper Supervisors having acquainted the Comm^s. of Excise that none could be procur'd.

[1] For the folios in the original the pages of this volume are substituted.

A LIST OF PERSONS IN ABERDEEN DISTRICT REBELLION, WITH EVIDENCES TO

Names.	Designations.	Abode.	Parish.	County.
George Alexander	Glover	Spittal	Oldmachar	Aberdeen
John Burnet, Junr	of Campfield	Campfield	Kincarden	do.
Peter Byres	of Toneley	Toneley	Touch	do.
James Duff, Esqr	Son to Hatton	Aberdeen	Aberdeen	do.
Alex. Durom, Junr	Writer's Servt	do.	do.	do.
Peter Duguid	of Auchenhove	Auchenhove	Lumfannan	do.
Hen. Elphinston, Senr	late a Land Waiter	Aberdeen	Aberdeen	do.
James Farquharson, Esq.	of Balmurle	Craigmile	Kincarden	do.
Fra. Farquharson, Esq.	of Monaltry	Brackley	Glenmuch	do.
George Gordon, Esq.	of Hallhead	Aberdeen	Aberdeen	do.
Francis Gordon, Esq.	of Kincarden Miln	do.	do.	do.

WHO HAVE BEEN CONCERN'D IN THE PROVE THE DIFFERENT FACTS.

Yearly rent.	Condition of Mansion House.	Evidences.
70 0 0	Pretty good	Alexander Paterson, Farmer in Todlochy & Parish of Monymusk, William Touch, Servant in Couly in s^d Parish & James Thomson, Town's Serjeant in Aberdeen, all in Aberdeen Shire. James Simpson, Servant in Charlestown in the Parish of Aboyn, John Shaw, Ground Officer there and the above William Towch. James Sinclair, Servt in Kirktown in Aboyn Parish & the s^{ds} James Simpson & John Shaw. Rod^k M'culloch, Town Serjeant in Aberdeen, James Thomson, also Town's Serjeant there and James Sutherland, merchant there.
30 0 0	Burnt	The s^{ds} Rod^k M'culloch, James Thomson & James Sutherland. The s^{ds} James Simpson, John Shaw, James Sutherland & William Touch.
40 0 0	very bad	The s^{ds} Rod^k M'culloch, James Sutherland & James Thomson. The s^{ds} James Simpson, John Shaw & Will. Touch.
50 0 0	Burnt	Do.
400 0 0	Indifferent	The saids James Sutherland, Will. Towch & James Thomson.
30 0 0	do.	Do.

Names.	Designations.	Abode.	Parish.	County.
Alex. Garrioch	Merchant	Aberdeen	Aberdeen	Aberdeen
Francis Gordon	Shoemaker	do.	do.	do.
Charles Gordon	of Blelock	Miln of Galland	Coul	do.
Charles Halket	Writer's Servant	Aberdeen	Aberdeen	do.
John Innes	Wright	do.	do.	do.
Alex. Irvine, Esq.	of Drum	Drum	Drumoak	do.
James Innes, Esq.	of Balnacraig	Balnacraig	Aboyn	do.
Patrick Leggie	Writer	Aberdeen	Aberdeen	do.
William Moir, Esq.	of Lonemay	Nether miln	Cruden	do.
Thomas Mercer	Merchant	Aberdeen	Aberdeen	do.
James Moir, Esq.	of Stonnywood	Stonnywood	Newhills	do.
Charles Moir		Aberdeen	Aberdeen	do.
Gilbert Menzies, Junr	of Pitfoddels	Pitfoddels	Maryculter	Kincarden
James Petrie	Sheriff Depute	Aberdeen	Aberdeen	Aberdeen
Robert Reid	Merchant	Aberdeen	do.	do.
James Ross	Cooper Apprentice	do.	do.	do.
John Ross	Sailor	do.	do.	do.
John Scott	do.	do.	do.	do.
George Steel	Merchant	do.	do.	do.
Daniel Smith	do.	do.	do.	do.
Robt Sandilands	Writer	do.	do.	do.
Will. Strachan	late Clk. of Cust^{os}	do.	do.	do.
William Trowp	Dancing M^r	do.	do.	do.
John Thomson	Merchant	Old Aberdeen	Old Machar	do.

ABERDEEN DISTRICT—Continued.

Yearly rent of their Estates.			Condition of Mansion House.	Evidences.
				The saids Rod. M'culloch, James Sutherland & James Thomson.
				Do.
50	0	0	Burnt	The above James Sinclair, James Simpson & John Shaw.
				The saids Rod^k M'culloch, James Sutherland and James Thomson.
				Do.
100	0	0	Pretty good	James Adamson, Gairdner in Drum in the parish of Drumoak, Andrew Clark in Colarly in Echt Parish, & Pat. Davidson in Balnacraig in Aboyn Parish.
30	0	0	very good	The s^{ds} Andrew Clerk & Pat. Davidson & James Davidson, Ground Off^r in Charlestown.
				Alex. Aiken & James Cook, Porters in Aberdeen & Pat. Harvie also Porter there.
150	0	0	Indifferent	Do.
200	0	0	None	Do.
80	0	0	very good	Do.
				Do.
				Do.
				Do.
				Do.
				Do.
				Do.
				Do.
				Do.
				Do.
				Do.
				Do.
				Do.
				Do.
				Do.

A LIST OF PERSONS IN OLD MELDRUM IN THE REBELLION, WITH

Names.	Designations.	Abode.	Parish.	County.
John Douglas	of Fechel	Fechel	Ellon	Aberdeen
Cha. Cumming	of Kinninmont	Kinninmont	Longmay	do.
Alex. Cumming	Farmer	Meikle Crichie	Old Deer	do.
William Cumming	of Pittully	Pitully	Pitsligo	do.
John Cruikshank	Surgeon	Fraserburgh	Fraserburgh	do.
Alex. Craig		Pitsligo	Pitsligo	do.
Will. Christie	Shipmaster	Fraserburgh	Fraserburgh	do.
Will. Chalmers	Baxter	do.	do.	do.
George Chain	Sailor	do.	do.	do.
Alexander Forbes	Lord Pitsligo	Pitsligo	Pitsligo	do.
William Fraser	Brother to	Inveralichy	Rathen	do.
James Ferrier	Sailor	Fraserburgh	Fraserburgh	do.

DISTRICT WHO HAVE BEEN CONCERN'D EVIDENCES TO PROVE THE FACTS.

Yearly rent of their Estate.	Condition of Mansion house.	Evidences.
83 6 8	very good	James Ryan Officer of Excise at Newburgh, Alex. Ritchie at Kirk of Methlick, Mrs Chalmers, Vintner in Ellon & Elizabeth Chalmers in Ellon.
150 0 0	do.	James Arthur in Kinninmont, John Wilkin in Cassiefoord, John Webster in Clockean and John Dalgarno in New Deer.
600 stock		John Lawrence at Old Deer, John Webster in Clockean, John Dalgarno in New Deer and James Arthur in Kinninmont.
300 0 0	a good house	John Foreman at House of Pitully, John Pirie at Roscarty & Eneas Campbell at Pittully.
		John Pirie at Roscarty, John Hepburn at Ardla & John Foreman at Pitully.
		Do.
		William M'Kay & Alex. Jamison in Philorth in the parish of Fraserburgh.
50 stock		Do.
400 0 0	a fine house	Do.
		John Pirie, Servt to Lord Pitsligo, John Hepburn in Ardla & Jno Foreman at Pitully.
1000 stock		Alexander Low in Fraserburgh, Alex. Russel there, John Pirrie at Roscarty, John Foreman at Pitully & John Hepburn at Ardla.
		William Hay & Alex. Jamison, both in Philorth & Fraserburgh Parish.

Names.	Designations.	Abode.	Parish.	County.
John Fullerton, Junr	of Dudwick	Slains	Ellon	Aberdeen
Mary Farquharson	Lady Turnerhall	Turnerhall	do.	do.
Geo. Forrest	Servt to C. Errol	Slains	Cruden	do.
Jonathan Forbes	Farmer	Brux	Kildrumie	do.
Robert Gordon	of Logie	Logie	Crimond	do.
Alex. Gill	Shipmaster	Fraserburgh	Fraserburgh	do.
Mary Hay	Count. of Errrol	Slains	Slains	do.
Adam Hay	of Cairnbanno	Cairnbanno	New Deer	do.
Peter Kilgour	Merchant	Ellon	Ellon	do.
Lawrence Leith	Farmer	Newflinder	Kinethmond	do.
Anthony Leith	do.	Leith hall	do.	do.
Alex. Morrison	Sailor	Fraserburgh	Fraserburgh	do.
Will. Moir	of Longmay	Nethermiln	Longmay	do.
William Miln	Merchant	Ellon	Ellon	do.
Alex. Ogilvie	of Auchiries	Corthie	Rathen	do.
W^m & Jno. Ogilvies	B^{rs} to Auchiries	Auchiries	do.	do.

OLD MELDRUM—Continued.

Yearly rent of their Estate.	Condition of Mansion houses.	Evidences.
166 13 8		Will. Nisbet at Waterside in Slains parish & Ja. Forrest at Nethermiln in Cruden Parish.
		Gilbert Davidson in Turnerhall, Will. Brechin in Hillhead & William Wilson in Kirkhill, all in Ellon parish.
		John Shewan in Braehead & John Lendrum in College, both in Cruden Parish.
1000 stock		Mr Will. Min^r at Kildrumie & David Ramsay in Old Rain
260 0 0	a fine house	John Pirrie at Roscarty in Pitsligo Parish, John Hepburn at Ardla in Tyrie Parish, Alex. Low in Fraserburgh, & Alex. Russel there.
		Will. M'Kay & Alex. Jamison both in Philorth & that parish.
3000 0 0		Will. Nisbet in Waterside in the parish of Slains, James Strachan, George Paul and William Ogston all in Slains & in Cruden parish.
50 0 0	a bad house	John Dalgarno in New Deer, John Lawrence in Old Deer & James Forbes in Turnerhall house in Ellon parish.
100 stock		Alex. Ritchie in Methlick, Geo. Catto & Geo. Cantlo both in Ellon.
		Alex. Tower, John Sey & Alex. Mathison all in Old Rain.
		David Ramsay in Old Rain, Alex. Bettie & John Chevas both in Premno that Parish.
		William M'Kay & Alex. Jamison both in Philorth & that parish.
166 13 8		John Hay of Auch Wharney, Mr Alexander Keith at Sand and James Gordon of Affluchrees all in the parish of Cruden & Provost Muirison of Aberdeen.
100 stock		Alex. Ritchie in Methlick, Geo. Catto & Geo. Cantlo both in Ellon.
200 0 0	very good & new	Aeneas Campbell and John Foreman at Pitully in Pitsligo Parish.
300 0 0	stock each	The s^{ds} Campbell & Foreman & Alex. Low & James Mathew, both in Fraserburgh.

Names.	Designations.	Abode.	Parish.	County.
Alex. Ramsay	Merchant	Roscarty	Pitsligo	Aberdeen
John Souter		Ellon	Ellon	do.
Alex. Smith	of Meany	Meany	Belhelvie	do.
John Turner	of Turnerhall, J^r	Turnerhall	Ellon	do.
George Leggat	Merchant	Ellon	Ellon	do.
Alex. Thomson	of Fechfield	Old Deer	Old Deer	do.
James Thomson, Jn^r	of Fechfield	Fechfield	do.	do.
David Tyrie, Junr	of Dunnydeer	Dunnedeer	Inch	do.
Alex. White, Junr	of Ardlahill	Aberdowr	Aberdowr	do.
Tho. Arbuthnot	Merch^t	Peterhead	Peterhead	do.

OLD MELDRUM—Continued.

Yearly rent.	Condition of their houses.	Evidences.
300 0 0	Stock	John Pirrie in Roscarty in Pitsligo Parish, John Hepburn in Ardla in Tyrie Parish, George Mathers & William Cruden, both in Fraserburgh.
		Charles Pirrie in Craighall, Andrew Pirrie in Piltachie & Andrew Bettie in Ellon, all in Ellon parish.
83 6 8	good house	John Wishart in Tillicorthy in Udny Parish, John Morice in Miln of Fiddess and Foveran parish & William Nisbet at Waterside in the parish of Slains.
300 0 0	do.	James Forbes in Turnerhall & Cha. Pirrie in Craighall, both in Ellon parish.
		Andrew Pirrie in Piltachy in Ellon Parish, Alex. Ritchie in Methlick in that vizt Methlick Parish, George Catto & George Cantlo, both in Ellon.
200 0 0	a fashionable house	Alex. Dalgarno, Tennent in Feckfield, Tho. Thomson in Parkhill, both in Longside Parish.
		John Webster in Clochean in Old Deer Parish & Jn° Marshall in Invervedy in Longside Parish.
80 0 0		David Ramsay & Alex. Mathison, both in Old Rain & that parish & John Chevas in Premno & Premno parish.
30 0 0	not good	William Cruden & Tho. Shirras, both in Fraserburgh.
		Alex. Cumming & James Moir, both in Longside & that parish, & Robert and Thomas Arbuthnot's both Merchants in Peterhead.

A LIST OF PERSONS FROM BANFF DISTRICT
EVIDENCES TO

Names.	Abode.	Parish.	Yearly Rent of their Estates.
James Abercrombie	Deskford	Deskford	
Alex. Anderson	Knocky miln	Turriff	
James Bicky	Turriff miln	do.	
George Bremner	Carmoucie	Forglen	
John Brown	do.	do.	
James Crighton	of Auchingoul	Inverkething in Banff	40 0 0
William Davidson	Turriff	Turriff	
James Duncan	Servt in do.	do.	
Alex. Gordon, sen^r	of Dorlathers	do.	56 0 0
Alex. Gordon, jun^r	of do.	do.	
John Garvock	Servt to do.	do.	
John Garvock	Dorlathers	do.	
Arthur Gordon	Carnoucie	Forglen	9000 0 0
John Gordon	his Servt	do.	
John Gillespie, Junr	Turriff	Turriff	
George Gill	Bridgend	do.	
Alex. Gall	Cormucie	Forglen	
George Hay, Junr	Montblairy	Alva, in Banff	56 0 0
John Hay Wright	Dalgity	Turriff	
Alex. Halket	Druckla miln	do.	
Charles Halket	a younger Br of Alex$^{r's}$	do.	

CONCERN'D IN THE REBELLION, WITH PROVE THE SAME.

Condition of Mansion House.	Evidences.
	James Donaldson, George Urquhart & Alex. Kennedy, Merchants in Turriff.
	Do.
	Do.
	Thomas & Alexander Davidsons in Wak Miln of Carmucie in Forglen parish.
	Do.
pretty good	James Donaldson, Geo. Urquhart, & Henry Jeans, in Turriff.
	Do.
	Do.
pretty good	William Irvine at Miln of Leuthers, & Alexander Irvine in Yonderstown parish.
	James Willox & Henry Jeans with the above Merchants in Turriff.
	Do.
very good	George Cow, James Lumisdale, & James Porter, all in Newton in Forglen Parish.
	Do.
	James Brodie Esqr Muresk, & Mr Fiddes his Chaplain both in Turriff Parish
	James & John Smarts & Tho. Davidson all in Bridgend & Turriff Parish & their wives.
	Janet Smith in Knocky burn, Marg^t Cowie her Servt & Wm Pirrey, Shoemaker in Turriff
	James Donaldson & others above nam'd in Turriff.
	Do.
	Do.
	Well known in Aberdeen.

Names.	Abode.	Parish.	Yearly Rent of their Estates.
Peter Hepburn	Ardin	Turiff	
John Innes	Turriff	do.	
James King	Darrow	do.	
John Kynnach	Burntbrae	Alva	
Alex. Leith	Turriff	Turriff	
William Lesslie	Hillhead	do.	
William Maver	Turriff	do.	
James Maver	do.	do.	
George Miln Sen[r]	do.	do.	
George Miln Jun[r]	Bridgend	do.	
Will. Miln	Turriff	do.	
Robert Massie	do.	do.	
Alex. Morrison	Knockyburn	do.	
Alexander Panton	Turriff	do.	

Condition of Mansion House.	Evidences.
	James Ramsay Farmer in Sigget in Auchterless Parish & Wm Porter, Hepburn's Subtennent.
	Merchants in Turriff above mention'd.
	Do.
	Do.
	Do.
	John Hay Wright & John Morrison both in Hillhead & Turriff Parish.
	Merchants in Turriff above mention'd.
	James Ramsay, Farmer in Sigget in Auchterless Parish.
	Merchants in Turriff above mention'd.
	James & John Smarts & Tho. Davidson all in Bridgend and Turriff parish.
	Merchants in Turriff before mention'd.
	George Urquhart, office keeper in Turriff & family & Henry Jeans, Mer^t there.
	William Morrison & Alex. Morrison his Son in Muckholp in Turriff Parish.

Names.	Designations.	Abode.	Parish.
John Pirrie	Servt to Dorlathers		Turriff
John Roy	Servant	Turriff	do.
James Stewart		do.	do.
John Skeen		do.	do.
William Scott		Carnuice	Forglen
George White		Miln of Gask	Turriff
William Wilson		Turriff	do.
George Gordon	Farmer	Muirifield	Grange
John Gordon	Young dominy	Jannycroy	Keith
Hercules Paterson	Surgeon	Keith	do.
John Simpson	Bleacher	Auchenhoof	Grange
Patrick Stewart	Farmer	Kinninder	Mortlech
Angus Stewart	do.	Park beg	do.
James Gordon Junr	of Aberlour	Aberlour	Aberlour
Alexander Lesslie	Farmer	Auchen-hanach	Mortleck
Alex. Grant	do.	Nether Clunie	do.
William Stewart	do.	Oleek	Aberlour
William Forbes	do.	West Cald-wald	Boharm
Arthur Gordon	of Carnouice	Forglan	Forglen
James Crighton	of Auchingowl		Inverkeithing
Alex. Gordon of	Dorlaithers		Turriff

Rental.	Condition of Mansion ho.	Evidences.
		George Mitchel at Mains, Leuthers & Mr Jno Duncan, Govr to Dorlather's Children, both in Turriff Parish.
		Merchants in Turriff before ment^d.
		Do.
		Do.
		Thomas & Alex. Davidsons in Walk Miln of Carnuice in Forglen Parish.
		Merchants in Turriff before mention'd.
		Janet Smith in Knockiburn, Marg^t Cowie, her Servt & Wm Pierrie, Shomaker in Turriff & all in that parish
		Mess^s Arch^d Campbell, asis^t Preacher in Carnie, & Alex. Chalmers, Probationer at Cairnwhelp in Carnie Parish.
		William Taylor & John Saunders, Messengers in Keith.
		Do.
		James Martin near Mortleck, Donald M'donald at Hidehaugh, & Alexander Day at Kirkton of Mortleck all in Mortleck parish.
		No Evidences ag^t these persons.
500 0 0		John Troup, Tenn^t in Greendykes, Geo. Cow, Ten^t in Old town of Carnouice, James Alexander in Boginhilt, & Geo. Leggat in Bogton, all in Forglan Parish.
40 0 0		James Brember, Mer^t in Mamock kirk, James Allan in Braehead, John Andrew in Euchry & Pat. Thain there, all in Inverkeithing Parish.
60 0 0		Geo. Mitchel in Mains of Laithers, John Ranny in Burnthall, Wm Ranny in Braefoot & Geo. Ranny, blacksmith there all in Turriff Parish.

Names.	Designations.	Abode.	Parish.
Alex. M'Rae		Banff	Banff
Robert Fraser		do.	do.
Angus Campbell		do.	do.
Thomas Marr		do.	do.
John Duff		do.	do.

Names.	Designations.	Abode.	Parish.
David Wilson	Brewer	Gardenhead	Ordowhill
Donald Fraser	Servant	Portsoy	Fordyce
George Hay	Sailor	do.	do.
George Paterson		New Durn	do.
James Bowman	Gardiner	Portsoy	do.
James Joiner		do.	do.
Robert Kennedy		Durn	do.
Sir Wm Gordon	of Park	Park	Ordowhill
Sir Wm Dunbar		Durn	Fordyce
William M'donald	Piper	Portsoy	do.
William Petrie		do.	do.

BANFF DISTRICT—*Continued.* 315

Rental.	Condition of Mansion ho.	Evidences.
		Provost James Innes, Baillies Duffus & Thain & Wm Reid all in Banff. Do. Do. Do. William Bruce.

County.	Evidences.
Banff do. do. do. do. do. do. do. do. do. do.	Pat. Gordon, Merchant in Portsoy & Rod. Davidson, Weaver there, both in the Parish of Fordyce.

A LIST OF PERSONS FROM STIRLING LION, WITH EVIDENCES TO

Names.	Designations.	Abode.	Parish.	County.
James Graham Junr	of Airth	Airth	Airth	Stirling
James Gardner	Servt to do.	do.	do.	do.
James Murray	Merchant	do.	do.	do.
Alex. Miln	of Newmiln	Newmiln	do.	do.
David & Thomas	sons to do.	do.	do.	do.
William Baad	Brewer	Lethem	Lethem	do.
John Simpson	Brewer	Falkirk	Falkirk	do.
James Kincaid	of Degren	Degren	do.	do.
John Henderson	Merch^t	Clackmannan	Clackmanan	do.
Da. & Ja. Rollos	Sons of Pows Rollo	Pows Rolls	St. Ninians	do.
Andrew Steven	Farmer	Ferrytown	Clackmanan	do.
James Robertson	Weaver	Bannockburn	St. Ninians	do.
Peter Lockhart	Smith	do.	do.	do.
Mr Wm Harper	Epis. Min^r	Bothkenner	Bothkenner	do.
John Lochead	Merch^t	in Alloa	Alloa	do.

DISTRICT CONCERN'D IN THE REBEL-PROVE THE DIFFERENT FACTS.

Yearly Rent.	Condition of Mansion House.	Evidences.
		Inhabitants of Airth.
40 0 0		James Raith, Barber in Airth & Alex. Archibald, Shoemaker there.
		John Watson, Shipmaster in Airth & John Scott, Wright there.
		} John Dick, Shipmaster in Airth & Alex. Hodge, Brewer there.
		James Rae, Barber in Airth & Alex. Arch^d, Shoemaker there.
25 0 0		James Cowan of Powside in the Parish of Airth & Henry Corbet off^r of Excise there.
		Robert M^{c}kie, Depute Baillie in Airth & his Spouse & Arch^d Gilchrist, Baxter there.
		John Clark, Mer^t in Airth, Henry Corbet, Excise Off^r there.
		John Baad, Mer^t in Airth, Christ. Davidson, Spouse to Wm Logan Brewer there & the Ex. officer.
		James Cowan of Powside in Airth Parish & Ja. Buchan, Mer^t in Borrowstouness.
		{ Margaret Logan, Spouse to John Logan, Brewer in Bannockburn, Robert Davidson, Weaver in Glasgow & Henry Corbet, Officer of Excise in Airth.
		James M'Near, Sclater in Falkirk & Robt & James M'nears his sons.
		Robert Adam & John Dick, Shipmasters in Airth.

LIST FROM

Names.	Designations.	Abode.	Parish.	County.
Robert Anderson			St. Ninians	Stirling
Robert Watt	Sclater	Down	Down	do.
Robert Caddel	Gunsmith	do.	do.	do.
Henry Oat Junr	Mason	do.	do.	do.
Pat. Ridoch	Sclater	do.	do.	do.
Don. Mitchell	Do.	do.	do.	do.
John M'lachlan	Wright	do.	do.	do.
John Squair	Weaver	Bridgend		do.
Tho. Caddel, Senr	Gunsmith	Down	Down	do.
Tho. Caddel, Junr	Do.	do.	do.	do.
Duncan Wright	Carrier	do.	do.	do.
Andrew Watt	Sclater	do.	do.	do.
Will. Oatt		do.	do.	do.
Duncan Mitchel	Carrier	do.	do.	do.
Thomas M'farlane	Smith	do.	do.	do.

STIRLING DISTRICT—*Continued.* 319

Yearly Rent.	Condition of Mansion House.	Evidences.
		Alex. Bow & Geo. M'Vie, Smiths in Carnock & Pat. Robertson, Mer^t in Elphingston. John Christy Multerer in Down Miln, John Michell, Merchant in Down, Robert Mitchel, Merch^t there, Alex. Campbell, Gunsmith there, James Kemp, Innkeeper there & James & William Taylors both Innkeepers there. Allan Stewart, Vintner in Down, & John Christy, Multerer in the Mill there. The above Mr Christy & Alex. Campbell, Gunsmith in Down. Robt & John Mitchels, Mer^{ts} in Down & Marjory Paton, Spouse to Robt Balfour there. Thomas Gibson, Wright in Down. Donald Campbell, Gunsmith in Stirling & James Taylor, Merch^t in Down. Pat. Ferguson, Mer^t in Down & James Taylor, Mer^t there. William M'lellan, Purse Master in Down & his Spouse, Will. Christy, Baxter there, Duncan M'niccol, Brewer there, & his Spouse, & Allan Stewart, Vintner there.

A LIST OF PERSONS IN MONTROSE REBELLION, WITH EVIDENCES

Names.	Designations.	Abode.
John Erskine	Mer^t Apprentice	Montrose
John Lindsay	Surgeon App.	do.
John Stephen	Wright	do.
Wm Jamieson	Reedmaker	do.
Walter Young	Sailor	do.
John Fettes	Maltman	do.
George Hay	Recidenter	do.
Wm Mackie	do.	do.
William Williamson	Shoemaker	do.
Alex. Young	Sailor	do.
David Smith	do.	do.
William Low	Smith	do.
Andrew Beattie	Ropemaker	do.
Robt Wright	Shoemaker	do.
Will. Lindsay	do.	do.
Will. Gordon	Writer App^{ce}	do.
Hugh Fraser	Smith	do.
Will. Mowat	Recidenter	do.
Dav. Pyot	Wright	do.
Robert Irons	Residenter	do.
Wm Baird	Gardiner	do.
George Dakers	Residenter	do.
George Guthrie	do.	do.
Da. Martine	Weaver	do.
Cha. Carnegy	Sailor	do.
John Gordon	Surgeon App^{ce}	do.
Geo. Carnegie	Mer^t do.	do.
John Ouchterlony	Writer do.	do.
John Scott	Merchant	do.
Alex. Grey	Mer^t App^{ce}	do.
John Low	Wigmaker	do.
James Henderson	Shipmaster	do.
Pat. Beattie	do.	do.
John Orkney	do.	do.
John Orkney	do.	do.
Will. Lesslie	Mariner	do.

DISTRICT CONCERNED IN THE TO PROVE THE FACTS.

Evidences.
John Fettes, Maltman in Montrose, & John Mackie, Residenter there, being both Rebells.
John Ritchie & Tho. Lesslie, Merch^{ts} in Montrose, & John Fettes above design'd.
Geo. Burnet, Shoemaker in Montrose & Ja. Fraser & Alex. Tweedale, Fishers & pilots there.
Robt Arbuthnot & Wm Miln, Shipmasters in Montrose. James Fraser, & Alex. Tweedale above design'd.

Names.	Abode.	Parish.
Alex. Alexander	Johnshaven	Benhom
Wm Anderson	do.	do.
Da. Burness	do.	do.
Robt Crookshank	do.	do.
John Forbes	Bervie	Bervie
John Freeman	Milton	St. Cyrus
James Gray	do.	do.
John Lessley	Miln of Morphy	do.
John Mitchell	Johnshaven	Benholm
Robt Mitchell	do.	do.
Will. Robison	do.	do.
Wm Wiseheart	do.	do.
John Durie	Stonehaven	Dunnoter
Wm Smith, mariner	do.	do.
John Ritchie, pilot	do.	do.
Geo. Reid, mason	do.	do.
Wm Gibbon	do.	do.
Pat. Cushnie, Mer{t}	do.	do.
Da. Keith, Ten{t}	Fetteresso	Fetteresso
Geo. Bisset, Pilot	Stonehaven	Dunnoter
John Martine, weaver	do.	do.
Rob. Johnston, sh. off{r}	do.	do.
Wm Gilmer, Shoemaker	do.	do.
Sr Alex. Bannerman of Elsick worth £350 p.an.	Elsick	Fetteresso
Alex. Garioch of Margie, worth 50 p.ann.	Margie	do.
Ja. Barclay	Findleston	do.

MONTROSE DISTRICT—*Continued.* 323

County.	Evidences.
Mearns	John Murray, Fisher in Johnshaven & Ja. Gibson. Carpenter there.
do.	John Hodge & Geo. Watson, Brewers in Johnshaven.
do. do.	} John Barclay & Ja. Blaber in Johnshaven.
do.	Ba. Tho. Christie in Bervie.
do. do.	} John Petrie & Wm Law in Milnton.
do.	Wm Dorret & Eliz. Anderson, his servants.
do.	Alex. Alexander in Johnshaven & Ja. Miln, Mer^t there etc.
do.	Do. & many others there.
do.	John Young, Sh. Dep. his wife & his daughter.
do.	Robt Grieve & Tho. Gove, Fishers at Melton.
Kincarden	
do. do. do. do. do. do. do. do. do. do. do. do.	} John Duncan, Not. Publick in Stonehaven, Wm Wyse, Mer^t there, Andrew Brown, Fisher there, Ja. Caldinghead & Geo. Taylor also Fishers there, James Duncan Junr Shoemaker there, James Falconer, Fisher there, George Schoola, Farmer in Guly Brands in the parish of Fetteresso, Paul Lyon, Farmer in Burn of Phepie in that parish & Ja. Gray, Farmer in the Kirktown of Fetteresso.

A LIST OF PERSONS FROM CAITHNESS EVIDENCES TO PROVE

Names.	Designations.	Abode.	Parish.
Geo. Sinclair	of Geese	Holburnhead	
Hector Campbell	Farmer	Houstry	Halkirk
Ken. M'Keamish	Tennant	Cathell	do.
Benj. Sinclair	Tennent	Brackachy	Lathron
Don. Stuart	Farmer	Quoycrook	Hallkirk

CONCERN'D IN THE REBELLION, WITH THE CRIMINAL FACTS.

County.	Evidences.
Caithness	Robert Winchester, Mer^t in Wick & Wm Mullican, Brewer there.
	John Bain, Customer in Thurso & Andrew Taylor Writer there.
do.	Geo. Mowat, Land Waiter in Thurso, John Donaldson, Merchant there & Mr Stuart, Coll^r of Excise.
do.	Theod. Dunnet & John Miln, Merch^{ts} in Thurso & Ja. Hosack, Brewer there.
do.	Theod. Dunnet & John Donaldson, Mer^{ts} in Thurso, & Mr Stuart, Coll^r of Excise.

A LIST OF PERSONS FROM ARGYLE IN THE REBELLION,

Rebells' Names.
Hector M'Alister, Mer^t in Glencoy in Arran
Ja. M'donald, Sea Coast Trader, Beallacheyran in Kintyre
William M'Alister in Marignecraig in Kintyre
Adam Fullerton, Brewer in Brodick, in Arran
James Bain Fullarton, Mer^t in Glencloy in Arran
Wm Miller, Brewer in Brodwick in Arran
Cha. Blaikie, Sailor at Campbelltown miln
John Cunnison, Excise Officer at Campbelltown miln

A LIST OF PERSONS FROM IN THE REBELLION,

Rebells' Names.
William Cochran of Ferguslie Esq. in the Parish of Paisley & County of Renfrew, worth £100 p. ann.
James Stirling, at the house of Erskine & the parish of that name & Renfrew County
Will. Weir, Coalier at Cathcart

A LIST OF PERSONS IN DUNSE DISTRICT CONCERN'D IN THE REBELLION, AND EVIDENCES TO PROVE THE SAME.

David Home, son to the Laird of Whitfield in the parish of Dunse
William Home, Indweller in Dunse
Arch^d Lawder, son to Bailmouth in Dunse Parish
The above persons are prisoners at Carlisle where are two of Hamilton's Dragoons as Evidences ag^t them

SOUTH COLLECTION, CONCERN'D WITH EVIDENCES.

Evidences.
{ Archibald Paterson a Rebell in Congary in Islay & Don. More M'Alister in Surn in Islay also a Rebell.
{ Pat. Gray, Taylor in Brodick in Arran & Wm Maitland Surgeon there, both Rebells.
{ Hugh White, Mer^t in Glasgow, Arch^d Obrolochon Taylor in Campbelltown & Capt Neil M'Neill of Machrihanish in Kintyre.

NEWPORT DISTRICT CONCERN'D WITH EVIDENCES.

Evidences' Names.
William Pollock, Writer, Hugh Montgomery, Ferrier, & Ja. King, Smith, all in Renfrew. Magistrates of Renfrew.
Tho. Bowes & Gavin Lawson & many others in Cathcart.

A LIST OF PERSONS IN ROSS DISTRICT EVIDENCES TO

Names.	Designations.	Abode.	Parish.
John Chisholm	Groom to Erchiles	Erchiles	Kilmorak
John Erskine	Ex. Officer	Dingwall	Dingwall
John Forbes	Merchant	Tain	Tain
Simon Fraser	Master of Lovat	Castledowny	Kilmorak
Will. Fraser	Junr of Culbocky		Kiltarlaty
Will. Fraser	Son to Culmiln	Culmiln	Kirkhill
Alex. Fraser	Tennent		do.
Alex. Fraser	do.		do.
Simon Fraser	Tacksman	Achnaclouch	Kiltarlaty
Cha. Graham		Tain	Tain
Alex. John Kenneth & Colin Grants	} Sons to Pat. Grant		Contine
Jo. & Finl. Glassess	Brogmakers, Miln of Redcastle		Kelerman
Alex. Gordon		Cromarty	Cromarty
Andrew Hood		Tain	Tain
George Hood		do.	do.
Theod. M'kenzie		East Culbock	Urquhart
Colin M'kenzie	Merchant	Edinburgh	Edin.
Ken. M'kenzie	Tennent	Hillend	Avoch
Rod. M'Culloch	of Glastlick	Glastlick	Fearn

CONCERN'D IN THE REBELLION, WITH PROVE THE SAME.

County.	Yearly Rent.	Evidences' Names.
	Merks Scotts.	
Inverness		Mr Tho. Chisholm, Min^r at Kilmorak & Mr Pat. Nicolson, Min^r in Kiltarlaty.
Ross		Alex. M'kenzie & Wm Fraser, Merchants in Dingwall.
do.		David Ross, Town Clerk & Alex. Ross, Sheriff Clerk in Tain.
do.	35,000	Wm Fraser Tennent Simon Fraser alias Miller there, Peter Gow alias Smith Gardiner &c. all in Bewly
do.	900	Do.
Inverness		Do.
do.		Do.
do.		Do.
Ross		Do.
do.		Ballies John Manson & Hugh Ross in Tain.
do.		Donald Rioch in Contine & Geo. M'kenzie, Dyer there.
Ross		James Calder, Tenn^t in Milnton & Rodk. M'kenzie, Ten^t in Hiltown both of Redcastle.
Cromarty		Tho. Gair & Mr Geo. Balfour &c. in Nigg in the County of Ross.
Ross		David Ross, Town Clk. & Alex. Ross, Sheriff Clerk in Tain.
do.		Do.
do.		Ja. Grant Ex. Off^r Jerom Williamson, Wigmaker & Wm Fraser, Mer^t all in Culbocky.
Mid Lothian		Do.
Ross		Do.
do.	3000	Baillies Hugh Ross & John Manson both in Tain & others there.

LIST FROM

Names.	Designations.	Abode.	Parish.
William Man	Servant	Pettford	Avoch
John More		Templand	do.
William Man		do.	do.
John M'kenzie	of Tarriden	Tarriden	Contine
Alex. M'kay	of Achmony	Achmony	Kilmore
Alex. M'Leod	Son to Muravenside	Muravenside	Muravenside
Ken. M'kenzie	Br to Fairburn		Urra
Alex. M'kenzie	of Lentron	Lentron	do.
Colin M'kenzie	Br to Lentron	do.	do.
Ken. M'kenzie	do.	do.	do.
Will. M'kenzie		Kinnellan	Contine
Alex. M'kenzie		Milnton of Ord	Urra
John M'urrachy			do.
Don. M'kenzie	Tennent	Inchavanny	Fottertay
Geo. M'kenzie		Milton of New Tarbet	Kilmoor
James M'lachy			
Ken. M'lennan			
Will. M'kenzie	Br to Allangrange	Allangrange	Kilmuir
Rod. M'farquhar		Spittal	Kilernan
John M'farquhar, Junr		do.	do.
Colin M'kenzie	Tennent	Chapeltown	do.
Don. M'farquhar, Junr		West Culmore	do.
Farq. M'farquhar	Tennent	Newton	do.
John M'kenzie, Junr		Burnton of Redcastle	do.
M'kenzie	of Ardloch		do.
James Niccoll		Avoch	Avoch

ROSS DISTRICT—*Continued.* 331

County.	Yearly Rent.	Evidences' Names.
	Merks Scotts.	
Ross		Ken. & Charles Thomsons, Tennents in Auchterfloo in the parish of Avoch.
do.		Do.
do.		Do.
do.	2000	Sir Alex. M'kenzie of Coul, W^m M'kenzie & Ken. Grant, Ten^{ts} in Echilty &c., in the Parish of Contine.
Inverness	1800	—— Grant, Factor to the Laird of Grant in Urquhart & the Minister there.
Linlithgow		Provosts Hossack & Fraser of Inverness & others in Cromarty.
Ross		William Fraser, Tennent in Kinnellan & Don. Reoch in the Parish of Contine.
do.	500	William M'kenzie & Ken. Grant, Tennents in Echilty.
do.		Do. & Don. Reoch, Ten^t in Contine & Wm Fraser, Ten^t in Kinnellan.
do.		Do.
do.		Rod^k M'kenzie of Reidcastle & Geo. M'kenzie of Allangrange, Esq^{rs}, &c.
do.		Alex. M'kenzie of Ord & John M'kenzie, Ten^t in Ardua Crack in Urra Parish.
do.		Do.
do.		Mr Colin M'kenzie Min^r at Fottertay & John M'kenzie, Tenn^t in Inchavannan.
do.		Dav. M'kenzie Smith in Milnton of Newtarbet & Alex. Ross Tennent there.
do.		Lairds of Kilcoy & Reidcastle.
do.		Rod. M'kenzie, Ten^t in Hilton of Redcastle, Don. Nobble, Ten^t there & Ja. Caldor, Ten^t in Milton of Redcastle.
do.		Do.
do.		Do.
do.		Do.
do.		Do.
do.		Do.
do.	3000	David Ross, Town Clk. in Tain & Alex. Ross, Sheriff Clerk there & others.
do.		William Reid, Miller & Alex. Reid, Shoemaker in Milton of Avoch.

Names.	Designations.	Abode.	Parish.
Murdoch Paterson		Lettoch of Redcastle	Kilmure
Don. Paterson, Sen[r]		East Kessock	do.
Donald Paterson, Jun[r]		do.	do.
Lauch Paterson		Blairdow	do.
And. Paterson, Jun[r]		Kessock	do.
George Reid		Templand	Avoch
Alex. Reid	Servant	Knockmuir	do.
John Reid, Jun[r]		Pitfoord	do.
John Robertson		Milnton	Kilmuir
W[m] Ross alias Rioch		Tain	Tain
Malcolm Ross	Son to Pitcalny	Arboll	Tarbet
Hugh Smith		Brackachy	Kilmorak
Peter Smith		Bewley	do.
Calum Stewart, Sn[r]		Milnton of Redcastle	Kilernan
Ken. Simpson		Dunvarny	Urquhart
Will. Urquhart		Kinnellan	Contine

ROSS DISTRICT—*Continued.*

County.	Yearly Rent.	Evidences' Names.
Ross		Murdoch M'kenzie, Ten^t in Kissock, Rod. M'kenzie & Don. Noble, Ten^{ts} in Hilton of Redcastle.
do.		Do.
do.		Do.
do.		Do.
do.		Do.
do.		The Ministers of Avoch & Suddy & Robt Forbes, Ten^t in Pitonachty in Suddy parish.
do.		Do.
do.		Do.
Cromarty		David M'kenzie, Smith, & Alex. Ross, Tenn^t both in Milnton of Newtarbet.
Ross		Do.
do.		And. Ross, Ex. Off^r, Abner Gallie, Ten^t in Tarbet Parish & the Laird of Cadboll.
Inverness		Mr Tho. Chisholm, Min^r at Kilmorak & his two sons.
do.		Do.
Ross		James Calder in Milnton & Rod. M'kenzie in Hiltown both of Reidcastle.
Nairn		James & Tho. Gordons, Maltsters in Dunvarnay.
Ross		Donald Rioch, Merch^t in Contine, & William Fraser, Tennant in Kinnellan.
		Most of the above Persons refuse to be Evidences although they are able to Inform the publick of the behaviour of those ag^t whom they are placed.
		Sign'd LAWRENCE ANGUS.

A LIST OF PERSONS FROM ELGIN DISTRICT
EVIDENCES TO

Names.	Designations.	Abode.	Parish.
James Cumming	Residenter	Inverness	Inverness
Ja. Dallas	of Cantray	Cantray	Croy
Alex. Fordyce	Servt	Windyhill	
Hugh Fraser	Mer^t	Inverness	Inverness
Wm Fraser	of Daleragg		Baleskine
Don. Fraser	Smith	Moy	
Cha. Fraser, J^r	Fairfield	Kinmyles	Inverness
Hugh Fraser	Green of Muirton		
James Fraser	of Phoyers	Phoyers	Boleskine
Simon Fraser	Farmer	Delehapple	
Alex. Fraser	Calduthul	Inchnacar-doch	
Wm Fraser	Mer^t	F^t Augustus	
Hugh Fraser	Farmer	Borlum	
John Fraser, Junr	Bochrubine	Castledowny	Kiltarlaty
Alex. Fraser	Farmer	Letelune	
Simon Fraser	Vintner	Gen^{es} Nutt	Kiltarlaty
John Fraser	Tacksman	Birnehen	Boleskine
Hugh Fraser	Son to do.	do.	do.
Don. Farquharson, Jn^r	Achreashean	Glencoles	
Lud. Gordon	Mer^t	Elgin	Elgin
Wm Grant	Wright	Windehill	
John Gray	Servant	Ironside	
Alex. Grant	Writer	Inverness	Inverness
John Gordon	Glenbucket	St. Budget	Kirkmichel
Lewis Gordon	at the Miln of	Lagan	
Tho. Hutcheson	Mer^t	Elgin	Elgin
Tho. Houston	Farmer	Deynample	Boleskine
Wm Jack	Messenger	Elgin	Elgin
Lud. Key	Gentleman	Ironside	
Cha. Lessley	B^r to Findrossie	Findrossie	
Rod. Mitchell	Shoemaker	Fort Aug^{tus}	
John M'lenan	Vintner	do.	
Don. M'donald	Lochgarry	Culachy	
Don. M'donald, Jn^r	of Scotas		

CONCERN'D IN THE REBELLION, WITH PROVE THE FACTS.

County.	Yearly Rent.	Condition of House.	Ex. Officers' Evidences.
Inverness			John Grant
do.		Good	Arch^d Graham
do.			William Porter
do.			Arch^d Graham
do.		Poor	do.
			do.
do.	150 0 0	Burnt	do.
			John Grant.
do.		Indiff^t	do.
			do.
			do.
			do.
			do.
Inverness		No house	do.
			do.
do.		Burnt	do.
do.		Indifferent	do.
do.			do.
			do.
Murray	28 0 0	Good	Roderick Merchant
Inverness			Arch^d Graham
Banff	83 0 0	Burnt	
Murray	8 0 0	Good	
Inverness		Indiff^t	John Grant
Murray	30 0 0		Alex. Dallas
			John Grant
			do.
			do.
Inverness		Burnt	do.
do.			do.

Names.	Designations.	Abode.	Parish.
Angus M'donald	of Greenfield	Garioloch	
Don. M'donald	of Shian	Shian	
John M'donald	of Arnabee	Arnabee	
Don. M'donald	B^r to do.	do.	
Alex. M'donald	of Octera	Octera	
All. M'donald	Son of Leck	Leck	
Don. M'donald	of Lundie	Lundie	
Don. M'donald, Junr	of Lundie	do.	
Alex. M'donald	Servant	Fort Aug^s	
Alex. M'donald	Vintner	Laggan	Laggan
Don. M'donald	Chelsea man	Inverness	Inverness
Lauch. M'Intosh	Merch^t	do.	do.
Evan. M'pherson	of Cluny	Cluny	Laggan
— M'pherson	Farmer	Dalwhiny	
Lewis M'pherson	do.	Delrady	
Mal. M'pherson	Son of Phoness	Phoness	Kingussie
— M'pherson	of Strathmassie	Strathmassie	Laggan
John M'pherson	Farmer	Garvamore	
Don. M'pherson	do.	Brachachy	
And. M'pherson Junr	of Bonasher	Bonasher	
John M'pherson	of Etridge	Etridge	Kingussie
John M'pherson	Farmer	Pitachuran	
Hugh M'pherson	do.	Coraldy	
Evan M'pherson	do.	Legan of Nood	Kingussie
Lauch M'pherson	do.	Pitmain	
Lauch M'pherson J^r	Strathnessie	Strathnessie	
Ken. M'pherson	Mer^t	Ruthven	
Angus M'bean	Farmer	Faillie	
Gilles M'bean	do.	Birnaghton	
Dun. M'intosh	do.	Drummond	
Gilleas M'bean	Servant	Aldourie	
John M'lean	Writer	Inverness	Inverness
Alex. M'Gilivray	of Dunmaglass	Dunmaglass	
Alex. M'Gilivray	Taxman	Pettie	
Robt. M'Gilivray	Farmer	do.	
Angus M'Intosh	of Pharr	Pharr	
John Perrie	Servant	Elgin	Elgin
Hugh Ross	do.	do.	do.
Hugh Stewart	Gairdner	Ft. Augustus	
James Shaw	Servant	Moy	
William Taylor	Carter	Elgin	Elgin
Tho. Watson	Servant	do.	do.
George Young	Taylor	do.	do.

ELGIN DISTRICT—*Continued.* 337

County.	Yearly Rent.	Condition of House.	Excise Officers' Evidences.
Inverness			John Grant
do.		Burnt	do.
do.		Burnt	do.
do.			do.
do.		Burnt	do.
do.			do.
do.		Burnt	do.
do.			do.
			do.
			do.
Inverness			Arch^d Graham
do.	30 0 0	Good	John Findlay
			James Brown
			do.
			do.
Inverness			do.
do.			do.
			do.
			do.
			do.
Inverness		Indiff^t	do.
			do.
			do.
Inverness		Indiff^t	do.
			do.
			do.
			do.
			Daniel M'Lennan
			do.
			do.
			do.
Inverness			John Grant
do.			do.
			do.
			do.
			do.
Murray			Alexander Dallas
do.			do.
			John Grant
			Arch^d Graham
Murray			Alex. Dallas
do.			do.
do.			do.

A LIST OF PERSONS IN EDINBURGH REBELLION, WITH EVIDENCES

Names.	Designations.	Abode.
James Allan	Merchant	Edin^r
Will. Brodie	Gunsmith	Cannongate
John Break	Merchant	Edin^r
James Brand	Watch maker's son	Edin^r
John Bayne	late Servt to Broughton	
John Bowie	Journey Taylor	Cannongate
Edw. Callander	Goldsmith	Edin^r
Alex. Coutts	Goldsmith's serv^t	do.
Henry Clark	Residenter	Cannongate
Cha. Colquhoun	Wright	Pleasants
Andrew Coupar	Son to Da. Coupar y^r	Cannongate
Robt Drumond	Mess^r at Arms	Edin^r
Alex. Davidson	Shoemaker	do.
John Esplin	Merchant	do.
Alex. Fife	Taylor's Son	Potter row
John Ferguson	Taylor	Edin^r
Richd Giles	Residenter	Cannongate
Robt Gordon	Alehouse keeper	do.
John Goodwillie	Writer	Edin^r
Geo. Hamilton	of Reidhouse	do.
James Hepburn Racart	of Keith	
Geo. Home	late Writer's son	Edin^r
Andrew Johnston	Servt to D. Hamilton	
James Johnston	Merch$^{t's}$ Son	Edin^r
Arch^d Kennedy	Goldsmith Apprentice	do.
Patrick Keir	Wright	Edin^r
James Lawder	Merch^t Apprentice	do.
Robt Mitchel	Goldsmith's Servt	do.
Anth. Murray	Goldsmith App.	do.
Ken. M'Kenny	Journey Goldsmith	do.

AND PRECINCTS CONCERN'D IN THE
TO PROVE THE SAME.

Evidences.
George Porteous, Ex. Officer.
Nin. Trotter, Geo. Robertson & Fra. Pringle, Ex. Officers.
James Murray, Taylor, in Cannongate.
Geo. Porteous, Ex. Off^r & Ja. Miller, Writer in Selkirk.
Wm Bennet, Ex. Off^r & Wm Younger in Linton in Tweedale.
Robt Ramsay, Taylor in St. Mary's Wind, Ed^r.
Geo. Porteous & John Smith, Ex. Officers.
Robt Gordon & Robt Low, Goldsmiths in Ed^r.
Nin. Trotter, Geo. Robertson & Fra. Pringle, Ex. Officers.
Da. Morison, Brewer, & John Davidson, Wright in the Abbay.
Ja. Easson, Ex. Off^r & Cromwell Easson, Shoemaker, Ed^r.
Geo. Robertson, Ex. Officer.
John Smith, Geo. Porteous & John Anderson, Ex. Officers.
Da. Morrison, Brewer & Jno Davidson, Wright. both in Abbay.
Robt Ramsay, Taylor, St. Mary's Wynd, Edin^r.
Do.
Jo. Wood, Vintner, & Alex. Spark, ale seller, Cannongate.
John Izat, Chandler & Colin Mitchel, Goldsmith, Cannongate.
Ja. Thomson & Geo. Robertson, Ex. Officers.
Nin. Trotter, Geo. Robertson & Fra. Pringle, Ex. Off^{rs}.
Ro. Brown, Geo. Robertson & Geo. Porteous, Ex. Officers.
Geo. Robertson, Ex. Officer.
Da. Morrison, Brewer & Jno Davidson, Wright in the Abbay.
Alex. Strang, Geo. Robertson & Fra. Pringle, Ex. Officers.
Ja. Ker, Goldsmith, & Ro. Brown, Excise Off^r both in Ed^r.
Robt Harvie & Ja. Jack, Brewers in Ed^r.
Geo. Porteous, Ex. Off^r & Robt Ramsay, Taylor, Ed^r.
Robt Gordon & Robt Low, Goldsmiths in Ed^r.
Dougal Ged & Robt Low, Goldsmiths in Ed^r.
Dougal Ged & Edward Lothian, Goldsmiths in Ed^r.

Names.	Designations.	Abode.
Marmaduke M'beath	Powder Flask maker	Cannongate
Alex. M'kenzie	Shoemaker	do.
Robt Maxwell	Writer	Edin^r
John Mitchel	Alehouse keeper	Cannongate
John M'Grigor	Gardiner	do.
Tho. Mitchel	Goldsmith	Edin^r
Wm Muschet	Wright App.	Edin^r
W^m M'Leish	Servt to Roy Stewart	Ed^r
Robt Niccol	Mason	Cannongate
Walter Orrok	Shoemaker	Ed^r
John Petrie	Aleseller	Ed^r
Tho. Robertson	Goldsmith's Servt	Ed^r
Alex. Reid	do.	do.
Ja. Rutherford	do.	do.
Alex. Stevenson	Journey Wright	do.
Cha. Stewart	Wright	Cannongate
Arch^d Stratton	Watchmaker	Edin^r
Dougal Souter	Mess^r at Arms	
Adam Tait	Goldsmith	Ed^r
John Wilson	Barber	Cannongate
James Winram	Son to the late Eymouth	do.
James Walker	Candlemaker's Servt	do.
Will. Wilson	Turner	Edin^r
John Aikman	Porter	Leith
Cha. Allan	Cooper	do.
David Beat	Mer^t	do.
Ro^t Bisset	Brickmaker	do.
Alex. Brymer	Baxter	do.
Robt Brymer	do.	do.
John Brown	Vintner	do.
John Bruce	do.	do.
Andrew Cooper	Cooper	do.
Walt. Drummond	Porter	do.
Da. Hodge	do.	do.
Hector M'lean	do.	do.
David Murray		do.
Adolphus Muir	Servant	do.
Chas Paterson	do.	do.
James Peth	Porter	do.
John Punton	do.	do.
Adolphus Riddel	Glasier	Leith
Reid James	Innkeeper	do.

EDINBURGH, ETC.—Continued.

Evidences.

Nin. Trotter, Geo. Robertson & Ja. Easson, Ex. Officers.
John & Will. Parks, Journey Shoemakers, Ed^r.
Geo. Robertson & Fra. Pringle, Ex. Officers.
Wm Lithgow, Maltster, Jno. Brown &c. his serv^t, Caldton.
Ja. & Wm Fleemings &c. Brewers in Caldton.
Robt Ramsay, Taylor, St. Mary's Wynd, Ed^r.
Robt Ramsay, Taylor, St. Mary's Wynd, Ed^r.
James Easson, Ex. Officer.
James Purdie, Skinner, & Geo. Robertson, Ex. Off^r Ed^r.
John & Ja. Aitkin's, Wrights, Tho. Beatson, Baxter & David Beatson, Hosier in Cannongate.
Robt Beatson, Baxter, Jo. Smith & Ro. Brown, Ex. Officers.
Wm Ayton & Pet. Spalding, Goldsmiths.
Wm Ayton & Robt Low, Goldsmiths, Ed^r.
   Do.
Ro. Brown, Ex. Off^r & Alex. Jackson, Shoemaker, Ed^r.
Jno. & Ja. Aitkins, Wrights in Cannongate & Tho. Wallace, Smith there.
Mark Sprott, Skinner & Geo. Areskine, Chandler, Ed^r & Ex. Officers.
Geo. Robertson, & Fra. Paterson, Ex. Officers.
Cha. Blair & Robt Low, Goldsmiths in Ed^r.
Geo. Porteous Ex. Off^r and Fra. Montgomery, Barber, Cannongate.
Geo. Robertson, Nin. Trotter & Fra. Pringle, Ex. Officers.
John Izate, Candlemaker in Cannongate & Fra. Paterson, Ex. Officer.
Da. Morrison, Brewer, & Jno. Davidson, Wright, both in the Abbay.
John Balfour in Leith, Stage Coach master.
Hen. Morison, Wm Gibson, Geo. Calder & Ja. Boyle, Ex. Officers.
   Do.
   Do.
All his neighbourhood.
   Do.
Thomas Miln, Mason, Powderhall.
The neighbourhood & Henry Morison, Ex. Officer.
Wm Gibson, Hen. Morrison, Geo. Calder & Ja. M‘duff, Ex. Officers.
Robt Osburn & Ja. Boyle, Ex. Off^{rs}.
The above John Balfour.
The neighbourhood.
Fullarton & Cairns, Distillers in Leith.
The above John Balfour.
   Do.
His neighbour Porters.
   Do.
Mr Balfour of the old Stage Coach Office.
   Do.

Names.	Designations.	Abode.
Robert Scott	Baxter	Leith
George Scott	Carter	do.
Will. Spark	Porter	do.
Alex. Steven	do.	do.
John Fyre	Carter	do.
Roy Bain M'intosh		
Patrick Butchard		
Tho. Dey	Turner	Edin^r
John Gordon		
Tho. Halliburton		
Mark Kerr		
Willison		

Evidences.

The neighbourhood & Hen. Morrison, Ex. Off^r.
The above Mr Balfour.
      Do.
Henry Morrison, Ex. Off^r.
The above Mr Balfour.
John Chapman Junr Ex. Off^r & Ensign Jno. M'Kay of the Suthrland Milittia.
John Chapman & Geo. Porteous, Ex. Off^{rs}.
Wm Simpson, Da. Murray & J. Burnlee all in Hamilton.
John Sloss, Ex. Off^r & Deacon Lawson, Weaver, Ed^r.
Wm Begg & Jno Chapman, Ex. Off^{rs}.
Jno Chapman, Ex. Off^r & Robt Kerr, Porter in the Ex. Office.
Wm Begg & Cha. Campbell, Ex. Officers.

LIST OF REBELLS FROM KIRKALDY

Names.	Designations.	Abode.	Parish.
Da. Boswell	Mer^t	Dubieside	Markinch
Alex. Balfour	Farmer	Colingsburgh	Kilconquar
Alex. Gall	Salt Off^r	Kirkaldy	Kirkaldy
Robt Hamilton	Junr Kilbrachm^t		Kilconquair
Ja. Malcolm, Junr	Balbeddie		Balingary
Christ. Seton		Methill	Weems
Alex. Seton	Son to above Ch^r	do.	do.

DISTRICT, WITH EVIDENCES.

County.	Witnesses.
Fife	Ja. & Wm Wall Walker & Da. Goodsir all in Leven.
do.	Tho. Bogle, Surgeon & Bessie Thom, Spinster in Colinsburgh.
do.	His Receipts to Brewers in Fife for Excise.
do.	Alex. Gourly, Smith in Colinsburgh, Tho. Henderson, Servant in Bowes in Ely Parish.
do.	John M'Gill, Mer^t Kirkaldy, Messrs Alex. Steedman late Provost & others in Kirkaldy.
do.	Elizabeth Dowie, Spouse to Da. Ramsay, Sailor in Leven & Isobell Burns his niece.
do.	His Receipts to Traders in Fife.

A LIST OF PERSONS IN GLASGOW & THE REBELLION, WITH EVIDENCES

Rebell's Names as in former List.	Designations.
Peter Bell	
Robert Duff	
James Finnie	
William Gray	
John Graham of	Kilmordinny
John Graham	painter
Robt Hamilton	
Tho. Robertson	
Ja. Stirling of	Craigbarnet
Ja. Stirling	Son to Northside
Hugh Stirling	Son to Keir
William Stirling	Son to do.
Walter Stuart	
Peter Stuart	
Andrew Sprewl	
Ja. Stirling	of Keir
Robt White	
Al. Graham in Glasgow	Chapman
Andrew Wood	Shoemaker
Grigor Grant	Glass grinder

COUNTRY ADJACENT CONCERN'D IN THE TO PROVE THE SAME.

Evidences' Names.
Matt. Wilson, Maltman, & Wm Brownlee, Innkeeper, both in Glasgow.   Will. Tennent & Robt Kerr, painters in Glasgow.   Malcolm Cowbrugh, Tennent, & Malcolm Cowbrugh, his son, both in the parish of Campsie, & Ja. Reid, Gardiner in Herriot's Work, Ed^r.   Ja. Aird, Weaver & Ja. Picken, Innkeeper, both in Gorbals, at Glasgow.   Alex. Forrester, Vintner, Ja. Forrester, Maltman, both in Kilsyth, Wm Adam, Farmer in Craigston in Kilsyth, Alex. Dick, Maltman & John Rob, Town Officer, both in Glasgow.   Wm Tennent, Robt Kerr & Jno Borland, painters in Glasgow.   Da. Findlay of Bogside, Robt Miller, portioner & Robt Finnie, Wright all in Balmor & Baldernock parish, Alex. Dick, Maltman in Glasgow & James Buchanan, Stabler there.   Tho. Breakenrig, Barber, Will. Currie, Innkeeper & Tho. Robins, Founder, all in Gorbals at Glasgow.   Arch^d Graham, Jno Muir, Will. Muir & Jno Calder, portioners in Burdstone in the parish of Campsie & many others in that parish.   } Robert Tennent, Vintner in Glasgow, David Dun his Drawer, Will. Cunningham, his Gardiner & Will Anderson, Hostler to said Tennent.   Malcolm Cowbrugh's Senr & Junr in Campsie Parish & Ja. Reid, Gardiner in Herriot's Work.   Ja. Cousland, Servt to Tho. Borland in Udston in Blantyre Parish, Jno Borthwick, Servt to Major Robertson in Emock near Hamilton & Ja. Scott, Servt to Jno Henderson in Emock hill in s^d parish.   John Rob & John Johnston, Town Off^{rs} in Glasgow, Alex. Dick, Maltman there & Ja. Buchanan, Stabler there.   Robt Rea of Littlegovan near Glasgow, John Hamilton, Innkeeper in Glasgow, Alex. Dick, Maltman there & Ja. Buchanan, Stabler there.   Jno Borland, Wm Tennent & Robt Kerr, all painters in Glasgow.   Ja. Graham, Taylor, Al. Dick, Maltman, & Ro. M'Nair, Mer^t all in Glasgow.   Ja. M'Kettrick, Ex. Off^r & his son, both in Glasgow.   Jno Jamison, Wright & Ja. Alison, Maltman, both in Glasgow.

LIST OF PERSONS FROM DUNFERMLINE WITH EVIDENCES TO

Rebell's Names.	Designations.	Abode.
John Allan	Wright	Alloa
Charles Blaw	Son to Castlehill	Castlehill
Hary Bruce	of Clackmanan	
James Bruce	Gentlemen	Clackmanan
Ja. Callender	Baker	Innerkeithing
Dan. Cameron	Coachman	Kincarden
Will. Comry	Stewart to E. Moray	
Fra. Craich	Mercht	Clackmanan
Da. Henderson	Glasier	do.
John Henderson	Mercht	do.
James Main	Brewer	Alloa
Fra. Masterton	of Parkmiln	
Robt Mercer	of Aldie	Aldie
John Marshal	Labourer	Alloa
John Marshal	Writer	Kinross
Alex. Montieth	Residenter	do.
Anth. Murray	of East Grange	
John Murray	Clerk to Collr of Customs	Alloa
Wm Verty	Carpenter	Alloa

DISTRICT CONCERN'D IN THE REBELLION, PROVE THE SAME.

Evidences' Names.

Anthony Newby Ex. Off^r at Stirling & William and James Davidson Elders in Alloa.
John Rolland & Robert Geddes, Baillies in Culross & John Halkerston Town Clerk there.
Will. & Alex. Anderson, James Dempster, John Ferguson, Robert Lindsay, William M'viccar, Wm Steen & Robt Wilson, all Residenters in Clackmanan.
The persons immediatly preceeding.
William Roxburgh, John Kirkaldie & Adam Turnbull, all Baillies in Kirkaldie.
William Wilson, Town Clerk of Dunfermline, John Pearson, Wright in Torry & And. Glen, Ex. Off^r in Torryburn.
The persons witnesses ag^t James Callander.
Alexander Anderson, James Dempster, Jno Donaldson, John Ferguson & many others Inhabitants in Clackmanan.
John Donaldson, Robt Henderson, Betty Nasmith, Andrew Tasy, Residenters in Clackmanan & Marg^t Paterson, residenter in Kinnet.
James Dempster, Jno Donaldson, Da. M'viccar, W^m M'viccar, Da. M'laren, Betty Nasmith, Wm Steen, & Robt Wilson, Residenters in Clackmanan.
James Haig, Innkeeper in Alloa & W^m & James Davidsons, Baillies there.
The persons Evidences ag^t the Laird of Clackmanan.
John Kelly of Newbigging, Adam Colvill, Tacksman of Aldie Parks & Wm Colvill, Brewer in Crook of Daven.
Robert Thomson, Charles White and Ja. Paton all Brewers in Alloa.
James Stuart, Sheriff Depute in Kinross, Wm Lendrum Ex. Off^r in Kirkintilloch & Ja. Dunbar, Servitor, to Sir John Bruce Hope of Kinross.
Those immediately preceeding.
Those opposite to Charles Blaw as above.
James Haig, Innkeeper in Alloa, Tho. Paterson, Ex. Off^r in Clackmanan & Fra. Brodie, Clerk in Alloa Custom house.
Those opposite to James Main.

FOLLOWS A LIST OF THOSE FORMERLY MENTION'D WHO HAVE ESTATES.

Names.	Designations.	Rental.			Condition of Mansion House.
Mr Bruce of	Clackmanan	100	0	0	Habitable
Mr Masterton of	Parkmiln	250	0	0	do.
Mr Mercer of	Aldie	400	0	0	do.
Mr Murray of	East Grange	72	0	0	do.

LIST OF PERSONS FROM DUNDEE DISTRICT CONCERN'D IN THE REBELLION WITH EVIDENCES TO PROVE THE CHARGE AG^T THEM.

Rebell's Names.	Designations.	Evidences' Names.
Thomas Birrell	Merchant	Joseph Peck Excise Officer at Dundee.
David Graham	do.	Geo. Paton, Ex. Officer at Montrose & the s^d Joseph Peck.
Alex. Graham	Son to s^d David	do.
Charles Horn	Shoemaker	The above Joseph Peck.
James Kernegie	of Balmachie	do.
Peter Ouchterlony	Coffeehouse keeper	do.
Charles Rattray	late of Dunoon	do.
William Low	Chapman	Tho. Wilson, Ex. Off^r at Benvie.

LIST OF PERSONS FROM ST. ANDREWS WITH EVIDENCES TO

Rebell's Names.	Designations.	Abode.	Parish.
Will. Aytone	Residenter	Craill	Craill
George Cleland		Pittenweem	Pittenweem
Robert Cleland		Craill	Craill
Henry Crawford		do.	do.
Elizabeth Crawford		Anstruther Wester	Anstruther
George Findlay	Heelmaker	Anstruther	do.
Robert Haxton	Surgeon	St. Andrews	St. Andrews
Robert Leith		Pittenweem	Pittenweem
Andrew Lothian		Cellardyke	Pittenweem
Maiden	Surgeon	Craill	Craill
George M'Gill		Cambuck	Cambuck
Alex. Oram	Coupar	Coupar	Coupar
Tho. Oliphant	Wright	West Anstruther	Anstruther
Robt. Philip		Craill	Craill
Reid	Spouse to John Skeen	do.	do.
Cha. Sibbald		St. Andrews	St. Andrews
Alex. Steven	Porter	Leith	Leith
Will. Thomson		Pittenweem	Pittenweem
Da. Weems	Surgeon	Coupar	Coupar
John Wright	do.		do.

DISTRICT CONCERN'D IN THE REBELLION PROVE THE SAME.

Evidences' Names.

John Black & Tho. Taylor, Shoemakers in Craill.
Janet Todie, Victualer in Pittenweem & Janet Mason, Spouse to Will. Thomson, Brewer there.
John Ross, Ex. Officer & the Town Councill.
Alex. Oliphant & John Brown Brewers in Craill.
Geo. Brown & Kath. Reid both Serv^{ts} to the s^d Eliz. Crawford & John Brown, Town Treasurer in Anstruther Wester.
John Dawson Servt to James Fleeming, Shoemaker in Anstruther Easter, James Fleeming & John Traill & others, Shoemakers there.
Robt Bell, Mer^t in Couper & —— Daw, Relict of Will. Coupar late Baillie there & David Nicoll Stabler there.
Janet Todie, Victualer in Pittenweem & Janet Mason, Spouse to Will. Thomson, Brewer there.
James Simpson, Town Treasurer of Cellardyke, Marjory Alison his Spouse, Marjory Alison their Servt & Tho. Anderson Brewer there.
Alex. Oliphant, Alex. Mapsie, Andrew Jamieson, all in Craill, & John Ross, Ex. Officer there.
David Paterson in Dearsie & Tho. Shepherd in Cambuck Miln.
Mary Dott, Spouse to Wm Melvill, Brewer in Coupar. Helen Morris & Grisell Kelkpatrick, Serv^ts to Mr Oram.
Alex. Stephen, porter in Leith, George Robertson & Kath. Reid, then Serv^{ts} to Mrs Rolland, &c.
John Morris & Geo. Anderson, both in Craill.
John, Ja. & Tho. Watson &c. in Craill.
Da. Coupar in Colinsburgh, Robt Bell, Mer^t in Coupar, John Arnot, Surgeon & Da. Nicol Stabler there.
Geo. Robison & Kath. Reid late Serv^{ts} to Mrs Rolland in Anstruther Wester.
John Skinner, Compt. of the Customs at Anstruther & John Fullen, Ex. Off^r there.
Robt Bell, Mer^t in Coupar, John Arnot, Surgeon there, David Nicol, Stabler there & Mr Halket Schoolmaster there &c.
The above witnesses.

APPENDIX

I.
ANALYSIS OF THE LIST.

The whole number of rebels here reported upon may be stated at 2590. The number returned in the first List, in obedience to the General Letter of instructions from the Excise Commissioners on the 7th May 1746, was 2520. But it appears that on receipt of the first returns further instructions were issued requiring the names of the 'evidences,' or witnesses, who could testify to the facts, and perhaps fuller information with regard to the value of the property held by the parties implicated. In collecting the evidence for this second or supplementary List the officers seem to have discovered about 70 additional names of rebels. There are some variations between the two Lists in the spelling of names and the description of persons, which are noticed below. It may be assumed that the List as a whole is the most authentic muster-roll of the Pretender's army now extant, having been compiled by Government officers stationed in the respective districts, within a year after the battle of Culloden, when the parties giving the information were not likely to incur jeopardy by stating the facts fully and freely. In the matter of numbers, however, the List is at variance with the common traditional estimates, which usually rest on the statements of contemporary newspapers, or the writings of some of the actors in the campaign. From such sources we learn that Charles brought with him from France a retinue consisting of four Irishmen—Sheridan, Macdonald, Kelly, and Sullivan; three Scotsmen—the Marquis of Tullibardine, Macdonald, and Buchanan; one Englishman —Strickland, with a squad of 100 soldiers, partly Irish and partly French. When, on the 20th of August 1745, the young Chevalier unfurled his father's standard at Glenfinnan, it is said to have been saluted with the cheers of 800 Camerons ready armed for the war. Six days after, at Aberchallader, his following numbered over 1800. The Edinburgh newspapers of 2d September inform us that 'the Highland Army' amounted by one account to 2000, by another to 3000 or 4000 men. On their arrival in Edinburgh on the 17th of September, Mr. Home the historian visited their camp, and estimated their number at 'less than 2000.' At the same time a requisition was laid upon the city for 6000 pairs of shoes, 1000 tents, 2000 targets, and other commodities in proportion. Four days later the battle of

Prestonpans was fought, in regard to which the *Caledonian Mercury* records, that 'after the most strict enquiry, it now most obviously appears that only 1456 of the Highland army engaged and foiled that commanded by Mr. Cope.' After this success the rebel force was considerably augmented, but almost entirely from the north.

The strength of these accessions was, as usual, exaggerated. Thus it was said that 'the Macdonalds and MacLeods from the Western Isles were expected in Athole on Friday last to the number of 3000.' These, it need hardly be said, did not join the movement; while for the royal cause they mustered little more than one-tenth of the number above reported.

Further, it was announced at the same time that 'the Lord Pitsligo will arrive in town this week at the head of 500 gentlemen and others, who have been raised in the shires of Aberdeen and Banff.' Two days later the same journal contains the following official note :—

'*From the Scots army at Duddingston, Octr.* 9 :—This afternoon the Prince reviewed that part of his army which is encamped here. His Royal Highness appeared in Lowland Dress. Before the Review was over the Right Hon. the Lord Pitsligo came into the camp from Linlithgow, at the head of a squadron of Horsemen, consisting of 132 Knights, Freeholders, and landed Gentlemen, besides their servants, all extremely well mounted and accoutred: They are all Gentlemen of experience, and are mostly above 40 years of age. There came in at the same time 6 companies of Foot raised in the shire of Aberdeen by the said Noble Lord Pitsligo.

'*N.B.*—The Lord Pitsligo's squadron are all in Highland Dress, amounting in all to 248 men.'

To these somewhat indefinite quantities there was added a force of '1400 men from the countries of Strathavin, Glenlivet, Strathdon, etc., as brave fellows as ever stept under arms, mostly Grants and Farquharsons,' and also '480 brave fellows from the countries of Strathbogie, and Enzie.' Besides some other minor accessions, the *Courant* reports on 22d October : 'The army increases, and several strong Bodies are on the Road to join it.' And six days after, the *Mercury* reports : 'We hear the Duke of Athol with a great Body of Troops has already passed the Forth, in order to rejoin the Prince's army, and more are still behind.' Gordon of Glenbucket was, about the same time, reported to be on the way with a following of 2000; a later account puts the number at 1400, and Aikman, who usually follows Home, estimates Glenbucket's force at 400. On 2d November, when Charles assembled his forces at Dalkeith, in order to march toward the English border, it is reported that Macpherson of Cluny and Menzies of Shian arrived with about 1000 followers. Putting these various figures together the army that invaded England should have amounted to nearly seven thousand. It is, however, asserted by Lord George Murray, who had a chief command, that they were 'not above 5000 fighting men, if so many.' There was also, it should be noted, a considerable force remaining in the north of Scotland, under Viscount Strathallan and Lord Lewis Gordon, to keep in check the royal army under Lord Loudon. When both divisions were brought together before the battle of Falkirk, Mr. Patullo, muster-master of the rebel forces, states their entire number at 9000.

On the other hand, to the general impression resulting from these various statements the List now published presents some interesting points of comparison, or of contrast, as the case may be.

The rebellion of 1745 is almost always referred to as if peculiarly a Highland affair. Both by contemporary or later writers the movement is regarded, with little or no discrimination, as exemplifying, on the one hand, the ignorance and barbarism of the Highlanders, or, on the other, their heroic valour and devoted loyalty to a dethroned and exiled dynasty. It is true that the people actively concerned in it belonged almost entirely to those parts of Scotland lying north of the river Forth : but the inhabitants of that region are not all 'Highlanders.' Of the surnames recorded in the List considerably less than the half are Highland clan names—and the persons denoted by them are not all from the clan districts. The great bulk of the rebel force, or about two-thirds of it, is derived from about Dundee, Kincardine, Aberdeen, and other north-eastern parts, which are no more Highland than are Fife and the Lothians. It will be observed from the table of surnames given below, that the Camerons, for instance, are reckoned at 33 clansmen. What has become of the 800 of that name who cheered the uplifted standard at Glenfinnan? And where in these meagre rows of Celtic patronymics can the material be found of the famous clan battalions, of which even the cautious Lord George Murray boasts?

The clan names are thus approximately enumerated:—

Buchanans	5	MacArthurs	1
Camerons .	33	MacBains .	5
Campbells .	9	MacColls .	7
Drummonds	19	MacCullochs	2
Duffs	2	MacDonalds	60
Farquharsons	25	MacDougalds	1
Forbeses .	11	MacEwans	5
Frasers	52	MacFarlanes	4
Gordons .	71	MacFarquhars	5
Grahames .	5	MacGillivrays	4
Grants	57	MacGregors	17
MacAlisters	3	Mackintoshes	7
MacAlpines	1	MacIntyres	3
MacAndrews	1	Mackays and Mackies	8

APPENDIX I.

Mackenzies	32	MacTavishes	3
MacLarens	4	MacWilliams	5
MacLachlans	19	Menzies	8
MacLeas	6	Ogilvies	27
MacLeans	13	Robertsons	41
MacLennans	2	Rosses	29
MacLeods	2	Stewarts	104
MacNabs	2	Sutherlands	5
Macphersons	28	Tullochs	2
MacRaes	1	Urquharts	5
MacRobies	4		

These, with some other names not belonging to distinct clans, amount to about 780.

This summary may suggest that the List must be very incomplete: absolutely complete it is not, but from a comparison with other sources of information it will be found that the omissions are probably few.

In regard to about 200 of the whole number the remark occurs that they were 'forced out,' or 'compelled,' or 'pressed.' About 130 are described as 'hired' by others in the country as substitutes. The forcing out appears to have been somewhat general, as many of the rebel leaders were charged with so coercing their people.

The conditions of the various individuals at the time when the list was compiled are thus summarised:—

Prisoners	about 300
Lurking	460
Absconding	10
Left the country	24
Bailed out	13
Wounded	6
Killed	103
Dead	20
Hanged (by the rebels for robbery)	1
Beheaded	1
Not known	620

There are many of whose condition nothing is stated.

In regard to the social position of the followers of Charles named in the List, the subjoined summary may be of interest.

Of peers, including two countesses, there are fourteen—of knights, lairds or landowners, great and small, with members of their families, there are about 320. These, reckoned according to their districts, stand thus:—

Aberdeen	15
Argyle	43
Banff	20

ANALYSIS OF THE LIST. 361

Caithness	1
Dumfries	14
Dundee	42
Dunfermline	5
Duns	2
Edinburgh	6
Elgin (including Inverness)	52
Glasgow	5
Haddington	5
Kirkcaldy	2
Lanark	2
Linlithgow	6
Montrose	9
Old Meldrum	17
Paisley	1
Perth	30
Ross	27
St. Andrews	3
Stirling	15

The designations and trades of the rank and file are thus tabulated:—

Alehouse-keepers	3	Coachmen	2
Apprentices	28	Coalgrieve	1
Bakers (or baxters)	10	Coalhewers	2
Bailies	8	Coffeehouse-keepers	2
Barbers	17	Collectors of Cess	3
Beggar	1	Cook	1
Bellman	1	Coopers	2
Blacksmiths	4	Cottars	10
Bleacher	1	Dancing-master	1
Boatmen	2	Deserters from royal army	8
Bookseller	1	Doctors	2
Boys	5	Drummer	1
Brazier	1	Dysters	9
Brewers and maltsters	58	Extraordinary tidesmen	2
Bricklayers	1	Factors	9
Brickmaker	1	Farmers	117
Brogmakers	4	Feuars	2
Butchers or fleshers	8	Fiddlers	3
Buttermaker	1	Gaoler	1
Candlemaker	1	Gardeners	16
Carpenters	3	Gentlemen	25
Carriers	8	Glass-grinder	1
Carters	2	Glaziers	6
Change-keepers	2	Glovers	2
Chapmen	8	Goldsmiths	10
Clerks	3	Grieves	5

Groom	.	1	School-boys	2
Gunsmiths		4	Schoolmasters	4
Heelmaker	.	1	Servants .	280
Hookmakers	. .	2	Shepherd .	1
Horsehirers	. .	8	Sheriff-officers	6
House carpenters	.	2	Shipmasters	11
Householders	. .	3	Shoemakers	51
Huxster	. .	1	Silkdyer . .	1
Idlers	. .	3	Silversmiths . .	4
Indwellers	. .	43	Skinners and tanners	6
Innkeepers	. .	16	Slaters . .	4
Joiner	. .	1	Smiths . .	31
Labourers .	. . .	116	Snuff-grinder . .	1
Lieutenant in navy	. .	1	Sorter of yarn .	1
Mathematical Instrument maker	. . .	1	Stablers . Steward .	2 1
Masons	. . .	32	Stranger .	1
Mealmongers	. .	2	Subtenants .	11
Merchants	. .	106	Surgeons . .	28
Messengers-at-Arms .	.	5	Tacksmen .	7
Messengers	. .	2	Tailors . .	27
Millers	. . .	5	Tenants . .	44
Ministers (non-juring)	.	8	Threadmakers .	3
Musician	. . .	1	Tinker . .	1
Notary	. . .	1	Tobacconists .	3
Officers (civil)	. .	35	Town Cadie	1
Painters	. .	5	Town Clerk	1
Pedlar	. .	1	Town Officer	1
Pendiclemen	. .	5	Tradesmen	3
Physicians	.	2	Troneman	1
Picture Drawers	.	2	Turners . .	4
Pilots	. .	2	Vagabond .	1
Pipers	. .	5	Valet de Chambre	1
Ploughmen	. .	36	Victuallers .	2
Popish priests	. .	4	Vintners .	12
Porters	. .	15	Waiter . .	1
Postmaster	. .	1	Watchmakers .	2
Powder-flask maker	.	1	Waulker (fuller)	1
Printers	. . .	2	Weavers . .	84
Procurator	. .	1	Wigmakers .	8
Ropemakers	. .	3	Workmen .	100
Saddlers	. .	5	Wrights .	48
Sailors	. .	37	Writers .	23
Salmon-fishers .	.	13	Young men .	3
Salt-officers	.	20	Not designed .	260

The names of about half a dozen ladies are mentioned as rebels acting either with or without the co-operation of their husbands.

II.

BIOGRAPHICAL NOTES.

Of the great majority of persons named in the List nothing is generally known beyond what is therein recorded. Having been suddenly drawn or driven from their quiet homes into the vortex of a revolutionary movement, most of the survivors, after the final disaster, would be content to glide again into safe obscurity.

The few notes which follow in reference to some of the names are necessarily of an incidental and fragmentary character.

ABERDEEN DISTRICT.

P. 2. *William Aberdeen, vintner.*—It would appear he had not 'lurked' very long, as the inventory of his estate, given up in 1749, bears that he died in April 1746. His widow, Ann Dalgarno, claimed £339, 4s. 11d. under marriage-contract provision. The children called as parties to the appointment of executors were James, William, Rachel, Margaret, Anne, and Helen.

P. 2. *John Alexander, picture drawer.*—A descendant of George Jamesone, the eminent painter, who was a fellow-student with Vandyck, and his senior by some years. Marjory, the elder daughter of Jamesone, was married to Mr. John Alexander, advocate, Aberdeen; and Mary, her younger sister, was the wife of Professor James Gregory, of Edinburgh, the distinguished mathematician. The two sisters were served heirs-portioners to their father George in half of the lands of Cowhill, in the barony of Esslemonth, Aberdeenshire.[1] The artistic faculty seems to have lingered in the family, as Mary Jamesone is credited with the execution of the fine tapestries in St. Nicholas Church, Aberdeen. John Alexander, descended of the marriage of Marjory Jamesone, early in the subsequent century studied his art upon the Continent, and, on his return to his native district, was favoured with the patronage of the Duchess of Gordon, and executed various historical pieces, besides many portraits. It seems probable that *Cosmo Alexander*, mentioned along with John, and with the same designation, was his brother or near relative.

P. 4. *Peter Byers, Esq. of Tonley.*—Second and only surviving

---

[1] Sheriff Court Records of Aberdeen, 20th May 1653.

son and heir of Robert Byres by his wife Jean, daughter of Patrick Sandilands, of Cottoun, near Aberdeen. Robert Byres (understood to have sprung from the family of Byres of Coates, Edinburgh), was a merchant of some note, first in the Netherlands, then in Aberdeen, and latterly in Dublin, where Peter (or rather Patrick), was born, 13th May 1713. About the time of his birth his father was accidentally drowned in Dublin Bay, and the widow soon after returned with her family to Aberdeenshire, where, in 1718, she purchased the barony of Tonley. Patrick married, in 1733, Janet, daughter of James Moir of Stoneywood. Of this marriage there were four sons and three daughters. After the defeat at Culloden, the Jacobite laird of Tonley remained for some time in hiding in the castle of Cluny, not far from his own house, until he found opportunity to escape to France. His friends having interceded for him, and represented that his name was erroneously entered on the list of proscribed persons as *Peter* instead of Patrick, he was, after some years, allowed to return home and to enjoy his estate.[1]

P. 6. *Peter Dogood of Auchinhove.*—This laird seems to be identical with Patrick Leslie Duguid of Auchinhove, son of Robert Duguid of Auchinhove by his wife Teresa, daughter of Patrick Count Leslie of Balquhain, by his wife Elizabeth, grand-daughter of William, Earl of Angus.

P. 8. *James Farquharson of Balmurret.*—A kinsman of the laird of Monaltrie. The company under his command appears to have taken part in the battles of Inverury, Falkirk, and Culloden. James Farquharson did not participate in the indemnity granted in 1747. From the Commissary Records of Aberdeen it appears that he was much in debt before the rebellion began. His estate was also named Balmurrel, and is now known as Balmoral, the Highland residence of Queen Victoria.

P. 8. *Francis Farquharson of Monaltrie.*—Second son of Alexander Farquharson of Monaltrie by his wife Anna Farquharson. The eldest son, John, though married, died without issue about the end of 1741. The third son, Robert, is described as 'in Kinaldine.' Alexander Farquharson of Monaltrie died on the eve of the rebellion, in July 1745. The family had taken part in the previous attempts to restore the Stewarts in 1689 and 1715, but do not appear to have been hardly dealt with by the Government on that account. Fidelity to the old dynasty was, however, preferred to gratitude to the new, when, in 1745, another opportunity arose to put their loyalty to the test. While the Pretender was at Edinburgh, after the victory at Prestonpans, waiting for

---

[1] *The Houses of Moir and Byres*, by A. J. Mitchell Gill. Edinburgh, 1885.

recruits, he was joined by the laird of Monaltrie, as the *Mercury* records, 'with a considerable corps of men' on the evening of 3d October 1745. The Farquharsons were present at the battles of Inverury, Falkirk, and Culloden. On this last occasion their leader was taken prisoner, and confined for some weeks at Inverness. Thence he was, with many others, conveyed to London in June, brought to trial in September, found guilty, and on 15th November condemned to death. On the evening before the day fixed for his execution he was reprieved, and soon afterwards pardoned; but whether he was sent with other pardoned rebels to America, has not been ascertained. In 1775 he petitioned the commissioners on the forfeited estates that they would allow him to rent a portion of his former estate on which to spend his old age. After some time this was granted. In a letter from his nephew, William Farquharson of Braxie, dated in 1784, Francis Farquharson, late of Monaltrie, is described as 'the only forfeiting person now alive,' and as having no children.

P. 8. *John Farquharson, farmer.*—Probably the same who is mentioned in the list of prisoners at Inverness on 19th April 1746.

P. 8. *Henry Farquharson, Whitehouse Miln.*—This is doubtless the Captain Farquharson of Whitehouse mentioned in the list of reported killed at Culloden. In the same list is the name of *Captain Farquharson of Auchrechan.*

P. 10. *George Gordon, Esq. of Halhead.*—Son and heir of Robert Gordon of Halhead by his wife Isabel Byres. The estate of Esslemont also belonged to the family. George Gordon, mentioned in the List, married Amy Bowdler, an English lady, and their descendant and eventual heiress, Anne Gordon, about the middle of this century, married Henry Wolrige-Gordon, now laird of Halhead and Esslemont. Mr. Thomas Bowdler, brother of Mrs. Gordon, professed to have copied a letter from her, and also to have taken down from her own mouth a statement, in reference to a visit paid by the Duke of Cumberland to her house of Halhead in February 1746. She affirmed that General Hawley, in spite of contrary orders from the Duke, 'packed up every bit of china I had, which I am sure would not be bought for £200, all my bedding and table linen, every book, my repeating clock, my worked screen, every rag of Mr. Gordon's clothes, the very hat, breeches, nightgown, shoes, and what shirts there was of the child's, twelve tea-spoons, strainer, and tongs, the japanned board on which the chocolate and coffee cups stood, and put them on board a ship in the night time, directed to himself at Holyrood House, Edinburgh. The flutes, music, and my cane, he made presents of. I had five pounds and a half of tea, seven loaves of fine sugar, half a hundred of lump, seven pounds of chocolate, a great stock of salt beef, pickled pork, hams, pease, butter, coals, peats, ale, verme-jelly, rice and spice, some cheese, brandy, rum, sago, hartshorn, salop, sweetmeats, Narbonne honey, two dozen washballs, with many other things which 'tis impossible to mention, all which he kept for himself, nor would he give me any share of them, even my empty bottles he took. The morning he went away, which was on Tuesday the 8th, he took the blankets and pillows off the beds, even the larding pins, iron screws, the fish kettle, and marble mortar.'

There is a *Lieutenant George Gordon* in a return of prisoners at Inverness dated 19th April 1746.

P. 10. *Francis Gordon of Kincardin Miln, writer.*—He did not long survive the campaign, as his will, subscribed at London 19th October 1746, was soon after confirmed at Aberdeen. He bequeathed his whole personal estate to William Duff of Corsindae and Alexander Chalmers of Balnacraig, for the use and benefit of Hugh Gordon, his only son, then an infant, and also for the maintenance and education of his daughters Helen and Ann, referring to the portions settled upon them in the marriage contract between him and Barbara Rose, his late spouse. The personal estate consisted entirely of debts due to him by various parties, chiefly Jacobites, including *John Burnet of Campfield*, Robert Mackie, in Mains of Midbelty, whose son *Peter* seems to have been an ensign in the rebel force (see page 16 of List), *James Farquharson of Balmurret*, who owed 1000 merks, and others.

P. 10. *Lord Lewis Gordon.*—Son of Alexander, second Duke of Gordon, by his wife Lady Henrietta, daughter of the Earl of Peterborough and Monmouth. Lord Lewis, a Lieutenant in the Royal Navy, declared for the Pretender, and was appointed to a command in the rebel force. His accession is thus chronicled by the *Mercury* of 16th October 1745 : 'Yesternight the Right Hon. Lord Lewis Gordon, third son of the deceast Alexander, Duke of Gordon, came and kissed the Prince's hand, and joined his Royal Highness's Standard. The Court, which was very numerous and splendid, seemed in great joy on this occasion, as several gentlemen, not only of the name of Gordon, but many others in the shires of Aberdeen, Banff, and Murray, who had declined joining the Prince's Standard unless some one or other of the sons of the Illustrious House of Gordon was to head them, will now readily come up and join the Army.' He was in command of the companies in the north until shortly before the battle of Falkirk. His chief exploit was the defeat of the Royalist detachment near Inverury in December 1745. The name of Lord Lewis Gordon was reported among the prisoners taken at Culloden; but whether that was so or not, he escaped abroad and was attainted. He died in France, unmarried, in 1754.

P. 12. *Mr. George Law, Nonjurant Minister.*—In list of prisoners at Inverness, 19th April 1746, he is described as chaplain.

P. 12. *David Lumsden, farmer.*—On 24th May 1746 edict was issued by the Sheriff of Aberdeen, citing James, Harry, John, and Margaret Lumsden, lawful children of the deceased David Lumsden in Mains of Auchlossan, who died in April of that year, to see executors appointed. Those named for the office were Charles Farquharson of Inverey, Alexander Grant of Grantfield, and Alexander Hunter in Craigens. In a subsequent deed the names of the trustees upon the estate are Lewis Barclay in Inverchat, Alexander Lumsden in Miln of Wester Coull, and *John Lumsden in Miln of Coull* (also named in List as a rebel). The value of the estate was considerable, and included several debts due by Jacobite neighbours, such as *Patrick Duguid of Auchinhove, James Farquharson of Balmurret,* and *James Innes of Balnacraig.* The widow is referred to, but not named.

P. 14. *Duncan M'Grigor, farmer.*—His name appears in list of prisoners at Inverness, 19th April 1746. He is there styled Ensign.

P. 14. *Thomas Mercier, Esq.*—A merchant citizen of Aberdeen, whose ancestors were cadets of the Mercers of Aldie, Perthshire. After the collapse of the rebellion he escaped to France, and resided in Paris. His eldest son James was afterwards an officer in the British army, and did good service in various campaigns. He published a volume of *Lyric Poems* in 1797.

P. 14. *James Moir, Esq. of Stonywood.*—Third laird of that name ; he married Jean, daughter of William Erskine of Pittodrie. Of this gentleman the following notice occurs in the *Caledonian Mercury* of October 7, 1745: 'A letter from Aberdeen says Mr. Moire of Stonywood has raised a Troop for the Prince's service. and I can assure you for certain that the whole free-holders of Aberdeen (four only excepted) have actually declared themselves for the Prince's Interest, and will get on horseback as soon as possible and head their people.' After the failure of the rebellion Mr. Moir escaped to France, and died in 1782.

P. 18. *Robert Reid, merchant.*—Son to Sir Alexander Reid of Barra. Sir Alexander was second baronet, the title having been created in 1703. He married Agnes, eldest daughter of Sir Alexander Ogilvie of Forglen, baronet, and had four sons, viz.

Alexander, James, Robert (the rebel officer), and William, and two daughters, Helen and Barbara. Alexander, the eldest son, died before August 1745, for on the 6th of that month his brothers and sisters were cited by the Commissary of Aberdeen to see executors appointed to the deceased Captain Alexander Reid, younger, of Barra, their brother. They disregarded the citation, and his goods, consisting chiefly of wearing apparel, were rouped for £67, 16s. Scots, for behoof of a creditor.

P. 18. *John Reid, stabler.*—This person, from his designation, may have been connected with four 'suspected rogues' of the name of Reid, belonging to Aberdeen, one of them being a horse-hirer, who, by advertisement in the *Mercury* of 22d October 1745, are described as having broken prison at Dunblane, leaving in the custody of the bailie of regality there the plunder for which they had been incarcerated, viz. 'a sorel Galloway, about 40s. value, an old black horse, about the value of £4 sterling, a skirt of blue watered stuff, a pair of blankets, a little woollen floor cloth, a lined stuff cloak, a pair coarse linen sheets, a small thin shoulder belt, an old short tartan coat, a snuffle bit, a pocket napken, with 3 old shirts in it of little value, two cutlasses, a durk, a pocket-pistol, and two tartan plaids, pretty much used, with some money.'

P. 20. *Robert Sandilands, writer.*—He took part in the rebellion along with his kinsman Patrick Byres of Tonley, whose daughter Isabella he afterwards married.

P. 20. *William Strachan, clerk, etc.*—Inventory of William Strachan, merchant in Aberdeen, is given up by William Strachan, his eldest son, and confirmed on 2d June 1747. Among the debtors are *Henry Elphinstone, senior*, merchant in Aberdeen (whose name occurs in the List), the representatives of *Alexander Farquharson of Monaltrie, Adam Hay of Asleed* (also a rebel), and others.

P. 20. —— *Steuart of Auchoily.*—The Commissary Records of Aberdeen, of 19th May 1746, contain a citation of Anna Gordon, relict of the deceased Alexander Stuart of Auchollie, and Margaret and Helen Steuart, his lawful daughters, as his executors. His death is stated to have occurred in the month of May 1746. The inventory of his estate amounts to £925, 17s. Scots, one-third of which is claimed by the widow in virtue of their marriage contract. An 'eik' is added to the inventory in the following year, to the extent of £208, 6s. 8d. Scots, as the value of grain in the 'corn-yard of Auchollie, a mare, two cattle, and certain articles of furniture' sold under warrant of the commissary. The cautioners are William Durward, in Gilcomston, and Samuel Gordon, in Miln-toun of Braichly. A further 'eik' in 1748 contained a debt of

£735 Scots, due by Alexander and Francis Farquharson, elder and younger, of Monaltrie.

BANFF DISTRICT.

P. 24. *George Abernethie, merchant, etc.*—He was a Captain in Ogilvie's Company, and was taken at the surrender of Carlisle, tried, convicted of high treason, and sentenced to death. His wife was Elizabeth Forbes, who claimed upon his forfeited estate her liferent of a house in Banff. He died in April 1747, and was buried in the churchyard of St. Margaret's, Westminster.

P. 28. *Sir William Gordon of Park.*—Eldest son of Sir James Gordon by Dame Helen Fraser, his spouse. He was attainted, and his estates forfeited. He died abroad in 1751, and his younger brother John succeeded to the estate in terms of a judgment of the House of Lords. Dame Janet Gordon, wife of Sir William, claimed her terce.

P. 28. *Charles Gordon, younger, of Terpersie.*—Taken at Carlisle, and attainted. His widow, Margaret Gordon, and his daughters, Margaret and Helen, were allowed as creditors upon his forfeited estate, which was heavily burdened with debt. His father, *James Gordon*, is also mentioned in the List as a rebel officer.

P. 30. *John Gordon of Glenbucket.*—Joined the Pretender's army soon after the battle of Prestonpans. On Wednesday, 25th September 1745, the *Caledonian Mercury* thus reports his approach: 'A letter from Forfar, dated Tuesday morning last, says, "General Gordon of Glenbucket is arrived here, and will march this evening, in order to join the Highland army in the Lothians. He has under command a numerous Body of Select Gentlemen and private people."' The number of his followers was by one account 2000, by another 1400, and latterly it was stated at 400. The *Mercury* of 8th November 1745 reports the following item of news from London: 'The crew of the *Fox* man-of-war, hearing that the Laird of Glenbucket was passing the Forth with a party of his clans, manned two Boats, went off, and took him with his whole company.' He was along with the rebel force in the rest of the campaign, and is thus referred to in the narrative by Lord George Murray, in connection with the skirmish at Clifton: 'Glenbucket, who was very infirm, stayed at the end of the village on horseback. He was sorry he was not able to go on with me. He gave me his targe; it was convex, and covered with a plate of metal, which was painted; the paint was cleared in two or three places with the enemy's bullets.' After the failure of the rebellion he made his way to the Continent, but

2 A

his estates were forfeited. His wife's name was Jean Forbes. In 1771 claims upon the estate were sustained on behalf of John Gordon, his eldest son, George and David, younger sons, and Clementina, Henrietta, and Cecilia, his daughters.

P. 32. *Adam Hay of Asslid.*—Eldest son of Andrew Hay of Asleed, in the parishes of Monquhitter and New Deer. Adam was entered apprentice to James Hay, W.S., Edinburgh, in 1738, so that he was probably quite a youth when he joined the Jacobite movement. He was taken and convicted of treason. The forfeited estate was claimed and eventually purchased by James Hay, Clerk to the Signet, uncle and tutor to the rebel. The burdens on the estate were heavy, and included a provision to Anna Forbes, grandmother, and Christian Cumming, mother of the said Adam, besides certain claims by Anna and Jean Hays, his aunts.

P. 32. *John Innes, younger, of Edingight.*—This family was related to the Inneses of Balveny, baronets of Nova Scotia. The title was claimed, after the death of the eighth baronet in 1817, by John Innes, then of Edingight.

P. 38. *Peter Stuart, gentleman.*—This person appears to be identical with Patrick Stuart of Tannachy, cited by edict of the commissary of Aberdeen on 7th June 1749, as eldest son of the deceased George Stuart of Tannachy, who died in December 1748; the other members of the family cited are James, Cosmo-George, Andrew, Alexander, Mary. Elspet, and Jean Stuart, brothers and sisters of said Patrick.

PERTH DISTRICT.

P. 42. *Robert Bresdie (or Brydie).*—This may be the person whose birth is recorded in the Episcopal register of baptisms for Muthill, on 15th January 1724, as son of John Brady and Jean Ure.

P. 42. *David Carmichael of Balmedie.*—This family is said to have descended from Robert, second son of Sir John de Carmichael of that ilk, who fought at the battle of Beaugé in 1421. David, mentioned in the List, was probably not the Laird of Balmedie, who at that time is understood to have been Thomas Carmichael, who died in 1746, leaving an only son James, afterwards distinguished as a physician. *John Carmichael of Baiglie*, in the same parish, whose representative is now an officer in the French navy, was also out in the '45. The person named on the same page of the List as collector of the stent may well have been the laird of Baiglie; he was related to the Balmedie family.

P. 44. *James Drummond, called Duke of Perth.*—Son of James, Duke of Perth, by his wife, Lady Jean Gordon, daughter of George, Duke of Gordon. James, the father, was in the rebellion of 1715, and, escaping to France, resided there until 1730, when he died at Paris. Although attainted, his son succeeded to the estates under a disposition executed by him in 1713. On the arrival of the Pretender at Perth in September 1745, he was joined by the Duke of Perth, who was appointed Lieutenant-General in conjunction with Lord George Murray. He and his following were conspicuous throughout the campaign. After the defeat at Culloden he embarked for France, but died at sea on 11th May 1746, at the age of thirty-three. His younger and only brother, Lord John Drummond, was his heir: he was an officer in the service of the French King, for whom he raised the regiment then called the Royal Scots, of which he was colonel. In November 1745 he arrived at Montrose with some French auxiliaries and a train of artillery for the service of the Chevalier, whom he joined just before the battle of Falkirk. After Culloden he returned to France, and died in 1747.

P. 46. *James Lindsay, shoemaker.*—Described as an Ensign in Strathallan's horse; was taken prisoner at Culloden, tried in London on 28th October, found guilty, and sentenced to death. A reprieve was granted just as he was about to be led to the scaffold.

P. 46. *Martin Lindsay, writer in Edinburgh.*—Was tried at York, and acquitted.

P. 46. *Mr. Robert Lyon, minister.*—An Episcopalian; was tried at York, found guilty, and executed in November 1746. He is said to have read at the place of execution a lengthy paper, declaring his unswerving attachment to the Jacobite cause.

P. 46. *Lord George Murray.*—Younger son of John, first Duke of Atholl. He was implicated in the Spanish enterprise on behalf of the Pretender in 1719, which ended with the skirmish at Glenshiel in June of that year. He then escaped abroad, and was some years an officer in the army of the King of Sardinia; but, having obtained a pardon, he returned, and was presented to George I. When the standard of rebellion was again unfurled in 1745, Lord George yielded to the temptation, and accepted the chief command of the Pretender's forces. In this position he greatly distinguished himself as a skilful leader and intrepid soldier. Upon the disastrous conclusion of the campaign he withdrew to the Continent, and died in Holland in 1760. A liferent provision which he had out of the estate of Glencarse was forfeited. His eldest son, John, born in 1729, succeeded as third Duke of Atholl in 1764.

P. 48. —— *Murray, younger of Dollaire.*—Mr. Murray of Dollary, Sheriff-Depute of Perthshire, is mentioned, on the occasion of the arrival of the Chevalier at Perth, as having left that town along with the officers of the revenue. It is doubtless his son who is named in the List.

P. 48. *Laurance Oliphant of Gask*, elder and younger.—Their estates were confiscated; but, in 1753, Mrs. Amelia Nairne, spouse to Lawrence Oliphant, late of Gask, was found entitled to her liferent of portions of the estate, in terms of her marriage contract, in the event of her surviving her husband. On 24th February 1754 he is mentioned as deceased. The daughter of the younger Lawrence, named Carolina, was married to Lord Nairne, and is celebrated as the writer of 'The Laird of Cockpen' and other favourite songs.

P. 48. *George Robertson of Faskilly.*—On the retreat of the rebel army from Stirling northwards, in February 1746, they were reinforced at Perth by this laird. The *Scots Magazine* reports that on 2d February 'there came in from Crieff 140 men, commanded by Mr. Robertson of Fascally and *Mr. James Robertson of Blairfetty*, and brought in seven pieces of brass cannon and four covered waggons.' They crossed the Tay on the 4th of the same month, on the way northwards.

P. 48. —— *Robertson of Strowan.*—Alexander Robertson succeeded to the estate in 1688, was involved in the Jacobite risings in 1689 and 1715, was eventually pardoned, and lived upon the estate for several years before 1745. Though then an old man, he gave all the countenance and aid in his power to the cause of the Pretender, for which he was attainted, and his estates forfeited. He died in his own house of Carie in 1749, in the 81st year of his age, leaving a volume of poems in MS. which was afterwards published.

P. 50. *The Lord Strathallan.*—William Drummond, fourth Viscount: was in the rebellion in 1715, and taken prisoner at Sheriffmuir, but was not subjected to forfeiture for that occasion. He received a leading command in the army of the Chevalier in 1745, and fell at Culloden. His wife was Lady Margaret Murray, daughter of the Baroness Nairne, by whom he had seven sons and six daughters. His eldest son, *James*, having also taken part in the rebellion was attainted, and died abroad in 1765. The attainder was taken off in 1824.

STIRLING DISTRICT.

P. 54. *Alexander Buchanan.*—Described as *Captain*: taken prisoner at Culloden. On 15th November 1746 he was tried and acquitted, being only nineteen years of age.

P. 56. *John Halden of Laurick* and *Alexander his son* are mentioned in precognition taken by the sheriff at the town of Lanark on 21st September 1748, when Christopher Bannatyne, merchant and bailie there, deponed that, upon Christmas Day 1745, a party of rebels came to Lanark, amongst whom were the said John and Alexander Halden, and that the latter came into a room where the declarant and Bailie Wild were sitting, with a party of the *rebels* with drawn swords, in order to force them to come out to the cross to witness a proclamation of the Pretender, which they were forced to do. The Haldens escaped to the Continent, and the father died at Paris in 1765.

P. 58. *Sir Archibald Primrose of Dunipace.*—A Baronet, son of George Foulis, of the family of Ravelston, who assumed the name Primrose in terms of entail. He was captured near Aboyne in July 1746, was tried at York, pleaded guilty, and executed at Carlisle on 15th November 1746. Mrs. Janet Cuningham claimed upon the forfeited estate for an annuity of 1000 merks due to her, as widow of George Primrose of Dunipace. Her claim is dated 30th May 1746, and she is then described as 'now spouse to William Innes, Writer to the Signet.'

P. 60. *David Stuart of Ballahallan.*—This is most probably Major Stewart, brother to the laird of Ardvorlich, who, along with six other rebels, was surprised in a hut on the Braes of Leny, where they were in hiding after Culloden. Their assailants were a party of the Perth volunteers, who, after a tough conflict, overpowered Stewart and his comrades, and carried them to Stirling, where the Major died of his wounds. The others taken with him were *Captain Malcolm Macgregor* of Cornour, *Captain Donald MacLaren, Serjeant King*, alias *Macree*, late of Lord Murray's regiment, and three privates. It is related of Captain MacLaren that when being carried towards Carlisle, strapped to a dragoon, he cut the strap, threw himself over a cliff, and escaped.

ST. ANDREWS DISTRICT.

P. 64. (*Alexander*) *Erskine, Earl of Kelly.*—Of this nobleman the *Caledonian Mercury* of 9th October 1745 reports: 'The Right Hon. the Earl of Kellie, who, after his joining the Prince's standard, had gone over to Fife in order to raise men to complete his regiment, is returned to camp, and brought a considerable body of men with him.' Having been attainted, he surrendered himself to the Lord Justice-Clerk at Edinburgh, in July 1746. After being detained in prison for three years, he was liberated, and died at Kellie in 1756.

P. 64. *Heleneas Haxton, gentleman.*—Of the well-known family of Hackston (or Halkerston) of Rathillet. The predecessor of this gentleman fought against the Jacobites in 1715. Heleneas evidently got the benefit of the indemnity, as he lived for many years after the rebellion, and sold his estate in 1772.

P. 66. *Peter Lindsay, gentleman.*—This is probably the Captain Patrick Lindsay, who was taken prisoner in Angus in July 1746, and carried to Dundee. There was a Patrick Lindsay executed at Brampton, but he is described as a farmer at Wester Deans, Tweeddale.

P. 68. *David Rue, gentleman.*—Described also as an officer of customs. He was brought before the judges at York in October 1746, and having pleaded guilty, was executed there on 8th November.

P. 68. *William Sharp, gentleman.*—Son of Alexander Sharp, merchant, St. Andrews. He was arraigned at York in September 1746, and having pleaded guilty, was sentenced to die, but his name does not appear among those executed.

ROSS DISTRICT.

P. 72. *Roderick Chisholm.*—Son of the chief of that name. The clan took part in the rising of 1715, and the estates of the chief were forfeited; but he was afterwards pardoned, and the lands restored to the family. This Roderick, styled Colonel, was reported by the prisoners taken at Culloden as among the killed.

P. 74. *Simon Fraser, Lord Lovat.*—Chief of the Frasers. His history is well known. At first he contrived to show himself friendly both to the Government and to the Pretender. He did not himself take part in the campaign, but sent his eldest son, a youth of nineteen, against his inclination, as leader of the clan. The treachery of the aged chief was soon manifest, and the journals of December 24th, 1745, report his apprehension at his house of Beauly, whence he was taken to Inverness. A later account states that early in December he was apprehended by Lord Loudoun at Castle Downie, and having been brought to Inverness, there managed to escape through the back door of the house in which he was lodged. After Culloden he was found by a party of the royal troops concealed in a hollow tree on an island in Loch Morar, and taken on a horse-litter to Fort Augustus on 15th June 1746. On his apprehension he wrote a letter to the Duke of Cumberland, in which he says: 'I did more essential service to your Royal family in suppressing the great

Rebellion in the year 1715, with the hazard of my life, and the loss of my only brother, than any of my rank in Scotland; for which I had three letters of thanks from my royal master, in which his Majesty strongly promised to give me such marks of his favour as would oblige all the country to be faithful to him; therefore the gracious king was as good as his word to me, for as soon as I arrived at Court and was introduced to the king by the late Duke of Argyll, I came by degrees to be as great a favourite as any Scotsman about the Court; and I often carried your Royal Highness in my arms in the parks of Kensington and Hampton Court to hold you up to your Royal grandfather that he might embrace you.' He then recounts some instances of the clemency of the king, and concludes with the wish. 'I hope I shall feel that the same compassionate blood runs in your Royal Highness' veins.' Whether or not the Duke was compassionate, the chief of the Frasers was found guilty of high treason and beheaded on Tower Hill. His son was pardoned in 1750, and in 1774 the estates were restored to him. After a long and honourable service in the British army, in which he rose to the rank of General, he died in 1782.

P. 74. *Donald Fraser, Balagalken.*—This is probably the soldier of Lovat's company who is said to have killed seven men at the battle of Falkirk, whose son John, born in 1750, was well known as a botanist and traveller, and who, with his sons, is said to have introduced the dahlia into Europe. See *Curtis Magazine.*

P. 76. *(George) Mackenzie, Earl of Cromarty.*—This rebel peer, with his son, *Lord Macleod,* and the clan Mackenzie, were engaged for the Pretender almost exclusively in their own district, against the loyal clans in Sutherlandshire on the one hand, and the troops under Lord Loudoun on the other. They were not at Culloden, for on the previous day they were attacked by the Earl of Sutherland at Golspie and routed, and Cromarty and his son, with 150 of their men, taken prisoners. The Earl and his son were taken to London for trial. The father was sentenced to death, but reprieved, chiefly through the intervention of his lady, who presented personally a petition to the king. The estates were forfeited. The Earl died in 1766. His son, styled Lord Macleod, received a pardon in 1748, served for some years in the Swedish army, and afterwards in the British, where he rose to the rank of General. He raised the 71st Regiment of Highland Light Infantry, which he commanded in India. The estates were restored to him in 1784, and he died in 1789.

P. 76. *Roderick M'Culloch.*—Laird of Glastullich, captain in Cromarty's regiment. He was tried in London. and on 15th November sentenced to death.

LANARK DISTRICT.

P. 84. *Andrew Cassie.*—One of the Chevalier's Life Guards.

P. 84. *John Murray of Brughton.*—Secretary to the Chevalier, and his confidential adviser. When his master had escaped after the dispersion of his followers, Murray sought refuge with his relative Mr. Hunter of Polmood, but was seized and carried to London. There he turned King's evidence against Lovat, who thereupon charged him as being 'the most abandoned of mankind.' Mr. Murray, as the representative of Murray of Stanhope, succeeded in 1770 to the baronetcy which belonged to that family.

OLD MELDRUM DISTRICT.

P. 90. *John Forbes, Lord Pitsligo.*—His name was Alexander. Joined the army after the battle of Prestonpans. The *Mercury* of 4th October 1745 reports thus: 'A letter from Aberdeen assures that the Rt. Hon. Alexander Lord Pitsligo has put himself at the head of his friends and tenants, and is on the march to join the Prince's army.' The letter adds, 'This most worthy peer cannot fail of becoming an honour and ornament to either camp or cabinet.' After the final defeat he remained in hiding for many years in the neighbourhood of his own estate, which was forfeited. He died at the House of Auchiries, belonging to Mr. Ogilvie, in 1762, at the age of eighty-five.

P. 104. *Donald Fraser, smith.*—The famous 'smith of Moy.' When Prince Charles was at Moy Hall, on his way to Inverness, in February 1746, Lord Loudoun marched from that town with a large force, said to be 1500, to seize him by night. The enterprise was frustrated by Donald the smith, who, with five or six comrades, fired on the royalists, ordering at the same time imaginary Macdonalds and Camerons to advance on the right and left, and to give no quarter. The royalists, assuming that the whole Jacobite forces were upon them, retreated hastily to Inverness. This incident is known as the *Rout of Moy.*

P. 116. *Gillice M'Bain, brewer.*—This is the hero referred to by Chambers as signalising himself at Culloden by resisting to the last and defending himself against the dragoons, of whom it is said he slew thirteen before he himself was cut down.

P. 116. *Alexander M'Gillarrae of Dimmaglass.*—Chief of his clan, a sept of the Clan Chattan. He led the Mackintoshes at Culloden, and fought his way into the centre of the royal army, killing, it is said, a dozen men with his sword. He was at length killed at the well still known as the *Well of the Dead.*

P. 118. *Donald M'Bean, Auldaury.*—His daughter was married to Alexander Grant, Inchbrene, Glenurquhart, who was in the rebel army, and killed in the flight after Culloden, leaving an infant son Charles, who became Chairman of the East India Company, and father of Lord Glenelg and of Sir Robert Grant.

P. 118. *Evan M'Pherson of Clunie.*—Was an officer in the royal army, but threw up his commission when the rebellion began. His accession to the Pretender's cause is thus announced in the *Mercury* of 30th October 1745 : 'Yesterday, Evan Macpherson of Clunie, Esq., attended by a detachment of his Clan, came to the Abbey of Holyroodhouse, kissed the Prince's hands, and had the honour to dine with his Royal Highness. This gentleman left 400 more of his followers at Alloa, who serve as Escorte to 300 waggons with artillery, ammunition, arms, etc., which are expected at Dalkeith to-morrow.' Cluny and his men took a prominent part at the battles of Clifton and Falkirk, but were not forward in time at Culloden. After that fatal field the chief of the Macphersons lived for several years in hiding not far from his own house, which was burned down by Cumberland's soldiers. In 1755 he escaped to France, and died the following year. His estate was forfeited.

P. 128. *John Stewart, late bailie, Inverness.*—A cousin of the noted rebel leader, John Roy Stewart. The bailie was a leading merchant in Inverness. His grandson was General Sir John Stuart, Count of Maida. His daughter Ann was married to Richard Hay Newton of Newton, Haddingtonshire, with whom he found refuge after Culloden.

HADDINGTON DISTRICT.

P. 134. *Arthur Elphingston, Lord Balmerino.*—He was involved in the rebellion of 1715, and thereafter spent many years in France. His father having obtained for him a pardon from the Crown, he returned to Scotland, after an absence of about twenty years. On the outbreak of the new rebellion in 1745, Elphinston was one of the first to join the movement, and was appointed Colonel of the second troop of Life Guards to the Chevalier. He was in all the important conflicts of the campaign, was taken prisoner at Culloden, and carried to London along with other noble prisoners. When arraigned he pleaded not guilty, but was condemned. When brought to the block he behaved with great firmness. Having succeeded to the title and estates only in January 1746, he never enjoyed the latter. He left no issue.

P. 138. *Andrew Porteus of Burnfoot.*—One of the Life Guards of Prince Charles. When brought to trial he pleaded guilty, and was condemned, but his name does not appear in the list of those executed.

DUMFRIES DISTRICT.

P. 142. *John Henderson of Castlemains.*—By profession a writer in Lochmaben: found guilty, sentenced to death, and executed at Carlisle.

DUNFERMLINE DISTRICT.

P. 146. *Charles Blair, son to Castlehill.*—It is probably this man's father who is referred to in the *Mercury* of 25th September 1745: 'The same day (Sept. 19), John Bleau of Castlehill, Esq., was committed to Newgate, after long examination, by the Marquis of Tweeddale, his Majesty's principal Secretary of State for the Kingdom of Scotland.'

P. 148. *James Main, brewer, Alloa.*—When brought to trial he pleaded guilty, but does not appear in the list of those executed.

DUNDEE DISTRICT.

P. 202. *John Catinoch.*—Was apprehended by the royal dragoons, in the autumn of 1746, and shortly after set at liberty. Having been afterwards observed to go on several occasions between the place of his former residence and the quarters of the royal troops, he was suspected of being an informer, and murdered. Some of the neighbours were apprehended on suspicion of the crime, and brought to Edinburgh for trial.

P. 218. *Sir James Kinloch of Kinloch.*—Third Baronet, was accompanied in the Rebellion by his brothers *Alexander* and *Charles*, and all taken prisoners. On 15th November 1746 Sir James was sentenced to death. The counsel for his two brothers moved for arrest of judgment in their case, and the debate was adjourned for a month. On 15th December they were again at the bar, and after considerable debate they were again remanded till the 20th, when the Court, with the exception of one of the judges, decided against the plea, and sentence was passed upon them, and executed. Sir James, however, managed to escape from prison, went to France, and was at length pardoned.

P. 222. *Thomas Lawson, chapman.*—Was tried at Carlisle, found guilty, and probably transported.

P. 226. *Laurence Mercer of Lethenday.*—Son to Laurence Mercer of Melginch, deceased. His kinsman, *Robert Mercer*, of Aldie, was a captain in the rebel force. Laurence was taken prisoner in June 1746, brought to trial at Carlisle, pleaded guilty, and was condemned, but died in prison.

P. 228. *David Ogilvy of Pool.*—One of this name was tried at York, found guilty, but recommended to mercy by the jury.

P. 232. *James Rattray of Corb.*—Of Tullibardine's regiment. He is described in account of his trial as 'of Ranagullian,' and as brother-in-law of Sir James Kinloch. Though a true bill was found against him, he was acquitted.

P. 234. *James Stormout of Pitscauly.*—One of this name is mentioned as on trial before the Lord Chief-Justice, London, on 16th December 1746. A true bill was found against him, but his ultimate disposal is not specified.

P. 238. *Sir John Wedderburn.*—Fifth Baronet, was taken prisoner at Culloden. When brought to trial in November 1746, he pled that the rebels had taken him four times out of his own house by force, and that during the greater part of the time specified in his indictment he was at home. There were produced, however, twelve receipts for excise collected at Perth and Dundee for behoof of the Pretender written and subscribed by him; and it was proved that he owned himself to have been a volunteer in Ogilvie's second battalion. He was found guilty and executed. By his wife, Jean Fullerton, he had several children, of whom *John*, the eldest, was also in the Rebellion, but having escaped, he afterwards assumed the title notwithstanding the attainder.

P. 240. *Charles Webster.*—Tried at York and acquitted.

EDINBURGH DISTRICT.

P. 246. *Henry Clark, gentleman.*—When arraigned at Carlisle he pleaded guilty, and was sentenced to death, but died in prison before the 14th of November 1746.

P. 246. *Alexander Davidson, shoemaker.*—Was brought to trial at Carlisle, and, pleading guilty, was sentenced to death.

P. 248. *James Gedd, printer.*—Son of William Ged, goldsmith, Edinburgh, who in 1725 invented the art of stereotyping. After an unsuccessful venture in partnership with some London tradesmen, the Geds in 1738 resumed business in Edinburgh, and in the following year issued an edition of *Sallust* printed by the new process. Their labours were interrupted by the Jacobite rising of 1745, in which James Ged took part. He was made prisoner at Carlisle and condemned to death, but through the influence of some friends, and especially on account of his father's useful invention, he was reprieved, and emigrated to Jamaica.

P. 250. *George Hamilton* of *Redhouse.*—Tried at York, found guilty, and executed there on 1st November 1746.

P. 250. *Andrew Johnston.*—One of this name, styled 'son to Knockhill,' was brought to trial at York, and, pleading guilty, was sentenced to death.

P. 250. *Patrick Keir, wright.*—Tried at Carlisle, pleaded guilty, and executed at Carlisle on 15th November 1746.

P. 250. *Simon Lugton, tailor.*—Was tried at Carlisle, found guilty, and sentenced.

P. 252. *John M'Naughton, journeyman watchmaker.*—This is the 'stalwart Highlander' who killed the famous Colonel Gardner at the battle of Prestonpans. He is described as an Edinburgh workman. Tried at Carlisle, he was found guilty, and executed there on 18th October 1746.

P. 252. *James Murray, surgeon.*—Was tried at Carlisle, and acquitted.

P. 252. *Richard Morrison, barber.*—Is described also as valet and barber to the young Pretender; tried at Carlisle and found guilty, but reprieved. It is added that he was carried off to London from Carlisle by one of the King's messengers, on the morning of the 21st October 1746. Probably he could tell a good deal of the domestic history of his unhappy master.

P. 252. *Robert Murray, writer, Edinburgh.*—Also described as 'son to Spittlehaugh,' was brought to trial at Carlisle, pleaded guilty, and was condemned.

P. 252. *Sir David Murray (of Stanhope.)*—Fourth Baronet: was brought to trial at York, and, pleading guilty, was condemned, but afterwards received a pardon on condition of his leaving the country. His estates were confiscated, and he died in exile.

P. 254. *James Nicolson, coffee-house keeper, Leith.*—Also described as a Lieutenant in Perth's regiment. Was taken at the surrender of Carlisle, tried in London on 31st July, and condemned to death.

P. 254. *John Petrie, alehouse keeper.*—Tried at Carlisle, and acquitted.

P. 256. *James Smith, writer, Edinburgh.* Described as son of James Smith, writer, deceased. Was brought to trial at Carlisle, pleaded guilty, and was condemned, but died in prison.

P. 256. *Andrew Swan, shoemaker.*—Brought to trial at Carlisle, pleaded guilty, and was executed at Penrith, on 28th October 1746.

P. 258. *David Wymes, Lord Elcho.*—Eldest son of James, fourth Earl of Wemyss, was aged about twenty-four years when he joined the Rebellion. He is thus referred to in the *Mercury* of 30th

September 1745: 'There is now forming and pretty well advanced a body of Horse Life-Guards for his royal highness the Prince, commanded by the Right Hon. the Lord Elcho; their uniform is blue trimmed with red, and laced waistcoats; they are to consist of four squadrons of gentlemen of character.' In the *Scots Magazine* the troops commanded by Lord Elcho and Lord Kilmarnock are said to have numbered 160 men. After Culloden he escaped to the Continent, and, having been attainted, was debarred from the succession. On his death in 1787 his younger brother Francis became Earl of Wemyss.

LINLITHGOW DISTRICT.

P. 264. *James Ancrum, salt grieve.*—Tried at Carlisle, found guilty, but was reprieved.

P. 264. *George Boyd.*—Was tried at York, pleaded guilty, and condemned.

P. 266. *Kilmarnock, William, Earl of.*—Fourth Earl. His estates, greatly encumbered when he succeeded, were not relieved by his mode of living, which he himself acknowledged to be 'careless and dissolute.' The embarassments under which he lay on these accounts impelled him to risk all in the cause of the Pretender. He was taken at Culloden, and tried at Westminster along with the other rebel lords. He pleaded guilty, was condemned, and beheaded on Towerhill 18th August 1746. His Lady, Anne Livingstone, daughter of the Earl of Callendar, who was attainted in 1716, seems to have sympathised with the Jacobites, and went north with their army when they left Stirling. The eldest son of Lord Kilmarnock succeeded in 1758 to the Earldom of Erroll.

GLASGOW DISTRICT.

P. 272. *Andrew Wood, shoemaker, Glasgow.*—Captain in the Pretender's army, taken prisoner at Culloden, tried and found guilty, and executed on Kensington Common, 28th November 1746.

P. 278. *Andrew Sprewl, writer.*—Taken prisoner at Culloden, tried in London, and acquitted 'by consent of the Attorney-General, without entering into the evidence for the Crown.'

KELSO DISTRICT.

P. 280. *Henry Kerr of Greden.*—Colonel in the rebel force, and aide-de-camp to the young Pretender. Tried at St. Margaret's, Westminster, and found guilty. His counsel alleged 'that he was an officer in the Spanish service; but soon gave up that point.' The evidence showed that he was very active in the Rebellion; took and harshly treated Captain Vere. on 2d December 1745 within three miles of the royal army, then at Newcastle—the said Captain Vere being called 'principal spy' of the Duke's army 'by the rebel journal published at Glasgow.' Kerr was also alleged to have 'endeavoured to rally the rebels at Culloden after they were broke.' He was condemned.

ARGYLL DISTRICT.

P. 282. *Allan Cameron of Callart.*—Was wounded at Culloden and taken prisoner. Tried at St. Margaret's, London, in November 1746, he pleaded that 'he was forced from his family, a wife and ten children, by Lochiel, whose tenant he was.' It appeared by the evidence that he had behaved with great humanity, and in Edinburgh prevented one of the King's officers from being murdered by the rebels. He was, however, found guilty and condemned, but no notice of his death appears.

P. 282. *Donald Cameron of Lochiel.*—Captain of the Clan Cameron, his father, the chief, being then alive, but in exile under attainder for his share in the rising of 1715. Donald Cameron, though a very warm friend to the Jacobite cause, did his best to dissuade Charles from venturing to take the field without foreign aid. But the young adventurer was headstrong, and his adviser yielded. He is alleged to have led 1400 of his clan into the field, but they do not appear in the List. He did much to prevent dishonourable excesses in the rebel army, and ordered one of his own men to be shot for theft. He and his men were in all the battles of the campaign. At Culloden he was wounded in both ankles, and carried from the field. After lurking for some months in Rannoch and Badenoch, he escaped, in the company of Prince Charles, to France. There he received the command of a regiment of his compatriots in exile in the service of the King of the French. He died in 1748.

P. 282. *Ewen Cameron, Callart's uncle.*—There was a *Hugh* Cameron (probably Ewen), described as of Lochaber, tried at Carlisle, found guilty, and executed there on 18th October 1746.

P. 284. *Alexander M'Lauchlan, in Ladill.*—An Archibald Maclauchlan, of Fort-William, was tried at Carlisle, and acquitted. He was most likely the person here named *Alexander*, as such mistakes are frequent.

P. 284. *Angus M'Donald, younger, of Glengarry.*—He was colonel of the Glengarry men, who distinguished themselves throughout the campaign by their bravery. Their young chief was accidentally killed at Falkirk.

P. 284. *Alexander M'Donald of Keppoch.*—Of an old and ardent Jacobite family, involved in the various rebellions since the Revolution. He and his men did brave service during the entire campaign, but at Culloden the clansmen, wounded in their pride by being placed on the left wing, were broken and dispersed by the royal troops, when Keppoch, ashamed at their retreat, advanced alone to face the foe, and was shot dead.

P. 284. *Donald M‘Donald, Tirindrish.*—A captain in Keppoch's regiment. Taken prisoner at Falkirk in a singular way. Having mounted a spirited horse, which had lost its royalist rider, the animal carried its new master right into the lines of the enemy, where MacDonald was at once made prisoner. He was brought to trial at St. Margaret's on the last of July 1746, found guilty, and executed at Carlisle on 18th October.

P. 286. —— *M‘Donald of Kinloch Moidart.*—His name was *Donald*. When the rebel army was marching towards England, this officer was taken prisoner by Mr. Linning, a minister, at Lesmahagow, in Lanarkshire. He was brought to trial at Carlisle, in September 1746, and being found guilty, was executed. After Culloden two of his brothers submitted to Major-General Campbell; one of them, *Eneas*, was formerly a banker at Paris, and came over with Charles. He was brought to Edinburgh on 31st August 1746, and confined in the castle. Soon after he was carried to London under charge of two officers, who watched him every night by turns.

Pp. 286-288.—In regard to the *Stewarts of Appin* and their followers, the subjoined list of their killed and wounded at Culloden is taken from a manuscript left by Alexander Stewart, eighth of Invernahyle, and printed in *The Stewarts of Appin*, 1880:—

Ardsheal's family—	Killed.	Wounded.
John Stewart of Benmore	1	...
John, son to Alexander Stewart of Acharn	1	...
James, son to ,, ,,	1	...
John Stewart	1	...
John Stewart	1	...
William Stewart	...	1
John Stewart	1	...
Duncan Stewart, uncle to Ardsheal	1	...
Dugald Stewart, standard-bearer	1	...
Alan Mor Stewart	...	1
William Stewart	...	1
	8	3
Fasnacloich's family—		
James Stewart, uncle to Fasnacloich	...	1
James Stewart, younger, of Fasnacloich	...	1
John Stewart, son to Fasnacloich	...	1
John, son to Duncan Stewart	...	1

APPENDIX II.

	Killed.	Wounded.
James Stewart, from Ardnamurchan	1	...
Alan Stewart, son to Ardnamurchan	1	...
	2	4
Achnacone's family—		
Alexander Stewart, brother to Achnacone	1	...
Duncan Stewart	1	...
	2	...
Invernahyle's family—		
Alexander Stewart, son to —— Ballachelish	1	...
Duncan, Donald, Dugald, and Alan Stewart, nephews to Ballachelish	...	4
John Stewart, from Ardnamurchan	...	1
Charles Stewart, from Bohallie	...	1
Alexander Stewart, of Invernahyle	...	1
James Stewart, brother to Invernahyle	...	1
Duncan Stewart, from Inverphalla	...	1
Donald Stewart, from Annat	...	1
Alan Stewart, died in the East Indies	...	1
Donald Stewart, nephew to Invernahyle	1	...
John Stewart, from Balquhidder	1	...
Duncan Stewart	1	...
John Stewart	...	1
	4	12
Stewarts, followers of Appin—		
Duncan Stewart, from Mull	1	...
Duncan, Hugh, and John Stewart, from Glenlyon	...	3
John Stewart—Macalan Vane	...	1
John Stewart, *alias* Macalan	1	...
Duncan Stewart, *alias* Macalan	...	1
Malcolm Stewart	1	...
Dugald Stewart	1	...
Donald Stewart, natural son to Ballachellan	1	...
Robert Stewart, natural cousin to Appin	...	1
	5	6
Ardsheal's family	8	3
Fasnacloich's family	2	4
Invernahyle's family	4	12
Achnacone's family	2	...
Stewarts, followers of Appin	5	6
	21	25
Commoners, followers of Appin—		
M'Colls	18	15
Maclarens	13	4

BIOGRAPHICAL NOTES. 385

	Killed.	Wounded.
Carmichaels	6	2
M'Combichs	5	3
M'Intyres	5	5
M'Innises	4	2
M'Ildeus, or Blacks	1	...
Mackenzies	1	3
M'Corquadales	1	...
M'Uchaders	...	1
Hendersons	1	1
M'Rankens	1	...
M'Cormacks (Buchanans)	5	1
Camerons	...	1
M'Donalds	...	1
M'Lachlans	2	...
M'Leas, or Livingstones	4	1
M'Arthurs	1	...
Volunteers—George Haldane, nephew to Lanrick Ardsheal having married Haldane of Lanrick's sister	1	...
Total of killed and wounded	90	65

Dugald Stewart of Appin was a boy when the Rebellion broke out, so that the clan was led by the Tutor, *Charles Stewart*, fifth of Ardsheal. They were among the most valiant warriors of the Pretender's army. Ardsheal was attainted, as was Haldane of Lanerick, his brother-in-law. The former remained in hiding, in a cave upon his own estate, until, on 17th September 1746, he and four other gentlemen got on board a French vessel, and escaped to the Continent. Shortly after Culloden the estate was plundered by the royal troops. Major-General John Campbell, who commanded in the district, was humane enough to show kindness to the wife and children of the fugitive, as appears by a letter from him to the lady, dated Appin, 25th May 1746, in which he says: 'MADAM,—Your misfortune, and the unhappy situation Ardsheal has brought you and your innocent children into, by being so deeply concerned in this unjust and unnatural rebellion, makes my heart ache. I know the King to be compassionate and merciful. I know the brave Duke, under whose command and orders I act, to have as much humanity as any man on earth; from which, and my own natural inclination, I have taken the liberty of ordering back your milk cows, six wethers, and as many lambs; the men who pretend a right to them shall be paid. I have taken the freedom at the same time of ordering two bolls of meal, out of my own stores, to be left here for you, which I desire you to accept for the use of yourself and little ones; and if what I write can have any weight, I most earnestly entreat you to bring up your children to be good subjects to his Majesty. I wish your husband, by surrendering himself to the Duke of Cumberland, had given me an opportunity of recommending him to his Majesty's mercy. I feel for you, and am, Madam, your most obedient and humble servant,

JOHN CAMPBELL.

It would appear that General Campbell misjudged the humanity of the Duke, for in December following Ardsheal House was sacked, and the lady compelled to flee for refuge to a hut. From this also she was driven, the very night after her confinement, to seek, with her new-born infant and five children, another shelter from the falling snow. These cruel details are inscribed upon the stone erected to her memory in Northampton, where she died in 1782.

ROSS DISTRICT.

P. 330. *Alexander M'Kay, of Achmony, Glenurquhart.*—He made himself very active in the Jacobite cause in his district, and induced the people of Glenurquhart to join the Rebellion. After Culloden he concealed himself in a cave in Craig-Achmony, and so escaped. In 1777 he sold the property to Sir James Grant, and died shortly afterwards at Nairn. His wife was Angusia M'Donell, daughter of Angus M'Donell, younger of Glengarry, who was killed at Falkirk.

NOTES ON SUPPLEMENTARY LIST.

(Those marked with an asterisk are additional names.)

ABERDEEN DISTRICT.

P. 298. *Alexander Durom, junior.*—This name is on page 6 spelled *Decorm*. It stands, in all probability, for Durham, a frequent surname in the north-east of Scotland.

P. 298. *Balmurle.*—The name of the estate of James Farquharson is *Balmurret* on page 8, and is now represented by Balmoral, the royal residence on Deeside.

P. 300. *Charles Halket, writer's servant.*—Doubtless the same who, on page 10, is erroneously styled a 'wright lad.'

P. 300. *Patrick Leggie.*—Probably the same as Patrick Logie, on page 12.

OLD MELDRUM DISTRICT.

P. 302. *William Cumming of Pittully.*—The blank on page 88 is thus filled up.

NOTES ON SUPPLEMENTARY LIST. 387

P. 302. *John Cruikshank, surgeon.*—The full name of the *doctor,* on page 88, thus appears.

P. 302. *Alexander Forbes, Lord Pitsligo.*—The error on page 90 is here corrected.

P. 304. *Mary Farquharson, Lady Turnerhall.*—We have thus the full name of this Amazon, mentioned only by her title on page 98.

P. 304. *Robert Gordon of Logie.*—Apparently the father of him mentioned on page 90.

*P. 306. *Alexander Smith of Meany.*—Does not occur in corresponding list, page 96.

P. 308. *James Abercrombie, Deskford.*—May be the same who, on page 24, is styled farmer at Skeith.

*P. 308. *John Brown, Carmoucie.*—Does not occur on similar list, page 26.

*P. 308. *John Garvock.*—There are here two of this name, neither of whom seems identical with John Garvich, described on page 30.

*P. 308. *John Gordon.*—Not plainly identified with any of the same name on pages 28 and 30.

P. 308. *Alexander Gall.*—Is probably the correct form of Alexander Gatt, on page 30.

*P. 310. *John Innes.*—Is not clearly identified with the young laird named on page 32.

*P. 310. *John Kynnach, William Maver, George Miln, senior,* and *Robert Massie,* are additional names.

*P. 312. *John Pirrie, George White, George Gordon, Alexander Grant, William Stewart, William Forbes,* are additional names.

*P. 314. *Robert Fraser, Robert Kennedy, William Petrie,* are additional names.

STIRLING DISTRICT.

*P. 316. *James Murray, merchant.* P. 318. *Robert Watt, Robert Caddel, Henry Oat, junior, Patrick Ridoch, Donald Mitchell, John M'Lachlan, John Squair, Thomas Caddel, senior, Thomas Caddel, junior, Duncan Wright, Andrew Watt, William Oatt, Duncan Mitchell, Thomas M'Farlane,* all additional names.

MONTROSE DISTRICT.

P. 320. *John Stephen.*—Is doubtless the same as John *Stiven*, page 186.

P. 320. *David Pyot.*—May be a connection of Alex. Pyot on page 184.

P. 320. *Alex. Grey, merchant apprentice.*—May stand for Alexr. Greig, with same designation, on page 168.

*P. 320. *John Orkney.*—Here there are two of this name, and on 184 only one.

P. 322. *Alex. Alexander.*—May be a correction for Alexr. Anderson on page 150.

P. 322. *Da. Burness.*—Seems to be the correct form of David Bumoss, on page 154.

P. 322. *John Freeman.*—Is evidently the proper reading of John Framan on page 164.

P. 322. *Pat. Cushnie.*—Seems identical with Peter Cashnie on page 160.

ARGYLE DISTRICT (SOUTH).

*P. 326. *Hector M'Alister, Ja. M'Donald, William M'Alister, Adam Fullerton, James Bain Fullarton,* and *William Miller,* are additional names.

PAISLEY DISTRICT (NEWPORT).

*P. 326. *James Stirling.*—Not mentioned on page 292.

P. 326. *William Weir.*—May be a correction for John Weir, on page 292.

ROSS DISTRICT.

P. 328. *Will. Fraser, junior of Culbocky.*—Supplies the blank on page 74.

*P. 328. *William Fraser, son to Culmiln.*—Probably not the same as William Fraser of Culmiln, page 74.

*P. 328. *John, Kenneth,* and *Colin Grants.*—Sons to Patrick Grant (not *Perter* Grant, as on page 74). He had thus four sons in the field.

P. 328. *Kenneth M'Kenzie, Hillend.*—Not *Killend*, as on page 76.

*P. 330. *Alexander M'Kay, of Achmony.*—Already noted on page 386.

*P. 330. *Alexander M'Leod.*—Additional name.

P. 330. *Colin* and *Kenneth M'Kenzie.*—Brothers to the laird of Lentron. First names blank in list on page 76.

P. 330. *Alex. M'Kenzie, Milnton of Ord.*—More fully described at page 76.

*P. 330. —— *M'Kenzie of Ardloch.*—Additional name.

*P. 332. *Malcolm Ross, Hugh Smith, Peter Smith.*—Not mentioned on pages 80, 82.

ELGIN DISTRICT.

P. 334. *James Cumming.*—May be the same as John Cumming, page 102.

*P. 334. *Wm. Grant, wright.*—Additional name; so also is *Wm. Jack, messenger.*

P. 334. *John M'Lenan, vintner.*—Probably the same as John M'Laren, on page 116.

P. 336. *Don. M'Donald of Shian.*—Seems the same as Ronald M'Donald, page 116.

P. 336. *Don. M'Donald, brother to Arnabee.*—Probably the same as Ronald M'Donald, brother to Arnabell, page 116.

*P. 336. *Don. M'Donald, Chelsea man* (or pensioner).—Does not occur in former list.

*P. 336. *Mal. M'Pherson, son of Phoness.*—Additional.

P. 336. *Angus M'Bean, farmer.*—Same as Angus M'Bear, on page 118.

*P. 336. *George Young.*—Not in principal list.

EDINBURGH DISTRICT.

*P. 340. *Wm. M'Leish.*—Additional; so also is *David Murray*, without designation, unless he is intended for Sir David Murray described on page 252.

P. 342. *John Fyre.*—May be a mistake, or a correction for John Tyrie on page 256.

*P. 342. *Tho. Dey* and —— *Willison* are additional names.

KIRKCALDY DISTRICT.

*P. 344. *Alex. Seton.*—Additional.

GLASGOW DISTRICT.

*P. 346. *James Finnie* and *Alexander Graham.*—Additional.

DUNFERMLINE DISTRICT.

P. 348. *William Verty.*—Seems identical with William Verly, page 148.

DUNDEE DISTRICT.

P. 351. *Thomas Birrell.*—Is probably the full form of Thomas Bire, on page 198.

*P. 351. *Alexander Graham.*—Additional.

III.

ILLUSTRATIVE DOCUMENTS.

I.

The following accounts are copied from the originals in the Signet Library:—[1]

ROYAL INFIRMARY: Account of the Charge of Subsisting the Rebel prisoners.

To the 28th of April, 1746,	£19 1 4
To the 31st of May, 1746,	11 14 8
To the 30th of June, 1746,	7 0 0
To the 31st of July, 1746,	3 12 8
	£41 8 8
Paid by Mr. James Finlayson to Mr. Gavin Hamilton, Treasurer,	£22 8 8

7th August 1746.

MR. GRAY,

Pay to Mr. Gavin Hamilton, Treasurer to the Royal Infirmary, the sum of twenty-two pounds, eight shillings, and eightpence, remaining unpaid of the subsistence furnished to the Rebel prisoners in the Royal Infirmary, to the 31st of July, 1746, inclusive, and take the said Mr. Hamilton's receipt for the same.

(Signed) GEO. FRAZER.

To Mr. William Gray, appointed to subsist the
    Rebel prisoners in and about Edinburgh.

---

[1] A collection of Papers, printed and manuscript, including contemporary numbers of the *Caledonian Mercury* and *Edinburgh Evening Courant*, relating to the Rebellion in Scotland in the year 1745.

STATE of the Cash Drawn for the 16th of December 1747.

	Subsistence to the Well and Sick.			Cures.			Funerals.			Contingencies.			Total		
	£	s.	d.	£	s.	d.	£	s.	d.	£	s.	d.	£	s.	d.
Aberdeen Goal to the 30th of September, 1746,	94	11	10	...			...			1	15	0	96	6	10
Canongate Goal for the months of { October,	22	0	8	1	13	4	0	8	0	...			24	2	0
November,	18	15	4	...			...			...			18	15	4
Dumfermling Goal for October,	3	2	0	...			...			...			3	2	0
Dumfries Goal for the months of { July,	4	2	8	...			...			...			4	2	8
August,	3	14	4	...			...			...			3	14	4
September,	3	10	0	...			...			...			3	10	0
October,	3	12	4	...			...			...			3	12	4
Edinburgh Castle for the months of { August,	13	12	0	2	13	4	0	8	0	...			16	13	4
September,	9	12	0	...			...			...			9	12	0
October,	10	14	8	1	0	0	...			...			11	14	8
November,	12	6	4	1	13	4	...			...			13	19	8
Edinburgh Goal for the months of { October,	25	18	0	1	6	8	...			...			27	4	8
November,	25	12	4	2	13	4	...			...			28	5	8
Haddington Goal for the months of { September,	2	3	0	...			...			...			2	3	0
October,	1	14	0	...			...			...			1	14	0
Stirling Castle for the months of { July,	36	5	6	...			...			...			36	5	6
August,	29	14	11	10	13	4	0	8	0	...			40	16	3
September,	18	16	10	...			...			...			18	16	10
October,	19	12	8	3	0	0	...			...			22	12	8
November,	19	0	0	2	13	4	...			...			21	13	4
Stirling Goal for the month of September,	0	8	8	...			...			...			0	8	8
Royal Infirmary for the months of { October,	3	12	4	...			...			...			3	12	4
November,	3	9	0	1	0	0	...			...			4	9	0
Musselburgh Goal for the time ended 31st August,	9	6	4	...			...			...			9	6	4
	395	7	9	28	6	8	1	4	0	1	15	0	426	13	5
Surgeons' Fees, Haddington Goal, short charged in last state,													0	13	4
To Mr. Fleming, Printer, per his bill and acquittance,													1	1	0
Agency for the months of October and November,													15	5	0
													443	12	9

Exd. per Geo. Frazer.

APPENDIX III.

WILLIAM GRAY, Dr.

1746.
14 July. To Cash from James Finlayson, per Receipt, £5 0 0
17 Do. To ditto from ditto, per ditto, . . 40 0 0
31 Do. To Cash from the Right Honble. the Lord Justice Clerk, ... 38 0 0

	£83 0 0
By Balance due to W. Gray, . . .	0 7 8
	£83 7 8

WILLIAM GRAY, Cr.

1746.

		£	s	d
	By Cash paid to the Rebell prisoners in the Castle of Edinburgh from the 14th July to the 8th August, per particular attestations,	19	16	2
	By ditto from the 4th October to the 24th of said month, per do.,	5	19	0
17 July.	By Cash paid to James Smith for subsisting the rebell prisoners in the Goal of Dumfries to the 31 May, as per Precept of Mr. Fraser and receipt of Mr. Smith,	3	15	0
21 Do.	By Cash paid David Lyon, prisoner in the Canongate, from the 27 May to the 21 July inclusive, on Mr. Home, solicitor's order, and Lyon's receipt in terms of said order,	0	18	4
25 Do.	Paid to Mr. Park, surgeon in the Castle of Edin^r., on Mr. Frazer's precept and Mr. Park's receipt,	10	0	0
26 Do.	Paid said Mr. Park on Mr. Fraser's order and do.,	14	2	10
30 Do.	Paid the Funeral expenses of William Sutherland who dyed in the Canongate Goal, per receipt,	0	8	0
1 Aug^t.	Paid Robert Meldrum, Jaylor in Dumfermline, for maintaining rebell prisoners to the 30th June, per receipt,	5	13	0
4 Do.	Paid to David Maitland, as per receipt of the Magistrates of Haddington, for maintaining rebell prisoners to the 30 June, as per Mr. Frazer's order,	8	12	0
5 Do.	Paid Mr. Fleeming, printer, per Mr. Frazer's precept and Mr. Fleeming's receipt,	2	1	0
7 Do.	Paid to Mr. Park, surgeon in Castle of Edinburgh, per Precept of Mr. Frazer and receipt,	3	0	0
Do.	Paid Mr. James Smith for John Donaldson, goaler in Dumfries, for maintaining the Prisoners in said goal to the 30th June, per precept and receipt,	3	12	8
Do.	Paid to Robert Meldrum, Jaylor in Dumfermline, for maintaining the Prisoners in said Goal to the 31st July, per precept and receipt,	2	16	4
2 Oct.	Paid William Chrystie, surgeon, for taking care of the rebell prisoners in the Castle and goal of Stirling, per precept and receipt,	2	13	4
		£83	7	8

Exd. per Geo. Frazer.

II.

LIST OF THE REBELL PRISONERS in the different places of confinement, shewing when they became indisposed and when they recovered for the months of December and January last, and their cures.

No.	Men's Name.	When Become Indisposed.		When Recovered.		Cures.		
						£	s.	d.
	Edinburgh Goal.							
1	Colin M'Lachlan	Dec.	1	Dec.	29	...	6	8
2	James Stewart	Do.	9	Do.	30	...	6	8
3	Magnus Macavy	Do.	12	Do.	Do.	...	6	8
4	William M'Intosh	Do.	Do.	Do.	29	...	6	8
5	William Frazer	Do.	28	Janry.	27	...	6	8
6	Thomas Ross	Jany.	15	Do.	30	...	6	8
	Canongate Goal.							
1	Robert Robertsone	Dec^r.	16	Dec^r.	31	...	6	8
2	Charles Millar	Do.	Do.	Do.	28	...	6	8
3	Arch^d. Lamond	Do.	26	Janry.	29	...	6	8
4	Alex^r. Cattah	Jan.	13	Do.	Do.	...	6	8
5	James Jacksone	Do.	Do.	Do.	30	...	6	8
	In sick quarters.							
1	John Dalmahoy	Aug^t.	11	Dec.	13	...	6	8
						£4	0	0

18th February 1746-7.

MR. GRAY,—I have examined the above account of Recoveries of the Rebell Prisoners, and find that the same agrees to the account sworn to by George Cunningham, surgeon, for the months of December and January last, amounting to four pounds.
(Signed)   GEO. FRASER.

To Mr. William Gray, appointed to subsist the
Rebel prisoners in Edinburgh, &c.

Edr., 19 Feb. 1747.

Then received payment of the above four pounds sterling money per the hands of the above Mr. William Graye, and discharges the same by me.   (Signed)   GEO. CUNNINGHAME.

Office for Sick and Wounded Seamen,
the 29 January 1746.

Sir,—Colⁿ. Brown, who is now a Prisoner at Berwick, having acquainted us that one Mr. Lafarque, lieutenant on board his Majesty's sloop the Hazard, when she was retaken from the French, is now at Inverness with four soldiers and one sailor, who was left there dangerously wounded; and that Mr. Lafarque complains they receive but a pound of oat meal and water a day: We must desire you will enquire and let us know what truth there is in this, and whether any method can be found out to remove the People from thence; for they ought to be treated as Prisoners of War, and subsisted at the rate of 6 pence a man a day.—Your most humble servant, (Signed) W. Bell.
Nath. Hills.
Cha. Allix.

E.
   Mr. Grey
      at Edinburgh.

Office for Sick and Wounded Seamen,
26 Feby. 1746.

Sir,—We have received your letter of the 21st instant, and the several accounts mentioned in the schedule which came enclosed, your Bill for £302, 4s. for the amount whereof shall be duely paid.

We approve your conduct with respect to the Prisoners at Inverness; as likewise in regard to what passed between the Earl of Albemarle and yourself concerning his demand of £172, 9s. 6d.: and it may be well for you to let his Excellency know it is not in our power to satisfy that Demand without special order.

What you have said about an allowance for the Gaolers of the Prisons where the Rebel Prisoners were confined in Scotland shall be considered, and you shall then have our thoughts about it.— We are, Sir, your very humble servants, W. Bell.
Cha. Allix.

E.
   Mr. Gray,
      Edinburgh.

APPENDIX III.

STATE of the CASH drawn for the 14th April 1747.

	Subsistence.			Cures.			Funerals.			Contingencies.			Total.		
	£	s.	d.	£	s.	d.	£	s.	d.	£	s.	d.	£	s.	d.
Aberdeen for the month of February,	14	0	0	...			...			3	15	0	17	15	0
Do. for March 1747,	17	0	0	...			...			...			17	0	0
Canongate { Feb. 1746/7,	16	7	4	1	6	8	...			...			17	14	0
Goal for { March 1747,	10	12	8	0	13	4	...			...			11	6	0
Dumbarton Castle for { 1st account to 31 Jany. 1746/7	49	19	9	...			0	5	8	1	2	7	51	8	0
{ Feb. 1746/7,	4	13	4	...			...			...			4	13	4
{ March 1747,	4	15	4	...			...			...			4	15	4
Edinburgh { Castle for Feb. 1746/7,	3	10	0	0	13	4				...			4	3	4
{ Goal for Do.	22	8	0	4	13	4				...			27	1	4
{ Royal Infirmary Do.	2	16	0	...									2	16	0
{ Castle for March 1747,	5	1	8	1	6	8	...						6	8	4
{ Goal, Do.	22	13	4	2	13	4	...						25	6	8
{ Royal Infirmary Do.	1	11	0	1	0	0	...			...			2	11	0
Haddington { February 1746/7,	1	8	0	0	6	8	...			...			1	14	8
{ March 1747,	1	10	0	...			...			...			1	10	0
Glasgow, February 1746/7,	10	16	0	...			...			...			10	16	0
Irvine, from 30th Novr. 1746 to 28th February 1746/7,	1	9	8	...			...						1	9	8
Kinghorn, from 31st July to 11th March,	3	4	0				...			...			3	4	0
Musleburgh { Sep. 1746,	1	10	0				...			...			1	10	0
{ Oct. Do.	1	11	0				...			...			1	11	0
{ November,	1	10	0				...			...			1	10	0
{ December,	1	11	0				...			...			1	11	0
{ January, 1746/7,	1	11	0	...			...			...			1	11	0
{ February Do.	1	8	0	...			...			...			1	8	0
Stirling { February 1746/7,	14	6	8	...			...			...			14	6	8
Castle { March 1747,	8	16	8	...			...			...			8	16	8
	226	0	5	12	13	4	0	5	8	4	17	7	243	17	0
For Agency for Feby. and March,				...			...						14	15	0
Odd pence in last state not drawn for,				...			...			...			0	0	5
N.B.—The five pence not drawn for.													258	12	5

Exd. per GEORGE FRAZER.

Inverness, 21st February 1746/7.

Sir,—I am favoured with your letter of the 10th Instant, and if any of the Prisoners have not been paid sixpence per man a day, or have not had a larger allowance than a pound of oat meal per man a day, it has been for want of proper application to my commanding officer, for I never refused giving the officers what money they desired to have.

Mr. Dundas's Deputy is the Person that has supplied all the prisoners here with a pound of oatmeal per man a day, the magistrates having refused to do it.

I have paid to the French and Spanish officers, prisoners here, £172, 9s. 6d., and the vouchers are lodged with the Earl of Albemarle's secretary. Yesterday I paid to Lieutenant Lafarque £9, 8s. to subsist himself and six men, and to Lieutenant Morgan M'Mahon of Ultona's Regiment £3, 3s. They are all to set out next Monday for Edinburgh. These two Lieutenants and six men are all the prisoners that are here belonging to the French and Spanish service; but there are many Rebel Prisoners of whom the Deputy Sheriff has given an account to my Lord Justice Clerk.

My Paymaster, who is now at Forres, has given these officers more money than is mentioned here, of which I will give you an account in my next letter.—I am, Sir, your most obedient humble servant, (Signed) WILL. BLAKENEY.

To Mr. William Gray,
Writer in Edinburgh.

Inverness, 28th February 1746/7.

Sir,—Underneath is an account of the money paid by my Paymaster to Lieutenant Lafarque, and to J. Baptist Dubois of Fitz James's Horse in Capt. Cook's Company, amounting to seven pounds one shilling sterling, which is not included in the last account I sent you.—I am, etc., WILL. BLAKENEY.

Feb. 6th, 1746/7.—To cash paid to Curon Lafarque, £5 5 0
To subsistence paid to J. Baptist Dubois as per receipt, 1 16 0
£7 1 0

To Mr. William Gray, etc.

Edinburgh, 10th December 1747.
Mr. William Gray. £207 3 0.

Please pay to James Sibbald Keeper of the Goal of Perth the sum of £207, 3/ sterling, as subsistance furnished to the Rebel prisoners in that Goal from the 6th February 1745/6 to August 1747 both inclusive, which you will pay to the said James Sibbald, and take his receipt for the same upon any of the magistrates and town clerk testing his subscription. (Signed) GEO. FRAZER.

To Mr. William Gray, etc.

(*Receipt is endorsed.*)

On 3d November 1749, the gentlemen of the 'Office for the Sick and Hurt Seamen,' intimate to Messrs. Frazer and Gray that it was 'thought proper to suppress the present expense of Agency for Rebel prisoners,' and that their allowance of half a crown a day should cease on the 10th of that month.

On 23d November 1749, the same gentlemen acknowledge receipt of letters from Mr. Gray, and add, 'As there is a gentleman Goaler in the Tower of London, it was very easy for us to conceive there might be a like officer in the castle of Edinburgh; but as there is not, and you are willing to carry on the payment of subsistence to the Rebel prisoners in that place, we should be glad to make you an allowance for it of twenty shillings per quarter. We are sorry for the decrease of your other business, but, however, hope that will revive again as people come to cool thinking.'

A scroll of Mr. Gray's letter thus answered contains reference to accounts, and mentions that the Lord Justice-Clerk had communicated the letter intimating the intended suppression of the agency. Mr. Gray then refers to the Commissioner's order to pay the prisoners by the Goaler, and informs them that 'there is no goaler, but a centinel every two hours'; and adds that the prisoners should not be neglected by him (Mr. Gray) though he should receive nothing for his trouble. He concludes by a reference to the decrease of his business since he was employed in the public service during the rebellion and at Carlisle, which, he adds, 'is well known, and I hope is not unknown to your Honours.'

On the 8th August 1750, the Commissioners write to Mr. Gray, acknowledging receipt of two letters and two 'states,' which, they remind him, should have been 'attended with the usual receipts,' or 'at least the accustomed affidavit to the truth of the payments,' and requiring these by return of post; desiring him also to explain 'the article of John Graham, for whom there seems to be no charge in the first ten days of November; nor does it appear at what rate *per diem* he was subsisted between the 1st of December 1749 and the 30th of June following.'

On 31st July 1752, Messrs. Bell and Hills again write as follows: 'SIR,—We have just now received your letter of the 25th instant, with an account annext of what was due to you for subsistance of Mr. Graham of Kilmardine, and for agency to the time therein mentioned, together with two pence short drawn upon last occasion, amounting in the whole to £8, 2s. 2d., and acquainting us with your having drawn upon this office for so much, which shall be duly paid. But we desire you to let us know, by the return of the post, whether Mr. Graham be not at Glasgow, whether there be at present any more Rebel prisoners in custody, and where, if this be ; and the reasons, if there be any, why your allowance of agency should be still continued.'

On 28th August 1752, they again write : 'We have received your letter of the 20th instant, and in answer thereto it may be sufficient to say, that as now only Mr. Graham remains a prisoner of state under your care, it is thought proper to reduce your agency to twenty shillings the year for him ; but if you can give any good reason why it should be more, and let us know it, it shall be candidly considered by your very humble servants,' etc.

The correspondence between the Commissioners of the 'Office for Sick and Hurt Seaman' and Mr. William Gray concludes, so far as this collection shows, with the following letter, dated 6th October 1752 : 'SIR,—We have received your letter of the 30th September relating to your agency for the Rebel prisoners. This Board has really conceived a good opinion of you, and should be very glad it were reasonable for them to make you a greater allowance than was mentioned to you in their last, for your care of Mr. Graham.—We are, your very humble servants, W. BELL, NATH. HILLS.'

The following receipts are in the same collection :—

'Edr. Castle, 15th Janry. 1751.—Received by me, Thomas Ogilvy of East Mill, from William Gray, writer in Edinburgh, one pound sterling money, as twenty days subsistance allowed me by the Government as a prisoner, at the rate of one shilling sterling per day, and that from the 31st ultimo to and for the nineteenth curt., both first and last days included.

(Signed) THO. OGILVY.'

On 8th February Mr. Ogilvy grants a receipt in similar terms for the same alimentary allowance between 20th Janry. and 10 Febry. And similar receipts for twenty or twent -one days' subsistence each are granted onwards till 7th May 1751, when receipt is given for the previous twenty-five days. And on 12th July 1751, Mr. James Smyth, clerk to the Signet, grants receipt on behalf of the said Mr. Ogilvy to 'William Gray of Newholm, wryter in Edinburgh,' for fourteen shillings, as allowed for subsistence of the prisoner from 8th to 21st May last, 'and eight shillings sterling for a coffin to the said Thomas Ogilvy, I say received by me as depurser of the expence of his funeralls.

(Signed) JA. SMYTH.'

III.

The charges of outrage and cruelty against both parties in the campaign of 1745-6 have since then been matter of controversy; and the following notes, copied verbatim, by kind permission of Mr. Erskine of Cardross, from a Manuscript in his possession, contributes somewhat as to the state of the question at the time. The paper is described on the back by this title: 'Facts that ingross the present conversation: May 1746'; and is headed thus: 'Facts reported; some true.' The *facts* follow:—

'Lady Gask, after a protection and allowance to lift tenants rests [arrears], brought to her house 150 bolls meal, quhich she sent to Lord George Murray at Blair Athol.

'Kingston had 700 £ st. taken from him. The church of St. Ninians blown up of design.

'Lord Cromarty burnt a mans legs for not discovering money or arms.

'Lord Elcho threatened to hang Mr. Maitland, and proposed to maim the officers prisoners.

'All the Carse country rifled and nothing paid for about Falkirk.

'Lord Menzies house plundered.

'Money exacted arbitrarily, without regard to valuation: and heavy quarterings and pillaging quhen refused to be paid.

'Shops rifled by the rebels in England.

'My Lord Finlater's house plundered, and My Lord Elchies's, and severall other gentlemen's houses in that country.

'The rebels took not only hay and straw, but meal and all provisions in the north country, without payment: and wherever a gentlemen submitted voluntarily to the government they forced him to pay double.

'They imposed cess and levied it long before it fell due in Perthshire.

'Quaker Erskine's house plundered by the rebels.

'Sir Robert Munro barbarously murdered with his brother, and severall other officers murdered after quarter given.

'No sogers wound drest after the battle of Preston for 2 days.

'The rebels ignominiously whipt a minister for favouring the escape of some of Lord Loudon's men.

'D. Douglas' house rifled, and money forced from him.

'Where they were cantond in towns, they lived on free quarter.

'Immense numbers of horses and quantities of hay, corn, &c.'

[What follows is written as *per contra* in column right opposite the foregoing.]

'The ministers at Edinburgh left their charges.
'The King's troops quartered within Edinburgh.

'A particular set of persons assumed the government of the town : they ordered all who wanted back their blankets to give up their names.

'The publisher of the *Mercury* restrained his liberty ; and no accounts but the Government's to be published.

'Shirreff-Substitute of Haddington ordered horses to transport Blyth's regiment, etc., under pain of 10 £ Scots : and hay to be furnished by the gentlemen for bedding to the foot as they should be answerable without bargaining with any officer.

'Messrs. Clerk, Drummond, etc., piniond when going from Stirling, by order of Hawley.

'Mrs. Mathison's house plundered, and the Ds. of Perth's in Canongate ; Gask's, Cunochies, Strathalans, Sir H. Stirling's, Lady Barrowfield's, Mrs. Gordon's, etc.

'D. once resolved to plunder Montrose.

'Meeting-houses gutted, and prayer-books burnt.

'People not belonging to the military hanged as spies, without tryal.

'Orders given to ministers to read declarations in the pulpits ; and to inform the Government of the dissaffected persons in their paroches.

'Officers who were under parole liberated.

'Officers incouragd and prompted the breaking windows at the Duke's coming to Edinburgh.

'Orders to pillage eight miles round Blair. Above 100 M'Intoshes killed in cold blood without proof.

'Glenesk, Cameron's country, etc. burnt, and innocent persons put to starve after the danger was over.

'Haliburton of Dryburghs house plundered by order of an officer. Sir Robert Morton and Lord Dundonald shot at, with a servant killed, no inquiry ; and thanks given by the ministers to guest.

'Free quarters on Jo. Mar; —— Wright, baxter; and ——, butcher, in Haddington, plundered.

'Free quarters at Longformacus.

'Highlanders plaids stole by country people at Preston.

'The orders to carry the water from the town.

'Sending of the Glenmoristons.

'The Highlanders everywhere killed after Culloden : above 100 not resisting shot next day in a wood hard by ; 18 or 20 wounded taken out of a barn or church, and shot at as marks.

'Disclamation in doubtful cases.

'Unnatural, perverse, wilful, wicked.

'Carlisle prisoner to be tryed.

'I had no honour.

'Hobby :—owned to me the killing of 40 wounded—Lockhart, with the man and wife and two sons. It : offerd to force one after burning : but was hindered by ——. Car. Scot hangd up 3 brought into him by Maxwell.'

2 c

APPENDIX III.

In connection with the reference in the preceding paper to the ministers of Edinburgh deserting their charges, it may be of interest to note that, on 29th August 1745, the Presbytery of Edinburgh enacted that the 5th of September should be observed 'as a day of solemn fasting, humiliation, and prayer, within the bounds of this Presbytery.' They assign as the public grounds for such observance 'the dangerous and expensive war,' then carried on against 'powerful and united enemies' abroad, and the mark of the divine displeasure in permitting ' a popish and malignant party, with the Pretender's son at their head, to disturb the peace of our native country, by a wicked and rebellious insurrection at home.'

On 30th September following the *Mercury* reports :—

' There was no sermon yesterday in any church of this city, though the Bells invited the people thither as usual ; only Messrs. Macvicar and Pitcairn preached in the West Kirk parish, and prayed for King George.' In the same journal of 2d October the first article is an ' Advice to the Reverend ministers of Edinburgh ' strongly reflecting upon their cowardly desertion of their flocks, and exhorting them to return to their duty, assuring them that they might even pray for King George without incurring any risk of persecution from Prince Charles, 'who seems to wear religion pretty easy, and to be no Bigot.'

INDEX

INDEX

Abbot, James, 150.
Aberchallader, 357.
Abercrombie, James, Skeith, 24.
—— —— Deskford, 308, 387.
Aberdeen, Anne, 363.
—— Helen, 363.
—— James, 86, 363.
—— Margaret, 363.
—— Rachel, 363.
—— William, 363.
—— district, xvi, 2, 298, 386.
—— gaol, 391.
Aberdour, James, 2.
Abernethie, Alexander, 24.
—— George, Banff, 24, 369.
—— —— 194.
—— John, Strathbogie, 24.
—— —— Tyrie, 86.
Aboyn, Earl of, 11.
Aboyne, 373.
Achmeden, Laird of, 89, 91, 95.
Adam, James, 2.
—— John, 150.
—— Robert, 317.
Adamson, David, 196.
—— James, Drum, 2, 301.
—— —— Kingoldrum, 196.
—— John, 152.
—— William, 2.
Aiken, Alexander, 301.
Aikenhead, John, Brechin, 150.
—— —— of Jaw, 264.
Aikman, John, 244, 251.
Aitken, William, 244, 260.
Aiton, Andrew, 62, 63.
—— James, 150.
—— John, 150.
—— William, 62.
Albemarle, Earl of, 395, 397.
Aldie, David, 196.
Alexander, Alexander, 388.
—— Cosmos, 2, 363.
—— George, 2, 298.
—— James, 196, 313.
—— John, 2, 363.
—— Thomas, 196.
Alison, Mr., of Newhall, 215, 225, 233.
—— Marjory, 353.
Allan, James, 2, 244, 313.

Allan, John, 24, 146, 194, 196.
—— Robert, 2, 152.
Allanoch, John, 100.
Allardice, James, 152.
Allen, Charles, 244.
Allix, Charles, 395.
Alloa, 377.
Anandale, John, 244.
Ancrum, James, 264, 381.
Anderson, Alexander, 24, 150, 308.
—— Charles, 86, 152.
—— David, 152, 196, 206.
—— George, 132, 139, 353.
—— James, 2, 24, 150, 196.
—— John, 24, 132, 150, 196.
—— Laurance, 196.
—— Robert, 54, 132, 318.
—— Thomas, 72, 196, 353.
—— William, 100, 150.
Andrew, James, 150.
—— John, 198, 313.
Angus, district of, 374.
—— Robert, 132.
—— William, 86.
—— —— Earl of, 364.
Anson, Commodore, 21.
Anton, Alexander, 198.
Arbuthnot, Robert, 307.
—— Thomas, 86, 306, 307.
—— Lord, 190.
Archer, David, 198.
—— William, 150.
Archibald, Alexander, 317.
Argyll, district of, xiv, 282, 360, 382, 388.
—— Duke of, 375.
Arnot, John, 353.
Arrat, John, 196.
Arsil, David, 152.
Arthur, James, 303.
Athole, Duke of, 358, 371.
Attila, xii.
Auchenleck, Andrew, 62.
Auchinleck, David, 198.
Auld, William, 2.
Ayr district, xvi, 293.

Baad, John, 317.
—— William, 54, 316.

406 INDEX.

Bagrie, William, 86.
Baillie, Charles, 200.
Bain, Donald, 244.
—— James, 388.
—— John, 100.
—— Thomas, 100.
—— William, 244.
Baird, William, 4, 26, 156, 264, 320.
Balfour, Alexander, 260.
—— Henry, 62.
—— John, 42.
—— Robert, 319.
—— William, 260.
Ballingal, James, 200.
Balmerino, Lord, x, xiv, 377.
Balmoral, estate of, 364, 386.
Banff, district, xvi, 24, 308.
Banks, Alexander, 246.
Bannatyne, Christopher, 373.
Bannerman, Sir Alexander, of Elsick, 154, 183.
—— John, 42.
Barclay, Alexander, 62.
—— David, 154.
—— George, 200.
—— James, 154.
—— John, 24.
—— Lewis, 367.
—— Peter, of Johnstone, 154.
—— Robert, 4, 154.
Barnet, William, 200.
Barnie, John, 62.
Barrowfield, Lady, 401.
Barry, James, 200.
—— John, 200.
Baxter, David, 198.
—— Robert, 4.
Bayne, James, 42, 72.
—— John, 84, 244.
Bean, William, 200.
Beatt, David, 246.
Beattie, Andrew, 156, 320.
—— Patrick, 320.
—— Peter, 156.
Beaufort, Duke of, xii.
Beg, James, 198.
Begg, Alexander, 24.
Bell, Francis, 154.
—— Peter, 274.
—— Robert, 353.
—— W., 395, 399.
—— William, 200.
Belleisle, v.
Bennet, David, 154.
—— Robert, 24.
Berrie, John, xv, 132.
Berwick, 395.
Bettie, Alexander, 86, 305.
—— Andrew, 307.
Betty, Robert, 152.

Biberny, Patrick, 198.
Bicky, James, 26, 308.
Binnachie, John, 100.
Binny, Alexander, 200.
Bire, Thomas, 198.
Birrell, Thomas, 390.
Birse, William, 4.
Bisset, George, 156.
—— James, 4.
—— Robert, 246.
Black, Andrew, 198.
—— David, 200.
—— John, 353.
—— Thomas, 132.
Blackie, Charles, 290.
Blair, Thomas, of Glassclone, 198.
—— William, 200.
Blakeney, William, 397.
Blaw, Charles, of Castlehill, 146, 378.
Blyth, John, 198.
Blyth's Regiment, 401.
Boberno, John, 200.
Bocik, James, 62.
Boswald, Thomas, 244.
Boswell, David, 260.
Bouglass, Alexander, 132.
Bovey, Allan, 198.
Bow, Alexander, 319.
Bowar, Alexander, of Meathie, 200.
Bowdler, Amy, 365.
—— Mr. Thomas, 365.
Bower, Bartholomew, xvii, 132.
—— Meathie, 203.
Bowie, James, 24, 100.
—— John, 42, 244.
Bowman, James, 24, 86, 152, 314.
Boyd, Mr. Charles, 264.
—— George, 264, 381.
Brady, John, 370.
Brand, James, 244.
—— Robert, 4.
—— William, 152.
Break, John, 244.
Brebermackinteer, Angus, 100.
Brechin, Alexander, 152.
—— George, 152.
—— James, 152.
—— William, 305.
Bredy, John, 4.
Brember, James, 313.
—— George, 26, 308.
Bremner, Andrew, 156.
—— George, 24.
—— John, 100.
—— Robert, 24, 156.
—— William, 156.
Bresdie, Robert, 42, 370.
Bridgefoord, Magnus, 4.
Bristol Riots, vii.
Brodie, David, 134.

INDEX. 407

Brodie, James, 309.
—— Simon, 72.
—— Walter, 134.
—— William, 244.
Brounhills, Thomas, 200.
Brown, Andrew, 134, 135.
—— Colonel, 395.
—— David, 62, 198, 200.
—— Gavin, of Bishoptown, 142.
—— George, 353.
—— James, 100, 106, 112, 118, 120, 130, 198, 200.
—— John, 100, 154, 198, 246, 308, 353, 387.
—— Major, 145.
—— William, 26, 132.
Bruce, Andrew, 200.
—— —— Leith, 246.
—— David, 152.
—— George, 152.
—— Mr. Henry, of Clackmanan, 146.
—— Mr. James, 146, 152.
—— John, 152.
—— Robert, 86.
—— Thomas, 72.
—— William, 315.
Bryan, John, 156.
Brymer, Alexander, 246.
—— Robert, 246.
Buccleuch, Duke of, 281.
Buchan, David, 154.
—— George, 86.
—— James, 86, 317.
—— John, 86, 156.
Buchanan, Alexander, 54, 357, 359, 372.
—— John, 42, 54.
—— Patrick, 54.
—— Robert, 54.
Buckard, Patrick, 198, 244.
Buock, William, 156.
Burness (Bumoss), David, 154, 388.
Burnet, John, Campfield, 4, 298, 366.
—— William, 2.
Burt, —— Perth, 42.
Butcher, David, 198.
Bygowan, George, 24.
Byers, Peter, of Tonley, 4, 298, 363, 368.
Byres, Isabel, 365, 368.
—— Robert, 364.

CABLE, DAVID, 202.
Caddel, Thomas, 318, 387.
—— Robert, 318, 387.
Caird, James, 158.
Cairncross, Thomas, 202.
Cairns, James, 134.
—— John, 246.
Caithness district, xvi, 270, 324.

Calbreath, James, 54.
Calder, John, 4, 72.
—— Robert, 6.
Calinoch, John, 202, 378.
Callander, James, 146.
Callendar, Earl of, 381.
Callender, Edward, 246.
Cameron, Alexander, 102, 282.
—— Allan, of Callart, 282, 381.
—— —— of Lundarva, 282.
—— Angus, 282.
—— Daniel, 146.
—— Donald, 72, 282.
—— Duncan, 282.
—— —— More, 282.
—— Evan, 102, 282.
—— —— More, 282.
—— —— of Callart, 282, 382.
—— —— of Inverlochy, 282.
—— John, 72, 102, 282.
—— Malcom, 282.
—— Robert, 102.
—— of Lochiel, 246, 282, 382.
Camerons, 359, 376, 385.
Campbell, Alexander, 72, 319.
—— Angus, 26, 314.
—— Archibald, 313.
—— David, 156.
—— Donald, 102, 319.
—— Duncan, 42.
—— Eneas, 303, 305.
—— Hector, 270.
—— John, 42, 102.
—— —— Major-General, 383, 385.
—— Mungo, Creiff, 42.
—— William, 200.
—— of Glenlyon, 42.
Campbells, 39, 359.
Campbelltown district, xvi, 290.
Cando, John, 200.
Candow, John, 202.
Canongate, 401.
—— gaol, 391, 393.
Cantlo, George, 305, 307.
Cargil, John, 160, 204.
Carlisle, xii, 373, 378, 383, 398, 401.
Carmichael, David, Balmedie, 42, 370.
—— Donald, 282.
—— John, 42, 282.
—— Sir John de, 370.
—— John, of Baiglie, 370.
—— Malcom, 282.
—— Robert, 370.
Carmichaels, 384.
Carnegy, Charles, 156, 320.
—— George, 156, 320.
—— Mr., junior, of Bonny Moon, 168.
—— James, of Findaury, 158.
—— —— of Balmachy, 202.
—— Robert, 158.

Carre, Thomas, 204.
Carruthers, William, 142.
Cashie, Alexander, 160.
Cashnie, Peter, 160, 388.
Cassie, Andrew, 84, 376.
Catenoch, Alexander, 156.
Catineaugh, John, 204, 378.
Cathrae, Isobel, 215.
Catto, George, 305, 307.
Cato, James, 88.
Caw, Lodovick, 42.
Chadwick, Thomas, xiv.
Chalmers, Alexander, 313.
—— —— of Balnacraig, 366.
—— Andrew, 204.
—— Elizabeth, 303.
—— George, 4.
—— James, 95.
—— John, 88, 158.
—— Mrs., 303.
—— Thomas, 204.
—— William, 88, 158, 302.
Chape, Matthew, 42.
Chaplain, James, 202.
Chapman, John, 26.
Charles I., King, ix.
Chein, George, 88, 302.
Chevas, John, 305, 307.
Chisholm, John, 72.
—— Roderick, 72, 374.
Chives, John, 88.
Christy, John, 319.
—— Patrick, 26.
—— William, 88, 302, 319, 393.
Chrystie, Alexander, 64, 202.
—— Peter, 204.
Clanranald, Chief of, xiii.
Clapperton, Thomas, 26.
Clark, Alexander, 26, 202, 204.
—— Andrew, 6, 301.
—— Charles, 202.
—— David, 202.
—— Henry, 246, 379.
—— James, 202.
—— John, 44, 100, 204, 317.
—— Thomas, 156.
—— William, 88.
Claverhouse, ix.
Cleland, George, 64.
—— Robert, 64.
Clerk, Mr., 401.
Clifton, 369, 377.
Cochran, David, 202.
—— William, 200.
—— —— of Ferguslie, 292.
Collie, William, 160.
Collison, James, 160.
Colquhoune, Charles, 246.
Colvile, Dr. George, 204.
Comrie, Duncan, 44.

Comry, William, 146.
Congleton, John, 246.
Constable, John, 204.
Cook, James, 301.
—— Captain, 397.
—— John, 202.
Cooper, Andrew, 246.
—— Robert, 160.
Cope, General, xi, xii, 29, 357.
Copens, David, 202.
Corbet, Henry, 317.
Cormack, John, 26.
Cornall, Andrew, xvii, 202.
Corser, Archibald, 134.
Cosky, John, 158.
Coupar, James, 158.
—— David, 353.
—— William, 353.
Coutts, Alexander, 246.
—— David, 4.
—— James, 4.
—— John, 6.
—— Peter, 4.
—— William, 6, 102.
Covenant, The, ix.
Cow, George, 309, 313.
Cowan, James, of Powside, 317.
Cowie, Alexander, 26.
—— David, 158.
—— Margaret, 309, 313.
Cowper, Ashley, xiv.
Cowtie, David, 202.
Craich, Francis, 146.
Craig, Alexander, 88, 302.
—— George, 6.
Craik, David, 202.
—— John, 202.
Craw, Mr. Andrew, 246.
Crawford, Elizabeth, (or Rolland,) 64, 353.
Crawfurd, Henry, xvii, 62.
Creiff, 372.
Crichton, James, xvii, 26, 158, 197, 308, 312.
Crighton, Alexander, 158, 202, 204.
—— John, 202, 204.
—— Robert, 131, 135.
—— Thomas, 158, 202, 204, 206.
Cristal, David, 4.
—— John, 4.
Crockat, James, 202.
—— William, 204.
Crole, David, 156.
Cromartie, Earl of, xiv, 73, 75, 77, 79, 83, 263, 400.
Crombie, Patrick, 134.
Crook, Alexander, 204.
Crookshanks, Charles, 134.
Crow, James, 202.
Cruden, William, 307.

INDEX. 409

Cruickshank, Hector, 102.
—— James, 88.
—— John, 102, 302.
—— John, surgeon, 88, 387.
—— Robert, 102, 158.
—— William, 158.
Culloden, viii, xvii, 371-386, 400.
Cumberland, Duke of, xviii, 183, 291, 365, 374, 377, 385.
—— county of, xiv.
Cuming, Alexander, 44, 88, 302, 307.
—— Charles, of Kininmont, 88, 302.
—— Christian, 370.
Cumming, David, 4, 206.
—— James, 389.
—— John, 102.
—— Lachlan, 102.
—— William, of Pittully, 88, 302, 386.
Cuningham, Mrs. Janet, 373.
Cunison, John, 290.
Cunninghame, George, 394.
Cunochie, Laird of, 401.
Cuthbert, Archibald, 204.
Cuthberth, Robert, 100.

DALGAIRNS, ALEXANDER, 208.
Dalgarno, Ann, 363.
—— John, 303, 305, 307.
Dalglish, James, 206.
Dalgrean, John, 88.
Dalkeith, 141, 247, 358, 377.
Dallas, Alexander, 104, 124, 126.
Dallass, James, Cantra, 102.
Dalmahoy, Alexander, 264, 265.
Davert, David, 264.
Davidson, Alexander, 246, 309, 313.
—— Christopher, 317.
—— George, 102.
—— Gilbert, 305.
—— Hendry, 134.
—— James, Myreside, 64, 102, 301.
—— John, 102, 162.
—— Patrick, 301.
—— Peter, 6.
—— Robert, 317.
—— Roderick, 315.
—— Thomas, 280, 309, 311, 313.
—— William, 26, 206, 308.
Davie, John, 206.
Daw, ——, widow, 353.
Dawson, James, 26.
—— John, 353.
Day, Alexander, 313.
Deakers, George, 160, 320.
Deans, Andrew, 6.
—— James, 160.
Dear, William, 162.
Deary, Andrew, 160.
—— James, 160.
Dease, James, 162.

Decorm (Durom), Alexander, 6, 298, 386.
Denhame, John, 134.
Dennies, David, 160.
Denothy, John, 264.
Derby, vii, xii, xiii.
Derg, Angus, 102.
Dettingen, 279.
Deuar, John, 64.
Deughars, John, 208.
Dewar, John, 63.
Dey, Thomas, 342, 389.
Dick, John, 134, 317.
—— William, 206.
Ditch, Alexander, 88.
Doctor, Peter, 208.
Dodds, James, 134.
Dogood, Peter, of Auchenhove, 6, 298, 364, 367.
Doig, John, 206.
Don, Allan, 54.
Donald, John, 206.
Donaldson, James, 26.
—— Mr. James, 31, 309.
—— John, 393.
—— Thomas, 134.
—— William, 264.
Dorwood, David, 160.
—— John, 160.
Dott, Mary, 353.
Dougal, Andrew, 206.
—— James, 206.
Douglas, Alexander, 6.
—— Duke of, 400.
—— Erskine, 142.
—— Francis, 142.
—— John, 6.
—— —— of Fechel, 88, 302.
—— Sir John, of Hillhead, 143.
—— Robert, 64, 208.
—— Samuel, 102.
—— William, 162.
Douny, Alexander, 206.
—— Ebenezer, 206.
Dow, John, 206.
—— William, 44.
Downie, John, 6.
—— Castle, 374.
Drummond, Gavin, 44.
—— George, 44.
—— Gilbert, 206.
—— James, 44.
—— John, Perth, 44, 54, 371.
—— Lord, 27, 43, 147.
—— of Logie Almond, 206.
—— Mr., 401.
—— Peter, 44.
—— Robert, 246.
—— Walter, 246.
—— William, 44.

Drummonds, 359.
Drysdale, James, 44.
Dublin, 364.
Dubois, J. B., 397.
Duddingston, 358.
Duff, Alexander, 206.
—— James, 6, 298.
—— John, 26, 314.
—— Robert, 274.
—— Patrick, 37.
—— William, of Corsindae, 366.
Duffs, 359.
Duffus, Alexander, 26, 315.
Duguid, Peter, 88.
—— Robert, of Auchinhove, 364.
Dumbarton Castle, 277.
Dumfries district, 142, 361, 378.
—— gaol, 391, 393.
Dunbar, Archibald, 104, 126, 130.
—— Sir William, Durn, 26, 314.
Dunblane, 209, 368.
Duncan, Alexander, 160.
—— Charles, 206.
—— George, 26.
—— James, 26, 64, 160, 161, 206, 308.
—— John, 160, 162, 206, 313.
—— Peter, 206.
—— Robert, 162.
—— Thomas, 6.
—— William, 162.
Dundas, Mr., 397.
Dundee district, xvi, 196, 351, 378, 390.
Dundonald, Lord, 401.
Dunfermline district, xvi, 146, 348, 361, 378, 390; gaol, 391, 393.
Dunn, James, 6.
Duns district, xvi, 294, 326, 361.
Durie, John, 160.
Durom, Alexander, 298.
Durward, John, 88.
—— George, 6.
—— Robert, 6.
—— William, 368.
Dury, David, 160.
Duthie, Alexander, 162.
—— John, 206, 208.

EACIE, JOHN, 210.
Easson, Andrew, 208.
—— John, 8.
—— Robert, 8.
Edgar, John, of Keithlock, 162.
Edie, James, 155, 157, 175.
Edinburgh, vii, x.
—— district, xvi, 244, 338, 379, 389.
Edward, Alexander, 208.
—— Andrew, Newbigging, 208.
—— David, 208.

Edward, James, Ferryden, 162, 208.
—— John, Nethertoun, 208.
—— Michael, 8.
—— William, 8.
Elcho, Lord, 135, 245, 400.
Elder, John, 26.
Elgin district, xvi, 100, 334, 389.
Ellis, Alexander, 210.
—— John, 210.
Elphingston, Arthur, Lord Balmerino, 134, 377.
Elphinston, James, 134, 135.
—— Henry, 8, 298, 368.
Emly, Alexander, 248.
Enzie, 358.
Erskine, Jean, 367.
—— John, 72, 162, 320.
—— Thomas, 64.
—— William, of Pittodrie, 367.
—— —— gentleman, 248.
Espline, John, 248.
Essie, James, 162.
Esslemonth, barony of, 363, 365.
Ewing, Charles, 8.
—— Peter, 8.
—— Robert, 8.

FAIRWEATHER, PETER, 166.
Falconer, Alexander, 90, 164.
—— John, 248.
Falkirk, vii, xi, xiii, xvi, 359, 364-366, 371, 375, 377, 382, 386, 400.
Farquhar, David, 210.
—— Francis, 10.
—— James, 26.
—— Patrick, 212.
—— William, 212.
Farquharson, Alexander, 2.
—— —— of Monaltrie, 364, 368.
—— Andrew, 106.
—— Anna, 364.
—— Charles, 10.
—— —— of Inverey, 367.
—— Cosmus, of Tombea, 106.
—— Donald, of Auchrachan, 106.
—— Francis, of Monaltry, Brachly, 8, 298, 364, 365, 369.
—— Gregory, 106.
—— Henry, 8, 365.
—— James, of Balmurle, Craigmile, 8, 298, 364, 366, 367, 386.
—— —— Westertoun, 210.
—— John, 8, 210, 365.
—— —— Monaltrie, 364.
—— —— Dow, 102.
—— —— of Altery, 106.
—— Lewis, 90.
—— Mary, 98, 304, 387.
—— Robert, 10, 106, 364.
—— William, 8, 210.

INDEX. 411

Farquharson, William, of Braxie, 365.
Farquharsons, 358, 359, 365.
Feithie, Andrew, 210.
Feithy, John, 210.
Fenton, David, 210.
—— James, 210.
—— Silvester, 210.
—— Thomas, 212.
Ferguson, Hugh, 74.
—— James, 108.
—— John, 248.
—— Joseph, 210, 212.
—— Robert, 212.
—— Patrick, 319.
—— William, 164.
Ferrier, David, 90, 164, 171.
—— James, 90, 302.
—— John, 164.
—— Robert, 164.
Fethes, David, 164.
Fettes, John, 162, 320.
Fieldes, Mr., Turriff, 309.
Fife, Alexander, 248.
—— Charles, 212.
—— district of, xvi, 359, 373.
—— Gilbert, 248.
—— James, 212.
—— William, 28.
Filp, Thomas, 210.
Findaury, Laird of, 169.
Findlater, Earl of, 25, 29, 39, 400.
—— William, 8.
Findlay, Robert, 8.
Finlay, Alexander, 104.
—— George, 64.
—— James, 164, 210.
—— Mr., 116, 128.
—— William, 106.
Finlayson, James, 390, 392.
—— John, 136.
Finlyson, John, 248.
Finnie, James, 346, 390.
—— Robert, 274.
Frizel, John, 166.
Fleeming, James, 353.
—— Mr., 391.
Fleming, Donald, 108.
—— James, 106.
—— John, 106.
—— Robert, 106.
Fletcher, Robert, 210, 212.
Fogo, John, 212.
Forbes, Alexander, 90, 210.
—— —— Lord Pitsligo, 90, 302, 303, 376, 387.
—— Anna, 370.
—— Benjamin, 8.
—— Duncan, 260, 263.
—— Elizabeth, 369.
—— George, 26, 95, 212.

Forbes, James, 90, 305, 307.
—— Jean, 370.
—— John, 74, 106, 108.
—— —— Pitsligo, 90, 376.
—— —— 164, 248.
—— Jonathan, 90, 304.
—— Joseph, 136, 139.
—— Robert, 8, 28, 248.
—— Thomas, 90.
—— William, 312, 387.
Forbeses, 359.
Fordue, James, 164.
Fordyce, Alexander, 104.
Foreman, John, 303, 305.
Forres, 104, 393.
Forrest, George, 90, 304.
—— James, 90, 305.
—— William, 90.
Forrester, Silvester, 210.
Forret, James, 164.
Forsyth, George, 8.
—— James, 104.
Fort Augustus, 374.
—— William, 283.
Forth, the river, ix, xv.
Fotheringham, David, 212.
—— James, 166.
—— Thomas, of Bandaine, 212.
Foulis, George, 373.
Fowler, John, 106.
Frain, John, 10.
Framan, John, Miltown, 164, 322, 388.
France, 199, 357, 364, 367, 371, 377, 378, 382.
Fraser (Frazer), Alexander, 8, 74.
—— —— 26, 104.
—— Charles, 104.
—— David, 74, 164.
—— Donald, 26, 74, 104, 314, 375, 376.
—— George, 390, 393, 396, 398.
—— Dame Helen, 369.
—— Hugh, 74, 104, 166, 320.
—— James, 74, 104, 106.
—— John, 106, 108, 164, 210.
—— John, 74, 104.
—— Robert, 26, 314, 387.
—— Roderick, 74.
—— Simon, Lord Lovat, 74, 105, 107, 374.
—— —— 74, 75, 77, 104.
—— Thomas, 106.
—— William, of Culbocky, 74, 328, 388.
—— —— Culmiln, 74, 328, 388.
—— —— 74, 90, 104, 106, 302.
—— of Inverallochy, 75.
Frasers, 75, 359.
Freebairn, Mr., 175.

Freeman, John, 322, 388.
Frendraught, Viscount, xvii.
Froster, William, 210.
Fullen, John, 353.
Fullerton (Fullarton), Adam, 326, 388.
—— James B., 326, 388.
—— Joan, 379.
—— John, 90.
—— —— of Dudwick, 304.
Furnival, Thomas, xiv.
Fyre, John, 342, 389.

GALL, ALEXANDER, 260, 308, 387.
Gammack, William, 214.
Garden, David, 168.
Garder, Peter Gow, 74.
Gardner, Colonel, 380.
—— James, 56, 316.
—— William, 168.
Garmack, William, 10.
Garrioch, Alexander, 10, 300.
—— —— of Mergie, 168.
Garvich, John, 30, 308.
Garvock, John, 308, 387.
Gatt, Alexander, 30, 37, 41.
Gattahon, John, Dyce, 10.
Gauld, Alexander, 112.
—— John, 112.
—— Thomas, 110.
—— Robert, 110.
Gauldie, James, 112.
Gaw, Lewis, 112.
Ged (Gadd), James, xiv, 248, 379.
Geigie, George, 214.
Gelletlie, James, 216.
George II., viii, xi, xiv, xvii, 199, 402.
Gibb, James, 214.
Gibbon, Alexander, 168.
—— William, 168.
Gibenach, Donald, 110.
—— Thomas, 112.
Gibson, David, 214.
—— Gilbert, xv, 214.
—— John, 166, 214.
—— Thomas, 319.
Gilchrist, Archibald, 317.
Giles, Richard, 248.
Gill, Alexander, 30, 90, 304.
—— George, 30, 35, 308.
Gillespie, John, 30, 308.
—— William, 168.
Gilmer, William, 168.
Glasgow, vii, ix, 267, 279.
—— district, xvi, 272, 274, 346, 361, 381, 390, 396, 399.
Glashan, George, 28.
Glass, Finlay, 76.
—— James, 10.
—— John, 76.
Glassfoord, Thomas, 264.

Gleig, Adam, 170.
—— Robert, 170.
Glencarse, 371.
Glencoe, xi.
Glenday, James, 214.
Glendy, John, 216.
Glenelg, Lord, 377.
Glenesk, 401.
Glenfinan, 357, 359.
Glenlivet, 358.
Glenmoristons, the, 401.
Glenshiel, 371.
Glenurquhart, 377, 386.
Gleny, Peter, 214.
Gollan, Donald, 76.
Golspie, 375.
Goodbrand, John, 28.
Goodwillie, John, 248.
Gordon, Alexander, of Darlathis, 30, 308, 312.
—— —— 28, 76, 108, 112.
—— Anne, 365, 366, 368.
—— Arthur, of Carnousie, 30, 308, 312.
—— Cecilia, 370.
—— Charles, of Blelock, 10, 300.
—— Charles, Aberdeen, 28, 369.
—— Clementina, 370.
—— David, of Kirkhill, 108.
—— —— Glenbucket, 370.
—— Donald, 110.
—— Duchess of, 363.
—— Duke of, 366, 371.
—— Francis, 10, 298, 366.
—— George, of Hallhead, 10, 298, 365, 366.
—— —— of Foderleter, 110.
—— George, 28, 110, 248, 312, 387.
—— —— Glenbucket, 370.
—— Lord George, xii.
—— Helen, 366, 369.
—— Lady Henrietta, 366.
—— Henrietta, 370.
—— Henry Wolrige, 365.
—— Hugh, 366.
—— Ishmael, 112.
—— James, 28, 30, 108, 112, 305.
—— James, of Aberlour, 28, 312.
—— —— Sir, 369.
—— Dame Janet, 369.
—— Lady Jean, 371.
—— John, 28, 30, 108, 110, 168, 216, 248, 308, 312, 320, 387.
—— —— of Aberlour, 28, 312.
—— —— of Auchleuchres, 305.
—— —— of Avochie, 25, 30, 37.
—— —— of Glenbucket, 29, 30, 31, 108, 109, 237, 358, 369, 370.
—— Lord Lewis, 10, 27, 31, 35, 135, 137, 358, 366.

INDEX. 413

Gordon, Lewis, 108.
—— Lodovick, 112.
—— Margaret, 369.
—— Mrs., 401.
—— Patrick, of Cordregny, 108.
—— —— 315.
—— Peter, 28.
—— Robert, of Logie, 90, 304, 387.
—— —— of Halhead, 365.
—— —— 112, 248.
—— Samuel, 368.
—— Thomas, 108.
—— Walter, 248.
—— Sir William, of Park, 28, 314, 369.
—— William, 10, 28, 108, 110, 112, 168, 320.
—— Riots, vii.
Gordons, The, 359.
Gouck, David, 166.
Gourlie, George, 214.
—— James, 214.
Gow, Alexander, 110.
—— Donald, 216.
—— John, 216.
—— Thomas, 248.
—— William, 10.
Gowans, William, 168.
Gower, George, 214.
Graham, Alexander, 214, 346, 351, 390.
—— Archibald, 100, 102, 104, 112-116, 126.
—— Charles, 74.
—— David, 214.
—— James, Airth, 56, 316.
—— —— of Duntroun, 214.
—— John, 248, 274.
—— —— of Kilmardiny, 274, 398, 399.
—— Peter, 44.
—— Robert, 44.
—— Walter, 264.
Grahams, 359.
Grant, Alexander, 74, 108, 112, 312, 377, 387.
—— —— of Deskie, 110.
—— —— of Grantfield, 367.
—— Captain, 89, 91, 95.
—— Charles, 110.
—— Colin, 328, 388.
—— David, 90.
—— —— of Blarfinde, 108.
—— Donald, 110.
—— Gregor, 110, 172.
—— Humphrey, 28.
—— James, 30, 77, 108, 110, 168, 248.
—— Sir James, 31, 35, 37, 41, 386.
—— John, 28, 102-105, 108-116, 126-129, 248, 328, 388.

Grant, Kenneth, 75, 328, 388.
—— Lewis, 112.
—— Neil, 112.
—— Patrick, 110, 214, 216, 328, 388.
—— Peter, 110, 112, 126, 388.
—— Sir Robert, 377.
—— Walter, 248.
—— William, 108, 110, 112, 334, 389.
Grants, 358, 359.
Gray, Andrew, 214.
—— David, 168, 214.
—— James, 168.
—— John, 28, 112, 216.
—— William, 10, 28, 44, 168, 216, 274.
—— —— of Newholm, 390, 393-399.
—— & Bisset, Messrs., 183, 193.
Greek, David, 216.
Greenhill, Robert, 214.
—— William, 216.
Gregory, Prof. James, 363.
Greig, Alexander, 168.
—— James, 170, 212.
Grey, Alexander, 320, 388.
Grower, William, 216.
Guthrie, George, 168, 320.
—— Robert, 214.
Guthry, James, 28.

HALKET (HACKET), ALEXANDER, 308.
—— Mr., 353.
—— Charles, 10, 250, 300, 386.
—— —— 30, 300, 308.
—— James, 32.
Hackie, John, 218.
Haddington district, xvi, 132, 361, 377.
—— gaol, 391, 393, 401.
Haggart, David, of Cairnmuir, 218.
Haldane, Alexander, 56, 373.
—— George, 385.
—— John, of Lendrick, 56, 373, 385.
Haliburton, Thomas, 216, 250.
—— of Dryburgh, 401.
Hall, Alexander, 10.
Hamilton, Mr. Gavin, 390.
—— George, of Redhouse, 250, 379.
—— John, 30.
—— Robert, of Kilbrachmont, 260, 276.
Harper, Mr. William, 56, 316.
Harrel, William, 46.
Harvie, James, 266.
—— Patrick, 301.
Hawley, General, xii, 365, 401.
Haxton, Heleneas, 64, 373.

Haxton, Robert, 64.
Hay, Adam, Asslid, 32, 368, 370.
—— —— of Cairnbanno, 92, 304.
—— Alexander, 30.
—— Anna, 370.
—— Andrew, 30, 64.
—— —— of Asleed, 370.
—— George, 30, 172, 308, 314, 320.
—— James, 136.
—— —— W.S., 370.
—— Jean, 370.
—— John, 30, 305, 308.
—— Mary, Countess of Errol, 92, 95, 304.
—— Patrick, 250.
—— William, 303.
Hazard, sloop, 395.
Hector, John, 10.
Henderson, Alexander, 136, 216.
—— Charles, 218.
—— David, 56, 148.
—— Duncan, 46.
—— Francis, 216.
—— James, 172, 216, 218, 320.
—— John, 56, 148, 316.
—— —— of Castlemains, 142, 378.
—— Robert, 170.
—— William, 46, 218.
Hendersons, 385.
Hendrie, Alexander, 114.
Hendry, Robert, 30.
Henry, Alexander, 218.
Henryson, John, 250.
Hepburn, James, 250.
—— John, 303, 305, 307.
—— Peter, 30, 310.
Hill, Thomas, 46.
Hills, Nathaniel, 395, 398, 399.
Hobert, John, 216.
Hodge, Alexander, 317.
—— David, 250.
—— Robert, 170.
Hogg, John, 10.
Holyrood, vii, ix.
Home, David, 216, 294.
—— Mr., 393.
—— Norwald, 266.
—— William, 294.
Hood, Andrew, 76.
—— George, 76.
—— James, 170, 197.
—— Patrick, 218.
Horn, Charles, 216.
—— William, 218.
Houston, David, 260.
—— Thomas, 114.
How, Andrew, 216.
Hume, George, 250.
—— John, 216.
Hunter, Adam, 170.

Hunter, Alexander, 367.
—— David, 218.
—— Hary, 170.
—— James, 170, 172.
—— John, 10, 170.
—— Mr., of Polmood, 376.
Hutchen, John, 216.
Hutcheson, Thomas, 114.
—— William, 218.

IMBRY, ALEXANDER, 12.
Ingram, John, 12, 32.
Innes, ——, Coltfield, 114.
—— Alexander, 114.
—— Sir Henry, 109.
—— Colonel James, 32.
—— James, 32, 315.
—— —— of Banacraig, 12, 300, 367.
—— Sir James, xvii, 92.
—— John, 12, 32, 114, 300, 310, 370, 387.
—— Patrick, 32.
—— Robert, 114.
—— William, 32.
—— —— W.S., 373.
Inverarity, David, 172.
Inverness, 361, 374, 395, 397.
Inverury, 364-366.
Irons, Robert, 172, 320.
Irvine, Adam, 32.
—— Alexander, of Drum, 12, 300, 309.
—— Charles, 136.
—— Edward, of Wysbie, 142.
—— James, 142.
—— John, of Whitehill, 144.
—— William, of Gribton, 144.
—— —— 172, 218, 309.

JACK, DAVID, 46.
Jackson, Charles, 218.
Jaffrey, James, 12.
—— Thomas, 12.
James II., King, ix, xi, xiii, xvii, 139.
Jameson, George, 363.
—— Marjory, 363.
—— Mary, 363.
—— William, 172, 320.
Jamieson, Andrew, 353.
Jamison, Alexander, 303, 305.
Jeans, Henry, 309, 311.
Johnston, Andrew, 142, 250, 380.
—— George, 218.
—— James, of Knockhill, 142.
—— —— 218, 250.
—— John, 32.
—— Robert, 172.
—— William, of Lockerby, 144.
Johnstoun, Alexander, 218.
Joyner, James, 32, 314.

INDEX. 415

Kay, Lodovick, 114.
Keill, Thomas, 172.
Keir, Patrick, 250, 379.
Keith, W. A., 305.
—— David, 12, 174.
—— James, 174.
Kelly, Earl of, 63, 65, 69, 263, 373.
Kemla, James, 172.
Kemlar, Alexander, 172.
—— Thomas, 172.
Kemlay, Gideon, 172.
Kemloe, Joseph, Hardgate, 12.
Kemp, James, 319.
Kennedy, Alexander, 309.
—— Archibald, 250.
—— John, 114.
—— Robert, 314, 387.
Kermock, Andrew, 218.
Kerr, Alexander, 32.
—— Henry, 280, 381.
—— James, 84.
—— Mark, 250.
Kerrie, Alexander, 172.
—— John, 172.
Kerry, Robert, 218.
Key, John, 172.
Kilgower, Peter, 92, 304.
Kilmarnock, Earl of, xiv, 65, 127, 266, 267, 381.
Kilpatrick, Grisell, 353.
Kincaid, James, 56, 316.
King, James, 32, 310.
—— Lauchlane, 136.
—— Serjeant, *alias* Macree, 373.
Kinloch, Alexander, 220, 378.
—— Charles, 220, 378.
—— Sir James, 218, 231, 378, 379.
—— John, of Kildry, 218.
Kinnair, Peter, 220.
Kinnier, Thomas, 172.
Kirkcaldy district, xvi, 260, 344, 361, 389.
Kirkeant, Laird of, 141.
Knows, Robert, 12.
—— William, 12.
Kynnach, John, 310, 387.

Lacky, Alexander, 220.
Lafarque, Mr., 395, 397.
Lafusille, Major, 195.
Laing, John, 92, 174.
—— William, 32.
Laird, Andrew, 222.
—— James, 222.
—— John, 220.
—— Patrick, 222.
Lamb, William, 114, 176.
Lanark district, xvi, 84, 361, 373, 376.
Largo, Joseph, 12.

Lauder, Archibald, 294.
—— Charles, 136.
—— James, 250.
—— Robert, of Bailmouth, 294.
Laurance, James, 176.
Laurence, John, 92, 303, 305.
Lawrance, John, 32.
Law, Mr. George, 12, 367.
—— William, xvii, 12.
Lawrie, John, 136.
Lawson, David, 222.
—— James, 220.
—— John, 176, 220.
—— Patrick, 220.
—— Thomas, 220, 222, 378.
Leech, Archibald, 284.
Legat, George, 92, 306, 313.
Leggie, Patrick, 300, 386.
Leigh, Alexander, 114.
Leith, Alexander, 32, 310.
—— Anthony, 92, 304.
—— George, 12.
—— John, 32, 174.
—— Laurence, 92, 304.
—— Robert, 66.
—— William, 12, 174.
Lendrum, John, 305.
Lesmahagow, 287, 383.
Leslie, Alexander, 32, 312.
—— Charles, 114.
—— James, 92, 136.
—— John, 92, 174.
—— Patrick, Count, 364.
—— Teresa, 364.
—— William, 32, 174, 310, 320.
Ley, Thomas, 14, 174.
—— William, 12.
Lichton, ——, Kirriemuir, 220.
Lilly, Alexander, 136.
Lind, George, 92.
Lindsay, Alexander, 250.
—— James, 46, 371.
—— John, 176, 320.
—— Martin, 46, 371.
—— Peter, 66, 374.
—— Robert, 136.
—— Thomas, 176.
—— William, 114, 176, 320.
Lines, Andrew, 12.
Linlithgow district, xvi, 264, 358, 361, 381.
Linning, Mr., 383.
Littlejohn, Alexander, 176.
—— David, 174.
Livieth, John, 220.
—— William, 220.
Livingstone, Lady Anne, 381.
Livingston, James, 266.
Lochaber, 382.
Lochead, John, 56, 316.

Lochmaben, 378.
Lockhart, James, 46.
—— Peter, 56, 316.
London, vii, xi, xii.
Longformacus, 401.
Longmuir, Charles, 12.
Lorimer, William, 32.
Lothian, Andrew, xvii, 66.
Loudoun, Lord, 89, 127, 358, 374, 375, 376, 400.
Louper, John, 174.
Lovall, Andrew, 222.
Lovat, Lord, xiv. *See* Fraser.
Low, Alexander, 174, 303, 305.
—— David, xvii, 220.
—— James, 220.
—— John, 14, 46, 176, 320.
—— William, 174, 176, 222, 320.
Lownan, James, 220.
Lowper, Alexander, 32.
Lowthian, John, 220.
Lugtoun, Simon, 250, 379.
Lumgair, James, 222.
Lumsdaile, Andrew, 250.
Lumisdale, James, 309.
Lumsden, Alexander, 367.
—— David, 12, 367.
—— Harry, 367.
—— James, 367.
—— John, 12, 367.
—— Margaret, 367.
Lunan, David, 220.
—— John, 220.
Lundie, John, 220.
Lyon, Charles, 222.
—— David, 174, 393.
—— James, 222.
—— Mr. Robert, 46, 371.
—— Patrick, of Easter Ogle, 220.

MACKIE, ALEXANDER, 34, 178.
—— Peter, 16.
—— Robert, 180, 366.
—— William, 178, 320.
Mackies, 359.
Macvicar, Mr., 402.
Maiden, ——, surgeon, Craill, 66.
Main, Alexander, 176.
—— George, 176.
—— James, 148, 378.
—— William, 224.
Mair, James, 34.
—— William, 16, 176.
Maitland, David, 393.
—— Mr., 400.
—— Mr., of Pitrichie, 7, 19.
—— Mr. John, 180.
Malcolm, James, of Balbeddie, 262.
Malcom, William, 34, 224.
Man, Alexander, 34, 114, 226.

Man, James, 48.
—— John, 48.
—— William, 78.
Manchester, x.
Mansie, James, 178.
Mapsie, Alexander, 353.
Marischall, Earl, 87.
Marr, Alexander, 14.
—— David, 14.
—— Robert, 14.
—— Thomas, 34, 314.
Marshall, James, 224.
—— John, 148, 307.
Martin, Alexander, 120.
—— David, 178, 320.
—— George, 120.
—— James, 313.
—— John, 14, 46, 176.
Mason, James, 178.
—— Janet, 353.
—— John, 176.
Massie, Robert, 310, 387.
Masterman, Henry, xiv.
Masterton, Andrew, 226.
—— Francis, 148.
Mather, Alexander, 178.
—— Charles, 222, 224.
—— James, 180.
Mathers, George, 180, 307.
—— David, 180.
Matheson, Alexander, 94, 305, 307.
—— David, 34, 94.
Mathison, Mrs., 401.
Mathie, James, 178.
Mathew, James, 305.
Matthew, Peter, 114.
Maul, Henry, 252, 266.
—— John, 176.
—— Peter, 176.
Maver, James, 34, 310.
—— William, 310, 387.
Maxwell, James, of Kirkconnal, 144.
—— Lady Katharine, 144.
—— Robert, 252.
—— William, of Carruchan, 144, 145.
—— —— of Barncleugh, 144.
—— —— Earl of Nithsdale, 144.
—— Sir William, of Sprinkell, 144.
M'Adam, William, 122.
M'Alister, Alexander, 122.
—— Hector, 326, 388.
—— William, 326, 388.
MacAlisters, 359.
M'Allan, John, 120.
M'Alman, Nicol, 286.
M'Alpin, Patrick, 120.
MacAlpines, 359.
M'Andrew, Donald, 78.
MacAndrews, 359.
M'Angus, William, 124.

INDEX. 417

M'Arthur, John, 114.
MacArthurs, 359, 385.
M'Bain, Gillice, 116, 376.
—— Hugh, 76.
MacBains, 359.
M'Bean, Angus, 336, 389.
—— Donald, 118, 377.
—— Gillies, 118.
—— John, 118.
—— Major, 119.
M'Bear, Angus, 118.
—— Gillies, 118.
M'Beath, Marmduke, 252.
M'Callum, John, 100, 114, 126, 130.
M'Carro, James, 224.
M'Charmaig, Duncan, 284.
M'Chombich, Duncan Dow, 284.
M'Clacky, James, 78.
M'Coll, Archibald, 284.
—— Duncan, 284.
—— Hugh, 284.
—— —— Roy, 284.
—— John, 286.
MacColls, 359, 384.
M'Combichs, 384.
M'Connachy, Alexander, 76.
M'Connie, Robert, 262.
M'Cook, Hercules, 14.
M'Cormacks, 384.
M'Corquadales, 384.
M'Culloch, Roderick, 76, 299, 301, 375.
—— William, 266.
MacCullochs, 359.
M'Currathy, John, 76.
M'Donald, Alex., 14, 34, 116, 118, 122.
—— —— of Glencoe, 284.
—— - —— of Keppoch, 284, 382.
—— Allan, 46, 116, 124.
—— Angus, 116, 120, 122, 124.
—— - —— of Glengarry, 284, 382, 386.
—— Arch., of Clenaig, 284.
—— Coll., 124.
—— Don., 122, 284, 313, 336, 389.
—— - —— of Lochgarry, 284.
—— George, 124.
—— James, 78, 122, 124, 284, 326, 388.
—— John, 76, 116, 120, 122, 224, 286, 292.
—— Murdoch, 78.
—— Peter, 120.
—— Robert, 122.
—— Ronald, 16, 116, 286, 389.
—— William, 34, 122, 286, 314.
—— of Barrisdale, 77, 81.
—— of Kinloch Moidart, 286, 383.
MacDonalds, 357, 359, 376, 385.
M'Donell, Angusia, 386.
M'Dougal, Samuel, 224.

MacDougalds, 359.
M'Duff, James, 224.
M'Erick, Archibald, 284.
M'Erich, Donald, 284.
M'Evan, John, 120.
M'Ewan, Donald, 48.
—— James, 56.
—— John, 48, 226.
MacEwans, 359.
M'Farlan, Duncan, 284.
M'Farlane, Alexander, 262.
—— John, 48, 56.
—— Thomas, 318, 387.
MacFarlanes, 359.
M'Farquhar, Donald, 78.
—— — Farquhar, 78.
—— John, 78.
—— Donald, 78.
—— Kenneth, 78.
—— Roderick, 78.
MacFarquhars, 359.
M'Gee, Hugh, 14.
M'Ghie, William, 144.
M'Gill, George, 66.
M'Gillavrae, Alexander, 116, 376.
MacGillivrays, 359.
M'Gillawray, Archibald, 116.
—— Robert, 116.
M'Glashan, William, 34.
M'Grar, Alexander, 122.
M'Grigor, Alexander, 16, 58, 122.
—— —— Roy Callander, 58.
—— Donald, 224.
—— Dougal, 58.
—— Duncan, 14, 367.
—— Evan, 120.
—— Grigor, 120.
—— Roy, 126.
—— John, 120, 252.
—— Malcolm, 120, 122.
—— Captain, 373.
—— Patrick, 58.
—— William, 120.
M'Grigors, 175, 183, 359.
M'Growther, Alexander, xiv.
M'Gurman, John, 120.
M'Hardie, William, 124.
M'Herioch, Duncan, 284.
M'Humish, John, 58.
M'Ildeus, 384.
M'Ildonick, James, 78.
M'Inhonnel, John, 58.
M'Inish, Archibald, 284.
—— Donald, 284.
M'Innises, 384.
M'Intosh, Alexander, 116.
—— Angus, of Pharr, 116.
—— Duncan, 118.
—— Lady, 117, 119.
—— Lauchlan, 116.

2 D

418 INDEX.

M'Intosh, John, 122.
—— Simon, 116.
—— William, 224.
Mackintoshes, 359, 376, 401.
M'Intyre, ——, 46.
—— Donald, 78.
—— Duncan, 284.
MacIntyres, 359, 384.
M'Iver, Alexander, 78.
—— William, 84.
M'Javis. *See* M'Tavish.
M'Kaog, Patrick, 286.
M'Kay, Alexander, of Achmony, 330, 386, 388.
—— Donald, 34.
—— John, 124.
—— Robert, 122.
—— William, 303, 305.
M'Keamish, Kenneth, 270.
M'Kenzie, Alexander, 76, 78, 252, 330, 389.
—— Colin, 76, 78, 330, 389.
—— Donald, 34, 78.
—— Earl of Cromarty, 76, 375.
—— George, 78.
—— John, 78, 114, 120, 122, 286.
—— Kenneth, 76, 120, 252, 328, 330, 388, 389.
—— Lord M'Leod, 76, 375.
—— Murdoch, 78, 79.
—— Patrick, 224.
—— Roderick, 138.
—— Theodore, 78.
—— William, 76, 114, 138.
—— of Ardloch, 330, 389.
Mackenzies, 360, 384.
M'Kie, Robert, 317.
M'Knoby, Archibald, 262.
M'Laren, Archibald, 58.
—— Captain Donald, 373.
—— Daniel, 106, 118.
—— Hugh, 284.
—— John, 116.
—— Lauchlan, 286.
MacLarens, 360, 384.
M'Lauchlan, Alexander, 284, 382.
—— Dougald, 284.
—— Duncan, 284.
—— George, 124.
—— James, 286.
—— John, 58, 124, 286, 318, 387.
—— Kenneth, 286.
—— Lauchlan, of that Ilk, 286.
—— —— of Inishconel, 286.
—— Neil, 286.
—— Peter, 34.
MacLachlans, 360, 385.
M'Lea, Alexander, 122.
—— Allan, 124.
—— James, 122.

M'Lea, John, 122.
—— Robert, 122.
—— William, 124.
MacLeas, 360, 385.
M'Lean, Alexander, 46, 226.
—— Allan, 284.
—— Charles, of Drimnan, 284.
—— Hector, 252.
—— Hugh, 284.
—— John, Ferryhill, 14, 116, 286.
—— Lauchlan, 286.
—— Roderick, 78.
MacLeans, 360.
M'Leish, John, 48.
—— William, 340, 389.
M'Lellan, William, 319.
M'Lennan, Alexander, 77.
—— Donald, 78.
—— John, 334, 389.
—— Kenneth, 78.
MacLennans, 360.
M'Leod, Alexander, Muiravonside, 266, 330, 389.
—— Laird of, 31, 81, 93.
M'Leods, 23, 89, 99, 358, 360.
M'Mahon, Lieutenant Morgan, 397.
M'Nab, Donald, 58.
MacNabs, 360.
M'Naughton, John, 252, 379.
M'Near, James, 317.
—— Robert, 317.
M'Niccol, Duncan, 319.
—— William, 224.
M'Nully, Farquhar, 76.
M'Pherson, Alexander, 120, 124.
—— Andrew, of Banachar, 118.
—— Angus, 118.
—— Donald, 118.
—— Evan, of Clunie, 118, 377.
—— Hugh, 118.
—— John, 118, 120, 122, 358.
—— Kenneth, 118.
—— Lauchlan, 118.
—— Lewis, 118.
—— Malcolm, of Phoyness, 118.
—— Paul, 124.
—— —— Delwhiny, 118.
—— Thomas, 122.
—— William, Ringussie, 120.
—— of Strathmasy, 118.
Macphersons, 360, 377.
M'Phun, Archibald, 284.
M'Queen, Alexander, 120.
M'Ra, Alexander, 34, 314.
MacRaes, 360.
M'Rankens, 384.
M'Robie, John, 48.
—— Lewis, 48.
—— William, Morings, 122.
MacRobies, 360.

INDEX.   419

M'Tavish, Alexander, 116.
—— John, of Gartenbeg, 116.
MacTavishes, 360.
M'Uchaders, 384.
M'Vie, George, 319.
M'William, John, 76, 78.
—— Thomas, 78.
MacWilliams, 360.
M'Willie, David, 120.
—— Dun., 122.
—— James, 120.
Meal, John, 222.
Meathie, Laird of, 229, 235.
Meldrum, Robert, 393.
Meldrum, Old, district, xiv, 84, 302, 361, 376, 386.
Melvill, William, 353.
Mensat, John, 124.
Menzies, Mr. John, 252, 266.
—— Lord, 400.
—— —— of Sheen, 46, 267, 358.
—— David, of Pitfodels, 16.
—— Gilbert, of Pitfodels, 16, 300.
—— James, of Pitfodels, 16.
—— John, of Pitfodels, 16.
—— William, of Pitfodels, 16.
Menzies, 360.
Mercer, James, 367.
—— Laurence, of Lethenday, 226, 378.
—— Sir Laurence, of Aldie, 378.
—— Robert, of Aldie, 148, 226, 378.
—— Thomas, 14, 300, 367.
Mercers, of Aldie, 367.
Merchant, Roderick, 112, 114, 126, 130.
Merns, Alexander, 94.
Michie, John, 124.
Middleton, Alexander, 66.
—— James, 16, 122.
—— Patrick, 252.
—— Robert, 92.
—— Samuel, 16.
—— William, 16, 176.
Miles, James, 222, 224.
Mill, Alexander, 58, 178, 316.
—— David, 58, 224, 316.
—— George, 14, 178.
—— James, 222.
—— John, 178.
—— Robert, 222.
—— Thomas, 58, 247, 316.
—— William, 94.
Miller, Alexander, 252.
—— David, 180.
—— Duncan, 178.
—— James, 224, 226.
—— John, 222.
—— William, 120, 224, 326, 388.
Moillin, Alexander, 16.
Millne, George, 122.

Milne, George, 34, 310, 387.
—— James, 222.
—— John, 34, 176, 178.
—— Robert, 222.
—— Thomas, 224.
—— William, 34, 178, 304, 310.
Mitchell, Alexander, 34, 222.
—— Donald, 318, 387.
—— Duncan, 318, 387.
—— George, 16, 313.
—— James, 16, 34.
—— John, xv, 182, 187, 224, 226, 252, 319.
—— Murdoch, 78.
—— Robert, 14, 180, 193, 252, 319.
—— Roderick, 116.
—— Thomas, 224, 252.
—— William, 94, 138.
Moffat, 145.
Moidart, xiii.
Moir, Charles, 14, 300.
—— James, 14, 307.
—— —— of Stonywood, 14, 91, 300, 364, 367.
—— Janet, 364.
—— John, 16, 78.
—— Kenneth, 76.
—— Robert, 280.
—— William, of Longmay, 14, 92, 94, 300, 304.
Mollison, Robert, 176.
Moncrieffe, Mr. D., xiv.
Moncrife, Thomas, 46.
Moncur, John, 176.
Moncurr, Andrew, 224.
—— Patrick, 222.
Money, George, 222.
Monro, Donald, 120.
Monteith, Alexander, 148.
Montgomery, Peter, 34.
—— Robert, 14.
Montrose district, xvi, 150, 320, 361, 388.
Moodie, James, 178.
—— Thomas, 222, 224.
Moar, William, 224.
More, John, 124.
—— Peter, 122.
Morgan, Charles, 94.
—— David, 224.
—— John, 176.
—— William, 176.
Morrise, James, 94.
Morice, John, 307.
Morris, John, 353.
—— Helen, 353.
Morrison, Alexander, 34, 94, 304, 310, 311.
—— John, 34, 311.
—— Richard, 252, 380.

420 INDEX.

Morrison, William, 34, 311.
Morton, Sir Robert, 401.
Mossman, Thomas, 14.
Mouat, William, 178, 320.
Muir, Adolphus, 252.
—— Alexander, 122.
—— Robert, 14.
Muirison, Provost, of Aberdeen, 305.
Munie, Thomas, 222.
Munro, Sir Robert, 400.
Murdoch, William, 58.
Murray, Anthony, of Grange, 148.
—— —— Edinburgh, 252.
—— Sir David, 252, 380.
—— of Dollarie, 48, 372.
—— Lord George, 46, 267, 358, 359, 366, 369, 371, 373, 400.
—— James, 176, 252, 316, 380, 387.
—— John, Broughton, 84, 376.
—— —— 58, 135, 148, 252.
—— Lady Margaret, 372.
—— Mungo, 226.
—— Peter, 14.
—— William, 46, 176.
Murry, Lewis, 171.
—— Robert, 252, 380.
Mushet, William, 252.
Mussleburgh, 141.
Mutch, George, 94.
—— John, 94.

NAIRN, Lord, 201, 213, 227.
—— —— John, 226.
Nairn, 386.
Nairne, Mrs. Amelia, 372.
Napier, John, 48.
Nash, John, 226.
—— William, 226.
Neavy, David, 254.
Neil, Thomas, 226.
Netherbow Port, 255.
Netherlands, 364, 371.
Nevay, David, 226.
Newcastle, 381.
—— Duke of, ix.
Newport (Paisley), 326.
Newton, Richard Hay, of Newton, 377.
Nicoll, David, 353.
Niccol, James, 80, 182.
Nicol, Thomas, 48.
Nicolson, Alexander, 124.
—— James, 254, 380.
—— William, 34.
Niddry, Andrew, 94.
Nisbet, William, 94, 305, 307.
Nivie, James, 16.
Norald, Adam, 94.
Northampton, 386.
Nova Scotia, 370.
Nuccol, Robert, Canongate, 254.

OAT, HENRY, 318, 387.
Oatt, William, 318, 387.
Ogg, William, 16.
Ogilvie, Agnes, 367.
—— Lord, 33, 167, 179, 195, etc.
—— Sir Alexander, of Forglen, 367.
Ogilvies, 360.
Ogilvy, Alexander, 36, 94, 228, 304.
—— —— of Auchiries, 96, 376.
—— David, 226, 228, 379.
—— Henry, 228.
—— James, Mearns, 226, 228.
—— John, 96, 228, 304.
—— Patrick, 36.
—— Thomas, 226, 228, 399.
—— Walter, 36.
—— William, 16, 96, 228, 304.
Ogston, James, 266.
—— William, 305.
Oldman, James, 96.
Oliphant, Alexander, 353.
—— Caroline, 372.
—— Thomas, 66.
—— of Gask, 47.
—— Laurance, 48, 372.
Oram, Alexander, 66.
—— Mr., 353.
Ord, James, 36.
Orkney, John, 184, 320, 388.
Orrock, Walter, 254.
Orrok, John, 228.
Osburn, Robert, 341.
Ouchterlony, John, 184, 228, 320.
—— Peter, 228.

PAISLEY DISTRICT, xvi, 292, 326, 361, 388.
Palmer, Robert, 230.
—— William, 230.
Panton, Alexander, 36, 310.
Paris, 367, 371, 373, 383.
Park, Mr., 393.
Paterson, Alexander, 18, 230, 299.
—— Andrew, 80.
—— Charles, 254, 255.
—— David, 353.
—— Donald, 80.
—— George, 36, 314.
—— Hercules, 36, 312.
—— James, 31, 37, 41, 230.
—— Lauchlane, 80.
—— Murdoch, 80.
—— Robert, 96.
Paton, George, 16.
—— John, 84.
—— Marjory, 319.
—— William, 124.
Pattie, James, 68.
Patullo, George, 230.
—— Henry, xiii., 230, 359.

INDEX. 421

Paul, George, 305.
Peddie, John, 184, 230.
Peirie, Alexander, 96.
—— Charles, 96, 307.
Penrith, 380.
Penston, Robert, 138.
Perrie, John, 124.
Perth, Duke of, xvi, 45, 145, 247, 251, 371.
—— district, xvi, 42, 361, 370.
—— town of, 371, 379, 397.
Peterborough, Earl of, 366.
Peterloo, vii.
Peterson, James, 184.
Petrie, Andrew, 230.
—— James, xvii, 18, 300.
—— John, 254, 380.
—— William, 314, 387.
Philp, John, 230.
—— Robert, 66.
—— William, 16.
Pierson, Alexander, 184.
Piery, John, 84, 303, 305, 307.
Piggot, Alexander, 228, 230.
Pirrey, William, 309, 313.
Pirrie, Andrew, 307.
—— —— 96.
—— John, 312, 387.
Pitcairn, Mr., 402.
Pitcalny, Laird of, 75, 235.
Pith, James, 254.
Pitsligo, Lord, 11, 302, 358, 387.
Porter, James, 309.
—— William, 104, 126, 311.
—— —— 112, 114.
Porteous, Captain, ix.
Porteus, Andrew, 138, 377.
—— Samuel, 138.
Powrie, John, 48.
Preston, 61, 67, etc.
Prestonpans, xv, 141, 357, 364, 369, 376, 380, 400.
Primrose, Sir Archibald, of Dunipace, 58, 373.
—— George, of Dunipace, 373.
—— Janet, 138.
Prophet, Thomas, 228.
Punton, John, 254.
Pyot, Alexander, 184, 388.
—— David, 320, 388.

RAE, JAMES, 317.
Raith, James, 317.
Ramsay, Alexander, 96, 186, 306.
—— Christopher, 138.
—— David, 232, 305, 307.
—— George, 232.
—— James, 18, 234, 311.
—— John, 234.
—— Kenneth, 96.

Ramsay, Percy, 230.
—— Robert, 232.
—— William, 96.
Ranken, Duncan, 286.
Rannie, John, 96, 313.
—— Peter, 184.
—— William, 140, 313.
Ranny, George, 313.
Rattray, Charles, 232.
—— Henry, 232.
—— James, 50, 232, 379.
—— John, 126.
—— of Dunoon, 199.
Rea, Charles, 230.
—— James, 232.
Reat, William, 232.
Redpath, Thomas, 138.
Reekie, Peter, 186.
Reid, ——, Craill, 68.
—— Alexander, 80, 126, 186, 254, 368.
—— —— Sir, of Barra, 367.
—— David, 230.
—— Donald, 18.
—— George, Templand, 80, 184, 186.
—— James, 140, 254.
—— John, 18, 80, 81, 368.
—— Katharine, 353.
—— Peter, 184.
—— Robert, Barra, 18, 186, 300, 367.
—— William, 234, 315.
Renwick, Andrew, 230.
Reoch, Alexander, 126.
—— James, 126.
—— John, alias Ross, 80, 126, 232.
Retty, James, 184.
Rhind, John, 126.
—— William, 184.
Richy, Andrew, 18.
Riddel, Adolphus, 254.
Riddell, John, 138.
Riddoch, James, 50.
Ridoch, Patrick, 318, 387.
Rieth, Alexander, 18.
Rioch, Donald, 73, 75, 126.
Ritchie, Alexander, 184, 303, 305, 307.
—— James, 234.
—— John, 58, 184.
—— William, 186.
Robb, James, 18, 232.
Roben, William, 232.
Robert, Alexander, 186.
Robertson, Alexander, 18, 184, 232, 372.
—— —— of Blairfetty, 48, 372.
—— —— of Strowan, 372.
—— Charles, 48, 126, 232, 234.
—— David, 232.
—— Donald, 48, 230.
—— Duncan, 48, 234, 372.

2 D 2

Robertson, George, 48, 353, 372.
—— James, 36, 48, 60, 184, 266, 316.
—— John, 18, 80, 96, 230, 232.
—— Joseph, 137, 138.
—— Laurance, 50.
—— Patrick, 36, 319.
—— Peter, 36, 232.
—— Robert, 138.
Robertson, Thomas, 50, 256, 276.
—— William, 186.
Robertsons, 360.
Robison, John, 36.
Roger, John, 232.
—— Peter, 232.
Rollo, David, 58, 316.
—— James, 58, 316.
Ronald, John, 184.
—— William, 184.
Rose, Barbara, 366.
Ross, Alexander, 18, 36.
—— Andrew, 114.
—— Angus, 80.
—— Charles, 36.
—— district, xvi, 72, 328, 361, 374, 386, 388.
—— Francis, 96.
—— Hugh, 18, 80, 124.
—— James, 18, 80, 300.
—— John, 18, 80, 126, 300, 353.
—— Malcolm, 332, 389.
—— Master of, 81.
—— Robert, 18, 126.
—— Ronald, 80.
—— Thomas, 36, 80.
—— William, 80, 126.
Rosses, 360.
Rough, Alexander, 232.
—— Thomas, 230.
Roy, Duncan, 50.
—— John, 36, 230, 312.
Royston, Lord, 79.
Rue, David, 68, 374.
Russel, Alexander, 303, 305.
—— Hugh, 18.
—— John, 234.
Rutherford, James, 256.
—— Robert, 254.
Ryan, James, 303.

SALTER, DAVID, 236.
Sandilands, Jean, 364.
—— Patrick, of Cottoun, 364.
—— Robert, 20, 300, 368.
Sandyman, Andrew, 188.
Sangster, John, 236.
—— William, 96.
Sanyson, Peter, 22.
Saunders, John, 313.
Schaw, Alexander, 236.
—— James, 236.

Scot, Alexander, 96.
—— Francis, 280.
Scott, Charles, 234, 280.
—— David, 188, 234.
—— George, 256.
—— James, 52.
—— John, 20, 52, 157, 188, 300, 317, 320.
—— Mr., of Rossie, 151.
—— Robert, 256.
—— William, 38, 91, 96, 247, 312.
Scrogy, Robert, 20.
Seaton, Andrew, 236.
Semple, Francis, 288.
—— James, 266.
Seton, Alexander, 262, 344, 389.
—— Christopher, 262.
—— David, 262.
—— James, 262.
—— John, 262.
—— Robert, 256.
—— William, 234.
Sey, John, 305.
Shaddon, Charles, 266.
Shand, William, 38.
Shanks, Alexander, 186.
—— David, 188.
—— John, 188.
Sharp, Alexander, 374.
—— William, 68, 374.
Shaw, Duncan, 234.
—— James, 126.
—— John, 20, 299, 301.
—— William, 236.
Sheepherd, Charles, 236.
—— David, 188.
—— John, 186.
Shepherd, Thomas, 353.
Sheridan, Mr., 357.
Sherrif, John, 20.
Sherriff, Andrew, 140.
Shewan, John, 305.
Shirras, Thomas, 307.
Shives, Alexander, 96.
Showster, John, 50.
Shunger, John, 234.
Sibbald, Charles, 68.
—— James, 397.
Siddall, Thomas, xiv.
Sill, James, 20.
Simpson, Adam, 38.
—— Andrew, 236.
—— James, 20, 256, 299, 301, 353.
—— John, 38, 60, 234, 312, 319.
—— Kenneth, 82.
—— Patrick, 234.
—— William, 234, 236.
Sinclair, Æneas, 50.
—— Benjamin, 270.
—— George, of Geese, 270.

INDEX. 423

Sinclair, James, 84, 299, 301.
—— John, 36.
—— Lord, 29.
Skien, John, 38, 312.
Skinner, John, 353.
Smart, James, 309, 311.
—— John, 309, 311.
—— Walter, 188.
Smith, Alexander, 268.
—— —— of Meany, 306, 387.
—— Alexander, 20, 38, 96, 188.
—— Andrew, 128, 234.
—— David, 186, 234, 320.
—— Daniel, 20, 300.
—— Francis, 20.
—— George, 38, 186.
—— Hugh, 332, 389.
—— James, 20, 36, 96, 256, 380, 393, 399.
—— Janet, 309, 313.
—— John, 96, 126, 188.
—— —— of Ballcharry, 236.
—— Peter, 20, 332, 389.
—— Robert, 20, 128.
—— William, Keith, 38, 50, 96, 126, 188, 190.
Souter, Dougald, 256.
—— James, 190.
—— John, 96, 306.
Spark, William, 256, 257.
Speed, George, 188.
Spens, John, 96.
Sprewl, Andrew, 278, 381.
Squair, John, 318, 387.
Stalker, John, 50.
—— Peter, 50.
St. Andrews District, xvi, 62, 352, 361, 373.
Stark, Alexander, 234.
—— William, 234.
Stead, Thomas, 190.
Steill, George, 20, 300.
Stephen, Alexander, 353.
—— John, 320, 388.
—— William, 126.
Stewart, Alexander, of Invernachyle, 286, 383, 384.
—— —— Achnacon, 288, 383.
—— —— of Ballechalish, 288, 383.
—— Allan, 286, 288, 319, 383, 384.
—— Charles, of Ardsheil, 288, 384, 385.
—— Donald, 270, 271, 288, 384.
—— Dougald, 288, 383, 384.
—— —— of Appin, 384, 385.
—— Duncan, 288, 383, 384.
—— Helen, 368.
—— James, 22, 38, 50, 52, 288, 383, 384.
—— John, 22, 288, 383, 384.
—— Joseph, 22.

Stewart, Margaret, 368.
—— Peter, 22.
—— Robert, 288, 384.
—— William, 20, 288, 312, 383, 387.
—— —— Auchoily, 20, 368.
—— —— Drummond, 50.
Stewarts, 360, 364.
Stirling district, xvi, 54, 316, 361, 372, 387.
—— gaol, 393.
—— Hugh, 276, 277.
—— James, of Keir, 276.
—— James, 278, 326, 388.
—— Sir H., 397.
—— William, 276.
Stiven, Alexander, xvii, 68, 256.
—— Andrew, 60, 316.
—— James, 188.
—— John, Montrose, 186, 236.
—— William, 236.
Stivenson, Alexander, 256.
—— James, 36.
Stodhart, William, 38.
Stormond, James, 234, 236.
—— John, of Kinwhirie, 236.
Stormont, James, 234, 379.
Stot, James, 18.
Stouter, James, 188.
Strachan, James, 20, 305.
—— John, 188.
—— William, 20, 300, 368.
Strathallan, Lord, xvii, 358, 371, 372, 401.
Strathavin, 358.
Strathbogie, 358.
Strathdon, 358.
Strathmore, Lady, 199.
Stratton, Archibald, 256.
Strickland, Mr., 357.
Stuart, Alexander, 38, 50, 128, 236, 238, 368.
—— Alexander, 370.
—— Allan, 128, 130.
—— Andrew, 370.
—— Angus, 38, 102, 312.
—— Archibald Bain, 100.
—— Callum, 80.
—— Charles, 50, 236, 256.
—— —— Prince, vii-xviii, etc.
—— Cosmo-George, 370.
—— David, 60, 373.
—— Donald, 128, 236.
—— Elspet, 370.
—— Finlay, 50.
—— George, 128.
—— Hugh, 128.
—— —— Glenlyon, 384.
—— James, 128, 186, 188, 236, 370.
—— Jean, 370.

424 INDEX.

Stuart, John, 50, 60, 128, 130, 236, 262, 377.
—— John Roy, 126, 377.
—— Sir John, Count of Maida, 377.
Stuart, Laurance, 52.
—— Lewis, 130.
—— Malcolm, 50, 384.
—— Mary, 370.
—— Patrick, 38, 128, 278, 312.
—— Peter, 38, 128, 370.
—— Robert, 50, 52, 128, 130.
—— Roy, 39.
—— Thomas, 96.
—— Walter, 278.
—— William, 128.
Stuarts, 50.
Stubble, David, 236.
Sullivan, Mr., 137, 357.
Surrey, County of, xiv.
Sutherland, Alexander, 36, 186.
—— George, 38.
—— James, 299, 301.
—— John, 80.
—— William, 80, 393.
Sutherlands, 360.
Sutherlandshire, 375.
Sutor, William, 236.
Swan, Andrew, 256, 380.
Syme, James, 126.
—— Mr. Thomas, 236.
Symers, Alexander, 20.
—— Andrew, 256.

TAIT, ADAM, 256.
Talboth, John, 238.
Tasker, Alexander, 262.
Taylor, Charles, 238.
—— James, 38, 130, 319.
—— Peter, 130.
—— Robert, 98, 130.
—— Thomas, 82, 353.
—— William, 38, 130, 190, 238, 313, 319.
Tervas, Alexander, 98.
Thain, Bailie, 315.
—— James, 98.
—— John, 38.
—— Patrick, 313.
Thom, George, 238.
Thomson, Alexander, 98, 306.
—— Hector, 140.
—— James, 52, 98, 140, 238, 299, 301, 306.
—— John, 22, 300.
—— Robert, 52, 190.
—— Thomas, 307.
—— William, 68, 238, 353.
Thores, James, 256.
Threepland, Thomas, of Fingask, 238.
Thurso, 271.

Tillan, Alexander, 8.
Tilleray, Andrew, 22.
Tindal, Colin, 190.
—— David, 190.
Todd, Archibald, 140.
—— Thomas, 140.
—— Walter, 256.
—— William, 212.
Todie, Janet, 353.
Torry, James, 130.
Touch, William, 299.
Tower, Alexander, 305.
Townley, Colonel, xiv.
Traill, John, 353.
Troup, Charles, 22.
—— John, 313.
—— William, xvii, 22, 300.
Tullibardine, Marquis of, xvi, 49, 233, 357.
Tulloch, David, 38, 115.
—— Robert, 130.
—— Mr. Thomas, 181.
Tullochs, 360.
Turner, Duncan, 130.
—— John, 22.
—— of Turnerhall, 98, 306.
—— William, 130.
Turnerhall, Lady, 98, 304, 387.
Turras, John, 98.
Tweedale, 374.
—— Marquis of, 378.
Tydieman, John, 262.
Tyrie, David, 98, 306.
—— Mr. John, 130, 256, 389.

URE, JEAN, 370.
Urquart, Kenneth, 82, 130.
Urquhart, George, 309, 311.
—— James, 60.
—— William, Kennellan, 82, 130.
Urquharts, 360.
Ushet, Robert, 262.

VALLANTINE, ROBERT, 194.
Veitch, Patrick, 140.
Vere, Captain, 381.
Verly, William, 148, 390.
Verty, William, 348, 390.
Volume, James, 98.
—— Thomas, 98, 240.

WADDELL, JOHN, 140.
Wade, George, 194.
—— General, 209.
Wagrae, John, 238.
Wales, Prince of, 7, 19, 57, 61, 139, 155, 157.
Walker, Alexander, 194.
—— James, 258.
—— John, 40.

INDEX. 425

Walker, Robert, 192.
—— William, 22, 40, 190, 192.
Wallace, Patrick, 155, 192.
Walpole, Sir Robert, xii.
Warden, James, 194.
Wardlaw, Henry, 268.
Warsaw, ix.
Watson, Alexander, 238.
—— James, 38, 192, 242, 353.
—— John, 192, 317, 353.
—— Thomas, 130, 192, 240, 353.
—— William, 192, 240.
Watt, Andrew, 318, 387.
—— John, 40.
—— Robert, 318, 387.
—— William, 40, 240.
Webster, Andrew, 192.
—— Charles, 240, 379.
—— James, 22.
—— John, 192, 240, 303, 307.
—— William, 194.
Wedderburn, Sir John, 238, 379.
Weems, David, 63, 70.
Weir, George, 22.
—— John, 292.
—— William, 326, 388.
Welsh, John, 190.
—— William, 190.
—— The, xii.
Wemyss, David, Lord Elcho, 258, 380.
—— Francis, Earl of, 380.
—— James, Earl of, 380.
Westminster, 369, 381.
White, Alexander, 22, 98, 240, 306.
—— Daniel, 22.
—— George, 312.
—— James, 240.
—— John, 194, 240.
—— Robert, 262, 278.
—— William, 84, 197, 258.
Wightman, Charles, 68.
Wild, Bailie, 373.
Wilkie, David, 240.
—— George, 238, 240.
—— John, 240.
—— Thomas, 192.
Wilkin, Alexander, 98.
—— John, 303.

Wilkins, Joseph, 22.
Will, William, 242.
—— Mr., 305.
Williamson, Alexander, 130.
—— David, 238.
—— John, 238.
—— William, 22, 192, 320.
Willox, Charles, 194.
—— James, 309.
Wilson, Alexander, 38.
—— David, 38, 52, 192, 240, 314.
—— James, 240.
—— John, 192, 258.
—— Robert, 38.
—— Thomas, 240.
—— William, 40, 82, 98, 258, 305, 312.
—— —— 256, 258.
—— Windram, James, 258.
Wintoun, William, 240.
Wischart, John, 238, 307.
—— William, 192.
Wise, Ninian, 268.
Wood, Andrew, 272, 381.
Wood, Samuel, 262.
—— of Allardie, 192.
—— William, 238.
Wordie, William, 262.
Wright, Alexander, 38.
—— Duncan, 318, 387.
—— John, 40, 70, 240, 311.
—— Robert, 192, 258, 320.
—— Thomas, 201.
Wyllie, Alexander, 190.
—— Francis, 192.
—— Robert, 192.

York, city of, xiv, 371, 373, 374, 379-381.
—— Duke of, ix.
Yoully, David, 242.
Young, Alexander, 194, 242, 320.
—— David, 242.
—— George, 336, 389.
—— James, 242.
—— Robert, 194, 242.
—— Walter, 194, 320.
Yuill, James, 52.

Printed by T. AND A. CONSTABLE, Printers to Her Majesty,
at the Edinburgh University Press.

Scottish History Society.

THE EXECUTIVE.

President.
THE EARL OF ROSEBERY, LL.D.

Chairman of Council.
DAVID MASSON, LL.D., Professor of English Literature, Edinburgh University.

Council.
T. G. MURRAY, Esq., W.S.
J. FERGUSON, Esq., Advocate.
Right Rev. JOHN DOWDEN, D.D., Bishop of Edinburgh.
ÆNEAS J. G. MACKAY, LL.D., Sheriff of Fife.
JOHN RUSSELL, Esq.
Sir ARTHUR MITCHELL, K.C.B., M.D., LL.D.
Rev. GEO. W. SPROTT, D.D.
Rev. A. W. CORNELIUS HALLEN.
W. F. SKENE, D.C.L., LL.D., Historiographer-Royal for Scotland.
Colonel P. DODS.
J. R. FINDLAY, Esq.
THOMAS DICKSON, LL.D., Curator of the Historical Department, Register House.

Corresponding Members of the Council.
OSMUND AIRY, Esq., Birmingham; Very Rev. J. CUNNINGHAM, D.D., Principal of St. Mary's College, St. Andrews; Professor GEORGE GRUB, LL.D., Aberdeen; Rev. W. D. MACRAY, Oxford; Professor A. F. MITCHELL, D.D., St. Andrews; Professor W. ROBERTSON SMITH, Cambridge; Professor J. VEITCH, LL.D., Glasgow; A. H. MILLAR, Esq., Dundee.

Int. Hon. Treasurer.
J. T. CLARK, Keeper of the Advocates' Library.

Hon. Secretary.
T. G. LAW, Librarian, Signet Library.

RULES.

1. The object of the Society is the discovery and printing, under selected editorship, of unpublished documents illustrative of the civil, religious, and social history of Scotland. The Society will also undertake, in exceptional cases, to issue translations of printed works of a similar nature, which have not hitherto been accessible in English.

2. The number of Members of the Society shall be limited to 400.

3. The affairs of the Society shall be managed by a Council consisting of a Chairman, Treasurer, Secretary, and twelve elected Members, five to make a quorum. Three of the twelve elected members shall retire annually by ballot, but they shall be eligible for re-election.

4. The Annual Subscription to the Society shall be One Guinea. The publications of the Society shall not be delivered to any Member whose Subscription is in arrear, and no Member shall be permitted to receive more than one copy of the Society's publications.

5. The Society will undertake the issue of its own publications, *i.e.* without the intervention of a publisher or any other paid agent.

6. The Society will issue yearly two octavo volumes of about 320 pages each.

7. An Annual General Meeting of the Society shall be held on the last Tuesday in October.

8. Two stated Meetings of the Council shall be held each year, one on the last Tuesday of May, the other on the Tuesday preceding the day upon which the Annual General Meeting shall be held. The Secretary, on the request of three Members of the Council, shall call a special meeting of the Council.

9. Editors shall receive 20 copies of each volume they edit for the Society.

10. The owners of Manuscripts published by the Society will also be presented with a certain number of copies.

11. The Annual Balance-Sheet, Rules, and List of Members shall be printed.

12. No alteration shall be made in these Rules except at a General Meeting of the Society. A fortnight's notice of any alteration to be proposed shall be given to the Members of the Council.

PUBLICATIONS.

Works already Issued.

1887.

1. BISHOP POCOCKE'S TOURS IN SCOTLAND, 1747-1760. Edited by D. W. KEMP.

2. DIARY OF AND GENERAL EXPENDITURE BOOK OF WILLIAM CUNNINGHAM OF CRAIGENDS, 1673-1680. Edited by the Rev. JAMES DODDS, D.D.

1888.

3. PANURGI PHILO-CABALLI SCOTI GRAMEIDOS LIBRI SEX.—THE GRAMEID: an heroic poem descriptive of the Campaign of Viscount Dundee in 1689, by JAMES PHILIP of Almerieclose. Edited, with Translation and Notes, by the Rev. A. D. MURDOCH.

4. THE REGISTER OF THE KIRK-SESSION OF ST. ANDREWS. Part I. 1559-1582. Edited by D. HAY FLEMING.

1889.

5. DIARY OF THE REV. JOHN MILL, Minister of Dunrossness, Sandwick, and Cunningsburgh, in Shetland, 1740-1803, with original documents, local records, and historical notices relating to the District. Edited by GILBERT GOUDIE, F.S.A. Scot.

6. NARRATIVE OF MR. JAMES NIMMO, A COVENANTER. 1654-1709. Edited by W. G. SCOTT-MONCRIEFF, Advocate.

1890.

7. THE REGISTER OF THE KIRK-SESSION OF ST. ANDREWS. Part II. 1583-1600. Edited by D. HAY FLEMING.

8. A LIST OF PERSONS CONCERNED IN THE REBELLION (1745), transmitted to the Commissioners of Excise by the several Supervisors in Scotland, in obedience to a General Letter of the 7th May 1746, and a Supplementary List with Evidences to prove the same. With a Preface by the EARL OF ROSEBERY and Annotations by the Rev. WALTER MACLEOD. Presented to the Society by the EARL OF ROSEBERY.

9. GLAMIS PAPERS: The 'Book of Record,' a Diary written by PATRICK, FIRST EARL OF STRATHMORE, and other documents relating to Glamis Castle (1684-89). Edited from the original manuscripts at Glamis, with Introduction and Notes, by A. H. MILLAR, F.S.A. Scot.

In Preparation.

JOHN MAJOR'S DE GESTIS SCOTORUM (1521). Translated by ARCHIBALD CONSTABLE, with a Memoir of the author by ÆNEAS J. G. MACKAY, Advocate.

THE DIARY OF ANDREW HAY OF STONE, NEAR BIGGAR, AFTERWARDS OF CRAIGNETHAN CASTLE, 1659-60. Edited by A. G. REID, F.S.A. Scot., from a manuscript in his possession.

THE RECORDS OF THE COMMISSION OF THE GENERAL ASSEMBLY, 1646-1662. Edited by the Rev. JAMES CHRISTIE, D.D., with an Introduction by the Rev. Professor MITCHELL, D.D.

'THE HISTORY OF MY LIFE, extracted from Journals I kept since I was twenty-six years of age, interspersed with short accounts of the most remarkable public affairs that happened in my time, especially such as I had some immediate concern in,' 1702-1754. By Sir JOHN CLERK OF PENICUIK, Baron of the Exchequer, Commissioner of the Union, etc. Edited from the original MS. in Penicuik House by J. M. GRAY.

SIR THOMAS CRAIG'S DE UNIONE REGNORUM BRITANNIÆ. Edited, with an English Translation, from the unpublished manuscript in the Advocates' Library.

THE DIARIES OR ACCOUNT BOOKS OF SIR JOHN FOULIS OF RAVELSTON, (1679-1707), and the ACCOUNT BOOK OF DAME HANNAH ERSKINE (1675-1699). Edited by the Rev. A. W. CORNELIUS HALLEN.

PAPERS RELATING TO THE MILITARY GOVERNMENT OF SCOTLAND, AND THE CORRESPONDENCE OF ROBERT LILBURNE and GENERAL MONK, from 1653 to 1658. Edited by Mr. C. H. FIRTH.

A SELECTION OF THE FORFEITED ESTATE PAPERS PRESERVED IN H.M. REGISTER HOUSE.

COURT-BOOK OF THE BARONY OF URIE. Edited by the Rev. D. G. BARRON, from the original MS. in possession of Mr. R. BARCLAY of Dorking.

SCOTTISH HISTORY SOCIETY

As a general desire has been expressed for a fuller and more detailed Index to the 'List of Rebels,' a new Index has been prepared, and is now issued to Members, to be substituted for the Index bound up with the volume.

March 1891.

INDEX

ABBOT, JAMES, dyster, 150.
Aberchallader, 357.
Abercrombie, James, captain, 24, 308, 387.
Aberdeen, city, 7, 9, 11, 13, 23, 35, 89, 93, 95, 99, 167, 181, 193, 299, 301, 309.
—— district, xvi, 2, 298, 360, 386.
—— gaol, 391, 396.
—— old, 3, 5, 9, 15.
—— port of, 9.
—— sheriff of, 367.
—— Anne, 363.
—— Helen, 363.
—— James, 363.
—— —— labourer, 86.
—— Margaret, 363.
—— Rachel, 363.
—— William, quarter-master, 2, 363.
—— —— younger, 363.
Aberdour, James, brazier, 2.
Abernethie, Alexander, officer, 24.
—— George, captain, 24, 369.
—— —— servant, 194.
—— John, tanner, 24.
—— —— overseer, 86.
Aboyne, 9, 299, 301, 373.
—— Earl of, 11.
Achtertyre, laird of, 284, 289.
Adam, James, gardener, 2.
—— John, serjeant, 150.
—— Robert, shipmaster, 317.
—— Thomas, Cheitlay, 202.
—— William, farmer, 347.
Adamson, David, chapman, 196.
—— James, gardener, 2, 301.
—— —— serjeant, 196.
—— John, shoemaker, 152.
—— William, labourer, 2.
Aiken, Alexander, porter, 301.
Aikenhead, John, lieutenant, 150.
—— —— younger, of Jaw, 264.
Aikman, James, the historian, 358.
—— John, porter, 244, 251, 340.
Aird, James, weaver, 347.
Airly, Earl of, 224, 230, 232, 234.
Airth, 317.
Aitken, William, import waiter, 244.

Aitken, William, servant, 260.
Aitkin, James, wright, 341.
—— John, wright, 341.
Aiton. *See* Ayton.
Albemarle, Earl of, 395, 397.
Aldaury, 119.
Aldie, David, weaver, 196.
Alexander, Alexander, Johnshaven, 322, 323, 388.
—— Cosmos, artist, 2, 363.
—— David, Garlay, 196.
—— George, ensign, 2.
—— —— glover, 298.
—— James, servant, 196.
—— —— Boginhilt, 313.
—— John, artist, 2, 363.
—— Thomas, workman, 196.
Alford, parish of, 7.
Alison, Mr., of Newhall, 215, 225, 233.
—— James, maltman, 347.
—— Marjory, Cellardyke, 353.
—— —— servant, 353.
Allan, Charles, cooper, 340.
—— James, Braehead, 313.
—— —— cadie, 2,
—— —— merchant, 244, 338.
—— John, farmer, 24.
—— —— serjeant, 146, 194, 348.
—— —— workman, 196.
—— Robert, servant, 2.
—— —— Keithock, 152.
—— Thomas, Keithock, 152.
Allanoch, John, merchant, 100.
Allardice, James, Drums, 152.
Allen, Charles, cooper, 244.
Allix, Charles, 395.
Alloa, 149, 377.
Anandale, John, shoemaker, 244.
Ancrum, James, salt greive, 264, 381.
Anderson, Alexander, of Tynot, 24.
—— —— serjeant, 24.
—— —— servant, 24, 308.
—— —— Johnshaven, 150.
—— —— Clackmannan, 349.
—— Charles, merchant, 86.
—— —— shoemaker, 152.
—— David, workman, 152.
—— —— servant, 196.

Anderson, David, Eassie, 196, 206.
—— Elizabeth, servant, 323.
—— George, captain, 132, 139.
—— —— Craill, 353.
—— James, barber, 2.
—— —— ensign, 24.
—— —— fisher, 150.
—— —— Bougiehall, 196.
—— Linross, 196.
—— John, ensign, 24.
—— —— of Greens, 24.
—— —— sadler, 132.
—— —— wright, 132.
—— —— servant, 150.
—— —— Navoy, 196.
— — —— excise officer, 339.
—— Laurance, servant, 196.
—— Robert, brewer, 54, 318.
—— —— of Whitburgh, 132.
—— Thomas, officer, 72.
—— —— servant, 196.
—— —— brewer, 353.
—— William, wig-maker, 100.
—— —— Johnshaven, 150, 322.
—— —— hostler, 347.
—— —— Clackmannan, 349.
Andrew, David, Drumellie, 150.
—— James, Drumellie, 150.
—— John, cottar, 198.
—— Euchry, 313.
Angus, district of, 63, 159, 169, 374.
—— Laurance, 333.
—— Robert, salt officer, 132.
—— William, labourer, 86.
—— —— Earl of, 364.
Annandale, 145.
Anson, Commodore, 21.
Anton, Alexander, shoemaker, 198.
Arbroath, 155, 159, 169, 185, 193, 205, 215, 241.
Arbuthnot, Robert, merchant, 307.
—— —— shipmaster, 321.
—— Thomas, factor, 86, 306, 307.
—— —— sailor, 86.
—— Lord, 190, 191.
Archer, David, weaver, 198.
—— William, tailor, 150.
Archibald, Alexander, shoemaker, 317.
Ardsheal house, 386.
Argyle, districts, xvi, 282, 360, 382, 388.
Argyll, Duke of, xvii, 375.
Arnot, John, surgeon, 353.
Arrat, John, lieutenant, 196.
Arsil, David, Kincraig, 152.
Arthur, James, Kinninmont, 303.
Athole Brigade, 205, 221.
—— district, 279, 358.
—— Duke of, 371, 375.
Attila, xii.

Auchenleck, Andrew, of Cunnachie, 62.
Auchinleck, David, vintner, 198.
Auchiries, house of, 376.
Auchleishie, laird of, 54.
Auchmedden, laird of, 89, 91, 95. See Baird.
Auchterless, parish, 311.
Augustus, Fort, 374.
Auld, William, huxter, 2.
Avoch, parish of, 331, 333.
Ayr, burgh, x.
—— district, xvi, 293.
Ayrshire, x.
Ayton (Aiton) Andrew, 62, 63.
—— James, serjeant, 150.
—— John, surgeon 150.
—— William, 62, 352.
—— —— goldsmith, 341.

BAAD, JOHN, merchant, 317.
—— William, brewer, 54, 316.
Bagrie, William, labourer, 86.
Baillie, Charles, captain, 200.
Bain, Donald, labourer, 244.
—— John, Glenconles, 100.
—— —— Thurso, 325.
—— Thomas, shoemaker, 100.
—— William, innkeeper, 244.
Baird, William, of Auchmedin, 26.
—— —— coalhewer, 264.
—— —— dyer, 4.
—— —— gardener, 156, 320.
Baldernock, 277, 347.
Balfour, Alexander, farmer, 260, 344.
—— Mr. George, Nigg, 329.
—— Henry, of Dunboag, 62.
—— John, captain, 42.
—— —— Leith, 341, 343.
—— Robert, Down, 319.
—— William, surgeon, 260.
Ballingall, James, ensign, 200.
Balmedie, estate, 370.
Balmerino, Lord, x, xiv, 134, 377. See Elphinston.
Balmoral, 364, 386.
Banff, district, xvi, 24, 308.
Banffshire, 27, 31, 37, 89, 95, 358, 360, 366.
Banks, Alexander, weaver 246.
Bannatyne, Christopher, 373.
Bannerman, Sir Alexander, of Elsick, 156, 183, 322.
Bannerman, John, workman, 42.
Barclay, Alexander, bleacher, 62.
—— David, brewer, 154.
—— George, workman, 200.
—— James, Finlastown, 154, 322.
—— John, shoemaker, 24.
—— —— Johnshaven, 323.

INDEX. 407

Barclay, Lewis, 367.
—— Peter, of Johnstone, 154.
—— Robert, merchant, 4.
—— —— gentleman, 154.
Barnet, William, ploughman, 200.
Barnie, John, servant, 62.
Barrisdale's regiment, 77, 81.
Barrowfield, Lady, 401.
Barry, James, workman, 200.
—— John, tailor, 200.
Baxter, David, servant, 198.
—— Robert, labourer, 4.
Bayne, James, quarter-master, 42.
—— —— in Knockbelly, 72.
—— John, servant, 84, 224, 338.
Bean, William, mason, 200.
Beatson, David, hosier, 341.
—— Robert, baxter, 341.
—— Thomas, baxter, 341.
Beatt, David, merchant, 246. 340.
Beattie, Andrew, rope-maker, 156, 320.
—— Patrick, 320.
—— Peter, shipmaster, 156, 320.
Beaufort, Duke of, xii.
Beauly, 374.
Beg, James, cooper, 198.
Begg, Alexander, tanner, 24.
Begg, William, excise officer, 343.
Bell, Francis Denniln, of Fordon, 154.
—— Peter, Glasgow, 274, 346.
—— Robert, merchant, 353.
—— William, 395, 399.
—— —— ploughman, 200.
—— —— workman, 200.
Belleisle, vii.
Bennet, David, servant, 154.
—— Robert, merchant, 24.
—— William, excise officer, 339.
Bergen, 239.
Berrie, John, salt-watchman, xvii, 132.
Berwick, 395.
Bettie, Alexander, labourer, 86, 305.
—— Andrew, Ellon, 307.
—— John, Drumellie, 152.
Betty, Robert, Drumellie, 152.
Biberny, Patrick, mason, 198.
Bicky, James, apprentice, 26, 308.
Binnachie, John, weaver, 100.
Binny, Alexander, quarter-master, 200.
Bire, Thomas, ensign, 198.
Birrell, Thomas, merchant, 351, 390.
Birse, William, labourer, 4.
Bisset, George, mariner, 156, 322.
—— James, servant, 4.
—— Robert, brickmaker, 246, 340.
Blaber, James, Johnshaven, 323.
Black, Andrew, officer, 198.
—— David, ploughman, 200.
—— John, shoemaker, 353.

Black, Thomas, serjeant, 132.
Blackfoord, 145.
Blackie, Charles, sailor, 290, 326.
Blair, Charles, goldsmith, 341.
—— Thomas, of Glasclone, 198.
—— William, workman, 200.
Blakeney, William, 397.
Blantyre, Lady, 134.
—— parish, 347.
Blaw, Charles, Castlehill, 146, 348, 349, 378.
Blyth, John, shipmaster, 198.
Blyth's Regiment, 401.
Boberno, John, Mill of Loor, 200.
Bocik, James, indweller, 62.
Bogle, Thomas, surgeon, 345.
Borland, John, painter, 347.
Borthwick, John, servant, 347.
Boswell, David, merchant, 260, 344.
—— Thomas, writer, 244.
Bouglass, Alexander, mill-wright, 132.
Bovey, Allan, servant, 198.
Bow, Alexander, smith, 319.
Bowar, Alexander, of Meathie, 200, 203, 229, 235.
Bowdler, Amy, 365.
—— Mr. Thomas, 365.
Bower, Bartholomew, xvii, 132.
Bowes, Thomas, Cathcart, 327.
Bowie, James, brewer, 24.
—— —— deserter, 100.
—— John, mason, 42.
—— —— tailor, 244, 338.
Bowman, James, householder, 24, 314.
—— —— farmer, 86.
—— —— Brechin, 152.
Boyd, Mr. Charles, captain, 264.
—— George, servant, 264, 381.
Boyle, James, excise officer, 341.
Braddock, xii.
Brady, John, 370.
Brampton, 374.
Brand, Alexander, watchmaker, 244.
—— James, Edinburgh, 244, 338.
—— Mrs., Kinghorn, 262.
—— Robert, labourer, 4.
—— William, merchant, 152.
Break, John, merchant, 244, 338.
Breakenrig, Thomas, barber, 347.
Brebermackinteer, Angus, Achlounie, 100.
Brechin, 151, 153, 159, 165, 167, 171, 179, 181, 195.
—— Alexander, Achenblae, 152.
—— —— jun., Achenblae, 152.
—— George, Achenblae, 152.
—— James, tailor, 152.
—— —— jun., 152.
—— William, Hillhead, 305.

Bredie, Robert, 42, 370.
Bredy, John, labourer, 4.
Brember, George, wright, 26.
—— James, merchant, 313.
Bremner, Andrew, cooper, 156.
—— George, shoemaker, 24, 308.
—— —— shoemaker, 24.
—— John, servant, 100.
—— Robert, weaver, 24.
—— —— mariner, 156.
—— William, wright, 156.
Bridgefoord, Magnus, labourer, 4.
Bristol Riots, vii.
British Museum, xvii.
—— Warship, 163, 173.
Brodie, David, chaplain, 134.
—— Francis, clerk, 349.
—— James, of Muresk, 309.
—— Simon, 72.
—— Walter, shoemaker, 134.
—— William, gunsmith, 244, 338.
Brounhills, Thomas, labourer, 200.
Brown, Andrew, bailie, 134, 135.
—— —— fisher, 323.
—— Colonel, 395.
—— David, indweller, 62.
—— —— merchant, 198.
—— —— Kirry Muir, 200.
—— Gavin, of Bishoptown, 142.
—— George, servant, 353.
—— James, excise officer, 100, 106, 112, 118, 120, 130, 337.
—— —— tailor, 198.
—— —— ploughman, 200.
—— —— weaver, 200.
—— John, Balindouan, 100, 308.
—— —— Carnoucie, 308, 387.
—— —— lieutenant, 154.
—— —— jun., merchant, 198.
—— —— vintner, 246, 340.
—— —— servant, 341.
—— —— brewer, 353.
—— Major, 145.
—— Robert, excise officer, 339, 341.
—— William, servant, 26.
—— —— salt officer, 132.
Brownlee, William, innkeeper, 347.
Bruce, Andrew, ploughman, 200.
—— David, butcher, 152.
—— George, serjeant-major, 152.
—— Mr. Henry, of Clackmannan, 146, 348, 350.
—— Mr. James, 146, 348.
—— —— Brechin, 152.
—— John, butcher, 152.
—— —— vintner, 340.
—— Robert, labourer, 86.
—— Thomas, servant, 72.
—— —— vintner, 246.
—— William, 26, 132, 315.

Bryan, John, Montrose, 156.
Brymer, Alexander, baxter, 246, 340.
—— Robert, Leith, 246, 340.
Buccleuch, Duke of, 281.
Buchan, David, servant, 154.
—— George, labourer, 86.
—— James, labourer, 86.
—— —— merchant, 317.
—— John, labourer, 86.
—— —— mariner, 156.
Buchanan, Alexander, captain, 154, 372.
—— Baillie, of Boghastle, 54.
—— James, stabler, 347.
—— John, carrier, 42.
—— —— brewer, 54.
—— Patrick, brewer, 54.
—— Robert, captain, 54.
Buckard, Patrick, smith, 198, 244, 342.
Bumoss, David, Johnshaven, 154, 388.
Buock, William, servant, 156.
Burness, David, Johnshaven, 322.
Burnet, George, shoemaker, 321.
—— John, of Campfield, 4, 298, 366.
—— William, labourer, 2.
Burnlee, J. Hamilton, 343.
Burns, Isobell, 345.
Burt ——, shoemaker, 42.
Butcher, David, servant, 198.
Bygowan, George, servant, 24.
Byres, Isabel, 365, 368.
—— Peter, of Tonley, 4, 298, 363, 368.
—— Robert, 364.
—— of Coates, 364.

CABLE, DAVID, servant, 202.
Cadboll, laird of, 333.
Caddel, Robert, gunsmith, 318, 387.
—— Thomas, sen., gunsmith, 318, 387.
—— —— jun., gunsmith, 318, 387.
Caird, James, servant, 158.
Cairncross, Thomas, workman, 202.
Cairns, James, salt officer, 134.
—— John, merchant, 246.
—— —— distiller, 341.
Caithness, district, xvi, 270, 324.
Calbreath, James, 54.
—— William, miller, 54.
Calder, George, excise officer, 341.
—— James, in Red Castle 72, 80, 329, 331, 333.
—— John, servant, 4, 72.
—— —— Burdstone, 347.
—— Robert, sailor, 6.
Caldinghead, James, fisher, 323.
Calgarie, laird of, 284. See MacLean.
Calinoch, John, servant, 202, 378.

INDEX. 409

Callendar, Earl of, 381.
Callender, Edward, lieutenant, 246, 338.
—— James, baker, 146, 348, 349.
Cameron, Alexander, servant, 102.
—— —— of Dungallon, 282.
—— —— Stronlia, serjeant, 282.
—— —— Maryburgh, 282.
—— —— Altavullin, 282.
—— —— Drimnasall, 282.
—— Allan of Callart, 282, 382.
—— —— of Lundarva, 282.
—— Angus, Maryburgh, 282.
—— —— Altavullin, 282.
—— Daniel, coachman, 146, 348.
—— Donald, Teahrowat, 72.
—— —— Kilmorack, 72.
—— —— of Lochiel, 246, 282, 382.
—— —— brewer, 282.
—— Duncan, brewer, 282.
—— More, officer, 282.
—— Evan, tailor, 102.
—— Ewen, uncle of Callart, 282, 382.
—— —— brewer, 282.
—— —— More, Maryburgh, 282.
—— —— officer, 282.
—— —— of Inverlochy, 282.
—— John, in Kilmorack, 72.
—— —— serjeant, 102.
—— —— miller, 102.
—— —— Corran, 282.
—— —— officer, 282.
—— —— serjeant, 282.
—— Malcom, serjeant, 282.
—— Robert, Keppoch, 102.
Cameron's country, 401.
Camerons, the, 359, 376, 385.
Campbell, Alexander, ensign, 72.
—— —— gunsmith, 319.
—— Angus, carrier, 26, 314.
—— Charles, excise officer, 343.
—— Archibald, Carnie, 313.
—— David, Glenfarquhar, 156.
—— Donald, Foderleter, 102.
—— —— gunsmith, 319.
—— Duncan, officer, 42.
—— Eneas, Pittully, 303, 305.
—— Hector, tenant, 270, 324.
—— John, of Kinloch, 42.
—— —— Foderleter, 102.
—— —— major-general, 383, 385.
—— Mungo, ensign, 42.
—— William, lieutenant, 200.
—— of Glenlyon, 42.
—— son of Glenlyon, 42.
Campbells, the, 39, 359.
Campbelltown, district, xvi, 290.
Campsie, 275, 277, 347.
Cando, John, weaver, 200.

Candow, James, Longdrum, 202.
—— John, servant, 202.
Canongate, 255, 257, 401.
—— gaol, 391, 393.
Cantlo, George, 305, 307.
Cargil, John, tobacconist, 160.
—— —— ploughman, 204.
Carlisle, xiv, 9, 25, 31, 143, 145, 203, 205, 209, 217, 221, 239, 241, 243, 326, 373, 378, 383, 398, 401.
Carmichael, David, of Balmedie, 42, 370.
—— James, 370.
—— Donald, sergeant, 282.
—— John, collector, 42.
—— —— Achusragan, 282.
—— —— of Baiglie, 370.
—— Sir John de, 370.
—— Malcom, Kintalin, 282.
—— Robert, 370.
—— Thomas, 370.
Carmichaels, the, 384.
Carnegie, James, of Balmachy, 202, 351.
—— mason, Findaury, 158.
—— mason, 158.
—— surgeon, 158.
—— Mr., of Bonnymoon, 169.
Carnegy, Charles, sailor, 156, 320.
—— George, apprentice, 156, 320.
—— Robert, weaver, 158.
Carnie parish, 313.
Carnoucie, town of, 313.
Carre, Thomas, weaver, 204.
Carruthers, William, servant, 142.
Carse, the, 400.
Cashie, Alexander, merchant, 160.
Cashnie, Peter, merchant, 160, 322, 388.
Cassie, Andrew, of Kirkhouse, 84, 376.
Catenoch, Alexander, servant, 156.
Cathrae, Isobel, 215.
Catineaugh, John, ploughman, 204, 378.
Cattah, Alexander, 394.
Cato, James, carpenter, 88.
Catto, George, 305, 307.
Caw, Lodovick, surgeon, 42.
Chadwick, Thomas, xiv.
Chalmers, Alexander, Cairnwhelp, 313.
—— of Balnacraig, 366.
—— Andrew, ploughman, 204.
—— Captain, of Gadgart, 292.
—— George, fisher, 4.
—— Elizabeth, Ellon, 303.
—— James, printer, 95.
—— John, farmer, 88.
—— —— servant, 158.

Chalmers, John, St. Vigeans, 158.
—— Mrs., vintner, 303.
—— Thomas, Whitside, 204.
—— William, baxter, 88, 302.
—— —— Mains of Uris, 158.
—— —— Whitside, 204.
Chape, Matthew, sadler, 4.
Chaplain, James workman, 202.
Chapman, John, servant, 26.
—— —— jun., excise officer, 343.
Charles II., King, ix.
—— Edward, Prince, vii, xviii.
Charlestown, 299, 301.
Chein, George, sailor, 88, 302.
Chelsea, 117.
Chisholm, of that Ilk, 72, 374.
—— John, lieutenant, 72, 328.
—— Roderick, captain, 72, 374.
—— Mr. Thomas, Kilmorak, 329, 333.
Chisholmes, the, 73, 374.
Chives (Chevas), John, labourer, 88, 305, 307.
Christy, John, multerer, 319.
—— Patrick, sergeant, 26.
—— William, shipmaster, 88, 302.
—— —— baxter, 319.
—— —— sergeant, 393.
Chrystie, Alexander, servant, 64, 202.
—— Peter, ploughman, 204.
—— Thomas, Bervie, 323.
Clackmannan, 147, 149, 349.
—— laird of, 349.
Clanranald, chief of, xiii.
Clapperton, Thomas, weaver, 26.
Clark (Clerk), Alexander, dyster, 26.
—— —— workman, 202.
—— —— ploughman, 204.
—— Andrew, labourer, 6, 301.
—— Charles, workman, 202.
—— David, workman, 202.
—— Henry, gentleman, 246, 338, 379.
—— James, servant, 202.
—— —— sailor, 204.
—— John, mason, 44.
—— —— quarter-master, 100.
—— —— ploughman, 204.
—— —— merchant, 317.
—— Mr., 401.
—— Thomas, servant, 156.
—— William, labourer, 88.
Claverhouse, ix.
Cleland, George, shipmaster, 64, 352.
—— Robert, merchant, 64, 352.
Clifton, 369, 377.
Cluny Castle, 364.
Cochran, David, workman, 202.
—— William, sen., factor, 200.

Cochran, William, jun., servant, 200.
—— —— of Ferguslie, 292, 326.
Colinsburgh, 261.
Collie, William, carrier, 160.
Collison, James, bellman, 160.
Colquhoune, Charles, steward, 246, 338.
Colvile, Dr. George, 204.
Colvill, Adam, tacksman, 349.
—— William, brewer, 349.
Comrie, Duncan, indweller, 44.
Comry, William, steward, 146, 348.
Congleton, John, surgeon, 246.
Constable, John, wright, 204.
Contine, parish of, 331, 333.
Continent, the, viii.
Cook, captain, 397.
—— James, porter, 301.
—— John, workman, 202.
Cooper (Coupar), Andrew, servant, 246, 340.
—— —— Canongate, 246, 338.
—— David, gardener, 246, 338.
—— —— Colinsburgh, 353.
—— James, Arbroath, 158.
—— Robert, sen., sheriff officer, 160.
—— —— jun., sailor, 160.
—— William, bailie, 353.
Cope, general, xi, xii, 29, 357, 358.
Copens, David, workman, 202.
Corbet, Henry, excise officer, 317.
Cormack, John, servant, 26.
Cornall, Andrew, pendickle man, xvii, 202.
Cornwallise's Regiment, 105.
Corries, laird of, 284.
Corser, Archibald, weaver, 134.
Cortachie, 167.
Cosky, John, Binaves, 158.
Couly, 299.
Coupar, 67, 69, 205.
Cousland, James, servant, 347.
Coutts, Alexander, servant, 246, 338.
—— David, wright, 4.
—— James, poor man, 4.
—— John, apprentice, 6.
—— Peter, merchant, 4.
—— William, boatman, 6, 14.
—— —— Inverury, 102.
Covenant, the, ix.
Cow, George, 309, 313.
Cowan, James, of Powside, 317.
Cowbrugh, Malcolm, 347.
Cowhill, 363.
Cowie, Alexander, weaver, 26.
—— David, servant, 158.
—— Margaret, servant, 309, 313.
Cowper, Ashley, xiv.
Cowtie, David, bailie, 202.
Craich, Francis, brewer, 146, 348.

INDEX.

Craig, Alexander, merchant, 88, 302.
—— George, wright, 6.
Craig-Achmony, 386.
Craik, David, Nether Seythy, 202.
—— —— jun., Nether Seythy, 202.
—— James, Bridge End, 210.
—— John, workman, 202.
Craw, Mr. Andrew, Netherie, 246.
Crawford, Elizabeth (or Mrs. Rolland), merchant, 64, 352, 353.
—— Henry, Craile, xvii, 62, 352.
Crichton (Crighton), Alexander, sen., 158.
—— —— porter, 204.
—— —— workman, 202.
—— George, brulzeon, 202.
—— James, of Auchengoull, xvii, 26, 308, 312.
—— —— shoemaker, 158, 196, 197.
—— John, lieutenant, 204.
—— —— ploughman, 204.
—— —— sailor, 204.
—— —— servant, 202.
—— Robert, salt officer, 134, 135.
—— Thomas, mason, 158.
—— —— brulzeon, 202.
—— —— surgeon, 204.
—— —— lieutenant, 204.
—— —— ploughman, 204, 206.
Crieff, 55, 372.
Cristal, David, wright, 4.
—— John, wright, 4.
Crockat, Doctor, Coupar, 204.
—— James, workman, 202.
—— William, Coupar, 204.
Crole, David, weaver, 156.
Cromar, 9.
Cromartie, Earl of, xiv, 72, 73, 75, 76, 77, 79, 81, 83, 263, 375, 400.
Cromarty, 75, 81, 331.
Crombie, Patrick, workman, 13.
Crook, Alexander, sen., surgeon-major, 204.
—— —— jun., Coupar, 204.
Crookshanks, Charles, salt watchman, 134.
—— Robert, Johnshaven, 158, 322.
Crow, James, mason, 202.
Cruden parish, 305.
—— William, Fraserburgh, 307.
Cruickshank, Hector, Dalavoiar, 102.
—— James, labourer, 88.
—— John, deserter, 102.
—— —— surgeon, 88, 302, 387.
—— Robert, Dalavoiar, 102.
—— —— Badiglashean, 102.
Cruickshanks, William, subtenant, 158.
Cullcairn, laird of, 75.

Cullenhouse, 103, 113, 129.
Cullicuden, parish of, 75, 77.
Culloden, viii, xvii, 3, 5, 7, 9, 357, 371-386, 400, 401, *et passim*.
Cumberland, county of, xiv.
—— Duke of, xviii, 3, 143, 183, 291, 365, 374, 377, 385, 401.
Cuming, Alexander, sen., 44.
—— —— jun., 44.
—— —— farmer, 88, 302.
—— —— 307.
Cumming, Charles of Kininmount, 88, 302.
—— Christian, 370.
—— David, servant, 4.
—— —— Eassie, 206.
—— James, Inverness, 102, 334, 389.
—— John, officer, 102.
—— Lauchlan, Tomintowll, 102.
—— William, of Pitully, 88, 302, 386.
Cuningham, George, surgeon, 394.
—— Mrs. Janet, 373.
—— William, gardener, 347.
Cunison, John, excise officer, 290, 326.
Cunochie, laird of, 401.
Currie, William, innkeeper, 347.
Cushnie, Patrick, merchant, 322.
Cuthbert, Archibald, ploughman, 204.
Cuthberth, Robert, shoemaker, 100.

Dalgairns, Alexander, ploughman, 208.
Dalgarno, Alexander, Feckfield, 307.
—— Ann, 363.
—— John, New Deer, 303, 305.
Dalgearn, John, merchant, 88.
Dalglish, James, labourer, 206.
Dalkeith, 141, 247, 358, 377.
Dallas, Alexander, excise officer, 104, 124, 126, 130, 335, 337.
Dallass, James, of Cantra, 102, 334.
Dalmahoy, Sir Alexander, 264.
—— Alexander, jun., 264, 265.
—— John, 394.
Davert, David, gardener, 264.
Davidson, Alexander, shoemaker, 246, 309, 313, 338, 379.
—— Christian, 317.
—— George, Glenconless, 102.
—— Henry, mason, 134.
—— Gilbert, Turnerhall, 305.
—— James, servant, 64.
—— —— Glenconless, 102.
—— —— officer, 301.
—— —— Alloa, 349.
—— John, Inchnakeep, 102.
—— —— Achreachan, 102.
—— —— servant, 162.
—— —— wright, 339, 341.

Davidson, Patrick, Balnacraig, 301.
—— Peter, servant, 6.
—— Robert, weaver, 317.
—— Roderick, weaver, 315.
—— Thomas, Kelso, 280, 309, 311, 313.
—— William, tailor, 26, 308.
—— —— silversmith, 206.
—— —— Alloa, 349.
Davie, John, servant, 206.
Daw, ——, widow, Pittenweem, 353.
Dawson, James, wright, 26.
—— John, servant, 353.
Day, Alexander, Mortleck, 313.
Deakers, George, drummer, 160, 320.
Deans, Andrew, labourer, 6.
—— James, Cowie, 160.
—— Wester, 374.
Dear, William, meal-monger, 162.
Deary, Andrew, Glesla, 160.
—— James, servant, 160.
Dease, James, merchant, 162.
Decorm (Duvorm), Alexander, jun., lieutenant, 6, 298, 386.
—— —— sen., wright, 6.
Dempster, James, Clackmannan, 349.
Denhalme, John, gardener, 134.
Dennies, David, Binaves, 160.
Denothy, John, servant, 264.
Derby, vii, xii, xiii.
Derg, Angus, 102.
Dettingen, battle of, 279.
Deuar, John, indweller, 64.
Deughars, John, ploughman, 208.
Dewar, John, 63.
Dey, Thomas, turner, 342, 389.
Dick, Alexander, maltman, 347.
—— John, flesher, 134.
—— —— shipmaster, 317.
—— William, servant, 206.
Dingwall, 73, 79.
Disarming Acts, xi.
Ditch, Alexander, labourer, 88.
Doctor, Peter, ploughman, 208.
Dodds, James, Setonhill, 134.
Doig, John, pendicleman, 206.
Dollar, parish of, 59.
Donald, John, servant, 206.
Donaldson, James, servant, 26.
—— —— merchant, 31, 309.
—— John, merchant, 325.
—— —— Clackmannan, 349.
—— Thomas, salt officer, 134.
—— William, gardener, 264.
Dorret, William, servant, 323.
Dorwood, David, labourer, 160.
—— John, weaver, 160.
Dott, Mary, Coupar, 353.
Dougal, Andrew, servant, 206.
—— James, surgeon, 206.

Douglas, Alexander, labourer, 6.
—— Erskine, surgeon, 142.
—— Francis, sailor, 142.
—— John, cottar, 6.
—— —— of Fechel, 88, 302.
—— Sir John, of Hillhead, 143.
—— Robert, gentleman, 64.
—— —— ploughman, 208.
—— Samuel, collector excise, 102.
—— William, piper, 162.
Douny, Alexander, servant, 206.
—— Ebenezer, ploughman, 206.
Dow, Allan, labourer, 54.
—— John, servant, 206.
—— William, lieutenant, 44.
Dowie, Elizabeth, 345.
Downie, John, lieutenant, 4, 6.
—— Castle, 374.
Drumlethie, 179.
Drummond, Gavin, brewer, 44.
—— George, baxter, 44.
—— —— of Drummawhance, 44.
—— Gilbert, servant, 206.
—— James, tenant, 44.
—— —— Duke of Perth, 44, 247.
—— —— (Strathallan), 372.
—— John, messenger, 44.
—— —— captain, 44.
—— Lord, 27, 43, 147.
—— Peter, 44.
—— —— ensign, 44.
—— Robert, messenger-at-arms, 246, 338.
—— Walter, serjeant, 246, 340.
—— William, of Callander, 44.
—— of Logy Almond, 206.
—— factor, 54.
Drummonds, the, 359.
Drumoak, parish of, 301.
Drysdale, James, 44.
Dublin Bay, 364.
Dubois, J. B., 397.
Duddingston, 358.
Duff, Alexander, apprentice, 206.
—— James, apprentice, 6, 298.
—— John, baxter, 26, 314.
—— Patrick, 37.
—— Robert, painter, 274, 346.
Duffs, the, 359.
Duffus, Alexander, messenger, 26.
—— —— bailie, 315.
Duguid (Dogood), Patrick Leslie, of Auchinhove, 364, 367.
—— Peter, of Auchinhove, 6, 298.
—— —— vintner, 88.
—— Robert, of Auchinhove, 364.
Dumbarton Castle, 277, 396.
Dumfries, 143, 145.
—— district, xvi, 142, 361, 378.
—— gaol, 391, 393.

INDEX. 413

Dun, David, drawer, 347.
Dunbar, Archibald, excise officer, 104, 126, 130.
—— James, servitor, 349.
—— Sir William, of Durn, 26, 314.
Dunblane, 209, 368.
Duncan, Alexander, merchant, 160.
—— —— taxman, 160.
—— Charles, servant, 134.
—— —— workman, 206.
—— George, servant, 26.
—— James, servant, 26, 308.
—— —— innkeeper, 64.
—— —— shoemaker, 160, 323.
—— —— Henwells, 160, 161.
—— —— Shetrawhead, 160.
—— —— workman, 206.
—— John, shoemaker, 160.
—— —— brewer, 160.
—— —— merchant, 162.
—— —— carpenter, 206.
—— —— servant, 206.
—— Mr. John, governor, 313.
—— —— notary public, 323.
—— Peter, workman, 206.
—— Robert, servant, 162.
—— —— farmer, 162.
—— Thomas, labourer, 6.
—— William, farmer, 162.
Dundas, Mr., 397.
Dundee, district of, xvi, 196, 351, 378, 390.
—— town, 159, 161, 185, 199, 213, 229, 233, 239, 351.
Dundonald, Lord, 401.
Dunfermline, district of, xvi, 146, 348, 361, 378, 390.
—— gaol, 391, 393.
Dungarthle, laird of, 226.
Dunkeld, 225, 227.
Dunn, James, labourer, 6.
Dunnet, Theodore, merchant, 325.
Dunneves, laird of, 42.
Duns, district of, xvi, 45, 294, 326, 361.
Durham. *See* Durom.
Durie, John, merchant, 160, 322.
Durom, Alexander, jun., servant, 6, 298, 386.
Dury, David, feuar, 160.
Durward, George, labourer, 6.
—— John, saddler, 88.
—— Robert, labourer, 6.
—— William, 368.
Duthie, Alexander, smith, 162.
—— John, weaver, 206.
—— —— ploughman, 208.

EACIE, JOHN, labourer, 210.
Easson, Andrew, workman, 208.
—— Cromwell, shoemaker, 339.
Easson, James, excise officer, 339, 341.
—— John, cottar, 8.
—— Robert, labourer, 8.
Ecclefechan, 143.
Echt, parish of, 301.
Edgar, John, jun., of Keithlock, 162.
Edie, James, Drumlithie, 155, 157, 175.
Edinburgh, vii, x, 36, 46, 59, 65, 85, 87, 89, 91, 93, 97, 99, 137, 139, 141, 143, 145, 147, 149, 155, 163, 191, 193, 217, 277, 279, 281, 291, 339, 341.
—— Castle, vii, ix, 119, 391, 393, 396, 398, 399.
—— district of, xvi, 244, 338, 379, 389, 394-402.
—— gaol, 391, 394.
Edward, Alexander, labourer, 208.
—— —— workman, 208.
—— Andrew, workman, 208.
—— —— servant, 208.
—— —— chapman, 208.
—— David, workman, 208.
—— James, Ferryden, 162.
—— —— Pirsy, 208.
—— —— West Revearny, 208.
—— John, workman, 208.
—— —— Needs, 208.
—— —— servant, 208.
—— Michael, blacksmith, 8.
—— William, shoemaker, 8.
Elcho, Lord, 135, 245, 380, 381, 400.
Elder, John, servant, 26.
Elgin, district of, xiv, xvi, 100, 334, 389.
Elgine, 100, 104, 112.
Elie, parish of, 345.
Ellis, Alexander, labourer, 210.
—— John, labourer, 210.
Ellon, parish of, 303, 305, 307.
Elphingston, Arthur, Lord Balmerino. *See* Balmerino, x, xiv, 134, 377.
—— Henry, sen., tide-surveyor, 9, 298, 368.
—— —— jun., shipmaster, 8.
—— James, reg. bailie, 134, 135.
Emly, Alexander, shoemaker, 248.
England, vii, x, xii, 3, 7, 9, 17, 358, 383, 400, etc.
Enzie, 358.
Erroll, earldom of, 381.
Erskine (Areskine), George, chandler, 341.
—— —— gentleman, 248.
—— Jean, 367.
—— John, excise officer, 72, 328.
—— —— apprentice, 162, 320.
—— Thomas, merchant, 64.

Erskine, William, of Pittodrie, 367.
Espline, John, merchant, 248, 338.
Essie, James, weaver, 162.
Esslemonth, barony of, 363, 365.
Ewing, Charles, labourer, 8.
—— Peter, labourer, 8,
—— Robert, deserter, 8.
Excise Bill, the, xi.
Excise Districts, xvi.

FAIRBURN, Laird of, 76.
Fairweather, Peter, servant, 166.
Falconer, Alexander, sailor, 90.
—— —— farmer, 164.
—— James, fisher, 323.
—— John, shoemaker, 248.
Falkirk, viii, xi, xiii, xvi, xvii, 3, 5, 7, 9, 11, 13, 15, 19, 21, 23, 49, 55, 57, 59, 65, 73, 75, 77, 83, 87, 91, 93, 95, 117, 119, 127, 135, 137, 147, 151, 155, 157, 159, 161, 163, 165, 167, 169, 171, 173, 175, 177, 179, 183, 185, 187, 189, 191, 193, 195, 197, 199, 201, 203, 205, 207, 209, 211, 213, 215, 217, 219, 221, 223, 225, 227, 229, 231, 233, 235, 237, 239, 241, 243, 285, 289, 317, 359, 364-366, 371, 375, 382, 386, 400.
Falkland, 261.
Farquhar, David, labourer, 210.
—— Francis, servant, 10.
—— James, farmer, 26.
—— Patrick, servant, 212.
—— William, tailor, 212.
Farquharson, Alexander, Ingzeon, 206.
—— —— lieutenant, 210.
—— —— workman, 210.
—— —— Cordauch, 216.
—— —— of Monaltrie, 364, 368, 369.
—— Andrew, Balintom, 106.
—— Anna, 364.
—— Charles, ensign, 10.
—— Cosmus, jun., of Tombea, 106.
—— Donald, of Auchrachan, 106, 334.
—— —— servant, 106.
—— Francis, officer, 8.
—— —— of Monaltrie, 8, 298, 364, 365, 369.
—— Grigory, Tombea, 106.
—— Henry, captain, 8, 365.
—— James, of Balmurret, 8, 298, 364, 366, 367, 386.
—— —— Westertoun, 210.
—— —— jun., Westertoun, 210.
—— John, ensign, 8.
—— —— Dow, servant, 102.
—— —— of Altery, 106.

Farquharson, John, lieutenant, 210.
—— —— Monaltrie, 364.
—— —— Lewis, labourer, 90.
—— —— Mary (Lady Turnerhall), 98, 304, 387.
—— —— Robert, ensign, 10, 106, 364.
—— —— Dow, Eliet, 106.
—— —— William, farmer, 8.
—— —— workman, 210.
—— —— of Broughdurg, 210.
—— —— of Braxie, 365.
Farquharsons, the, 358, 359, 365.
Feithie, Andrew, labourer, 210.
Feithy, John, servant, 210.
Fenton, David, lieutenant, 210.
—— James, workman, 210.
—— Silvester, labourer, 210.
Fentor, Thomas, servant, 212.
Ferguson, Hugh, servant, 74.
—— James, Tomintoul, 108.
—— John, tailor, 248, 338.
—— —— Clackmannan, 349.
—— Joseph, labourer, 210.
—— —— weaver, 212.
—— Patrick, merchant, 319.
—— Robert, thread-maker, 212.
—— William, officer, 164.
Ferrier, David, labourer, 90.
—— —— merchant, 164, 171, 187.
—— James, sailor, 90, 302.
—— —— Kintrockat, 172.
—— John, cottar, 164.
—— Robert, ensign, 164.
Fethes, David, servant, 164.
Fettercairn, 155, 163, 173.
Fetteresso, parish of, 323.
Fetterneer, 183.
Fettes, John, maltman, 162, 320, 321.
Fiddes, Mr., chaplain, 309.
Fife, Alexander, Potterow, 248, 338.
—— Charles, surgeon, 212.
—— district, xvi, 138, 345, 359, 373.
—— Gilbert, tailor, 248.
—— James, servant, 212.
—— William, farmer, 28.
Filp, Thomas, sen., labourer, 210.
—— —— jun., labourer, 210.
Findaury, laird of, 169.
Findhorn, 104, 112, 114, 127, 183.
Findlater, Earl of, 25, 29, 39, 400.
—— William, shoemaker, 8.
Findlay, John, excise officer, 337.
—— Robert, labourer, 8.
Finlay, Alexander, weaver, 104.
—— David, workman, 164.
—— —— of Bogside, 347.
—— George, heelmaker, 64, 352.
—— James, Cairntoun, 164.

INDEX. 415

Finlay, James, workman, 210.
—— Mr., 116, 128.
—— William, Cruchly, 106.
Finlayson, James, 390, 392.
—— John, salt officer, 136.
Finlyson, John, instrument maker, 248.
Finnie, James, 346, 390.
—— Robert, servant, 274.
—— —— wright, 347.
Firzel, John, mason, 166.
Fisheraw, 141.
Fleeming, William, brewer, 341.
Fleming, Donald, Miln Achdregnie, 108.
—— James, Cruchly, 106.
—— —— brewer, 341.
—— —— shoemaker, 353.
—— John, Findran, 106.
—— —— servant, 106.
—— Robert, Miln Achdregnie, 106.
Fletcher, Robert, jun., of Balinsho, 210.
—— —— —— of Benchy, 212.
Fodd, William, pendickleman, 212.
Fogo, John, farmer, 212.
Forbes, Alexander, stabler, 90.
—— —— servant, 210.
—— —— Lord Pitsligo, x, 11, 31, 90, 191, 261, 267, 302, 303, 376, 387.
—— Anna, 370.
—— Benjamin, merchant, 8.
—— Duncan, Kirkcaldy, 260, 263.
—— Elizabeth, 369.
—— George, weaver, 26.
—— —— merchant, 95.
—— —— factor, 199, 212.
—— James, labourer, 90, 305, 307.
—— Jean, 370.
—— John, wright, 248.
—— —— Turnerhall, 307.
—— —— merchant in Tain, 74, 328.
—— —— labourer, 90.
—— —— merchant, 106.
—— —— Wester Achmore, 106.
—— —— Ballandie, 106, 108.
—— —— Bervie, 164, 322.
—— Jonathan, farmer, 90, 304.
—— Joseph, wright, 136, 139.
—— Patrick, Balivaler, 106.
—— president, xvii.
—— Robert, apprentice, 8.
—— —— farmer, 28.
—— —— Pitonachty, 333.
—— Thomas, vintner, 90.
—— gentleman, 248.
—— William, farmer, 312, 387.
Forbeses, 359.
Fordon Cross, 153, 179, 193.
Fordue, James, wright, 164.
Fordyce, Alexander, servant, 104, 334.

Fordyce, parish of, 315.
Foreman, John, Pitully, 303, 305.
Forfar county, 169, 201, 221, 235, 369.
Forglen, parish of, 309, 313.
Forres, 104, 114, 393.
Forrest, George, servant, 90, 304.
—— James, labourer, 90, 305.
—— William, officer, 90.
Forrester, Alexander, vintner, 347.
—— James, maltman, 347.
—— Silvester, workman, 210.
Forret, James, smith, 164.
Forsyth, George, servant, 8.
—— James, officer, 104.
Fort Augustus, 374.
Fort William, siege of, 283.
Forth, the river, ix, xv, 57, 61, 149, 358, 359, 369.
Fotheringham, David, governor, 212.
—— James, fishmonger, 166.
—— Thomas, of Bandaine, 212.
—— —— merchant, 212.
Foulis, George, 373.
Fourage, parish of, 181.
Foveran, parish of, 307.
Fowler, John, farmer, 106.
Frain, John, serjeant, 10.
Framan, John, Miltown, 164, 322, 388.
France, 199, 357, 364, 367, 371, 377, 378, 382.
Fraser, Alexander, captain, 104, 334.
—— —— officer, 104, 334.
—— —— West Cowlie, 164.
—— Charles, jun., of Fairfield, 104, 334.
—— David, piper, 74.
—— —— West Cowlie, 164.
—— Hugh, in Culbocky, 74.
—— —— merchant, 104, 334.
—— —— officer, 104, 334.
—— —— captain, 104, 334.
—— —— smith, 166, 320.
—— James, Balagalken, 74.
—— —— jun., Balagalken, 74.
—— —— of Foyers, 104, 334.
—— —— Upper Cults, 106.
—— —— fisher, 321.
—— John, in Bewly, 74.
—— —— serjeant, 74.
Fraser, John, in Tea Wigg, 74.
—— —— in Moydie, 74.
—— —— brogmaker, 74.
—— —— of Bochruben, 104, 334.
—— —— officer, 104, 334.
—— —— cottar, 106.
—— —— farmer, 106.
—— —— Auchrachan, 106.
—— —— Balnekeil, 108.

416   LIST OF REBELS.

Fraser, John, servant, 164.
—— —— stranger, 164.
—— —— maltman, 210, 375.
—— provost, Inverness, 331.
—— Roderick, in Limaire, 74.
—— Simon, Lord Lovat, xiv, 74, 105, 107, 374.
—— —— Master of Lovat, 74, 75, 77, 328.
—— —— of Achnacloich, 74, 328.
—— —— in Bewly, 74.
—— —— captain, 104, 334.
—— —— officer, 104, 334.
—— —— (*alias* Miller), 329.
—— Thomas, smith, 106.
—— —— serjeant, 106.
—— William, of Culmiln, 74, 328.
—— —— jun., of Culbocky, 74, 328, 329.
—— —— piper, 74.
—— —— merchant, 74.
—— —— Inveralichy, 90, 302.
—— —— of Dalernig, 104, 334.
—— —— captain, 104, 334.
—— —— farmer, 106.
—— —— merchant, 329.
—— —— Kinnellan, 331, 333, 394.
—— —— of Innervallachy, 75.
—— —— of Moydie, 74.
Fraserburgh, 303, 307.
Frasers, the, xiv, 75, 359.
Frazer, Alexander, servant, 8.
—— —— gentleman, 26.
—— —— of Rilich, 74, 328.
—— —— jun., captain, 74, 328.
—— —— of Balchreggan, 74.
—— —— in Limaire, 74.
—— —— in Kincardin, 74.
—— Donald, householder, 26, 314.
—— —— Balagalken, 74, 375.
—— —— captain, 104, 334, 376.
—— —— dame Helen, 369.
—— Robert, carrier, 26, 314.
Freebairn, Mr., schoolmaster, 175.
Freeman, John, Milton, 322, 388.
French auxiliaries, xii.
Frendraught, Viscount, xvii.
Friday (Black), vii, xi.
Froster, William, workman, 210.
Fullarton, James Bain, merchant, 326, 388.
—— Joan, 379.
—— —— jun., of Dudwick, 90, 304.
Fullen, John, excise officer, 353.
Fullerton, Adam, brewer, 326, 341, 388.
Furnival, Thomas, xiv.
Fyre, John, carter, 342, 389.

GAIR, THOMAS, Nigg, 329.

Gall (Gatt), Alexander, salt officer, 260, 344.
—— —— Cormucie, 30, 308, 387.
Gallow water, 141.
Gammack, William, clerk, 214.
Garden, David, jun., captain, 168.
Garder, Peter Gow, Bewly, 74.
Gardner, colonel, 253, 380.
—— James, servant, 56, 316.
—— William, servant, 168.
Garmack, William, workman, 10.
Garrioch, Alexander, ensign, 10, 300.
—— —— of Mergie, 168, 322.
Garvich, John, servant, 30, 308.
—— —— Dorlathers, 308.
Gask, Lady, 400, 401.
Gatt, Alexander, servant, 30, 37, 41, 308, 387.
Gattahon, John, turner, 10.
Gauld, Alexander, Achnagara, 112.
—— John, Achnagara, 112.
—— Robert (*alias* M'Pherson), Ruthven, 110.
—— Thomas, Auchlounie, 110.
Gauldie, James, jun., Pitchash, 112.
Gaw, Lewis, Knock of Achnhoil, 112.
Ged, Dougal, goldsmith, 339.
Gedd (Gadd), James, xiv, 248, 379.
—— William, 379.
Geddes, Robert, baillie, 349.
Geigie, George, weaver, 214.
Gelletlie, James, servant, 216.
George II., King, viii, xi, xviii, 199, 402.
Gibb, James, sailor, 214.
Gibbon, Alexander, ship carpenter, 168.
—— William, merchant, 168, 322.
Gibenach, Donald, Delavoiar, 110.
—— Thomas, Skala, 112.
Gibson, David, porter, 214.
—— Gilbert, weaver, xviii, 214.
—— James, carpenter, 323.
—— John, chapman, 166.
—— —— weaver, 214.
—— Thomas, wright, 319.
—— William, excise officer, 341.
Gilchrist, Archibald, baxter, 317.
Giles, Richard, Canongate, 248, 338.
Gill, Alexander, servant, 30.
—— —— shipmaster, 90, 304.
—— George, shoemaker, 30, 35, 308.
Gillespie, John, slater, 30, 308.
—— William, pilot, 168.
Gilmer, William, Stonehaven, 168, 322.
Ginglekirk (Chaunelkirk), 141.
Glasgow, vii, x, 145, 267, 273, 275, 277, 279, 317, 327, 347.
—— district, xvi, 272, 274, 346, 361, 381, 390, 396, 399.

INDEX. 417

Glashan, George, servant, 28.
Glass, Finlay, brogmaker, 76, 328.
—— James, rebel officer, 10.
—— John, brogmaker, 76, 328.
Glassfoord, Duncan, 264.
—— Thomas, 264.
Gleig, Adam, Drumlithie, 170.
—— Robert, smith, 170.
Glen, Andrew, excise officer, 349.
Glenbervie, kirk of, 171.
Glencarse, 371.
Glencoe, xi.
Glenday, James, greive, 214.
Glendy, John, weaver, 216.
Glenelg, Lord, 377.
Glenesk, 167, 187, 401.
Glenfinan, 357, 359.
Glenlivet, 358.
Glenlyon, laird of, 42.
Glenmoristons, the, 401.
Glenshiel, 371.
Glenurquhart, 377, 386.
Gleny, Peter, weaver, 214.
Gollan, Donald, in Avoch, 76.
Golspie, 375.
Goodbrand, John, wright, 28.
Goodsir, David, Leven, 345.
Goodwillie, John, writer, 248, 338.
Gordon, Alexander, farmer, 28.
—— —— captain, 28.
—— —— of Darlathis, 30, 308, 312.
—— —— jun., of Darlathis, 30, 308.
—— —— merchant, 76, 328.
—— —— lieutenant, 108, 112.
—— Anne, 365, 366, 368.
—— Arthur, of Carnousie, xviii, 30, 308, 312.
—— Cecilia, 370.
—— Charles, Esq. of Blelock, capt. 10, 300.
—— —— captain, 28, 369.
—— —— gentleman, 28.
—— —— of Binhall, 28.
—— —— of Terpersie, 28.
—— Clemintina, 370.
—— David of Kirkhill, 108.
—— —— of Glenbucket, 370.
—— Donald, Delavoiar, 110.
—— Duchess of, 134, 136, 363.
—— Duke of, 366, 371.
—— Francis, of Kincardin Miln, 10, 298, 366.
—— —— ensign, 10, 300.
—— Lord George, xii.
—— George, farmer, 312.
—— —— Esq. of Hallhead, 10, 298, 365, 366.
—— —— blacksmith, 28.
—— —— Foderleter, 110.
—— —— Newtoun, 110.
Gordon, George, Tomintowle, 110.
—— —— innkeeper, 248.
—— Helen, 366, 369.
—— Henrietta, 370.
—— Lady Henrietta, 366.
—— Henry Wolrige, 365.
—— Hugh, 366.
—— Ishmael, servant, 112.
—— James, of Affluchrees, 305.
—— —— maltster, 333.
—— —— of Clashtirum, 28.
—— —— lieutenant, 28.
—— —— of Aberlour, 28, 312.
—— —— of Beldornie, 30.
—— —— of Coubardie, 30.
—— —— sen., of Terpersie, 30.
—— —— officer, 108.
—— —— Minmore, 112.
—— —— messenger, 112.
—— Sir James, 369.
—— Dame Janet, 369.
—— Lady Jean, 371.
—— John, of Cordregny, 108.
—— —— jun., of Glenbucket, 108, 334.
—— —— of Minmore, 108.
—— —— ensign, 108.
—— —— officer, 110.
—— —— Inshnakap, 110.
—— —— Loynavere, 110.
—— —— weaver, 248, 342.
—— —— of Abochie, 25, 30, 37.
—— —— priest, 28.
—— —— serjeant, 28, 312.
—— —— farmer, 30.
—— —— apprentice, 168, 320.
—— —— jun., barber, 216.
—— —— servant, 308.
—— —— of Glenbucket, 29, 30, 31, 108, 109, 237, 358, 369, 370.
—— Lewis, Lagan, 108, 334.
—— Lord Lewis, 10, 27, 31, 35, 135, 137, 358, 366.
—— Lodovick, merchant, 112, 334.
—— Margaret, 369.
—— Mrs., 401.
—— Patrick, of Cordregny, 108.
—— —— merchant, 315.
—— Peter, innkeeper, 28.
—— Robert, jun., of Logie, 90, 304, 387.
—— —— serjeant, 112.
—— —— alehouse keeper, 248, 338.
—— —— of Becomie, 248.
—— —— goldsmith, 339.
—— —— of Halhead, 365.
—— Thomas, of Fodderleter, 108.
—— —— maltster, 333.
—— Walter, painter, 248.
—— William, farmer, 10, 28.

Gordon, Sir William, of Park, 26, 28, 38, 314, 369.
—— —— captain, 108.
—— —— serjeant, 110.
—— —— Glenrines, 112.
—— —— writer, 168, 320.
Gordon riots, vii.
Gordons, the, 359.
Gouck, David, servant, 166.
Gourlay, Alexander, smith, 345.
Gourlie, George, Panbridge, 214.
—— James, Panbridge, 214.
Gove, Thomas, fisher, 323.
Gow, Alexander, Ruthven, 110.
—— Donald, workman, 216.
—— John, servant, 216.
—— Peter (*alias* Smith), gardener, 329.
—— Thomas, shoemaker, 248.
—— William, fisher, 10.
Gowans, William, servant, 168.
Gower, George, workman, 214.
Graham, Al., chapman, 346.
—— Alexander, writer, 214, 351, 390.
—— Archibald, gauger, 100, 102, 104, 112, 114, 116, 126, 335, 337.
—— —— Burdstone, 347.
—— Charles, Tain, 74, 328.
—— David, merchant, 214, 351.
—— James, of Airth, 56, 316.
—— —— of Duntroun, 214.
—— —— tailor, 347.
—— John, barber, 248.
—— —— of Kilmordinny, 274, 346, 398, 399.
—— —— painter, 274, 346.
—— Peter, 44.
—— Robert, of Garrack, 44.
—— —— farmer, 216.
—— Walter, 264.
—— —— jun., surgeon, 264.
Grahams, the, 359.
Graitney, 143.
Grant, Alexander, captain, 89, 91, 95, 112, 334.
—— —— farmer, 112.
—— —— factor, 331.
—— —— Laird of, 331.
—— —— Inchbrene, 377.
—— —— Corromaly, 74, 328.
—— —— officer, 108, 312, 387.
—— —— lieutenant, 108.
—— —— ensign, 108.
—— —— Calier, 112.
—— —— of Deckie, 110.
—— —— of Grantfield, 367.
—— Angus, Tamvilan, 112.
—— Charles, lieutenant, 110.
—— —— 377.
—— Colin, Contine, 328, 388.

Grant, David, Old Meldrum, 90.
—— —— officer, 108.
—— —— Donald, Easter Galurg, 110.
—— —— Grigor, Delavoiar, 110.
—— —— —— glass-grinder, 272, 346.
—— —— Humphrey, lieutenant, 28.
—— James, fidler, 30.
—— Sir James, 31, 35, 37, 41, 386
—— James, excise officer, 77, 329.
—— —— ensign, 108.
—— —— Dalnabo, 110.
—— —— brewer, 168.
—— —— lieutenant, 248.
—— John, servant, 28.
—— —— tailor, 28.
—— —— servant, 28.
—— —— excise officer, 102, 104, 105, 114, 116, 118, 128, 129, 335, 337.
—— —— of Inverlochy, 108.
—— —— lieutenant, 108.
—— —— ensign, 108.
—— —— of Deskie, 108.
—— —— officer, 110.
—— —— weaver, 110.
—— —— merchant, 112.
—— —— Tamavelan, 112.
—— —— serjeant, 112.
—— —— farmer, 112.
—— —— Roy, Demickmore, 126.
—— —— barber, 248.
—— —— Contine, 328, 388.
—— Kenneth, in Contine, 75, 328, 331, 388.
—— Lewis, Little Neive, 112.
—— Neil, Tomahanan, 112.
—— Patrick, Inshnakap, 110.
—— —— captain, 214, 328, 388.
—— —— farmer, 216.
—— Perler, Corromaly, 74, 328, 388.
—— Peter, Delavoiar, 110.
—— —— Foderleter, 110.
—— —— Gaulurg, 112.
—— —— Roy, Badiglashean, 126.
—— Walter, barber, 248.
—— William, of Blairfinde, 108.
—— —— Findran, 110.
—— —— Tomintowle, 110.
—— —— Roy, Balnakeill, 110.
—— —— Foderleter, 110.
—— —— servant, 112.
—— —— Gaulurg, 112.
—— —— lieutenant, 112, 334.
—— Mr. —— priest, 110.
Grants, 358, 359.
Gray & Bisset, merchants, 183, 193.
Gray, Andrew, weaver, 214.
—— David, brewer, 168.
—— —— servant, 214.
—— James, Temple, 168.

INDEX. 419

Gray, James, cottar, 168.
—— —— Milton, 322.
—— —— farmer, 323.
—— John, servant, 28, 112, 334.
—— —— weaver, 216.
—— Patrick, tailor, 327.
—— William, fisher, 10, 28.
—— —— apprentice, 44.
—— —— painter, 168.
—— —— of Ballegerno, 216.
—— —— weaver, 274, 346.
—— —— of Newholm, 390, 393-399.
Greek, David, servant, 216.
Greenhill, Robert, serjeant, 214.
—— William, gardener, 216.
Gregory, prof. James, 363.
Greig, Alexander, clerk, 168.
—— James, 170.
—— —— Woodhill, 212.
Grey, Alexander, apprentice, 320, 388.
Grieve, Robert, fisher, 323.
Grower, William, servant, 216.
Gruar, William, Purgave, 208.
Guelph dynasty, vii.
Guthrie, George, Montrose, 168, 320.
—— Robert, merchant, 214.
Guthry, James, servant, 28.

HACKET (HALKET), ALEXANDER, 308.
—— Charles, 10, 300, 386.
—— —— farmer, 30.
—— —— jun., 30, 308.
—— —— barber, 250.
—— James, 32.
—— Mr., 353.
Hackie, John, weaver, 218.
Hackston (Haxton), Heleneas, gentleman, 64.
—— Robert, surgeon, 64, 352.
Haddington, district, xvi, 132, 361, 377.
—— town of, 137, 139, 400.
—— gaol, 391, 393, 401.
Haggart, David, of Cairnmuir, 218.
Haig, James, innkeeper, 349.
Haldane (Haddin), Alexander, 56, 373.
—— George, 385.
—— John of Laurick, 56, 373, 385.
Haliburton, Thomas, wright, 216.
—— —— carpenter, 250, 342.
—— of Dryburgh, 401.
Halkerton, Lord, 194.
Halkerston, John, town-clerk, 349.
Hall, Alexander, serjeant, 10.
Hamilton, Duke of, 250, 338.
—— Mr. Gavin, 390.
—— George, of Redhouse, 250, 338, 379.

Hamilton, John, gentleman, 30.
—— —— innkeeper, 347.
—— Robert, jun., of Kilbrachmant, 260, 262, 344.
—— —— sailor, 276, 346.
Hamilton's Dragoons, 326.
Hampton Court, 375.
Hanoverian dynasty, ix.
Hanton, Thomas, Easter Coull, 206.
Harper, Mr. William, minister, 56, 316.
Harrel, William, 46.
Harvie, James, quarter-master, 266.
—— Patrick, porter, 301.
—— Robert, brewer, 339.
Hawley, General, xii, 365, 401.
Hay, ——, 277.
—— Adam, of Asslid, 32, 368, 370.
—— —— of Cairnbanno, 92, 304.
—— Alexander, blacksmith, 30.
—— —— gentleman, 30.
—— Andrew, major, 30.
—— —— surgeon, 64.
—— —— of Asleed, 370.
—— Anna, 370.
—— George, lieutenant, 30, 314.
—— —— of Montblery, 30, 308.
—— —— Montrose, 172, 320.
—— James, Haddington, 136.
—— —— W.S., 370.
—— John W., officer, 30, 308.
—— —— of Auch Wharney, 305.
—— Mary, Countess of Errol, 90, 92, 94, 96, 98, 304.
—— Patrick, workman, 250.
—— William, Philorth, 303.
Hazard, sloop, 151, 153, 155, 159, 163, 165, 173, 175, 181, 187, 195, 395.
Hector, John, fisher, 10.
Henderson, Alexander, Tranent, 136.
—— —— merchant, 216.
—— Charles, servant, 218.
—— David, glazier, 56, 148, 348.
—— —— Duncan, lieutenant, 46.
—— Francis, merchant, 216.
—— James, ship-master, 172, 320.
—— —— servant, 216.
—— —— slater, 218.
—— John, merchant, 56, 316, 348.
—— —— of Castlemains, 142, 378.
—— —— brewer, 148.
—— —— Emock, 347.
—— Robert, Cottoun, 170.
—— —— Clackmanan, 349.
—— Thomas, servant, 345.
—— William, lieutenant, 46.
—— —— slater, 218.
Hendersons, 385.
Hendrie, Alexander, farmer, 114.

Hendry, Robert, servant, 30.
Henry, Alexander, dyster, 218.
Henryson, John, pupil, 250.
Hepburn (Riccart), James, of Keith, 250, 338.
—— John, Ardla, 303, 305, 307.
—— Peter, farmer, 30, 310, 311.
Highlanders, vii, viii, xii, xv, 359.
Hill, Thomas, brewer, 46.
Hills, Nathaniel, 395, 398, 399.
Hillhead, parish of, 311.
Hobert, John, workman, 216.
Hodge, Alexander, brewer, 317.
—— David, porter, 250, 340.
—— John, brewer, 323.
—— Robert, farmer, 170.
Hogg, John, tidesman, 10.
Holland, 371.
Holyrood, vii, ix, 365, 377.
Home, Mr., historian, xv, 357, 358.
—— Mr., solicitor, 393.
—— David, labourer, 216.
—— —— Whitfield, 294, 326.
—— George, of Whitfield, 294, 338.
—— Norwald, Boghall, 266.
—— Patrick, maltster, 294.
—— William, Duns, 294, 326.
Hood, Andrew, Tain, 76, 328.
—— George, Tain, 76, 328.
—— James, smith, 170, 197.
—— Patrick, weaver, 218.
Hope, Sir John Bruce, of Kinross, 349.
Horn, Charles, serjeant, 216, 351.
—— William, labourer, 218.
Hosack, James, brewer, 325.
—— Provost, Inverness, 331.
Houston, David, smith, 260.
—— Laird of, 266.
—— Thomas, farmer, 114, 334.
How, Andrew, weaver, 216.
Hume, Alexander, writer, 250.
—— George, Edinburgh, 250.
—— John, labourer, 216.
Huns, the, xii.
Hunter, Adam, excise expectant, 170.
—— Alexander, 367.
—— David, of Burnside, 218, 230, 234.
—— James, Lethan, 170.
—— —— Newbigging, 172.
—— John, labourer, 10.
—— —— Arbirlot, 170, 172.
—— Mary, Arbirlot, 170.
—— Mr., of Polmood, 376.
Hutchen, John, weaver, 216.
Hutcheson, Thomas, merchant, 114, 334.
—— William, labourer, 218.

IMBRY, ALEXANDER, 12.

India, 375.
Indians, North American, xii.
Ingram, John, miller, 32.
—— —— workman, 12.
Innes, Alexander, Balmdrowan, 114.
—— —— Coltfield, 114.
—— Sir Henry, 109.
—— James, of Banacraig, 12, 300, 367.
—— —— colonel, 32.
—— James, wigmaker, 32.
—— provost, James, 315.
—— Sir James, weaver, xvii, 92.
—— John, ensign, 12, 300.
—— —— of Edingight, 32.
—— —— Balmdrowan, 114.
—— —— Turriff, 310.
—— Patrick, weaver, 32.
—— Robert, West Foderleter, 114.
—— —— wright, 114.
—— William, wig-maker, 32.
—— —— W.S., 373.
Inverarity, David, meal-monger, 172.
—— —— shoemaker, 172.
Inverkeithing, parish of, 313.
Inverness, district of, xvi, 361, 374, 395, 397.
—— 15, 23, 79, 89, 91, 95, 102, 104, 106, 118, 127, 159, 167, 179, 181, 275.
Inverury, 3, 7, 11, 31, 89, 99, 151, 209, 213, 225, 233, 243, 364-366.
Irons, Robert, Montrose, 172, 320.
Irvine, 396.
—— Adam, of Bruchly, 32.
—— Alexander, of Drum, 12, 300.
—— —— Yonderstoun, 309.
—— Charles, salt-officer, 136.
—— Edward, of Wysbie, 142.
—— James, of Gribton, 142.
—— John, of Whitehill, 144.
—— William, of Gribton, 144.
—— —— Fetteresso, 172.
—— —— labourer, 218.
—— —— Leuthers, 309.
Izat, John, chandler, 339, 341.

JACK, DAVID, wright, 46.
—— James, brewer, 339.
—— William, messenger, 334, 389.
Jackson, Alexander, shoemaker, 341.
—— Charles, brewer, 218.
Jacksone, James, 394.
Jacobites, the English, xii, xiii.
Jaffrey, James, joiner, 12.
—— Thomas, gaoler, 12.
Jamaica, 379.
James VII., King, ix, xiii, 139.
—— VIII., King, ix, 241.

INDEX. 421

Jameson, Alexander, Philorth, 303, 305.
—— William, reedmaker, serjeant, 172, 320.
Jamieson, Andrew Craill, 353.
—— George, 363.
Jamison, John, wright, 347.
—— Marjory, 363.
Jeans, Henry, 309, 311.
Johnshaven, 183.
Johnston, Andrew, Knockhill, 142, 380.
—— —— servant, 250, 338.
—— George, factor, 218.
—— James Lesslie, of Knockhill, 142.
—— —— labourer, 218.
—— —— captain, 250.
—— —— merchant, 250, 338.
—— John, servant, 32.
—— —— town officer, 347.
—— Robert, sheriff officer, 172, 322.
—— William, of Lockerby, 144.
Johnstoun, Alexander, labourer, 218.
—— —— silversmith, 218.
Joyner, James, servant, 32, 314.
—— —— householder, 32.

KAY, LODOVICK, officer, 114, 334.
Keill, Thomas, servant, 172.
Keir, Patrick, wright, 250, 338, 380.
Keith, 29, 37, 39, 313.
Keith, Mr. Alexander, 305.
—— David, workman, 12.
—— —— farmer, 174.
—— —— Fetteresso, 322.
—— James, wright, 174.
Kelkpatrick, Grisell, servant, 353.
Kelly, Earl of, 63, 65, 69, 263, 373.
—— John, of Newbigging, 349.
—— Mr., 357.
Kelso, district of, xvi, 280, 381.
Kemla, James, Hyndwells, 172.
Kemlar, Alexander, Miln of Mundens, 172.
—— Thomas, miller, 172.
Kemlay, Gideon, merchant, 172.
Kemloe, Joseph, blacksmith, 12.
Kemp, James, innkeeper, 319.
Kennedy, Alexander, merchant, 309.
—— Archibald, apprentice, 250, 338.
—— John, servant, 114.
—— Robert, Durn, 314, 387.
Kensington, 375, 381.
Ker, James, goldsmith, 339.
Kermock, Andrew, workman, 218.
Kerr, Alexander, weaver, 32.
—— Henry, of Greden, 280, 381.
—— James, merchant, 84.

Kerr, Mark, lieutenant, 250, 342.
—— Robert, porter, 343.
—— —— painter, 347.
Kerrie, Alexander, sailor, 172.
—— John, merchant, 172.
Kerry, Robert, Panmuir, 218.
Key, John, tailor, 172.
Kilgower, Peter, dyster, 92, 304.
Killiwhinning, 77.
Kilmarnock, Earl of, xiv, 65, 127, 264, 266, 267, 381.
Kilmorie, 284.
Kincaid, James, of Degreen, 56, 316.
Kincardin, 7, 359.
—— Countess of, 146.
King, James, servant, 32, 310.
—— —— smith, 327.
—— Lauchlane, salt officer, 136.
Kinghorn, 396.
Kingston, 400.
Kinloch, Alexander, captain, 220, 378.
—— Charles, captain, 220, 378.
—— Sir James, of Kinloch, 218, 220, 231, 378, 379.
—— John, of Kildry, jun., 218.
Kinnair, Peter, labourer, 220.
Kinneil, parks of, 265, 267.
Kinnie, James, Onthank, 198.
Kinnier, Thomas, farmer, 172.
Kirk, the, ix.
Kirkaldie, John, bailie, 349.
Kirkcaldy, district of, xvi, 260, 344, 349, 361, 389.
Kirkeant, laird of, 141.
Kirriemuir, 207, 217.
Knows, Robert, fisher, 12.
—— William, fisher, 12.
Kynnach, John, Burntbrae, 310.

LACKY, ALEXANDER, workman, 220.
Lafargue, Mr., 395, 397.
Lafusille, major, 195.
Laing, John, labourer. 92.
—— —— servant, 174.
—— William, servant, 32.
Laird, Andrew, merchant, 222.
—— James, servant, 222.
—— John, workman, 220.
—— Patrick, lieutenant, 222.
Lamb, William, Achnhoyle, 114.
—— —— weaver, 176.
Lamond, Archibald, 394.
Lanark, district of, xvi, 84, 361, 373, 376.
Largo, Joseph, sadler, 12.
Lauder, Archibald, boy, 294, 326.
—— Charles, salt officer, 136.
—— James, merchant, 250.
—— —— apprentice, 250, 338.

Lauder, Robert, jun., of Bailmouth, 294.
Laurance, James, piper, 176.
Laurence, John, merchant, 92, 303, 305.
Laurencekirk, 155.
Law, Mr. George, nonjuror, 12, 367.
—— William, schoolboy, xvii, 12.
—— —— Milnton, 323.
Lawrance, John, mason, 32.
Lawrie, John, salt officer, 136.
Lawson, David, servant, 222.
—— Deacon, weaver, 343.
—— Gavin, Cathcart, 327.
—— James, servant, 220.
—— —— workman, 220.
—— John, jun., Stonhaven, 176.
—— —— labourer, 220.
—— Patrick, miller, 220.
—— Thomas, workman, 220.
—— —— chapman, 222, 378.
Leech, Archibald, Kirkmichael, 284.
Lee's regiment, 250.
Legat, George, merchant, 92, 306, 313.
Leggie, Patrick, writer, 300, 386.
Leigh, Alexander, wigmaker, 114.
Leith, 149, 203, 257, 380.
—— Alexander, farmer, 32.
—— —— mason, 32, 310.
—— Anthony, farmer, 92, 304.
—— George, tidesman, 12.
—— John, innkeeper, 32.
—— —— Brechin, 174.
—— Laurence, farmer, 92, 304.
—— Robert, bailie, 66, 352.
—— William, snuff-grinder, 12.
—— —— tobacconist, 12.
—— —— lieutenant, 174.
Lendrum, John, College, 305.
—— William, excise officer, 349.
Leochil, parish of, 7.
Leslie, Patrick, Count, 364.
—— Teresa, 364.
Lesmahagow, 287, 383.
Lesslie, Alexander, ensign, 32, 312.
—— Charles, Findracy, 114, 334.
—— James, labourer, 92.
—— —— gentleman, 136.
—— John, 92.
—— —— merchant, 174, 322.
—— Thomas, merchant, 321.
—— William, 32, 310.
—— —— mariner, 174, 320.
Leuthers, 313.
Ley, Thomas, labourer, 14.
—— —— Drumlethie, 174.
—— William, sergeant, 12.
Lichton, ——, workman, 220.
Lilly, Alexander, wright, 136.
—— Alexander, 136.

Lind, George, labourer, 92.
—— —— smith, 92.
Lindsay, Alexander, shoemaker, 250.
—— James, shoemaker, 46, 371.
—— —— apprentice, 46.
—— John, lieutenant, 176, 320.
—— Martin, writer, 46, 371.
—— Peter, gentleman, 66, 374.
—— Robert, weaver, 136.
—— —— Clackmannan, 349.
—— Thomas, Pennywells, 176.
—— William, Carchley, 114.
—— —— shoemaker, 176, 320.
Lines, Andrew, serjeant, 12.
Linlithgow, district of, xvi, 264, 358, 361, 381.
Linning, Mr., 383.
Lithgow, William, maltster, 341.
Littlejohn, Alexander, physician, 176.
—— David, servant, 174.
Livieth, John, labourer, 220.
—— William, labourer, 220.
Livingston, James, postmaster, 266.
Livingstone, Lady Anne, 381.
Lochaber, 382.
Lochead, John, merchant, 56, 316.
Lochiel, laird of, x. *See* Cameron.
Lockhart, James, wright, 46.
—— Peter, smith, 56, 316.
—— ——, 401.
Logan, John, brewer, 317.
—— Margaret, Bannockburn, 317.
—— William, brewer, 317.
Logie, Patrick, land-waiter, 12.
—— William, porter, 114.
London, vii, xi, xii, 365, 366, 369, 371, 375, 383.
—— Tower of, 398.
Longformacus, 401.
Longmuir, Charles, labourer, 12.
Longside, parish of, 307.
Lorimer, William, farmer, 32.
Lothian, Andrew, brewer, xvii, 66, 352.
—— Edward, goldsmith, 339.
Lothians, the, 359, 369.
Loudoun, Lord, 10, 89, 91, 95, 117, 119, 127, 287, 358, 374-376, 400.
Louper, John, smith, 174.
Lovall, Andrew, 222.
Lovat, Lord. *See* Fraser.
Low, Alexander, merchant, 174.
—— —— Brechin, 180.
—— —— Fraserburgh, 303, 305.
—— David, labourer, xviii, 220.
—— James, Colhaick, 220.
—— —— servant, 220.
—— John, serjeant, 14.
—— —— officer, 46.
—— —— servant, 176, 320.

Low, Robert, goldsmith, 339, 341.
—— William, chapman, 174, 351.
—— —— jun., smith, 176, 320.
—— —— serjeant, 222.
Lownan, James, weaver, 220.
Lowper, Alexander, mason, 32.
Lowthian, John, workman, 220.
Lugtoun, Simon, tailor, 250, 380.
Lumfannan, parish of, 7.
Lumgair, James, 222.
Lumisdale, James, 309.
Lumsdaile, Andrew, writer, 250.
Lumsden, Alexander, 367.
—— David, captain, 12, 367.
—— Harry, 367.
—— James, 367.
—— John, farmer, 12.
—— Margaret, 367.
Lunan, David, weaver, 220.
—— John, weaver, 220.
Lundie, John, workman, 220.
Lundin, laird of, 262.
Lyon, Charles, Dundee, 222.
—— —— apprentice, 222.
—— David, vintner, 174.
—— James, innkeeper, 222.
—— Mr. Robert, chaplain, 46, 371.
—— Mrs., 228.
—— Patrick, of Easter Ogle, 220.
—— Paul, farmer, 323.

M'ADAM, JOHN, Shanoal, 122.
—— William, Shanoal, 122.
M'Alister, Alexander, Tamavilan, 122.
—— Donald More, Surn, 327.
—— Hector, merchant, 326, 388.
—— William, Marignecraig, 326, 388.
MacAlisters, 359.
M'Allan, John, Tomintowl, 120.
M'Alman, Nicol, officer, 286.
M'Alpin, Patrick, ensign, 120.
MacAlpins, 359.
M'Andrew, Donald, in Fairly, 78.
MacAndrews, 359.
M'Angus, William, Letock, 124.
M'Arthur, John, brewer, 114.
MacArthurs, 359, 385.
Macavy, Magnus, 394.
M'Bain, Gillice, major, 116, 376.
—— Hugh, in Bewly, 76.
MacBains, 359.
M'Bean, Angus, officer, 118, 336.
—— Donald Auldaury, 118, 377.
—— Gillies, officer, 118, 336.
—— —— servant, 118, 336.
—— John, servant, 118.
—— major, 119.
M'Beath, Marmduke, flask-maker, 252, 340.

M'Callum, John, excise officer, 100, 114, 126, 130.
M'Carro, James, servant, 224.
M'Charmaig, Duncan, Achosrigan, 284.
M'Chombiech, Duncan Dow, Achosrigan, 284.
M'Clacky, James, Kilmuir, 78.
M'Coll, Archibald, Kintail, 284.
—— Donald, smith, 284.
—— Duncan, 284.
—— Hugh Roy, Appin, 284.
—— —— Glenstockidal, 284.
—— —— Aros, 284.
—— John, officer, 286.
—— —— Benderloch, 286.
MacColls, 359, 384.
M'Combichs, 384.
M'Connachy, Alexander, Balnamuik, 76.
—— —— lieutenant, 76.
M'Connie, Robert, brewer, 262.
M'Cook, Hercules, shoemaker, 14.
MacCormacks, 384.
MacCorquodales, 384.
M'Culloch, Roderick, of Glasstulich, 76, 299, 301, 328, 375.
—— William, servant, 266.
MacCullochs, 359.
M'Currathy, John, servant, 76.
M'Donald, Alexander, merchant, 14.
—— —— servant, 34, 118, 122, 336.
—— —— Inverness, 116.
—— —— captain, 116, 336.
—— —— officer, 116, 118, 336.
—— —— Dalnabo, 122.
—— —— of Glenco, 284.
—— —— of Keppoch, 284, 382.
—— Allan, brewer, 46.
—— —— officer, 116, 336.
—— —— Dalmloyn, 124.
—— Angus, captain, 116, 336.
—— —— servant, 120, 122, 124.
—— —— of Glengarry, 284, 286, 382, 386.
—— Archibald, of Glenaig, 284, 286.
—— Coll, Badivochal, 124.
—— Donald, lieutenant, 116.
—— —— of Lochgarry, 116, 284, 334.
—— —— of Scotas, 116, 334.
—— —— captain, 118, 284, 336.
—— —— officer, 118, 336.
—— —— Balintorn, 122.
—— —— of Sandaig, captain, 284.
—— —— officer, 284.
—— —— Hidehaugh, 313.
—— —— of Shian, 336, 389.
—— —— Inverness, 336.
—— Eneas, 383.
—— George, Nether Achdregnic, 124.

LIST OF REBELS.

M'Donald, James, tanner, 78.
—— —— Inveraven, 122.
—— —— Badivochal, 124.
—— —— Middle Achdregnie, 124.
—— —— officer, 284.
—— —— trader, 326, 388.
—— John, Balnamuik, 76.
—— —— of Arnabee, 116, 336.
—— —— Redorach, 120.
—— —— Achrachan, 122.
—— —— servant, 224.
—— —— Inverlochy, 280.
—— —— brewer, 286.
—— —— servant, 292.
—— Murdoch, Dingwall, 78.
—— Peter, Tomintowl, 120.
—— Robert, merchant, 122.
—— Ronald, servant, 16.
—— —— captain, 116, 336, 389.
—— —— officer, 116.
—— —— Morvern, 286.
—— —— Lochaber, 286.
—— —— officer, 286.
—— William, piper, 34, 314.
—— —— tailor, 122.
—— —— captain, 286.
—— —— of Kinloch Moidart, 286, 383.
Macdonald, Father, xiii.
MacDonalds, 357, 359, 376, 385.
M'Donell, Angusia, 386.
M'Dougal, Samuel, workman, 224.
MacDougalds, 359.
M'Duff, James, jun., of Forfechy, lieutenant, 224.
—— —— excise officer, 341.
M'Erich, Donald, piper, 284.
M'Erick, Archibald, 284.
M'Evan, John, Balacherach, 120.
M'Ewan, Donald, mason, 48.
—— James, 56.
—— John, shoemaker, 56.
—— —— lieutenant, 226.
MacEwens, 359.
M'Farlan, Duncan, deserter, 284.
M'Farlane, Alexander, doctor, 262.
—— John, tailor, 48.
—— —— servant, 56.
—— Thomas, smith, 318, 387.
M'Farlanes, 359.
M'Farquhar, Donald, 78, 330.
—— Farquhar, 78, 330.
—— John, lieutenant, 78, 330.
—— Kenneth, Red Castle, 78.
—— Roderick, captain, 78, 330.
—— William, in West Culmore, 78.
MacFarquhars, 359.
M'Gee, Hugh, sailor, 14.
M'Ghie, William, glazier, 144.

M'Gill, George, surgeon, 66, 352.
—— John, merchant, 345.
M'Gillavrae, Alexander, of Dimmaglass, 116, 336, 376.
—— —— captain, 116, 336.
M'Gillawray, Archibald, officer, 116.
—— Robert, officer, 116, 336.
MacGillivrays, 359.
M'Glashan, William, horse-hirer, 34.
M'Grar, Alexander, Foderleter, 122.
M'Grigor, Alexander, workman, 16.
—— —— tradesman, 58.
—— —— Roy, labourer, 58.
—— —— Inverachan, 122.
—— —— Balachnockan, 122.
—— Donald, town officer, 224.
—— Dougal, tradesman, 58.
—— Duncan, ensign, 14, 367.
—— Evan, Candelmore, 120.
—— Grigor, Loipuorn, 120.
—— —— Roy, deserter, 126.
—— John, Wester Gaulurg, 120.
—— —— gardener, 252, 340.
—— Malcom, Auchnahayl, 120.
—— —— Easter Gaulurg, 122.
—— —— of Cornour, 373.
—— Patrick, tradesman, 58.
—— William, Findran, 120.
M'Grigors, 175, 183, 359.
M'Growther (or Robertson), Alexander, xiv, xv.
M'Gurman, John, Wester Gaulurg, 120.
M'Hardie, William, Achrachan, 124.
M'Herioch, Duncan, Achosrigan, 284.
M'Humish, John, pedler, 58.
MacIldeus, 384.
M'Ildonick, James, Brackahy, 78.
M'Inhonnel, John, serjeant, 58.
M'Inish, Archibald, Maryburgh, 284.
—— Donald, Ballechelish, 284.
M'Innises, 384.
M'Intosh, Alexander, captain, 116.
—— Angus, of Pharr, 116, 336.
—— Duncan, officer, 118, 336.
—— John, East Inveroury, 122.
—— Lady, 117, 119.
—— Lauchlan, lieutenant-colonel, 116, 336.
—— Roy Bain, Leith, 342.
—— Simon, officer, 116.
—— Thomas, Daviot, 116.
—— William, servant, 224.
—— ——, 394.
M'Intosh's company, 104.
Mackintoshes, 359, 376, 401.
M'Intyre, Donald, servant, 78.
—— Duncan, brewer, 284.
—— —— officer, 46.

INDEX. 425

MacIntyres, 359, 384.
M'Iver, Alexander, serjeant, 78.
—— William, factor, 84.
M'Kaog, Patrick, Kerrera, 286.
M'Kay, Alexander, of Achmony, 330, 386, 388.
—— Donald, servant, 34.
—— John, merchant, 124.
—— —— ensign, 343.
—— Robert, serjeant, 122.
—— William, Philorth, 303, 305.
MacKays, 359.
M'Keamish, Kenneth, tenant, 270, 324.
M'Kenny, Kenneth, goldsmith, 338.
M'Kenzie, Alexander, officer, 76.
—— —— lieutenant, 76, 330, 389.
—— —— mason, 78.
—— —— grieve, 78.
—— —— merchant, 329.
—— of Ardloch, 330.
—— Alexander, of Lentorn, 76, 330, 389.
—— —— shoemaker, 252, 340.
—— Sir Alexander, of Coul, 331.
—— Alexander, of Ord, 331.
—— Colin, officer, 76, 328.
—— —— bailie, 78.
—— —— in Chapletoun, 78, 330.
—— —— of Lentorn, 76, 330, 389.
—— —— minister, 331.
—— David, smith, 331, 333.
—— Donald, mason, 34.
—— —— captain, 78, 330.
—— George, Auchternood, 78.
—— —— Kilmuir, 78, 330.
—— —— dyer, 329.
—— —— Allangrange, 331.
—— John, Red Castle, 78, 330, 331.
—— —— musician, 78.
—— —— of Tarriden, 330.
—— —— surgeon, 114.
—— —— Ruthven, 120.
—— —— merchant, 122.
—— —— Aldinlon, 122.
—— —— Ballachelish, 286.
—— —— Maryburgh, 286.
—— —— Ardua Crack, 331.
—— —— Inchavannan, 331.
—— Kenneth, captain, 76, 330.
—— —— servant, 120.
—— —— goldsmith, 252.
—— —— Hillend, 328.
—— —— of Lentorn, 76, 330, 389.
—— Lauchlan, in Miltown of Ord, 76.
—— Lord M'Leod, 76, 81, 375.
—— Murdoch, Dingwall, 78, 79.
—— —— Kissock, 333.
—— Patrick, servant, 224.
—— Roderick, merchant, 138.

M'Kenzie, Roderick, Hiltown, 329.
—— —— of Redcastle, 331, 333.
—— Theodore, Easter Culbocky, 78, 328.
—— Thomas, Redcastle, 78.
—— Mr. William, captain, 76, 330.
—— —— William, of Kilcoy, 76, 331.
—— —— Kennellan, 82.
—— —— Elgin, 114.
—— —— saltman, 138.
—— —— Echilty, 331.
Mackenzies, 360, 384.
M'Kettrick, James, excise officer, 347.
M'Kie, Robert, depute bailie, 317.
Mackie, Alexander, servant, 34.
—— —— Arbroath, 178.
—— John, Montrose, 321.
—— Peter, ensign, 16, 366.
—— Robert, servant, 180.
—— William, Montrose, 178, 320.
Mackies, 359.
M'Knoby, Archibald, servant, 262.
M'Lachy, James, Kilmoor, 330.
M'Lauchlan, Alexander, major, 284, 382.
—— —— captain, 284.
—— Colin, 394.
—— —— miller, 286.
—— Dougald, officer, 284.
—— Duncan Roy, Ardachork, 284.
—— ——, 284.
—— —— Ballemore, 284.
—— Ewen, Inversanda, 284.
—— James, lieutenant, 286.
—— John, wright, 318, 387.
—— —— Roy, brewer, 58.
—— —— Badivochal, 124.
—— —— brewer, 286.
—— —— weaver, 286.
—— Mr. John, of Kilchoan, 286.
—— Kenneth, of Kilinuchanich, 286.
—— Lauchlan, of that Ilk, 286.
—— —— of Inishconel, 286.
—— —— Appin, 286.
—— Neil, Balimore, 286.
—— Peter, weaver, 34.
M'Lauchlane, George, Calur, 124.
MacLauchlans, 360, 385.
M'Laren, Archibald, farmer, 58.
—— Daniel, excise officer, 106, 118.
—— David, Clackmannan, 349.
—— Donald, captain, 373.
—— doctor, Appin, 284.
—— Hugh, Appin, 284.
—— John, vintner, 116.
—— Lauchlan, doctor, Appin, 286.
MacLarens, 360, 384.
M'Lea, Alexander, serjeant, 122.
—— Allan, Badiglashean, 124.

M'Lea, James, Coull, 122.
— John, Clagan, 122.
— Robert, Coull, 122.
— William, Souie, 124.
MacLeas, 360, 385.
M'Lean, Alexander, apprentice, 46.
— — serjeant, 226.
— Allan, officer, 284.
— — lieutenant, 284.
— Charles, of Drimnan, 284, 286.
— Hector, servant, 252, 340.
— Hugh, captain, 284.
— John, servant, 14.
— — officer, 116, 336.
— — captain, 286.
— Lauchlan, officer, 286.
— Roderick, in Bridgehouse, 78.
MacLeans, 360.
M'Leish, John, 48.
— William, servant, 340, 389.
M'Lellan, William, purse master, 319.
M'Lenan, John, vintner, 334, 389.
M'Lennan, Alexander, 77.
— Daniel, excise officer, 337.
— Donald, Gurgastoun, 78.
— Kenneth, Kilmuir, 78, 330.
MacLennans, 360.
M'Leod, Alexander, Muiravonside, 266, 330, 389.
— Mr. John, advocate, 266.
MacLeod, Laird of, 31, 35, 37, 93.
MacLeods, 23, 89, 99, 358, 360.
M'Mahon, lieutenant Morgan, 397.
M'Nab, Donald, farmer, 58.
MacNabs, 360.
M'Nair, Robert, merchant, 347.
M'Naughton, John, watchmaker, 252.
M'Near, James, slater, 317.
— — jun., 317.
— Robert, Falkirk, 317.
M'Neill, Neil, captain, of Machrihanish, 327.
M'Niccol, Duncan, brewer, 319.
— William, workman, 224.
M'Nully, Farquhar, in Bewly, 76.
M'Pherson, Alexander, farmer, 120.
— — Achrachan, 124.
— Andrew, jun., of Banachar, 118, 336.
— Angus, farmer, 118.
— Donald, captain, 118, 336.
— — merchant, 118.
— Evan, of Clunie, 118, 336, 358, 377.
— — officer, 118, 336.
— jun., lieutenant-colonel, 118, 336.
— of Strathmasy, 118, 336.
— Hugh, officer, 118, 336.

M'Pherson, John, lieutenant, 118, 336.
— — captain, 118, 336.
— — officer, 118, 336.
— — farmer, 120.
— — Achrachan, 120.
— — Foderleter, 122.
— Kenneth, officer, 118, 336.
— Lauchlan, jun., of Strathmashie, 118, 336.
— — farmer, 118, 336.
— Lewis, major, 118, 336.
— Mal, Dow, farmer, 118.
— Malcolm, sen., of Phoyness, 118, 336.
— — younger, 389.
— Paul, St. Skola, 124.
— — Dalwhiny, 118.
— Thomas, servant, 122.
— William, farmer, 120.
— — wigmaker, 120.
Macphersons, 360, 377.
M'Phun, Archibald, tailor, 284.
M'Queen, Alexander, quarter-master, 120.
M'Ra, Alexander, lieutenant, 34, 314.
MacRaes, 360.
M'Rankens, 384.
M'Robie, John, 48.
— Lewis, 48.
— William, Morings, 122.
— — Tormachork, 122.
MacRobies, 360.
M'Tavis, John, of Gartenbeg, officer, 116.
M'Tavish, Alexander, officer, 116.
MacTavishes, 360.
MacUchaders, 384.
M'Urrachy, John, Urra, 330.
MacVicar, Mr., minister, 402.
M'Viccar, David, Clackmanan, 349.
— William, Clackmanan, 349.
M'Vie, George, smith, 319.
M'Willie, David, Achrachan, 120.
— Dun, East Corrie, 122.
— James, servant, 120.
M'William, Donald, Balavalick, 76.
— John, Balavalick, 76.
— — in Kilmorack, 78.
— Thomas, in Platchaick, 78.
MacWilliams, 360.
Maiden, —, surgeon, 66, 352.
Main, Alexander, servant, 176.
— George, servant, 176.
— James, brewer, 148, 348, 349.
— William, Panmuir, 224.
Mair, James, servant, 34.
— William, farmer, 16.
— — factor, 176.
Maitland, David, 393, 400.
— Mr. John, factor, 180

INDEX. 427

Maitland, Mr., of Pitrichie, 7, 19.
—— William, surgeon, 327.
Malcolm, James, jun., of Balbeddie, 262, 344.
Malcom, William, weaver, 34.
—— —— workman, 224.
Malt tax, xi.
Man, Alexander, servant, 34.
—— —— Grange, 114.
—— —— jun., servant, 226.
—— James, baker, 48.
—— —— farmer, 114.
—— John, shoemaker, 48.
—— William, servant, 78, 330.
—— —— Templand, 78, 330.
Manchester, x.
Mansie, James, jun., Ballfield, 178.
Manson, John, bailie, 329.
Mapsie, Alexander. Craill, 353.
Marischal, Earl, 87.
—— estate of, 175.
Marr, Alexander, flesher, 14.
—— David, flesher, 14.
—— Jo., 401.
—— Robert, tidesman, 14.
—— Thomas, mason, 34, 314.
Marshall, James, officer, 224.
—— John, labourer, 148, 348.
—— —— writer, 148, 348.
—— ——, 307.
—— William, Dundee, 212.
Martin, Alexander, Camdelmore, 120.
—— David, weaver, 178, 320.
—— George, Tomachlagan, 120.
—— James, 313.
—— John, ensign, 14.
—— ——, 46.
—— —— weaver, 176, 322.
—— —— Mortleck, 313.
Mason, James, quarter-master, 178.
—— Janet, Pittenweem, 353.
—— John, Powbare, 176.
Massie, Robert, Tarriff, 310, 387.
Masterman, Henry, xiv.
Masterton, Andrew, weaver, 226.
—— Francis, of Parkhill, 148, 348, 350.
Mather, Alexander, brewer, 178.
—— Charles, ploughman, 222.
—— —— wright, 224.
—— James, ensign, 180.
Mathers, David, Brechin, 180.
—— baker, 180.
—— —— George, Brechin, 180, 307.
Matheson, Alexander, labourer, 94, 305, 307.
—— David, tailor, 34.
—— —— labourer, 94.
Mathew, James, 305.
Mathie, James, servant, 178.

Matthew, Peter, farmer, 114.
Maul, Henry, writer, 252.
—— —— clerk, 266.
—— John, ensign, 176.
—— Peter, workman, 176.
Maver, James, Turriff, 34, 310.
—— William, Turriff, 34, 40, 310.
Maxwell, James, of Kirkconnal, 142, 144.
—— —— of Barncleugh, 144.
—— Lady Katharine, 144.
—— Robert, writer, 252, 340.
—— William, of Carruchan, 144, 145.
—— —— of Barncleugh, 144.
—— —— Earl of Nithsdale, 144.
—— Sir William, of Sprinkell, 144.
Meal, John, ploughman, 222.
Mearns, county of, 155, 181, 191.
Meathie, Laird of, 229, 235.
Medison, Alexander, Bulzeon, 224.
Meldrum, Old, district of, xvi, 84, 302, 361, 376, 386.
—— Robert, 393.
Melvill, William, brewer, 353.
Mensat, John, weaver, 124.
Menzies, David, Pitfodels, 16.
—— Gilbert, of Pitfodels, 16, 300.
—— James, Pitfodels, 16.
—— John, 16.
—— —— paymaster, 266.
—— Mr. John, captain, 252.
—— Mr., of Pitfodels, 16.
—— —— laird of, 400.
—— Robert, innkeeper, 266.
—— William, 16.
—— —— of Shian, 46, 267, 358.
Menzieses, 360.
Mercer, James, 367.
—— Laurence, of Lethenday, 226, 378.
—— Sir Laurence, of Aldie, 378.
—— Robert, of Aldie, 148, 226, 348, 350, 378.
Mercers of Aldie, 367.
Merchant, Roderick, excise officer, 112, 114, 126, 130, 335.
Mercier, Thomas, *aid du-camp*, 14, 300, 367.
Merns, Alexander, labourer, 94.
Methlick, parish of, 307.
Michie, John, West Achwauh, 124.
Middleton, Alexander, wright, 66.
—— James, labourer, 16.
—— —— Ballandie, 122.
—— Patrick, surgeon, 252.
—— Robert, porter, 92.
—— Samuel, labourer, 16.
—— William, labourer, 16.
—— —— baxter, 176.
Midmar, parish of, 7.

LIST OF REBELS.

Miles, James, ploughman, 222.
—— —— workman, 224.
Mill, Alexander, of Newmilln. 58, 316.
—— —— shepherd, 178.
—— David, 58, 316.
—— —— servant, 224.
—— —— weaver, 224.
—— George, labourer, 14.
—— —— lieutenant, 178.
—— James, ploughman, 222.
—— John, vagabond, 178.
—— Robert, ploughman, 222.
—— Thomas, 58, 316.
—, —— Leith, 247.
—— William, merchant, 94.
Millar, Charles, 394.
Miller, Alexander, servant, 252.
—— David, jun., shoemaker, 180.
—— Duncan, weaver, 178.
—— James, horse-hirer, 224.
—— —— brewer, 224, 226.
—— —— writer, 339.
—— John, ploughman, 222.
—— Robert, Balmor, 347.
—— William, Inshnkep, 120.
—— —— sailor, 224.
—— —— brewer, 326, 388.
Million, Alexander, shoemaker, 16.
Miln, George Balcathie, 158.
—— James, merchant, 323.
—— John, Skihowhead, 176.
—— —— wright, 176.
—— —— merchant, 325.
—— Thomas, mason, 341.
—— William, of Bonnytoun, 178.
Milne, David, Cotbank, 178.
—— George, innkeeper, 34, 310, 387.
—— —— jun., 34, 310.
—— —— Croft of Inverlochy, 122.
—— James, mason, 34.
—— —— Landends, 222.
—— —— jun., Landends, 222.
—— John, servant, 34.
—— —— Cotbank, 178.
—— Robert, servant, 222.
—— Thomas, workman, 224.
—— William, 34, 304.
—— —— Turriff, 310.
—— —— shipmaster, 321.
Mitchel, Colin, goldsmith, 339.
—— Duncan, carrier, 318, 387.
Mitchell, Alexander, farmer, 34.
—— —— ploughman, 222.
—— Donald, slater, 318, 387.
—— George, workman, 16.
—— —— Mains, 313.
—— James, workman, 16.
—— —— weaver, 34.
—— John, Fetterneir, xvii, 182, 187, 322.

Mitchell, John, drummer, 224.
—— —— wright, 226.
—— —— servant, 252, 340.
—— —— merchant, 319.
—— Murdoch, servant, 78.
—— Robert, serjeant, 14.
—— —— brewer, 180, 193, 322.
—— —— goldsmith, 252, 338.
—— —— merchant, 319.
—— Roderick, shoemaker, 116, 334.
—— Thomas, serjeant, 224.
—— —— goldsmith, 252, 340.
—— William, farmer, 94.
—— —— saltman, 138.
Moffat, 145.
Mohawks, vii.
Moidart, xiii.
Moir, Charles, captain, 14, 300.
—— James, of Stonywood, 14, 91, 300, 364, 367.
—— —— shoemaker, 14.
—— —— Longside, 307.
—— John, labourer, 16.
—— (More) John, Templand, 78, 330.
—— —— Aikimore, 124.
—— —— jun., 124.
—— Kenneth, brogmaker, 76.
—— Robert, 280.
—— William, of Longmay, 14, 92, 94, 95, 300, 304.
—— —— sailor, 92.
Mollison, Robert, barber, 176.
Moncrieffe, N. D., xiv.
Moncrife, Thomas, excise officer, 46.
Moncur, John, servant, 176.
Moncurr, Andrew, weaver, 224.
—— Patrick, Navoy, 222.
Money, George, ploughman, xviii, 222.
Moneymusk, parish of, 299.
Monquhitter, parish of, 370.
Monro, Donald, farmer, 120.
—— Sir Robert, 400.
Monteith, Alexander, wool sorter, 148, 348.
——, 148.
Montgomery, Francis, barber, 341.
—— Hugh, ferrier, 327.
—— Peter, sadler, 34.
—— Robert, beggar, 14.
Montrose, district of, xvi, xvii, 150, 320, 361, 388.
—— town of, 151, 153, 157, 163, 167, 169, 171, 175, 179, 183, 189, 193, 199, 321, 351.
Moodie, James, Auchmithie, 178.
—— Thomas, ploughman, 222.
—— —— weaver, 224.
Moor, William, horse-hirer, 224.
Morar, loch, 374.
More, Peter, Knockindo, 122.

INDEX. 429

Morgan, Charles, labourer, 94.
—— David, servant, 224.
—— John, tailor, 176.
—— William, glover, 176.
Morice, John, Miln of Fiddess, 307.
Morison, David, brewer, 339, 341.
—— Henry, excise officer, 341, 343.
—— John, servant, 34, 311.
—— Richard, barber, 252, 380.
—— William, servant, 34, 311.
Morris, Helen, servant, 353.
—— John, Craill, 353.
Morrise, James, labourer, 94.
Morrison, Alexander, 34.
—— —— farmer, 34, 310, 311.
—— —— sailor, 94, 304.
Mortleck, parish of, 313.
Morton, Sir Robert, 401.
Mossman, Thomas, writer, 14.
Mouat, William, Montrose, 178, 320.
Mowat, George, land waiter, 325.
Moy Hall, 376.
Muir, Adolphus, servant, 252, 340.
—— Alexander, serjeant, 122.
—— John, Burdstone, 347.
—— Robert, writer, 14.
—— William, Burdstone, 347.
Muirison, provost, of Aberdeen, 305.
Mullican, William, brewer, 325.
Munie, Thomas, ploughman, 222.
Murdoch, William, ensign, 58.
Murray, Anthony, of Grange, 148, 348, 350.
—— —— goldsmith, 252, 338.
—— Earl of, 146.
—— Sir David, captain, 252, 340, 380.
—— —— Hamilton, 343.
—— Lord George, 46, 252, 267, 358, 359, 366, 369, 371, 373, 400.
—— James, merchant, 58, 316, 387.
—— —— cooper, 176.
—— —— surgeon, 252, 380.
—— —— tailor, 339.
—— John, 58.
—— —— of Broughton, 84, 244, 376.
—— —— 135.
—— —— clerk, 148, 348.
—— —— surgeon, 252.
—— —— fisher, 323.
—— Lord John, 42.
—— of Dollarie, 48, 372.
—— Lewis, excise officer, 171.
—— Lady Margaret, 372.
—— Mungo, secretary, 226.
—— Mr. of Kincairnie, 226.
—— Peter, servant, 14.
—— Robert, writer, 252.
—— William, postmaster, 46.
—— —— weaver, 176.
Mushet, William, wright, 252, 340.

Musselburgh, 141.
—— gaol, 391, 396.
Mutch, George, labourer, 94.
—— John, labourer, 94.
Muthill, 370.

NAIRN, JOHN, Lord, 74, 148, 200, 201, 206, 213, 226, 236, 372.
Nairne, Mrs. Amelia, 372.
Napier, John, mason, 48.
Nash, John, servant, 226.
—— William, servant, 226.
Nasmith, Betty, 349.
Neavy, David, merchant, 254.
Neil, Thomas, servant, 226.
Netherbow Port, 255.
Nevay, David, servant, 226.
Newburgh, 89.
Newby, Anthony, excise officer, 349.
Newcastle, Duke of, xi.
——, 381.
Newgate, 378.
Newport (Paisley), 326.
Newton, R. Hay, of Newton, 377.
Nicholas, the emperor, ix.
Niccol, James, Avoch, 80, 330.
—— —— tailor, 182.
—— Robert, mason, 340.
—— Thomas, workman, 48.
Nicoll, David, stabler, 353.
Nicolson, Alexander, 124.
—— James, coffeehouse-keeper, 254, 380.
—— Patrick, minister, Kiltarlaty, 329.
—— William, servant, 34.
Niddry, Andrew, jun., weaver, 94.
Nisbet, William, farmer, 94, 305, 307.
Nithsdale, Earl of, 144.
Nivie, James, merchant, 16.
Noble, Donald, Redcastle, 331, 333.
Norald, Adam, labourer, 94.
Nuccol, Robert, mason, 254.

OAT, HENRY, jun., mason, 318, 387.
Oatt, William, Down, 318, 387.
Obrolochon, Archibald, tailor, 327.
Ogg, William, labourer, 16.
Ogilvie (Ogilvy), Agnes, 367.
—— Alexander, of Auchiries, 94, 96, 304, 376.
—— —— Braes, 228.
—— Sir Alexander, of Forglen, 367.
—— Alexander, shoemaker, 36.
—— Lord, 33, 151, 153, 159, 167, 169, 175, 179, 181, 187, 191, 195, 199, 201, 243.
Ogilvy, David, labourer, 226.
—— —— of Pool, 228, 379.
—— —— captain, 228.

LIST OF REBELS.

Ogilvy, David, lieutenant, 228.
—— Henry, innkeeper, 228.
—— James, labourer, 226.
—— —— lieutenant, 228.
—— —— servant, 228.
—— —— tinker, 228.
—— Sir John, 220, 226.
—— John, Auchires, 96, 304.
—— —— of Inshoan, captain, 228.
—— —— captain, 228.
—— —— of Quick, ensign, 228.
—— —— of Roughill, lieutenant, 228.
—— Patrick, servant, 36.
—— Thomas, captain, 226.
—— —— of East Miln, 226, 399.
—— —— lieutenant, 228.
—— Walter, officer, 36.
—— William, merchant, 16.
—— —— Auchires, 96, 304.
—— —— Meikle Kenny, 202.
—— —— servant, 228.
—— —— captain, 228.
—— —— dyster, 228.
Ogilvies, 360.
Ogstoun, James, weaver, 266.
Ogston, William, 305.
Oldman, James, labourer, 96.
Oliphant, Alexander, brewer, 353.
—— Caroline, 372.
—— Laurance, of Gask, 47, 48, 372.
—— —— younger, 48, 372.
—— Thomas, wright, 66, 352.
Oram, Alexander, vintner, 66, 352, 353.
Ord, James, wigmaker, 36.
Orkney, John, merchant, 184, 320, 388.
—— —— shipmaster, 320.
Orrock, Walter, shoemaker, 254, 340.
Orrok, John, land waiter, 228.
Osburn, Robert, excise officer, 341.
Ouchterlony, John, apprentice, 184, 320.
—— —— mason, 228.
—— Peter, coffeehouse-keeper, 228, 351.

PAISLEY, district of, xvi, 292, 326, 361, 388.
—— parish of, 326.
Palmer, Robert, workman, 230.
—— William, 230.
Panmuir, estate of, 159, 181.
—— Lord, 218.
Panton, Alexander, innkeeper, 36, 310.
Paris, 367, 371, 373, 383.
Park, John, shoemaker, 341.
—— William, shoemaker, 341.
Paterson, Alexander, labourer, 18, 299.

Paterson, Alexander, officer, 230.
—— —— servant, 230.
—— Andrew, Kessock, 80.
—— —— jun., Kessock, 80, 323.
—— Archibald, Congary, 327.
—— Charles, servant, 254, 340.
—— David, Dearsie, 353.
—— Donald, sen., East Kessock, 80, 332.
—— —— jun., East Kessock, 80, 332.
—— Fra., excise officer, 341.
—— George, householder, 36.
—— —— New Durn, 314.
—— Hercules, officer, 36, 312.
—— James, 31, 37, 41.
—— —— workman, 230.
—— John, Redcastle, 80.
—— Lauchlane, Redcastle, 80, 323.
—— Margaret, Kinnet, 349.
—— Murdoch, Redcastle, 80, 332.
—— Robert, labourer, 96.
—— Thomas, excise officer, 349.
Paton, George, shoemaker, 16.
—— —— excise officer, 351.
—— James, brewer, 349.
—— John, servant, 84.
—— Marjory, Down, 319.
—— William, Tomintowl, 124.
Pattie, James, servant, 68.
Patullo, George, ensign, 230.
—— Mr. Henry, muster-master, xv, 230, 359.
Paul, George, 305.
Pearson, John, wright, 349.
Peck, Thomas, excise officer, 351.
Peddie, John, merchant, 184.
Peddy, John, workman, 230.
Peirie, Alexander, labourer, 96.
—— Charles, 96, 307.
Penston, Robert, gardener, 138.
Perrie, John, Elgin, 124, 336.
Perth, district of, xvi, 29, 42, 51, 73, 147, 183, 213, 227, 239, 293, 361, 370.
—— town of, 371, 379, 397.
—— Duke of, x, xvi, 29, 43, 45, 145, 247, 251, 371.
Peterborough, Earl of, 366.
Peterhead, 5, 9, 15, 21.
Peterloo, vii.
Peterson, James, sheriff officer, 184.
Petrie, Andrew, workman, 230.
—— James, xvii, 18, 300.
—— John, alehouse-keeper, 254, 340, 380.
—— —— Milnton, 323.
—— William, Portsoy, 314, 387.
Philp, John, carrier, 230.
—— Robert, shoemaker, 66, 352.
—— William, weaver, 16.

INDEX.   431

Picken, James, innkeeper, 347.
Pierson, Alexander, shipmaster, 184.
Piery, John, servant, 84, 312, 387.
Piggot, Alexander, servant, 228.
—— workman, 230.
Pirie, John, Roscarty, 303, 305, 307.
Pirrey, William, shoemaker, 309, 313.
Pirrie, Andrew, labourer, 96, 307.
—— Charles, Craighall, 307.
Pitcalny, laird of, 75, 235.
Pith, James, porter, 254, 340.
Pitsligo, Lord, ii, 302, 358, 387.
—— parish of, 305, 307.
Pollock, William, writer, 327.
Porteous, George, excise officer, 339, 341, 343.
Porteous riots, ix.
Porter, James, 309.
—— William, excise officer, 104, 112, 114, 126, 311, 335.
Porteus, Andrew, of Burnfoot, 138, 377.
—— Samuel, salt officer, 138.
Portsoy, 29.
Powis, laird of, 58.
Powrie, John, shoemaker, 48.
Premney, parish of, 305, 307.
Prestonpans, xv, 49, 61-71, 87-99, 133-139, 147, 149, 199, 205, 207, 213, 217, 219, 229, 239, 245, 253-258, 261, 263, 275-277, 287, 289, 357, 364, 369, 376, 380, 400.
Pretender's army, xv-xvii, etc.
Primrose, Sir Archibald, of Dunipace, 58, 373.
—— George, of Dunipace, 373.
—— Janet, Dalkeith, 138.
—— John, excise officer 138.
Pringle, Fra., excise officer, 339, 341.
Prophet, Thomas, workman, 228.
Protestantism, xi, xiii.
Punton, John, porter, 254, 340.
Purdie, James, skinner, 341.
Pyot, Alexander, wright, 184, 388.
—— David, wright, 320, 388.

Rae, James, barber, 317.
Raith, James, barber, 317.
Ramoch, 382.
Ramsay, Alexander, merchant, 96, 306.
—— —— shoemaker, 186.
—— Christopher, labourer, 138.
—— David, workman, 232, 305, 307.
—— —— sailor, 345.
—— George, weaver, 232.
—— James, servant, 18.
—— —— tailor, 234.

Ramsay, James, farmer, Sigget, 311.
—— John, pendicleman, 234.
—— Kenneth, labourer, 96.
—— Robert, weaver, 232.
—— —— tailor, 339, 341.
—— William, labourer, 96.
—— —— workman, 230.
Ranken, Duncan, East Corran, 280.
Rannie, John, labourer, 96, 313.
—— Peter, serjeant, xvii, 184.
—— William, salt officer, 140.
—— —— Braefoot, 313.
Ranny, George, blacksmith, 313.
Rattray, Charles, of Dunoon, 232, 351.
—— —— ensign, 232.
—— Henry, servant, 232.
—— James, apprentice, 50.
—— —— of Corb., major, 232, 379.
—— —— clerk, 232.
—— John, Balno, 126.
—— —— of Dunoon, 199.
Rea, Charles, workman, 230.
—— James, servant, 232.
—— Robert, of Littlegovan, 347.
Reat, Dr., Dundee, 232.
—— William, surgeon, 232.
Redpath, Thomas, salt officer, 138.
Reid, Sir Alexander, of Barra, 18, 367.
—— Alexander, captain, 368.
—— —— servant, 80, 126, 186, 332.
—— —— goldsmith, 254, 340.
—— —— shoemaker, 331.
—— Barbara, 368.
—— David, workman, 230.
—— Donald, labourer, 18.
—— George, in Templand, 80, 332.
—— —— mason, 184, 322.
—— —— cottarman, 186.
—— Helen, 368.
—— James, salt officer, 140, 252.
—— —— innkeeper, 340.
—— —— gardener, 347, 368.
—— John, stabler, 18, 368.
—— —— Petfoord, 80, 81.
—— —— jun., Petfoord, 80, 332.
—— Katherine, servant, 353.
—— Peter, brewer, 184.
—— Robert, merchant, 18, 300, 367.
—— —— mason, 18.
—— —— jun., servant, 18.
—— —— jun., shoemaker, 186.
—— William, 368.
—— —— groom, 234.
—— —— bailie, 315.
—— —— miller, 331.
—— (Mrs. Skeen) 68, 352.
Renfrew, county of, 326, 327.
Renwick, Andrew, servant, 230.

Reoch, Alexander, Galurg, 126.
—— Donald, in Bogg, 73, 75, 80, 329, 331, 333.
—— —— jun., Culmores, 126.
—— —— Eliet, 126.
—— James, servant, 126.
—— John (*alias* Ross), sailor, 80.
—— —— West Foderleter, 126.
—— —— cooper, 232.
—— —— serjeant, 232.
Retty, James, servant, 184.
Rhind, John, brewer, 126.
—— William, workman, 184.
Richie, Peter, servant, 186.
Richy, Andrew, horse-hirer, 18.
Riddel, Adolphus, glazier, 254, 340.
Riddell, John, of Grange, 138.
Riddoch, James, 50.
Ridoch, Patrick, slater, 318, 387.
Rieth, Alexander, tailor, 18.
Ritchie, Alexander, threadmaker, 184.
—— —— Methlick, 303, 305, 307.
—— James, horse-hirer, 234.
—— John, of Sinks, 58.
—— —— pilot, 184, 322.
—— —— merchant, 321.
—— William, chapman, 186.
Rob, John, town officer, 347.
Robb, James, servant, 18, 232.
—— William, Burkhill, 174.
Roben, William, servant, 232.
Robert, Alexander, Bervie, 186.
Robertson, Alexander, labourer, 18.
—— (M'Growther), xiv, xv.
—— —— merchant, 184.
—— —— Gallowtown, 184.
—— —— servant, 184.
—— —— of Raimore, 232.
—— —— merchant, 232.
—— —— of Strowan, 48, 372.
—— Charles, officer, 48.
—— —— Balmlagan, 126, 232.
—— —— farmer, 232.
—— —— officer, 234.
—— David, of Bletton, 232.
—— Donald, of Woodsheel, 48.
—— —— workman, 230.
—— Duncan, of Drumaheen, 48, 372.
—— —— merchant, 234.
—— George, of Faskily, 48, 372.
—— —— excise officer, 339, 341.
—— —— servant, 353.
—— James, servant, 36.
—— —— of Gillichangie, 48.
—— —— jun., of Killichangie, 48.
—— —— of Blairfethy, 48, 372.
—— —— weaver, 60, 316.
—— —— servant, 184.
—— —— groom, 266.
—— John, wright, 18, 80, 332.

Robertson, John, labourer, 96.
—— —— of Crandirth, 230.
—— —— servant, 232.
—— Joseph, minister, 137, 138.
—— Laurance, mason, 50.
—— major, Emock, 347.
—— Patrick, servant, 36.
—— —— merchant, 319.
—— Peter, piper, 36.
—— —— apprentice, 232.
—— Robert, brewer, 138.
—— Thomas, captain, 50.
—— —— servant, 256, 340.
—— —— barber, 276, 346.
—— William (*alias* Bickers), 186.
—— —— Leven, 262.
Robertsone, Robert, 394.
Robertsons, 360.
Robins, Thomas, founder, 347.
Robison, George, servant, 353.
—— John, innkeeper, 36.
—— William, Johnshaven, 322.
Roger, John, servant, 232.
—— Peter, servant, 232.
Rolland, John, bailie, 349.
Rollo, David, 58, 316.
—— James, 58, 316.
Romanism, ix.
Ronald, John, fisher, 184.
—— William, merchant, 184.
Ross, Alexander, farmer, 18.
—— —— servant, 36.
—— —— sheriff clerk, 329, 331.
—— —— Milntown of Newtarbet, 331, 333.
—— Andrew, excise officer, 114, 333.
—— Angus (*alias* M'William), Tain, 80.
—— Charles, serjeant, 36.
—— David, town clerk, Tain, 329, 331.
—— Francis, surgeon, 96.
—— Hugh, labourer, 18.
—— —— Balavalich, 80.
—— —— turner, 124, 336.
—— —— Tain, 329.
—— James, ensign, 18, 300.
—— —— sen., sheriff officer, 18.
—— —— jun., drummer, 18.
—— —— Knockbreak, 80.
—— John, officer, 18, 300.
—— —— flesher, 18.
—— —— mason, 80.
—— —— farmer, 126.
—— —— servant, 126.
—— —— excise officer, 353.
—— Malcom, Arboll, 332, 389.
—— Robert, gardener, 18.
—— —— porter, 18.
—— —— kirk beadle, 126.
—— —— Tamorlan, 126.

Ross, Ronald, Miltown of Ord, 80.
—— Thomas, wright, 36.
—— —— Tain, 80.
—— —— Master of, 81.
—— ——, 394.
—— William (*alias* Reoch), 80, 332.
—— —— Ruthven, 126.
—— district of, xvi, 19, 72, 328, 361, 374, 386, 388.
—— county of, 329.
Rosses, 360.
Rough, Alexander, servant, 232.
—— Thomas, 230.
Roxburgh, William, bailie, 349.
Roy, Duncan, 50.
—— John, servant, 36, 104, 230, 312.
Royal Scots regiment, 371.
Royston, Lord, 79.
Rue, David, gentleman, 68, 374.
Russel, Alexander, Fraserburgh, 303, 305.
—— Hugh, apprentice, 18.
Russell, John, weaver, 234.
Rutherford, James, goldsmith, 256, 340.
—— Robert, shoemaker, 254.
Ruthven, 100, 106, 112, 118, 120.
—— laird of, 205.
Ryan, James, officer of excise, 303.

SALTER, DAVID, victualler, 236.
Sampson, William, serjeant, 236.
Sandilands, Jean, 364.
—— Patrick, of Cottoun, 364.
—— Robert, captain, 20, 300.
Sandyman, Andrew, workman, 188.
Sangster, John, servant, 236.
—— William, labourer, 96.
Sanyson, Peter, labourer, 22.
Sardinia, king of, 371.
Saunders, John, messenger, 313.
Schaw, Alexander, captain, 236.
—— James, servant, 236.
Schoola, George, farmer, 323.
Scot, Alexander, labourer, 96.
—— Car, 401.
—— Francis, barber, 280.
—— William, servant, 38, 312.
—— —— of Auchtydonald, 91.
—— —— farmer, 96, 247.
Scotland, ix, xiii.
—— lowlands of, x.
—— west of, x.
Scott, Charles, ploughman, 234.
—— —— chamberlain, 280.
—— David, tailor, 188.
—— —— servant, 188.
—— —— pendickleman, 234.
—— George, porter, 256, 342.
—— James, workman, 52.

Scott, James, servant, 347.
—— John, sailor, 20, 300.
—— —— mason, 52.
—— —— governor, 157.
—— —— cooper, 188.
—— —— governor, 188, 320.
—— —— wright, 317.
—— Mr. of Rossie, 151.
—— Robert, baxter, 256, 342.
Scrogy, Robert, servant, 20.
Seaton, Andrew, chapman, 236.
Selkirk, 245.
Semple, Francis, corporal, 288.
—— James, weaver, 266.
Seton, Alexander, merchant, 262, 344, 389.
—— Christopher, merchant, 262, 344.
—— David, greive, 262.
—— James, apprentice, 262.
—— John, baxter, 262.
—— Robert, Edinburgh, 256.
—— William, nonjuror, 234.
—— —— W.S., 256.
Sey, John, 305.
Shaddon, Charles, coal grieve, 266.
Shand, William, servant, 38.
Shanks, Alexander, Chapple Garty, 186.
—— David, weaver, 188.
—— John, weaver, 188.
Sharp, Alexander, 374.
—— William, gentleman, 68, 374.
Shaw, Duncan, factor, 234.
—— James, officer, 126, 336.
—— John, fidler, 20, 299, 301.
—— William, of Forter, 236.
Sheepherd, Charles, shoemaker, 236.
—— David, servant, 188.
—— John, captain, 186.
—— —— servant, 188.
Shepherd, Thomas, Cambuck Miln, 353.
Sherrif, John, tidesman, 20.
Sherriff, Andrew, salt officer, 140.
Shewan, John, Braehead, 305.
Shirras, Thomas, Fraserburgh, 307.
Shives, Alexander, labourer, 96.
Showster, John, indweller, 50.
Shunger, John, ploughman, 234.
Sibbald, Charles, gentleman, 68, 352.
—— James, 397.
Siddall, Thomas, xiv.
Sill, James, serjeant, 20.
Simpson, Adam, cottar, 38.
—— Andrew, drummer, 236.
—— James, servant, 20, 299, 301.
—— —— writer, 256.
—— —— Cellardyke, 353.
—— John, lieutenant, 38, 312.
—— —— brewer, 60, 316.

Simpson, John, servant, 234.
—— Kenneth, Dunvarny, 82, 332.
—— Patrick, West Dod, 234.
—— William, workman, 234.
—— —— Hamilton, 343.
Sinclair, Æneas, 50.
—— Benjamin, tenant, 270, 324.
—— George, of Geese, 270, 324.
—— James, Stobo, 84, 299, 301.
—— John, fiddler, 36.
—— Lord, 29.
—— William, salt officer, 140.
Skeen, Mrs. (or Reid), xvii, 68, 352.
Skien, John, tailor, 38, 312, 352.
Skinner, John, Anstruther, 353.
Slains, parish of, 305, 307.
Sloss, John, excise officer, 343.
Smart, James, 309, 311.
—— John, 309, 311.
—— Walter, workman, 188.
Smith, Alexander, labourer, 20.
—— —— of Meany, 306, 387.
—— —— servant, 38.
—— —— labourer, 96.
—— —— farmer, 188.
—— —— servant, 188.
—— —— barber, 188.
—— —— Linlithgow, 268.
—— —— writer, 268.
—— Andrew, Achnascra, 128.
—— —— servant, 234.
—— Daniel, lieutenant, 20, 300.
—— David, sailor, 186, 320.
—— —— servant, 234.
—— Francis, sen., servant, 20.
—— —— jun., 20.
—— George, farmer, 38.
—— —— lieutenant, 186.
—— Hugh, Brackachy, 332, 389.
—— James, workman, 20.
—— —— writer, 36.
—— —— labourer, 96.
—— —— writer, 256, 380.
—— —— clerk to the Signet, 393, 399.
—— Janet, Knockyburns, 309, 313.
—— John, labourer, 96.
—— —— carter, 126.
—— —— merchant, 126.
—— —— cooper, 188.
—— —— of Ballcharry, 236.
—— —— excise officer, 339, 341.
—— Peter, labourer, 20.
—— —— Bewley, 332, 389.
—— Robert, servant, 20.
—— —— Inverury, 128.
—— Thomas, writer, 268.
—— William, carrier, 38, 50.
—— —— labourer, 96.

Smith, William, farmer, 126.
—— —— skinner, 126.
—— —— thread maker, 188.
—— —— pilot, 190, 322.
—— —— wright, 210.
—— —— Kirrymuir, 222, 275.
Souter, Dougald, messenger at arms, 256, 340.
—— John, labourer, 96, 306.
Southesk, estate, 159, 181.
Soutor, James, servant, 190.
Spalding, Peter, goldsmith, 256, 341.
Spanish Ship, 5, 9, 15, 21.
Spark, Alexander, Canongate, 339.
—— William, porter, 256, 257, 342.
Speed, George, servant, 188.
Spens, John, labourer, 96.
Sprewl, Andrew, captain, 278, 346, 381.
Sprott, Mark, skinner, 341.
Squair, John, weaver, 318, 387.
St. Andrews, district of, xvi, 62, 352, 361, 373.
St. Cyrus, parish, 175.
St. Margaret's, Westminster, 369, 381-383.
St. Nicholas' church, 363.
St. Ninian's, church of, 400.
Stalker, John, 50.
—— Peter, servant, 50.
Stark, Alexander, servant, 234.
—— William, weaver, 234.
Stead, Thomas, maltster, 190.
Steedman, Alexander, provost, 345.
Steen, William, Clackmanan, 349.
Steill, George, merchant, 20, 300.
Stephen, Alexander, porter, 353.
—— John, wright, 320, 388.
—— William, merchant, 126.
Steuart, James, wigmaker, 38.
Stewart, Alan, Ardnamurchan, 384.
—— —— Mor, Ardsheil, 383.
—— —— Invernohyle, 384.
—— —— Ballachelish, 384.
—— Alexander, of Acharn, 383.
—— —— of Achnacone, 288, 384.
—— —— of Auchoily, 20, 368.
—— —— of Invernachyle, 286, 383, 384.
—— —— captain, 286.
—— —— officer, 286.
—— —— captain, 288.
—— —— of Ballechalish, captain, 288, 383.
—— Allan, serjeant, 286, 288.
—— —— captain, 286.
—— —— vintner, 319.
—— Ann, 377.
—— Charles, of Ardsheil, 288, 384, 385.

INDEX. 435

Stewart, Charles clerk, 288.
—— —— Bohallie, 384.
——Donald, serjeant, 288.
—— —— Annat, 384.
—— —— Ballachelish, 384.
—— —— Invernahyle, 384.
—— —— tenant, 270, 324.
—— —— Ballachellan, 384.
—— Dougald, Maryburgh, 288.
—— —— Appin, 384, 385.
—— —— Ardsheal, 383.
—— —— Invernachyle, 384.
—— Duncan, Ardsheal, 383.
—— —— Fasnacloich, 383.
—— —— Achnacone, 384.
—— —— Balquhidder, 384.
—— —— Inverncahyle, 384.
—— —— Inverphalla, 384.
—— —— *alias* MacAlan, 384.
—— —— officer, 288.
—— —— Inverfolla, 288.
—— —— Glenlyon, 384.
—— Elspet, 370.
—— James, 22, 394.
—— —— farmer, 38, 312.
—— —— Argour, 286.
—— —— officer, 288, 370.
—— Jean, 370.
—— John Roy, 39, 126, 340, 377.
—— Sir John, Count of Maida, 377.
—— John, Macalan Vane, 384.
—— —— farmer xvii, 22.
—— —— Glass, captain, 288.
—— —— serjeant, 288.
—— —— of Benmore, 383.
—— —— Acharn, 383.
—— —— Fasnacloich, 383.
—— Joseph, Borland, 22.
—— Peter, Borland, 22.
—— Robert, captain, 288.
—— —— Appin, 384.
—— William, lieutenant, 288.
—— —— farmer, 312, 387.
—— —— Ardsheal, 383.
Stewarts, 360, 364.
Stirling, Hugh, Calder, 276, 277, 346.
—— Sir H., 397.
—— James, of Keir, 276, 346.
—— —— of Craigbarnet, 276, 278, 346.
—— —— Glasgow, 278, 346.
—— —— Erskine, 326, 388.
—— William, Calder, 276, 346.
—— of Northside, 278.
—— castle, 391, 393, 396.
—— gaol, 393.
—— district of, xvi, 54, 316, 361, 372, 387.
—— town of, 13, 57, 147, 151, 153, 159, 167, 169, 173, 177, 181, 197,
199, 205, 209, 215, 217, 227, 233, 235, 241, 319, 349.
Stiven, Alexander, trone man, xvii, 68.
—— —— porter, 256, 342, 352.
—— Andrew, farmer, 60, 316.
—— James, apprentice, 188.
—— John, wright, 186.
—— —— workman, 236.
—— William, cooper, 236.
Stivenson, Alexander, wright, 256, 340.
—— James, servant, 36.
Stodhart, William, innkeeper, 38.
Stones, John, carrier, 262.
Stonhaven, 155, 157, 163, 169, 171, 173, 175, 179, 181, 185, 193.
Stormont, Alexander, Glenugg, 236.
—— James, of Pitscanly, 234, 235, 379.
Stormond, James, of Lidnathy, 234.
—— —— Glenugg, 236.
—— John, of Kinwhirie, 236.
Stot, James, slater, 18.
Stouter, James, brewer, 188.
Strachan, James, tidesman, 20, 305.
—— John, servant, 188.
—— —— butcher, 188.
Strachan, John, cottarman, 188.
—— William, clerk, 20, 300, 368.
Strang, Alexander, excise officer, 339.
Strathallan, Lord, xvii, 47, 50, 51, 275, 358, 371, 372, 401.
Strathavin, 358.
Strathbogie, 358.
Strathdon, 358.
Strathmore, Lady, 199, 212.
Stratton, Archibald, watchmaker, 256, 340.
Strickland, Mr., 357.
Stuart, Alexander, horse-hirer, 38.
—— —— sheriff officer, 50.
—— —— ensign, 128.
—— —— (*alias* Derg), 128.
—— —— serjeant, 236.
—— —— merchant, 238.
—— Allan, Gaulurge, 130.
—— —— Newtoun, 128.
—— Andrew, 370.
—— Angus, ensign, 38, 312.
—— Angus, Dow, Achnahayle, 102.
—— Archibald Bain, Delavoir, 100.
—— Callum, servant, 80, 332.
—— Charles, jun., of Ballachan, 50.
—— —— of Gowrdie, 236.
—— —— lieutenant, 256, 340.
—— Cosmo-George, 370.
—— David, of Ballahallan, 60, 373.
—— Donald, Ruthven, 128.
—— —— Glenconles, 128.
—— —— Findran, 128.
—— —— Auchnahayl, 128.

LIST OF REBELS

Stuart, Findran (*alias* Dow) 128.
—— —— schoolboy, 236, 271.
—— Finlay, sheriff officer, 50.
—— George, Badivochal, 128.
—— —— of Tannachy, 370.
—— Helen, 368.
—— Hugh, gardener, 128, 336.
—— —— Glenlyon, 384.
—— James, 50, 52.
—— —— tobacconist, 52.
—— —— East Inverury, 128.
—— —— Achnascra, 128.
—— —— merchant, 186.
—— —— Redmyre, 188.
—— —— workman, 236.
—— —— porter, 236.
—— —— sheriff depute, 349.
—— —— Acharn, 383.
—— —— Fasnacloich, 383.
—— —— Ardnamurchan, 384.
—— —— Invernahyle, 384.
—— John, Kirkaldy, 262.
—— —— Inverness, 377.
—— —— apprentice, 50.
—— —— of Glat, 60.
—— —— brewer, 60.
—— —— Roy, Tombreck, 126.
—— —— bailie, 128, 377.
—— —— Glenconles, 128.
—— —— Findran, 128.
—— —— Terbain, 128.
—— —— East Inverury, 128.
—— —— Tamavilan, 128.
—— —— jun., Baluhnockan, 128.
—— —— Achnascra, 128.
—— —— (*alias* M'Yoak), 128.
—— —— (*alias* Dow), 128.
—— —— Delavoiar, 130.
—— —— Stenton, 236.
—— —— Dundee, 236.
—— Thomas, gardener, 96.
—— Walter, servant, 278, 346.
—— William, 50.
—— —— baker, 20.
—— —— captain, 128.
—— —— Clashnaver, 128.
—— —— West Achivaich, 128.
—— of Kennoching, major, 50.
—— of Bohallie, officer, 50.
—— of Garth, officer, 50.
—— weaver, 50.
—— jun., of Findynet, 50.
—— Lieutenant-colonel, 278.
—— Laurance, tailor, 52.
—— Lewis, serjeant, 130.
—— Malcolm, Appin, 384.
—— Malcom, officer, 50.
—— Margaret, 368.
—— Mary, 370.
—— Mr., collector of excise, 325.

Stuart, Patrick, captain, 38, 312.
—— —— servant, 128, 278.
—— —— Tannachy, 370.
—— Peter, ensign, 38.
—— —— (*alias* Dow), 128.
—— ——, 346.
—— Robert, of Killihassy, 50.
—— —— servant, 52.
—— —— Dounan, 128.
—— —— Badivochal, 128.
—— —— servant, 130.
Stubble, David, workman, 236.
Suddy, parish of, 333.
Sullivan, Mr., 137, 357.
Surrey, county of, xiv.
Sutherland, Alexander, wright, 36.
—— —— shoemaker, 186.
—— Earl of, 375.
—— George, servant, 38.
—— James, 299, 301.
—— John, servant, 80.
—— William, dyster, 80, 393.
Sutherlands, 360.
Sutherlandshire, 73, 75, 77, 79, 81, 83, 271, 375.
Sutor, William, weaver, 236.
Swan, Andrew, shoemaker, 256, 380.
Syme, James, smith, 126.
—— Thomas, workman, xviii, 236.
—— Mr. Thomas, nonjuror, 236.
Symers, Alexander, gardener, 20.
—— Andrew, bookseller, 256.

TAIN, 77, 81, 329.
Tait, Adam, goldsmith, 256, 340.
Talbott, John, weaver, 238.
Tarbet, parish, 333.
Tasker, Alexander, servant, 262.
Tasy, Andrew, Clackmanan, 349.
Tay, river, 372.
Taylor, Andrew, writer, 325.
—— Charles, servant, 238.
—— George, fisher, 323.
—— James, shoemaker, 38.
—— —— (*alias* Robertson), farmer, 130.
—— —— innkeeper, 319.
—— Peter, farmer, 130.
—— Robert, labourer, 98.
—— —— dyster, 130.
—— Thomas, in Bridgehouse, 82.
—— —— shoemaker, 353.
—— William, ensign, 38.
—— —— Crachly, 130, 336.
—— —— brewer, 190.
—— —— mariner, 190.
—— —— coachman, 238.
—— —— messenger, 313.
—— —— innkeeper, 319.

INDEX. 437

Tennent, Robert, vintner, 347.
—— William, painter, 347.
Tervas, Alexander, merchant, 98.
Teviotdale, district, xvi.
Thain, James, servant, 98.
—— John, mason, 38.
—— bailie, 315.
—— Patrick, Euchry, 313.
Thom, Bessie, spinster, 345.
—— George, workman, 238.
Thomson, Alexander, of Feichfield, 98, 306.
—— —— sailor, 98.
—— Charles, Auchterfloo, 331.
—— Hector, salt officer, 140.
—— James, tenant, 52.
—— —— Feichfield, 98, 306.
—— —— brewer, 140.
—— —— gardener, 238.
—— —— serjeant, 299, 301.
—— —— excise officer, 339.
—— John, ensign, 22, 300.
—— Kenneth, Auchterfloo, 331.
—— Robert, tenant, 52.
—— —— factor, 190.
—— —— brewer, 349.
—— Thomas, Parkhill, 307.
—— William, boatman, 68, 352.
—— —— workman, 238.
—— —— brewer, 353.
Thores, James, weaver, 256.
Threepland, Sir David, of Fingask, 238.
—— Thomas, captain, 238.
Thurso, 271.
Tillan, Alexander, labourer, 8.
Tilleray, Andrew, horse-hirer, 22.
Tindal, Colin, serjeant, 190.
—— David, Nether, Pitforthy, 190.
Todd, Archibald, weaver, 140.
—— Thomas, town clerk, 140.
—— Walter, tanner, 256.
Todie, Janet, Pittenweem, 353.
Torry, James, dyster, 130.
Touch, parish of, 7.
—— William, servant, 299.
Touley, barony of, 364.
Tower, Alexander, 305.
—— James, 14.
Tower Hill, 375, 381.
Townley, colonel, xiv.
Traill, John, shoemaker, 353.
Tranent, 137, 139.
Traquair, earl of, 84.
Trotter, Ninian, excise officer, 339, 341.
Troup, Charles, servant, 22.
—— John, Greendykes, 313.
—— William, xvii, 22, 300.
Tullibardine, Marquis of, x, xvi, 49, 226, 233, 357.

Tulloch, David, captain, 38, 115.
—— Robert, lieutenant, 130.
—— Mr. Thomas, of Brigton, 181.
Tullochs, 360.
Turnbull, Adam, bailie, 349.
Turner, Duncan, Culmore, 130.
—— John, serjeant, 22.
—— —— jun., of Turnerhall, 98, 306.
—— William, Middle Dounan, 130.
Turnerhall, Lady, 98, 304, 387.
Turras, John, smith, 98.
Turriff, 31, 309, 311, 313.
Tweedale, Alexander, fisher, 321.
—— Marquis of, 378.
—— district of, 339, 374.
Tydieman, John, servant, 262.
Tyrie, David, labourer, 98.
—— —— jun., of Dinnedeer, 98, 306.
—— Mr. John, priest, 130.
—— John, servant, 256.
—— parish, 305, 307.

UDNY, parish of, 307.
Union, the, ix, x, xi.
Ure, Jean, 370.
Urquart, Kenneth, 82.
Urquhart, George, merchant, 309, 311.
—— —— Upper Cults, 130.
—— James, smith, 60.
—— Thomas, of Cullicuden, 82.
—— William, servant, 82, 332.
—— —— cooper, 130.
Urquharts, 360.
Urra, parish, 331.
Ushet, Robert, servant, 262.

VALLANTINE, ROBERT, servant, 194.
Vandyck, 363.
Veitch, Patrick, carter, 140.
Vere, captain, 381.
Verly (Verty), William, carpenter, 148, 348, 390.
Volume, James, surgeon, 98.
—— Thomas, surgeon, 98.
—— —— servant, 240.

WADDELL, JOHN, salt officer, 140.
Wade, George, workman, 194.
—— general, 209.
Wagrae, John, apprentice, 238.
Wales, Prince of, 7, 19, 57, 61, 139, 155, 157.
Walker, Alexander, Bervie, 194.
—— James, candlemaker, 258, 340.
—— —— Leven, 345.
—— John, servant, 40.
—— Robert, ensign, 192.
—— William, wauker, 22.
—— —— weaver, 40.
—— —— barber, 190.

Walker, William, Achenblea, 192.
—— —— Wall, Leven, 345.
Wallace, Provost Patrick, 155, 192.
—— Thomas, smith, 341.
Walpole, Sir Robert, xii.
Warden, James, drummer, 194.
Wardlaw, Henry, 268.
—— John, factor, 268.
Warsaw, ix.
Watson, Alexander, deputy governor, 238.
—— George, brewer, 323.
—— James, quarter-master, 38.
—— —— cottar, 192.
—— —— labourer, 242.
—— —— Craill, 353.
—— John, brewer, 192.
—— —— shipmaster, 317.
—— —— Craill, 353.
—— Thomas, drummer, 130, 336.
—— —— merchant, 192, 240.
—— —— Craill, 353.
—— William, weaver, 192.
—— —— jun., 192.
—— —— servant, 240.
Watt, Andrew, slater, 318, 387.
—— John, servant, 40.
—— Robert, slater, 318, 387.
—— William, servant, 40, 240.
Webster, Andrew, wright, 192.
—— Charles, workman, 240, 379.
—— James, servant, 22.
—— John, pensioner, 192.
—— —— workman, 240.
—— —— weaver, 240.
—— —— serjeant, 240.
—— —— Clockean, 303, 307.
—— William, chapman, 194.
Wedderburn, Sir John, of Blackness, 238, 379.
—— lieutenant, 238.
Weems, David, 63.
—— —— surgeon, 70, 352.
—— —— indweller, 70.
Weir, George, workman, 22.
—— John, coalhewer, 292.
—— William, coalier, 326, 388.
Welsh, John, porter, 190.
—— —— mason, 190.
—— William, servant, 190.
—— The, xii.
Wemyss, David, Lord Elcho, x, 135, 245, 252, 258, 260, 262, 380.
—— Francis, Earl of, 380.
—— James, Earl of, 380.
Western Isles, 358.
Westminster, 369, 381.
White, Alexander, hookmaker, 22.
—— —— jun., of Ardlahill, 98, 306.
—— —— servant, 240.

White, Charles, brewer, 349.
—— Daniel, hookmaker, 22.
—— George, Miln of Gask, 312, 387.
—— Hugh, merchant, 327.
—— James, workman, 240.
—— —— victualler, 240.
—— John, weaver, 194.
—— —— workman, 240.
—— Robert, gardener, 262.
—— —— painter, 278, 346.
—— William, servant, 84.
—— —— 197.
—— —— innkeeper, 258.
Wightman, Charles, merchant, 68.
Wigtown, Earl of, 268.
Wilkie, David, workman, 240.
—— George, apprentice, 238.
—— —— Auchleishie, 240.
—— John, servant, 240.
—— —— workman, 240.
—— Thomas, Arbroath, 192.
Wilkin, Alexander, farmer, 98.
—— John, Cassiefoord, 303.
Wilkins, Joseph, weaver, 22.
Will, William, wright, 242.
—— Mr., minister, 305.
William, Fort, siege of, 283.
Williamson, Alexander, Croft of Minmore, 130.
—— David, merchant, 238.
—— Jerom, wigmaker, 329.
—— John, cooper, 238.
—— William, fisher, 22.
—— —— shoemaker, 192, 320.
Willison, 342.
Willox, Charles, mason, 194.
—— James, 309.
Wilson, Alexander, servant, 38.
—— David, servant, 38, 52.
—— —— brewer, 192, 314.
—— —— weaver, 240.
—— James, workman, 240.
—— John, Farrie, 192.
—— —— barber, 258, 340.
—— Matthew, maltman, 347.
—— Robert, wright, 38.
—— —— Clackmanan, 349.
—— Thomas, Farrie, 192.
—— —— workman, 240.
—— —— excise officer, 351.
—— William, servant, 40, 312.
—— —— in New Tarbat, 82.
—— —— farmer, 98, 305.
—— —— turner, 258, 340.
—— —— town clerk, 349.
—— Mr., excise officer, 256.
—— Dundee, 256.
—— innkeeper, 258.
Winchester, Robert, merchant, 325.
Windrum, James, Abbeyhill, 258.

INDEX. 439

Windrum, James, of Eyemouth, 340.
Wintoun, William, weaver, 240.
Wischart, John, merchant, 238.
Wise, Ninian, 268.
Wisehart, William, Johnshaven, 192, 322.
Wishart, John, Tillicorthy, 307.
Wood, Andrew, captain, 272, 346.
—— John, vintner, 339.
—— Samuel, servant, 262.
—— William, mason, 238.
—— —— of Allardie, 192.
Wordie, William, merchant, 262.
Wright, Alexander, subtenant, 38.
—— Duncan, carrier, 318, 387.
—— James, Berie, 202.
—— John, tailor, 40.
—— —— surgeon, 70, 352.
—— —— workman, 240.
—— —— servant, 240.
—— —— Hay, Dalgety, 308, 311.
—— Robert, shoemaker, 192, 320.

Wright, Mr. Robert, gentleman, 258.
—— Thomas, 201.
Wyllie, Alexander, dyster, 190.
—— Francis, servant, 192.
—— Robert, brewer, 192.
Wyse, William, merchant, 323.

YONDERSTOWN, parish of, 309.
York, city of, xiv, 371, 373, 374, 379-381.
—— Duke of, ix.
Yoully, David, weaver, 242.
Young, Alexander, sailor, 194, 320.
—— —— workman, 242.
—— David, weaver, 242.
—— George, tailor, 336, 389.
—— James, servant, 242.
—— John, sheriff depute, 323.
—— Robert, captain, 194.
—— —— Coupar, 242.
—— Walter, serjeant, 194, 320.
Younger, William, Linton, 339.
Yuill, James, 52.